Praise for *Loot*

'Gripping… a must-read.'

Financial Times

'The storytelling is crisp, balanced and authoritative… As Britain continues to twist on the thorny issue of racism… this book's laser-sharp focus on the case notes from one instance of colonial cruelty allows for a much more informed understanding of the wider issue. Whereas before the now highly valuable Benin Bronzes might have had us looking in the attic for some forgotten heirloom, perhaps now we are left examining our consciences.'

Tim Butcher, *Spectator*

'[A] valuable guide to a complex narrative… Throughout this tortured history, Phillips writes with journalistic detail, gathering his accounts from many sources, attempting fairness.'

The Times

'His compelling book is full of African voices… It is balanced, sternly critical of the Brits when that is appropriate, but at the same time humane, reasonable and ultimately optimistic.'

Evening Standard

'Phillips is scrupulously fair yet damning. He points to the racist hypocrisy that rationalised colonial plunder… covers the ritzy, often clandestine, history of the Bronzes on the western market, where some objects have been sold for up to £10m. Above all, his tale is one of competing ways of assessing material culture.'

Prospect

'A veteran journalist based for years in Africa, Mr. Phillips has written a humane and thoughtful book, devoid of the sort of posturing that mars the debate over the repatriation of objects brought to the West during the colonial era.'

Wall Street Journal

'[A] balanced reconstruction of the Benin saga and probes the difficult choices facing European – and Nigerian – museums… Phillips excels at tracing the roundabout ways in which objects could find their way into museums.'

Times Literary Supplement

ALSO BY BARNABY PHILLIPS

Loot
Another Man's War

THE AFRICAN KINGDOM OF GOLD

Britain and the Asante Treasure

BARNABY PHILLIPS

A Oneworld Book

First published by Oneworld Publications Ltd in 2026

Copyright © Barnaby Phillips, 2026

The moral right of Barnaby Phillips to be identified as the Author of this work has been asserted by him in accordance with the Copyright, Designs, and Patents Act 1988

All rights reserved
Copyright under Berne Convention
A CIP record for this title is available from the British Library

ISBN 978-1-83643-133-6
eISBN 978-1-83643-134-3

Typeset by Geethik Technologies
Printed and bound in Great Britain by Clays Ltd, Elcograf S.p.A.

Every reasonable effort has been made to trace the copyright holders of material reproduced in this book, but if any have been inadvertently overlooked the publishers would be glad to hear from them.

No part of this publication may be reproduced, stored in a retrieval system, or transmitted, in any form or by any means, electronic, mechanical, photocopying, recording or otherwise, or used in any manner for the purpose of training artificial intelligence technologies or systems, without the prior permission of the publishers.

The authorised representative in the EEA is eucomply OU,
Pärnu mnt 139b–14, 11317 Tallinn, Estonia
(email: hello@eucompliancepartner.com / phone: +33757690241)

Oneworld Publications Ltd
10 Bloomsbury Street
London WC1B 3SR
England

Stay up to date with the latest books, special offers, and exclusive content from Oneworld with our newsletter

Sign up on our website
oneworld.co.uk

'The traveller who returns from a journey may tell all he has seen, but he cannot explain all'

Asante Proverb, from *Letters from the Gold Coast* by Princess Marie Louise

CONTENTS

A Note on Language	x
Dramatis Personae	xi
Timeline	xxi
Maps	xxviii

PREFACE:	'A Joyful Moment'	xxxi
1	'They Saw A Stool Descending from the Sky'	1
2	'King of Kings'	13
3	'An End to All the Peace and Quiet'	29
4	'The White Men Have Guns Which Hit Five Ashantees At Once'	45
5	'Every Doctor Looked Like A Butcher'	61
6	'Blew Up the Palace and Left Coomassie in Flames'	71
7	'Gold Is Always Pretty'	85
8	'Worthy to Find A Resting Place In the British and South Kensington Museums'	99
9	'Kumasi Was Falling Into A Ruinous State'	119
10	'Prepared to Sacrifice Myself to Save the Lives of My People'	131
11	'I Beg the Governor Not to Take My People and Myself Away'	143
12	'Simply A Policy of Robbery'	153
13	'Why Am I Not Sitting on The Golden Stool?'	169
14	'Gold Was A Perfect Curse'	183
15	'Consider How Wretched I Am'	193

16	'Return All Stolen Property to the People of Ashanti!'	209
17	'The Most Marvellous Experience of Our Lives'	227
18	'You Express The Views of A Civilian'	245
19	'The Past Should Not Dictate The Present'	255
20	'A Happy Day for Asante, for the Black African Continent'	271
21	'Which History We Remember'	285

Acknowledgements	299
Illustration List	301
Bibliography	305
Notes	317
Index	366

To Nicole

A NOTE ON LANGUAGE

This is a book about the Asante kingdom, located in modern-day Ghana. Asante is both the name of the kingdom, and the people. They belong to the larger Akan ethnic group.

But should we write Asante, Ashanti, Ashantii, Ashante, Ashantee, Achantis or even Assjantees? And is their capital city Kumasi, Kumase, Kumassi, Koomassee, Coomassie, Comassie or Commassie? Should the name of the king who resisted the British invasion in 1874 be written as Kofi Karikari, Koffi Kakari, Koffee Kalcalli or King Koffee? Or Coffee Calculli? Or Coffee Calcalli? Or just plain Coffee?

There are multiple spellings for many of the names and terms in this book. Although Twi, the language spoken by the Asante and many other Akan people in Ghana is written in the Roman alphabet, it has some unique digraphs and vowels; for example, 'ɛ' is like the e in bread and 'ɔ' is like the o in dog. So rendering Twi words into English results in many inconsistencies.

I have tried to choose the most common spellings or transliterations as used in written English in Ghana today. Hence, 'Asante', 'Kumasi' and 'Kofi Karikari'. When in doubt, I have synchronised my spellings with those of leading Asante scholars, or leading scholars of Asante history. I hope I have achieved at least an internal level of consistency and I apologise for any mistakes along the way. I have not changed spellings in quotations but have three or four times used asterisks to obscure a particularly offensive word.

DRAMATIS PERSONAE

The kings of Asante, known as the Asantehene, who feature prominently in this book, with the dates they reigned.

Osei Tutu, the first Asantehene (c. 1700–c.1717). Together with the great priest Okomfo Anokye, he founded the Asante nation after victory over the Denkyira at the Battle of Feyiase in 1701.

Opoku Ware, the second Asantehene (c. 1720–1750). Oversaw an expansion of Asante territory and gold reserves and accumulated vast wealth. Known as *Di Sika*, 'the one who ate gold.'

Osei Bonsu, the seventh Asantehene (1804–1824). Originally known as Osei Tutu Kwame, he took the name 'Bonsu', meaning 'whale', when he invaded the territories of the Fante people in 1806 and plunged his sword into the Atlantic Ocean. In 1817 he received the first British delegation to Kumasi and formed a friendship with Thomas Bowdich.

Osei Yaw Akoto, the eighth Asantehene (1824–1834). Suffered a great defeat to the British and their African coastal allies at the 1826 Battle of Katamanso (also called Dodowa).

Kwaku Dua I, the ninth Asantehene (1834–1867). Presided over a period of relative peace with the British.

Kofi Karikari, the tenth Asantehene (1867–1874). Ordered the Asante army to invade the Gold Coast in 1873, which in turn resulted in the catastrophic British invasion of Asante in 1874, when Sir Garnet Wolseley destroyed his palace and burnt Kumasi. Forced to abdicate by rivals thereafter, he died in 1884, apparently of dysentery, although some in Asante believe he was murdered.

Mensa Bonsu, the eleventh Asantehene (1874–1883). Younger brother of Kofi Karikari. Struggled to exert control in the confused period following the British invasion and abdicated when a crowd stormed his palace.

Kwaku Dua II, the twelfth Asantehene (1884). He ruled for only weeks during a period of unrest and division. Reportedly died of smallpox.

Agyeman Prempeh, the thirteenth Asantehene (1888–1931). He tried to preserve Asante's sovereignty at a time of aggressive British imperialism. Exiled by the British, 1896–1924, at first to Elmina, then Sierra Leone and finally the Seychelles, where he spent twenty-four years. Returned as a private citizen but was still regarded by the Asante as their king and was granted permission by the British to take the title of *Kumasihene*, or King of Kumasi.

Agyeman Prempeh II, the fourteenth Asantehene (1931–1970). Successor to Prempeh, installed on the Golden Stool with British permission in 1935, marking the official restoration of the Asante confederacy. Presided over the writing of the epic *History of Ashanti* and the delicate politics of Ghanaian independence in 1957.

Opoku Ware II, the fifteenth Asantehene (1970–1999). Pleaded with the British government for the return of Asante regalia to mark the centenary of Wolseley's invasion and supported landmark exhibitions celebrating Asante culture in London and New York.

Osei Tutu II, the sixteenth and current Asantehene (1999–). Successfully negotiated the long-term loan of some Asante regalia from the British Museum and Victoria and Albert Museum in 2024, as well as permanent returns of looted treasure from elsewhere.

OTHER SIGNIFICANT CHARACTERS

Adu Boahen, Albert (1932–2006). Renowned Ghanaian historian, activist and politician of Asante descent.

Adu Bofuo (c. 1815–1883). Asante general who seized European hostages in 1869 and favoured a policy of military expansion.

Dramatis Personae

Afua Kobiri (lived late nineteenth century, died c. 1900). Queen Mother, or Asantehemaa, to Kofi Karikari.

Agyeman-Duah, Ivor Kumasi-born historian, diplomat and Director of the Manhyia Palace Museum. His great grandfather, Kwame Boatin, was exiled with Prempeh in Sierra Leone and the Seychelles.

Akufo-Addo, Nana President of Ghana from 2017 to 2025.

Alison, Archibald (1826–1907). British soldier and Wolseley's deputy in 1873–4. A veteran of the Crimea and the Indian Uprising, where he lost an arm.

Amankwa Tia (early nineteenth century to 1874). Asante general who led the invasion of the Gold Coast protectorate in 1873. Killed at the Battle of Amoafo in January 1874.

Ansa, John Owusu (1851–1910). Led the Asante diplomatic mission to London in 1895, which failed to avert the British invasion of 1895–6.

Armitage, Cecil (1869–1933). British soldier and colonial official, who took part in the 1895–96 British invasion of Asante and survived the 1900 Siege of Kumasi Fort. Almost 500 of the Asante and Gold Coast objects he collected are now in the British Museum.

Asamoa Nkwanta (c. 1805–1875). Asante general who fought the British in 1873–4.

Baden-Powell, Robert (1857–1941). British soldier who served in the British expedition to Asante in 1895–96, became famous at the Siege of Mafeking in South Africa in 1899–1900 and later founded the Boy Scouts.

Barter, Charles (1857–1931). British soldier who brought the 'Asante Ewer' back to England in 1896 and sold it to the British Museum. Relieved of his command at the Battle of the Somme and spent the rest of his life trying to clear his name.

Bonnat, Marie-Joseph (1844–1881). French trader taken hostage by the Asante in 1869 and imprisoned in Kumasi. Freed in 1874, he guided Wolseley's officers through the Asantehene's palace, but regretted their plunder.

Bowdich, Thomas (1791–1824). Trained as a hatter in Bristol, he was a member of the first British delegation to Kumasi in 1817, after which he wrote the celebrated *Mission from Cape Coast Castle to Ashantee*. Died of malaria on the River Gambia.

Boyle, Frederick (1841–1914). Novelist, orchid collector and *Daily Telegraph* correspondent with Wolseley's expedition. Wrote the definitive account of the auction at Cape Coast Castle. Committed suicide in his Bayswater flat.

Brackenbury, Henry (1837–1914). Wolseley's trusted military secretary and a successful career soldier.

Bray, Xavier Director of the Wallace Collection since 2016.

Burleigh, Bennet (1840–1914). *Daily Telegraph* correspondent with the 1895–96 Asante expedition. Fought for the Confederates and reported on many wars thereafter.

Cade, Edwin Arthur (1856–1903). Pioneering gold miner with Ashanti Goldfields, died of malaria in Asante.

Cardwell, Edward (1813–1886). Liberal politician and Secretary of State for War, 1868–74, when his 'Cardwell Reforms' helped to modernise the British army.

Chamberlain, Joseph (1836–1914). Liberal and Liberal Unionist politician who served as Secretary of State for the Colonies between 1895 and 1903, when he pursued a policy of imperial expansion, especially in Africa. Father of Austen and Neville.

Cullinan, Nicholas Director of the British Museum since 2024. Art historian and formerly Director of the National Portrait Gallery.

Dawson, Joseph (late nineteenth century). Fante interpreter who was a prisoner in Kumasi 1872–74. Had the sensitive job of translating messages between Wolseley and Kofi Karikari.

Disraeli, Benjamin (1804–1881). Conservative politician who enjoyed two spells as Prime Minister, the first of which began in the midst of Wolseley's invasion of Asante.

Dupuis, Joseph (1789–1874). British envoy, led the second British mission to Kumasi in 1820.

Fagg, William (1914–1992). Influential ethnographic curator at the British Museum, 1938–74.

Fischer, Hartwig German art historian who resigned as Director of the British Museum in 2023 following revelations that some two thousand pieces of ancient jewellery had been stolen.

Franks, Augustus Wollaston (1826–1897). The first Keeper (curator) of British and Medieval Antiquities and Ethnography at the British Museum, where he bought some of the Asante regalia after Wolseley's return in 1874.

Freeman, Richard Austin (1862–1943). British writer of detective stories, often featuring forensic investigator Dr Thorndyke. He drew on his experience as a doctor in the Gold Coast. Visited Kumasi in 1889.

Freeman, Thomas Birch (1809–1890). Methodist minister, born in England to an African father and English mother. Worked as a missionary across West Africa. Visited Asante in the 1830s and 1840s.

Gavua, Kodzo Associate Professor of Archaeology at the University of Ghana in Accra.

Gladstone, William (1809–1898). Liberal politician, four times Prime Minister, including in 1873 when the decision was taken to send a British army to the Gold Coast under Wolseley's command.

Glover, John (1829–1885). British naval officer and colonial official, who led African soldiers to Kumasi in February 1874 in what became a diversionary expedition to Wolseley's main attack.

Grant, Frederick (late nineteenth century). 'Native of Accra', pioneering African photographer who took valuable photos of Kumasi in the 1880s and travelled to London to protect his copyright.

Henry, Prince of Battenberg (1858–1896). Son-in-law of Queen Victoria, who called him 'Liko'. Took part in the 1895–6 expedition to Asante as military secretary to Sir Francis Scott but contracted malaria and died.

Henty, George (1832–1902). Novelist and war correspondent, passionately pro-imperialist, accompanied Wolseley's expedition for the *Standard* newspaper.

Hingley, Samuel (1870–1939). British officer who received Yaa Asantewaa's surrender in 1901 when she gave him a wooden stool. His daughter, Dorothy Jackson, returned the stool to Kumasi in 1985, amidst great fanfare.

Home, Robert (1837–1879). British officer with the Royal Engineers. 'An able, daring and imaginative Irishman' according to Wolseley, who entrusted him with the destruction of the Asantehene's palace in February 1874. Died of typhoid contracted in Bulgaria five years later.

Hudson, Julie British Museum curator working on the African collections.

Hunt, Tristram Director of the V&A Museum since 2017, historian and former Labour MP.

Hodgson, Frederick (1851–1925). British colonial official who provoked the fifth and final Anglo-Asante war (also known as the 'War of the Golden Stool' and the 'Yaa Asantewaa War') of 1900–1 by demanding the Golden Stool. Survived the subsequent siege of the British fort in Kumasi with his wife Mary, who wrote a colourful account.

Kimberley, Earl; John Wodehouse (1826–1902). Liberal politician who was Secretary of State for the Colonies 1870–74 and 1880–82.

Kirby, Brandon (1852–1930). Australian-born colonial adventurer, self-styled 'English gentleman' who visited Kumasi in 1884 and took Asante gold regalia to Texas, where it remains.

Knox, William (1847–1916). British soldier who looted treasures from Maqdala in 1868 and Kumasi in 1874, which are now in the officer's mess of the Royal Artillery in Larkhill, Wiltshire.

Kofi Nti (late nineteenth to early twentieth century). Son of Asantehene Kofi Karikari, taken by the British to England and later lived in Trinidad and Sierra Leone. Returned to Kumasi and collaborated with the British after 1896.

Kufuor, John President of Ghana from 2001 to 2009, from a prominent Asante family.

Kwabena Dwumo (early to late nineteenth century). Appointed commander of the Asante army as Wolseley approached in December 1873, and wounded at the Battle of Amoafo. Had the title of *Mamponhene*.

Kwabena Kyere (late nineteenth century to 1900). Asante chief who fought alongside Yaa Asantewaa. Captured by the British, defiant at his execution.

Kwame Boatin (mid-nineteenth century to 1918). Asante aristocrat with the title *Kyidomhene*, took part in the London diplomatic mission of 1895. Deported with Prempeh to Sierra Leone and the Seychelles, where he died. Great-grandfather to Ivor Agyeman-Duah.

Kwasi Gyambibi (mid-nineteenth century to 1903). Father of Prempeh, in 1896 was arrested and deported with him to Elmina, Sierra Leone and the Seychelles, where he died.

Little, George (1850–?). British soldier who wrote a vivid diary of Wolseley's expedition of 1873–74. Left the army in 1883. His diary was donated to the V&A in 2022 by a family who are unsure of its origins.

MacCarthy, Charles (1764–1824). Soldier and colonial official, killed by the Asante at the Battle of Nsamankow. The subsequent fate of his skull – perhaps in Devon, or Kumasi – is an enduring mystery.

McCaskie, Tom British historian of the Asante and the editor of *History of Ashanti* by Prempeh II.

McLeod, Malcolm British anthropologist, taught in Ghana in the late 1960s, Keeper of the British Museum's Ethnographic Department 1974–90, Director of the Hunterian Museum, Glasgow, through the 1990s. In 2022, Asantehene Osei Tutu II asked him and Ivor Agyeman-Duah to work for the return of Asante regalia.

Mahama, John President of Ghana 2012–17 and re-elected in 2025.

Maurice, Frederick (1841–1912). British soldier and private secretary to Wolseley in 1873–74.

Maxwell, William (1846–1897). British Governor of the Gold Coast in 1896 when he ordered the arrest and exile of Prempeh and his entourage. He died of malaria the following year.

Nkrumah, Kwame (1909–1972). The first leader of independent Ghana and a pioneering Pan-Africanist, overthrown in a coup in 1966 and died in exile.

Okomfo Anokye (mid-seventeenth century to early eighteenth century). Legendary priest and adviser to the first Asantehene, Osei Tutu. The Asante believe he used special powers to defeat the Denkyira kingdom and summon the Golden Stool from the sky.

Owoo, Nii Kwate (1944–). Ghanaian filmmaker. Studied in London, where in 1970 he made the classic film on colonial loot in the British Museum, *You Hide Me*.

Paget, Arthur (1851–1928). British soldier on Wolseley's expedition, took a considerable collection of Asante loot. From a distinguished military family; his grandfather famously lost a leg at Waterloo.

Pope-Hennessy, John (1913–1994). British art historian and Director successively of the V&A and British Museum in the 1970s.

Prempeh, Molly Great-granddaughter of Asantehene Prempeh. Born in the Seychelles, lives in a village near Kumasi, speaks Old Creole.

Prior, Melton (1845–1910). War correspondent and artist for the *Illustrated London News*. Wolseley's expedition was his big break. Went to considerable lengths to hide his Asante loot. Commemorated in St Paul's Cathedral.

Ramseyer, Friedrich (1840–1914). Swiss missionary taken hostage with his family by the Asante in 1869, released in 1874. Later returned to Asante and survived the 1900 Siege of Kumasi Fort.

Rattray, Robert (1881–1938). British colonial official and anthropologist, who wrote seminal books on Asante language and culture. His memory is widely respected in Kumasi. Killed in a gliding accident.

Read, Charles Hercules (1857–1929). Succeeded Augustus Wollaston Franks as Keeper of British and Medieval Antiquities and Ethnography at the British Museum and played an important role in its acquisition of Asante gold and Benin Bronzes, as well as their dispersal amongst other museums and collections.

Richard, Henry (1812–1888). Welsh MP, 'the Apostle of Peace' and critic of imperial wars. Buried in an elaborate tomb in Abney Park, Stoke Newington.

Samori Toure (c. 1828–1900). African king of Mandinka origin who resisted the French in the 1880s and 1890s. The British worried he would form an alliance with the Asante. Died in a French prison camp in Central Africa, remembered as an anti-colonial hero.

Scott, Francis (1834–1902). British soldier, born in India, who led the

1895–6 expedition to Kumasi, which culminated in the arrest and exile of Prempeh.

Smith, Robert Soden (1822–1900). In charge of the Art Library at the South Kensington (later V&A) Museum 1857–1890. Took a keen interest in the museum's 1874 acquisitions of Asante gold.

Stanley, Henry Morton (1841–1904). Welsh-born explorer and journalist. Emigrated to the United States as a teenager. Reported on the 1868 Abyssinia expedition, found Livingstone in 1871 – 'Dr Livingstone I presume?' – and reported on Wolseley's expedition. Later explored Central Africa and worked for King Leopold of Belgium in the Congo.

Thomas, Joseph (late nineteenth century). British soldier with the Rifle Brigade who kept a diary on Wolseley's expedition, published by his father John as *A Full and Authentic Diary of the Ashanti Expedition*.

Torrane, George (late eighteenth to early nineteenth century). British Governor of the Gold Coast 1805–07, who tried to placate Asantehene Osei Bonsu in 1806.

Victoria (1819–1901). She became Queen in 1837. Her reign saw a phenomenal expansion of the British Empire, and more specifically, repeated conflict with the Asante, in which she took a keen interest.

Vyazemsky, Leonid (1848–1909). Russian aristocrat who invited himself on Wolseley's expedition in 1874, to the dismay of British officers. He bought some of the most precious Asante objects at the Cape Coast Castle auction. Both sons killed in the Russian Revolution, and the fate of his Asante loot is unclear.

Wallace, Richard (1818–1890). British aristocrat, illegitimate son of the Marquess of Hertford. Extravagant art collector who bought sixteen pieces of Asante regalia in 1874 following the return of Wolseley's expedition. The Wallace Collection was bequeathed to the nation after his death.

Wilks, Ivor (1928–2014). British historian of Asante, author of the seminal *Asante in the 19th Century*. Also an expert on working-class politics in his native Wales.

Willcocks, James (1857–1926). British soldier, born in India, who led the relief of the Kumasi Fort and subsequent campaign against

Yaa Asantewaa in 1900–1. Fought in the First World War and died back in India.

Winwood Reade, William (1838–1875). British writer who accompanied Wolseley's expedition as correspondent for *The Times*. Author of an 1872 history of mankind, *The Martyrdom of Man*, criticised for atheist leanings. Returned from Asante 'a broken man' and died the following year.

Wolseley, Garnet (1833–1913). One of Britain's most successful and influential soldiers in the heyday of Empire. Said his invasion of Asante in 1873–74 was 'the most horrible war I ever took part in', but it made him a household name. In Ghana it is still named after him: 'the Sagrenti War'.

Wood, Evelyn (1838–1919). British army officer, on Wolseley's staff in 1873–4 and injured at the Battle of Amoafo. 'The vainest but by no means the ablest of men', according to Wolseley, although they both rose to the rank of Field Marshal.

Yaa Asantewaa (late 1830s–1921). The Queen Mother of Ejisu, near Kumasi, who led the Asante in the fifth and final Anglo-Asante war (also known as the 'War of the Golden Stool' and more commonly in Ghana as the 'Yaa Asantewaa War') of 1900–1. Deported to the Seychelles, where she died. An icon of African resistance.

Yaa Akyia (c. 1843–1917). Influential mother of Prempeh and wife of Kwasi Gyambibi, arrested by the British alongside them in 1896 and deported to Elmina, Sierra Leone and the Seychelles, where she died.

TIMELINE

Perhaps thousands of years ago. The Akan people migrate southwards and westwards from the Sahel into what is today Ghana.

1471. The Portuguese arrive by ship on what they call the 'Costa da Mina', later known by Europeans as the 'Gold Coast'.

1482. The Portuguese start to build the fort of São Jorge da Mina, or 'Elmina'.

1660s. The British capture Cape Coast Castle from the Dutch. This will be their base on the Gold Coast for more than 200 years, from where they eventually subjugate the neighbouring coastline and territories to the north.

1701. Osei Tutu, a prince from Kumasi, leads his army to victory over the Denkyira at Feyiase, after which the Golden Stool reputedly descends from the sky and the Asante nation is born.

c. 1720. The second Asantehene, Opoku Ware, is enstooled. The Asante kingdom grows steadily richer and more powerful during the eighteenth century through trade in gold and slaves.

1800. Asante power and influence extends from the Atlantic seaboard some 600 kilometres inland and over 3–5 million people.

1806. Asantehene Osei Bonsu defeats the Fante near Cape Coast, and the British recognise Asante authority over the coastal people.

1807. The British parliament votes to abolish the slave trade.

April 1817. Thomas Bowdich travels 200 kilometres inland from Cape Coast to Kumasi as part of the first British delegation to visit the Asante capital and is received by Osei Bonsu.

September 1817. Bowdich leaves Kumasi with a short-lived 'Treaty of Trade and Friendship' between Britain and Asante and with a handful of gold objects donated by Osei Bonsu to the British Museum in London.

February 1820. Another British envoy, Joseph Dupuis, travels to Kumasi.

January 1824. The British, led by Sir Charles MacCarthy, are defeated by the Asante at the Battle of Nsamankow. Sir Charles is beheaded.

August 1826. The British, with their allies the Fante, the Ga, the Denkyira, the Akwamu, the Akyem and others, defeat the Asante army at Katamanso (Dodowa).

April 1831. The British and the Asante sign a peace treaty at Cape Coast Castle, bringing the First Anglo-Asante War to an end.

1844. The British start to establish more formal control of the southern Gold Coast as 'protected tribes' recognise British jurisdiction.

1850. The British buy Danish settlements on the Gold Coast.

1863. The Asantehene, Kwaku Dua, orders his army across the Pra River and into the British protectorate, in pursuit of a rebel chief. A British army, mainly comprised of West Indian soldiers, reaches the Pra but returns to the coast, weakened by disease. This is sometimes referred to as the Second Anglo-Asante War.

1867. Kwaku Dua dies and Kofi Karikari emerges as the new Asantehene.

1871. The British buy the fort of Elmina from the Dutch, despite Asante insistence it belongs to them. Britain is now the only European power on the Gold Coast and relations with the Asante kingdom to the north steadily deteriorate.

January 1873. An Asante army again crosses the Pra River and marches into the British protectorate. This is the beginning of the Third Anglo-Asante War, known by the Asante as the 'Sagrenti War'.

June 1873. The Asante army reaches the coast and is close to Cape Coast and Elmina.

July–August 1873. Heavy rains and smallpox and dysentery amongst the soldiers force the Asante to retreat.

August 1873. British ministers and soldiers, including Sir Garnet Wolseley, meet at the War Office to discuss the crisis in the Gold Coast.

September 1873. Wolseley and senior officers sail from Liverpool for the Gold Coast.

November 1873. Three battalions of British soldiers sail for the Gold Coast from England and Ireland to join Wolseley.

January 1874. Wolseley's army of some 2,500 soldiers starts to march towards Kumasi.

24 January 1874. Wolseley reaches Fomena, the first Asante settlement to be occupied by British troops.

31 January 1874. The British and Asante armies meet at the Battle of Amoafo. Many hundreds of Asante soldiers, but only four British, are killed.

4 February 1874. The armies meet again at the Battle of Odaso, as the Asante mount a desperate defence of their capital. After six hours of fighting, Asantehene Kofi Karikari orders his army to retreat and British soldiers enter Kumasi.

5 February 1874. Wolseley waits in vain in Kumasi for the Asantehene to surrender. In the evening, Wolseley orders his soldiers to plunder and destroy the Asantehene's palace and set Kumasi alight. They work through the night to fulfil his orders.

6 February 1874. The British army retreats, with Kumasi in flames.

13 February 1874. The Asantehene's envoys meet Wolseley at Fomena and agree that Asante will pay an indemnity of 50,000 ounces of gold, abandon territorial claims, stop human sacrifice and open its territory to trade.

23 February 1874. British soldiers at Cape Coast Castle auction treasure they looted from the Asantehene's palace.

21 March 1874. Wolseley returns to England to a hero's reception. He meets Queen Victoria the following day and Prime Minister Benjamin Disraeli the day after that.

April 1874. Asante treasure goes on display at Garrard, the Crown's jewellers in Piccadilly. Museums, as well as aristocrats and other wealthy individuals, compete to buy the best pieces.

June 1874. The South Kensington Museum (which later becomes the V&A) holds a special exhibition: 'A Collection of Gold and Other Objects from Ashanti'.

July 1874. Britain declares the Gold Coast forts a Crown Colony and increases legislative powers over the surrounding protectorate, up to the borders with Asante.

1883. Asantehene Mensa Bonsu, enstooled after the British invasion of 1874, is forced to abdicate amidst turmoil in a weakened Asante.

1884. Asantehene Kwaku Dua II dies, apparently of smallpox, after only six weeks on the Golden Stool.

1884–1888. Asante is engulfed in civil war.

1884–1885. European powers, meeting in Berlin, agree to carve up Africa between them.

1888. Agyeman Prempeh is chosen by Asante chiefs as the new Asantehene.

1891. Prempeh rejects Governor Brandford Griffith's suggestions that Asante become a British protectorate.

1894. Prempeh holds a coronation ceremony and formally assumes the Golden Stool.

March 1895. Asante envoys sail to England to make the case to Queen Victoria for continued independence. They do not meet the Queen and are ignored by the British government.

August 1895. Conservatives win the general election in Britain. The new Colonial Secretary, Joseph Chamberlain, adopts a policy of aggressive imperial expansion, especially in Africa.

October–December 1895. British soldiers, commanded by Colonel Sir Francis Scott, sail for the Gold Coast. The British give Prempeh an ultimatum: accept the imposition of a British protectorate or prepare for another invasion.

17 January 1896. Colonel Scott's army enters Kumasi unopposed. This is sometimes known as the Fourth Anglo-Asante War.

20 January 1896. In Kumasi, Prempeh begs Governor William Maxwell for forgiveness and accepts the imposition of a British protectorate. Maxwell orders Prempeh's arrest, along with several family members and chiefs. British soldiers loot Prempeh's palace.

22 January 1896. Prempeh and his senior chiefs and family members are carried off into exile, initially at Elmina. Many will never see Kumasi again.

4 March 1896. Joseph Chamberlain and officials at the Colonial Office admire the Asante treasure brought back by Colonel Scott's expedition. It is later put on display at the Royal United Services Institution in Whitehall Palace. Much of it is eventually bought by the British Museum.

November 1896. Prempeh and almost thirty other Asante prisoners are taken by the British from Elmina to Sierra Leone.

1899. Fifty-one countries, including Britain, sign the Hague Convention, which prohibits all seizure and destruction of religious and cultural objects.

March 1900. Gold Coast Governor Sir Frederick Hodgson visits Kumasi and demands the Asante chiefs produce the Golden Stool. Some chiefs, rallied by Queen Yaa Asantewaa of Ejisu, decide to resist, marking the beginning of the Fifth Anglo-Asante War, also known as the 'War of the Golden Stool' and 'The Yaa Asantewaa War'.

April–July 1900. British soldiers and officials are under siege at Kumasi Fort.

August 1900. The British send Prempeh and more than fifty other Asante exiles from Sierra Leone to the Seychelles in the Indian Ocean.

November 1900. British officers say they have crushed the last Asante resistance. One of Yaa Asantewaa's senior commanders, Kwabena Kyere, is publicly hanged in Kumasi.

March 1901. Yaa Asantewaa surrenders and is sent to join Prempeh in the Seychelles.

September 1901. Asante is formally annexed by the British and put under the direct control of the Gold Coast Colony.

September 1921. Road workers near Kumasi accidentally discover the Golden Stool, which had been hidden for two decades from the British. Some connive to melt down and sell attached artefacts, causing confusion and tension. British officials stress they have no desire to take the Stool.

October 1921. Yaa Asantewaa dies in the Seychelles.

April 1924. The British Empire Exhibition opens at Wembley and attracts millions of people. It includes an 'Ashanti village'.

12 November 1924. Prempeh returns to Kumasi as a private citizen after twenty-eight years in exile.

1926. Prempeh is installed as the king of Kumasi, or Kumasihene.

May 1931. Prempeh dies.

January 1935. Celebrations in Kumasi as Prempeh's successor, Agyeman Prempeh II, assumes the restored position of Asantehene with the blessing of the British.

1957. The Gold Coast becomes the independent nation of Ghana, led by Prime Minister, later President, Kwame Nkrumah.

November 1961. Queen Elizabeth visits Ghana and brings with her two Asante chairs and two stools looted in 1874 and 1896. She gives these to Nkrumah. She receives a warm reception in Kumasi.

January 1974. Asantehene Opoku Ware II and his chiefs in the Kumasi Traditional Council present a petition to the British government asking for the return of golden regalia to mark the centenary of the 'Sagrenti War'.

August 1974. The British government replies and regrets that it cannot help.

1974–1976. Opoku Ware II and the British Museum discuss the return of Asante regalia but do not reach agreement.

February 1981. The British Museum hosts a major exhibition, 'Asante, Kingdom of Gold', which is opened by Opoku Ware II.

1984. 'Asante, Kingdom of Gold' opens in New York.

1995. Opoku Ware II oversees the opening of the Manhyia Palace Museum in Kumasi.

November 2017. President Emmanuel Macron of France, visiting Burkina Faso, says European museums cannot hold on to Africa's cultural heritage.

November 2018. The Sarr-Savoy Report, commissioned by President Macron, says France should return 'objects taken by force or presumed to be acquired through inequitable conditions'.

May 2020. The murder of George Floyd by a policeman in the United States leads to Black Lives Matter protests around the world. In Europe, there is a renewed focus on the legacy of colonialism, including in museums.

July 2022. Germany transfers ownership of more than 1,000 Benin Bronze sculptures in its museums to Nigeria. They had been looted by the British in 1897.

December 2022. Germany's Foreign Minister Annalena Baerbock flies to Abuja with twenty-two of the Benin Bronzes, which she presents to the Nigerian government. 'It was wrong to take them and it was wrong to keep them', she says.

May 2023. Asantehene Osei Tutu II visits the British Museum and proposes the loan of some of the Asante regalia.

August 2023. The British Museum announces that some two thousand pieces of ancient jewellery have been stolen from its collection, apparently by a curator. Director Hartwig Fischer resigns.

February 2024. The Fowler Museum of Los Angeles returns seven objects taken by the British in 1874 to Osei Tutu II. They are unveiled at a durbar in Kumasi to mark the 150th anniversary of the 'Sagrenti War'.

1 May 2024. At the 'Homecoming ceremony' in Kumasi, the British Museum and V&A give thirty-two pieces of treasure – almost all of which were looted in 1874 and 1896 – to the Manhyia Palace Museum on long-term loan. 'Today is a happy day for Asante, for the black African continent', says Osei Tutu II.

July 2024. Osei Tutu II tells a packed hall at the British Museum that both those whose treasure was taken and the museums who hold looted objects are 'victims of a system that needs updating'.

November 2024. Asante celebrates the centenary of Prempeh's return from the Seychelles.

March 2025. President Donald Trump accuses Smithsonian museums of portraying 'Western values as inherently harmful and oppressive.' In 2022, the Smithsonian had transferred ownership of twenty-nine Benin Bronzes to Nigeria, which, it said, had been 'stolen' by the British.

June 2025. The Dutch government returns more than 100 Benin Bronzes to Nigeria.

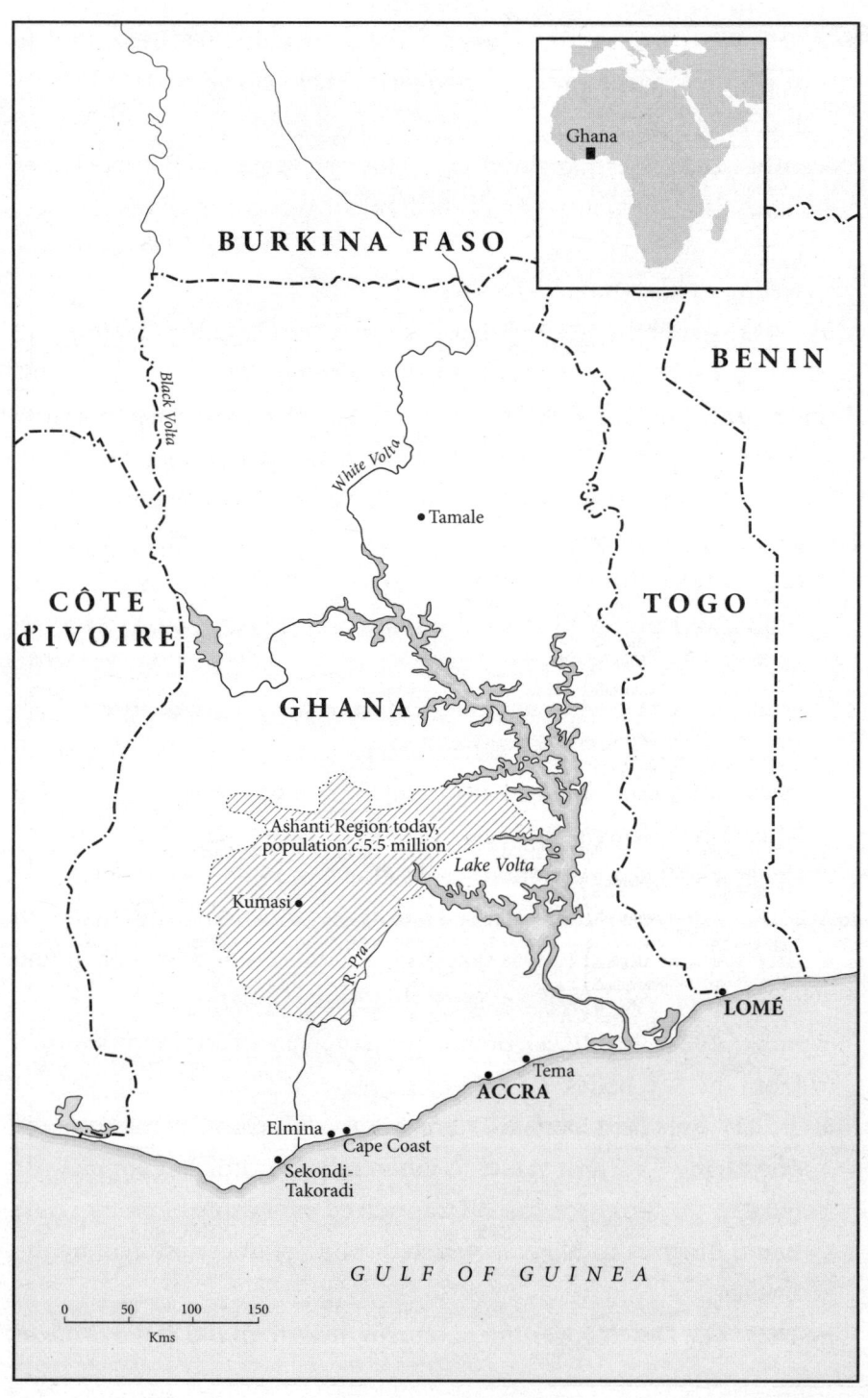

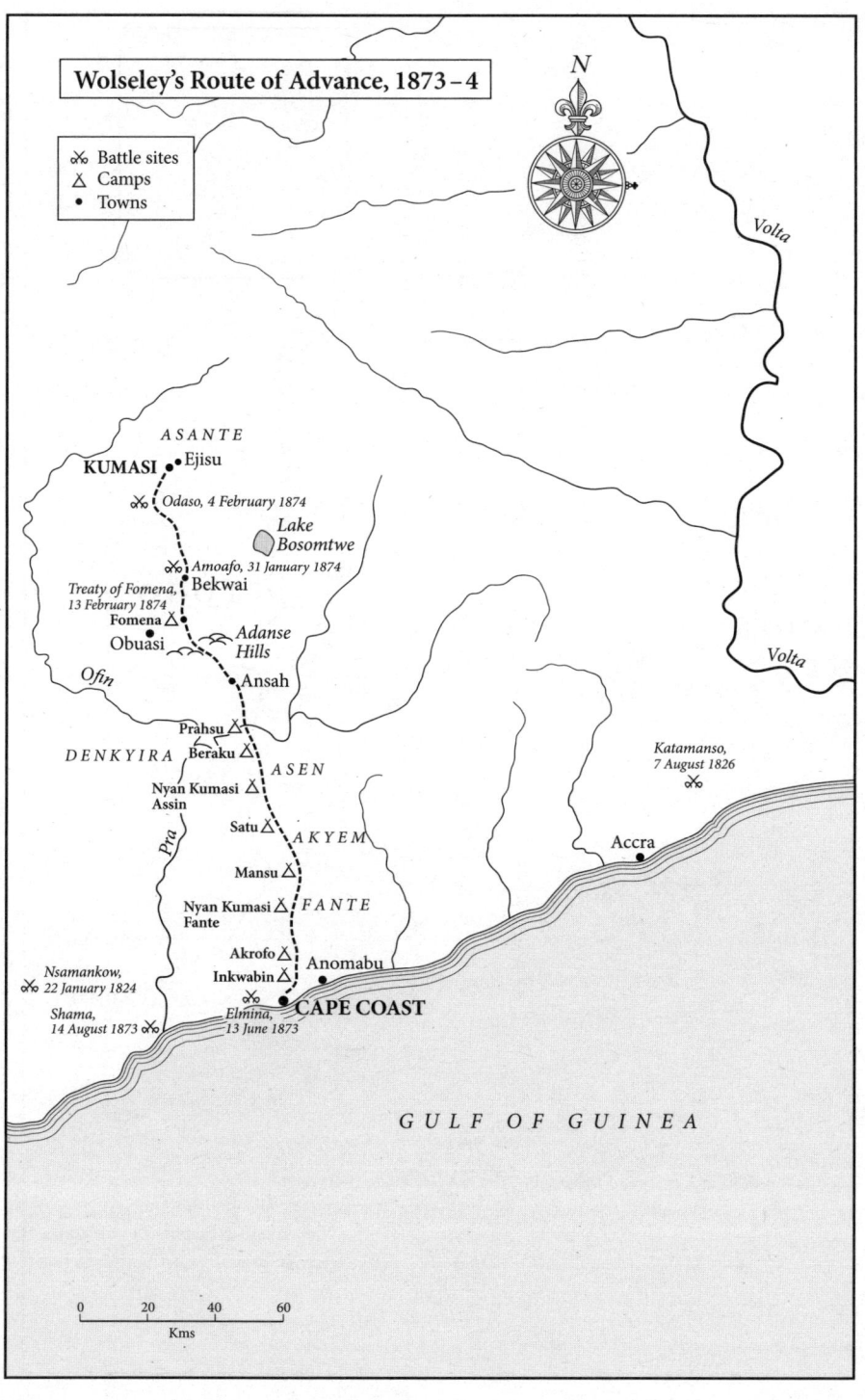

PREFACE

'A JOYFUL MOMENT'

On a hill above the city, an old man waited late into the night for his visitors. He could see the whole of Ghana's capital Accra below, a tableau of twinkling lights bordered by the abrupt black of the Atlantic. It was close to midnight, but he had no intention of going to bed.

His name is John Kufuor, and for many years he was the president of Ghana. His home, next to the presidential guesthouse known as Peduase Lodge, is protected by policemen and has a grand entrance of pseudo-classical columns and gilded furniture. Kufuor, however, is affable and unpretentious. He is very tall – about 1.9 metres – and many in Ghana call him 'the Gentle Giant', although in his old age he uses a wheelchair. I remember Kufuor when he was President, in the early 2000s. He would, unusually for a head of state, often stop to chat to journalists on his way in and out of summit meetings. Civil wars in Liberia or Côte d'Ivoire, Commonwealth rows about Pakistan or Zimbabwe; we liked Kufuor, because he had time for our questions.

The visitors were driven fast up the winding road to the top of the Aburi escarpment. They had come from Accra's airport with a police escort, speeding through empty streets. Kufuor greeted them: Ivor Agyeman-Duah, a Ghanaian scholar, and Julie Hudson, a curator from the British Museum. Carefully, Kufuor's staff unloaded four wooden crates from the back of their van. And inside these were thirty-two pieces of ceremonial gold and silver.

These ornate objects included a cast gold peace pipe, seventy-five centimetres long (*abua*); an antelope-skin helmet decorated with cast and leaf gold (*denkyemkye*); a ceremonial sword with a gold leaf and leopard skin pommel (*Mpomponsuo*); a dagger with handle and sheaf covered in sheet gold (*sikay*); and several intricate gold badges (*akrafokonmu*). All of these had once belonged to the kings of Asante, whose lands fall within what is today Ghana, and almost all of them had been looted by British soldiers in the nineteenth century. They had been in London ever since, in the collections of two of Britain's most famous museums: the British Museum itself and the Victoria and Albert, or V&A. Now they were coming home.

John Kufuor and Ivor Agyeman-Duah both belong to prominent Asante families. The memories and legacy of the Anglo-Asante Wars, a series of conflicts that began in the early nineteenth century and ended only at the beginning of the twentieth, are woven into their family histories. Kufuor later told me that Ivor had got in touch and explained that he needed a safe place to store the treasures for a couple of nights before they could be moved to the Asante capital Kumasi, some 250 kilometres to the north-west of Accra. 'I was thrilled, and readily offered,' Kufuor said.[1]

When the crates were unloaded, John Kufuor invited his guests to stay for a celebratory drink. 'It was a joyful moment,' said Julie Hudson. The temporary storage of the treasure at Peduase was an unconventional arrangement, but only Kufuor, Julie and Ivor were in on the plan and they trusted each other. And yet, after the others had gone, Kufuor took no chances. He ordered his staff to carry the crates into his bedroom. There, for two nights, the former president slept right beside the treasure. 'Naturally we didn't want any embarrassments, so I became a watchman,' he recalled, and gave a deep chuckle.

It had been a long day for Julie Hudson. She'd flown from London that morning, already exhausted after weeks of discussions and negotiations over the politics and practicalities of returning the treasure to Kumasi. When she landed at Accra's airport, she had been taken to a cargo area so the crates could be cleared through Ghanaian customs.

About a dozen people – cargo and customs officials, police, the air freight company – crowded around her. She pulled the pieces out one by one. 'No touching, and please, no photos,' she said. Everyone respected her instructions. 'There was a hushed silence, and gasps of amazement. But often just silence, and people gathered close together,' she remembers.[2]

★★★

Gold runs through the story of Asante, integral to both its rise as one of Africa's most powerful kingdoms and its near downfall. It was the lure that brought outsiders to this part of the world: a metal cherished since ancient times for its beauty and malleability and because it does not rust or tarnish. These qualities give gold a mystical power and make it a desirable adornment, but combined with its scarcity they also make it a store of value and unit of currency. 'Neither moth or rust devoureth it, but the mind of man is devoured by this supreme possession,' wrote the Greek poet Pindar.[3] Herodotus wrote of how the Carthaginians travelled along Africa's coast until they came to a mysterious land where they traded with a reclusive but trusting people, who would leave their gold on the beach and then withdraw. 'Neither party deals unfairly by the other: for [the Carthaginians] never touch the gold until it comes up to the worth of their goods, nor do the natives ever carry off the goods until the gold is taken away.'[4] For hundreds of years, Arab traders crossed the Sahara by camel to buy the precious metal in West Africa. When Henry III issued England's first golden pennies in the thirteenth century, he used West African gold.[5] Europeans arrived by ship on what is today the coast of Ghana in the fifteenth century. They called it 'the Gold Coast'. By the early sixteenth century, historians estimate, about one tenth of all the world's gold came from the Gold Coast.[6] In the 1660s, when the English Royal Mint issued a new gold coin they called it the 'guinea', a then common term for West Africa, and many were stamped with an elephant below Charles II's head to show the origin of the metal.

In 1817, a young British official, Thomas Bowdich, paid his respects at the court in Kumasi, where he met the king, known as the Asantehene. Bowdich described his reception: 'The sun was reflected, with a glare scarcely more supportable than the heat, from the massy gold ornaments, which glistened in every direction.'⁷ His account of fabulous opulence was met with both incredulity and excitement in Britain. In 1874, the British army, led by one of its most celebrated soldiers, Sir Garnet Wolseley, fought its way to Kumasi, only to discover that the Asantehene, Kofi Karikari, had abandoned the city. On Wolseley's instructions, British soldiers looted the three-storey palace. An eyewitness, a Frenchman who knew the palace and guided the soldiers through its chambers as they hunted for gold, described their behaviour as 'repulsive and shameful'.⁸ When the British had taken what they wanted, Wolseley ordered the Royal Engineers to blow up the palace and set Kumasi on fire. This was not straightforward. The engineers were short of gunpowder and Kumasi's thatched roofs were soaked by rain. Nonetheless they worked all night and an official British account records that Kumasi was 'set ablaze in every quarter and altogether destroyed' and the palace was 'reduced to a crumbling ruin'.⁹ The celebrated explorer and journalist Henry Morton Stanley accompanied Wolseley's expedition as correspondent for the *New York Herald* and described it as 'heroic', undertaken by England on 'behalf of her honour, her dignity, humanity, and justice'.¹⁰

The British army returned to Kumasi twenty-two years later, in 1896. This time the Asantehene, Agyeman Prempeh, did not resist or run away. He was brought before a British official, Governor William Maxwell, who sat above him on a platform of biscuit tins. Prempeh and his mother kissed Maxwell's feet and begged for forgiveness but could produce only a small part of the 50,000 ounces of gold the British demanded. Maxwell ordered the king's arrest and then gave permission to his soldiers to loot the palace, which the Asante had rebuilt after 1874. One of those who took part was Robert Baden-Powell, who would go on to found the Boy Scouts. 'There could be no more interesting, no more tempting work than this,' he wrote, 'To poke about in a barbarian king's palace.'¹¹ The British soldiers carried Prempeh, and their treasure, down to the coast. He spent more than two decades in exile on the Seychelles islands in the midst of the faraway Indian Ocean. In 1924, the British allowed Prempeh, by now an old man who called himself Edward, to come home.

★★★

Two days after her arrival in Accra, Julie Hudson was on the road to Kumasi, with Ivor Agyeman-Duah, having collected the treasures from John Kufuor's house. Before they left, an Asante chief poured a libation of gin, wishing them a safe journey and honouring the gods of the Ga people, traditional owners of the land around Accra. Police motorcycles went first, clearing the highway with blaring sirens and flashing blue lights. Julie was in a van with the regalia, with a policeman and his Kalashnikov ('Don't worry, Madam, for your safety') jammed uncomfortably next to her, watching the road ahead with trepidation. Ivor was in the car behind, asleep. Sitting next to him was a British man, Professor Malcolm McLeod.

Malcolm McLeod, in his eighties, lived in Ghana in the 1960s and was in charge of the British Museum's Africa collections in the 1970s and '80s. He has a soft Scottish accent and walks slowly with a stick after heart and eye operations. He is widely known and respected in Kumasi, where many refer to him as 'Prof'. In 2022, European and American universities and museums were embroiled in anguished debates about the legacy of colonialism, specifically the future of looted artefacts in museums. Restitution – the return of objects to a rightful owner after historic injustice – had become a fashionable and much discussed topic. That was when the current Asantehene, Otumfuo Osei Tutu II, telephoned Malcolm, an old friend, to discuss the possible return of treasures from the British Museum and the V&A. 'He said "Can you suggest how I can get some of my stuff back?"' recalls Malcolm. 'My advice was – don't make a lot of noise, but quietly contact the directors of the V&A and BM, and tell them you'd like to discuss things.' The Asantehene appointed Malcolm and Ivor as his advisers. 'I love Ghana, I love the Asante, they've been very kind to me over the decades, it seems natural to be involved,' Malcolm told me.[12]

They spent many months working on a deal. The British Museum and V&A would not permanently return the treasures – under the respective and controversial laws which govern their operations they are all but forbidden from doing so – but instead agreed to lend them to the Asantehene, for three years, which could be renewed. For many in Ghana, a loan was a bitter pill to swallow. 'It turns my stomach to be quite frank,' a Ghanaian filmmaker, Nii Kwate Owoo, told me. 'An armed robber comes into your house, mows down your family and grabs your valuables, and comes back later and says "Ok, you're making noises, I'll give this back as a loan!"'[13] And while the seventeen objects loaned by the V&A represent the entirety of its major Asante treasures, the fifteen objects from the British Museum are only a small part of its much larger Asante collection. In all, the British Museum has about 550 Asante objects taken in the Anglo-Asante Wars, of which about 220 are gold.[14]

The Asantehene took a pragmatic approach to the loan. He explained to me that after 'about fifty years of not making any headway we accepted that option.... We had wished they would not have come to us through loans, but they did.'[15] Ivor Agyeman-Duah agreed. Surely it was worth getting some treasure back, he argued, even if only for a few years. They would be on display, at the Asantehene's palace museum. 'Let's show our children these creations of 150 years ago, and say "your ancestors, your forebears, were able to do some of these marvellous productions." And it could inspire them to do similar things,' he said. Former President John Kufuor also looked on the positive side. 'It's history-making, even if it isn't a total return, it's a breakthrough,' he told me. 'In this world pragmatism must be the top-most ideology. We live in a globalised world. Maybe this loan will be renewed, maybe these objects can also travel around the world. The agreement is a credit to the King.'[16]

I've been writing about museums and looted objects for a number of years. In a previous book, I looked at the Benin Bronzes, also looted by the British from a West African kingdom in the late nineteenth century and which have taken on an emblematic status in discussions about restitution.[17] The story of how the British took the Asante gold is just as shameful as that of how they took the Benin Bronzes. I want to shed light on what happened, and why it still matters in West Africa, and by extension other once-colonised parts of the world. But I also want to confront readers with the complexities and contradictions within even such an apparently straightforward story. This is not a morality tale. Some readers will feel that there are plenty of villains in this book. Others will contend that not all of them are British, and that in any case many of them have redeeming features. The (invariably) men I write about are of their time. Nor is the way ahead always obvious. By the time I was writing this, universities and museums, especially in the United States, were reeling before a conservative backlash. The need for nuanced history, that challenges all of our prejudices, seems more urgent than ever.

★★★

The drive from Accra to Kumasi usually takes six hours, but with the police clearing the way it took barely three. The convoy arrived at the Asantehene's home in Kumasi, the Manhyia Palace, in the afternoon. 'We unpacked the treasures in the King's audience room, where we were joined by some twelve or fifteen palace chiefs,' Julie Hudson said. The objects were pulled out of their cases. Again, a hushed silence. Osei Tutu II was enthralled by all the objects but lingered especially over the helmet and sword. It was a very emotional moment. 'There was so much respect for the objects, and so much joy,' said Julie.

The King asked Malcolm McLeod to say a few words.

'We did it,' Malcolm said simply.

'Yes, we did it,' said the King.

Elmina Castle, 'the first true European building in the tropics'; trading post, slave fort and prison.

1

'THEY SAW A STOOL DESCENDING FROM THE SKY'

In the middle of Kumasi there is a large hospital, built in the 1950s in the tropical-modernist style, a time of optimism as the colonial era drew to an end. The sick and their families who gather each morning outside the now faded buildings convey the same repressed but potent mix of emotions that you feel in hospitals all over the world: silent fear, weary patience and hope. But in the middle of the hospital there is a small olive-coloured pavilion, with a history that is utterly unique to Kumasi. 'Okomfo Anokye Sword Site' reads the sign above the entrance. Inside, at the bottom of what looks like a shallow well, the hilt of a large sword protrudes from the gravel, surrounded by empty bottles of gin, whisky and other spirits, collectively known by Ghanaians as 'schnapps'. The drinks are poured as libations, for this is a holy place and Asante chiefs sacrifice a sheep here every month. The sword, the pavilion caretaker will tell you, was thrust into the ground on this precise spot by Okomfo Anokye himself, the original Asante high priest, in 1695. Anokye said that if anybody could pull his sword from the ground, the Asante kingdom would fall.

'The Cardinal Wolsey of Ashanti' is how some historians describe Anokye.[1] Not a king, but a kingmaker. But if Wolsey's flame flickered only briefly in Tudor England, Anokye is venerated by the Asante to this day. Over the centuries many have tried to free his 'immovable sword', but always in vain. Perhaps the most famous, in 1964, was Muhammad Ali, who had travelled to Ghana to celebrate the new dawn of African independence. In Kumasi, he was taken to the sword in the hospital grounds and could not resist the challenge. For several minutes he wrestled with the hilt, before admitting defeat. The onlookers were delighted. Even 'The Greatest' had failed. Asante had not fallen.

In their oral histories, the Asante – the word means both the people and the kingdom – say they migrated southwards thousands of years ago, from the drylands of the Sahel and beyond, down to the forests of West Africa. They belong to the larger Akan ethnic group, who make up about half of Ghana's population of 35 million and who also spill into the neighbouring country of Côte d'Ivoire to the west.[2] The Akan are linked by their language, which is called Twi, and many customs. But Asante's rise as the dominant power within the Akan only began at the end of the seventeenth century, and according to Asante legend, owes everything to the bond between that great priest Okomfo Anokye and Osei Tutu, a young and handsome Kumasi prince.

Okomfo Anokye was raised in a noble family, and even as a child displayed powers of prophecy. 'When he was playing with his fellow boys, if he informed them that a certain Tree would fall down', Asante legends recount, 'then it all happened so just as he said.'[3] But one day, when out hunting, Anokye accidentally killed a man and was imprisoned in the palace of a king outside Kumasi. Osei Tutu, the Kumasi prince, secured his release. After this, the Asante say, Anokye promised to serve Osei Tutu for the rest of his life.[4] They worked together to expand Kumasi's authority over the surrounding kingdoms. Anokye advised Osei Tutu on military appointments and used magic to ensure their supremacy in battle.

Osei Tutu's greatest victory was over the Denkyira kingdom, which lies to the south-west of Kumasi and had long held it in servitude, extracting tributes in wives and gold. The Denkyira king, Ntim Gyakari, had ten times more soldiers than Osei Tutu, but when their armies met at a place called Feyiase in 1701, Anokye's magic saved the day. In a scene reminiscent of *Macbeth*, Anokye was said to make the trees expand whenever Osei Tutu's soldiers needed to hide. This battle, 'sanguinary and fierce', was a turning point. 'With the vanquishment of Ntim Gyakari, King Osei Tutu the Great became the undisputed Ruler of all the Akan speaking peoples,' according to *History of Ashanti*, an epic account written in the mid-twentieth century by a distant successor of Osei Tutu, the Asantehene Agyeman Prempeh II, working with a committee of scholars.[5] Ntim Gyakari was executed and his head was cast in gold.[6] The word 'Asante' may have its origins in the war against Denkyira. In Twi, 'ɛsa nti' means 'because of war' and Kumasi and its neighbouring kingdoms came together through their shared ambition to overthrow Denkyira and achieve independence.[7]

After this victory, Okomfo Anokye summoned the people of Kumasi to a ceremony intended to elevate Osei Tutu, and his successors, above all other kings. Perhaps not entirely disinterestedly, Prempeh II describes this moment in reverential terms in his *History of Ashanti*: 'They saw a Stool descending down from the sky. It was shrouded in a thick cloud and it lighted gently on the lap of King Osei Tutu. Its appearance was acclaimed with repeated rousing and thunderous cheers by all of the people ... This Stool is known in History as "The Golden Stool of Ashanti." When the noise at last subsided Okomfo Anokye told the Assembly that the souls of all the Ashanti people had been fixed in and enshrined in the Golden Stool and that its occupant should be a father and Supreme Ruler over them all, before whom no one was to raise a hand in contempt.'[8]

The stool is much more than a mere wooden seat in Akan culture. Like a throne in English, it also means the office itself. 'To be enstooled' is to become a king, 'to sit on the stool' is to be a chief or king. 'Stool land', 'stool money' or 'stool farms' are those which belong to a chieftaincy or kingship.[9] But the Golden Stool – or *Sika Dwa* – which Anokye had conjured from the sky was different to any other stool. Osei Tutu, formerly the king of Kumasi or Kumasihene, was now King of all the Asante, or Asantehene. This did not make him a tyrant who could do as he pleased. Anokye told the crowd that 'their power, their health, their bravery their welfare were in this stool.'¹⁰ The Golden Stool embodied the soul of a single, united Asante nation and the Asantehene was the custodian of his people's welfare.

More than 300 years later, the Golden Stool retains its mystical status, its whereabouts known only to a select group of palace courtiers, who bring it out for major festivals and place it on its own throne, to the left of the Asantehene's. Nobody is allowed to sit on it, and it must never touch the ground. Perhaps inevitably, its actual appearance – it is some sixty centimetres high and wide, with bells, charms and effigies of vanquished rivals attached – falls short of its symbolic value. But context is everything. In May 2024, Osei Tutu II held a celebration to mark his Silver Jubilee, the twenty-fifth anniversary of his enstoolment. Thousands of people crowded onto the durbar ground outside the Manhyia Palace, including Ghana's then president, Nana Akufo-Addo. An American visitor told me that when she saw the Golden Stool there, perched beside the King, amidst all the drums, umbrellas, gold and shouts of praise, all the awe and extravagant majesty of Asante, 'it had such heft and solidity to it, it just looked every bit as wonderful as it is meant to look.'¹¹

★★★

Long before the rise of Asante, the Akan lands had been famous for the gold which lay beneath them. The metal was precious to the Akan themselves, but was also coveted by people much further away. In the eighth century, following the Arab conquest of North Africa, small amounts of gold dust were being carried across the Sahara Desert.¹² According to Peter Spufford, a historian who specialised in the medieval economy, this increased to 'considerable quantities at the end of the tenth century, and [the trans-Saharan trade] continued … almost uninterruptedly, until the fifteenth century.' By the eleventh century, meanwhile, West African gold had also reached as far east as Constantinople.¹³

In 1471, the Portuguese arrived by ship on the coast inhabited by the Akan and others, what they initially called the 'Costa da Mina' – the coast of mines – and were impressed by the quantities of gold on offer. In 1482, they sent a small fleet – ten caravels and two supply ships – to construct a permanent base, the fort of São Jorge da Mina ('Elmina'). An Akan king, Kwamena Elsa, watched the Portuguese arrive, loaded with masonry, lime and artillery and said with contempt: 'The Christians who have come here until now have been very few, dirty and base.'[14] But the Portuguese built an imposing white castle, which soon towered over the nearby fishing village and was 'the first true European building in the tropics' according to Ivor Wilks, a distinguished British historian of Asante and West Africa.[15] Portuguese enterprise was rewarded; within a few years traders from the interior flocked to Elmina, where they exchanged their gold for cloths, corals and brass bracelets known as manillas.[16] Other Europeans soon arrived on the coastline, all interested in buying gold, in return for which they sold guns, cloth, brass vessels and alcohol. Elmina, writes Wilks, 'had become transformed into a principal supplier of bullion to the world market and was exporting upwards of half a ton of gold annually'.[17] The Akan were being pulled into a new era of globalisation, full of opportunities but also dangerous unforeseen consequences.

For centuries the Akan panned the sediment of the lazy rivers which wind southwards towards the Atlantic through forests and rolling hills – especially the Pra and its tributary the Ofin – looking for alluvial gold. They dived, dredged and dug trenches and shafts in the gravel along the banks in search of fragments of ore which contained the glittering metal. This was often a seasonal activity, carried out by men, women and children when they were not busy on the farms.[18] But over time the Akan developed more sophisticated techniques, perhaps in response to the burgeoning demand for gold. By the end of the fifteenth century, Europeans learnt that Akan mining pits were 'very deeply driven into the ground'.[19] The Akan used iron-tipped sticks to dig these shafts, some so narrow that a miner could climb up and down by pressing their body against the walls.[20] A British soldier who travelled through Asante at the beginning of the twentieth century wrote that 'in many spots the ground on either side of the path is simply honey-combed with these "gold holes," which, overgrown by grass and small "bush," render walking by day dangerous, and by night impossible.'[21] Ivor Wilks speculates that the Asante were descending as deep as sixty metres below the surface, exploiting reefs as far as was possible without mechanical pumps.[22] They hacked away at the ore with crude chisels and picks made from stone, the discarded remnants of which they called God's axes, *Nyame Akuma*, thunderbolts which had fallen from the sky.[23]

In the 1610s a Portuguese trader, João Rodrigues Roxo, wrote cynically that if only a slave trade could be introduced alongside the gold trade at Elmina, 'there will soon be war among them and that will make them have to trade more gold to finance their wars.'[24] The musket guns – the so-called 'Long Danes' – which the Europeans sold to Africans, were in themselves a catalyst for conflict. According to the Ghanaian historian Kwame Yeboa Daaku, they 'shook the foundations of society', as they gave stronger African states the power to conquer weaker ones.[25] But the 'drastic change' came in the second half of the seventeenth century, with 'the sugar revolution in the New World and its resultant demand for West African slaves …. The Gold Coast, which had been a gold mine both literally and figuratively … now became a "slave mine" for virtually the whole of western Europe.'

Slavery had existed in West Africa long before the arrival of the Europeans, traditionally imposed on prisoners of war, debtors and criminals. One result of the European demand for gold was an increase in the internal West African demand for slaves; a visitor to Asante in the early nineteenth century was told thousands of slaves worked in the pits by river beds in the search for alluvial gold.[26] But West African slaves could traditionally inherit property and marry with their captors and thereby benefit from what the historian Basil Davidson describes as 'an organic absorption of subjected persons into the society that used them.'[27] In contrast, the soul-crushing irreversibility of the new transatlantic trade, not to mention its scale and racial underpinnings, introduced an entirely different degree of cruelty.

In 1637, the Dutch captured Elmina from the Portuguese. The English would soon establish their own stronghold a few kilometres to the east of Elmina, at Cape Coast Castle, which they themselves captured from the Dutch in the 1660s. The gold which England's Royal African Company brought home between 1673 and 1713 was minted into more than half a million guineas.[28] Ivory was a valuable supplement to the Gold Coast trade; elephants were not abundant in the coastal forests, but hunters brought tusks from further north. In 1706, an English ship loaded 339 tusks, each weighing twelve kilograms, described as something never seen 'before from the Gold Coast'.[29] By the eighteenth century there were some eighty forts and castles built by various European powers – the Portuguese, the Dutch, the British, the Swedes, the Danes, the French and the Brandenburg Germans – along a 250-kilometre stretch of the surf-pounded beaches and rocky promontories of the Gold Coast, each jostling to protect its foothold, each with a vested interest in the gold trade, the slave trade and war flourishing in the interior.[30] But if the West African coast was lucrative for Europeans, the high probability of fever – malaria, dysentery and yellow fever – also made it dangerous. In the blunt words of one historian, 'Their paramount interests were to maximize a quick profit and to leave before dropping dead.'[31]

★★★

Asante rose, just as it would one day fall, through conquest and plunder. Its army – not a permanent force but a sort of feudal levy that could be quickly assembled at times of war – developed a reputation for discipline and courage. After their victory in 1701, Osei Tutu and his soldiers entered the Denkyira capital and were 'astonished at the amount of gold there ... All the rooms of the palace were filled with bags and boxes of gold, not excepting the rooms where the King kept his wives.... It took more than two days to bring all this into the main street of the Denkyira capital. Denkyira people themselves who were captives were made to carry this gold back to Ashanti. It was a huge treasure that made King Osei Tutu rich beyond all his expectations,' wrote Prempeh II in *History of Ashanti*.[32]

Reports of a powerful emerging inland kingdom reached the Europeans on the coast. In November 1701, the Dutch recorded the victory of 'the Assjanteese' over the Denkyira, the first known European reference to Asante.[33] Indeed, Asante historians record that the Dutch had sold weapons – cannons, muskets and ammunition – on credit to both Osei Tutu and the Denkyira before the war and that Osei Tutu subsequently agreed to pay off these debts. In return the Dutch transferred the annual 'Rent' payment for Elmina Castle from Denkyira to Asante, thereby acknowledging the new predominant power of the interior.[34]

'The correlation between the growth of [African] empires and the European trade, especially the slave trade, is one of the most important phenomena in the history of the Gold Coast' according to Kwame Yeboa Daaku.[35] In the final quarter of the seventeenth century, shortly before the emergence of Asante, an estimated 75,000 people were forcibly taken from the Gold Coast to the Americas. But in the eighteenth century the transatlantic trade boomed. An estimated 460,000 people were taken from the Gold Coast between 1701 and 1750. 'Most of this massive increase came from Asante, and its name starts to appear with increasing regularity in the British, Dutch and Danish records,' writes the British historian Tom McCaskie. The new kingdom responded to European demand for slaves in 'quite spectacular fashion'.[36]

Osei Tutu was succeeded as Asantehene by Opoku Ware, who was enstooled around 1720. The Asante are ruled by a man, but like other Akan people have a matrilineal system of inheritance, in which almost all offices and property pass through the maternal line and in which the Queen Mother, or Asantehemaa, and royal sisters, wield considerable power. Opoku Ware was a great nephew of Osei Tutu, descended through his sister. 'The true nature of the Asante inheritance is that the clan properties belong to the women's line but the men act as caretakers' is how one Asante scholar explains it.[37]

Opoku Ware reigned for three decades. In Asante oral history he is remembered not only as *Katakyie*, 'the Impregnable Warrior' but also as *Di Sika*, 'the one who ate gold.'[38] He ordered an entire cloth of it, but when he discovered this was too heavy to wear, he told his courtiers to cut it into pieces and turn it into royal regalia.[39] Opoku Ware understood that gold was integral to Asante's power; to adorn its rulers in ornamental splendour, to trade with Europeans, to influence allies and to overawe and entice enemies.[40] In public, he appeared with copious amounts of gold jewellery. He walked under huge umbrellas with gold finials, his spokesmen, or *akyeame*, carried gold-topped staffs and his servants wore gold discs around their necks.

Kumasi was once a small settlement at the northern edge of the dense rainforest which reached down to the Atlantic coast. Its clay huts and narrow paths, gashes of bright red-brown from the laterite soil, were shaded by towering silk cotton and mahogany trees. But the gold and slave trade brought Asante not only guns but also New World crops, such as maize, cassava, cocoyam, groundnuts, tobacco and pineapples. The Asante cleared more land around Kumasi, their farms became more productive and their population grew. Kumasi was gradually developing into a city, its streets lined with two-storey houses and where craftsmen lived in specialist villages.

These craftsmen included skilled goldsmiths, who used the lost wax, or *cire perdue*, method to cast their pieces. The Asante and their trading partners needed accurate tools to measure gold dust and nuggets. The 'gold weights' or *mbrammoo* which the Akan developed for this purpose, cast from brass, are amongst West Africa's most wonderful artworks; small, intricate and full of humour and charm, they bring vibrant societies to life. Some depict people: a man blowing a horn, a woman smoking a pipe, a mother suckling a child, men playing the board game *oware* and so on. Many relate to Asante proverbs. They might portray a porcupine ('never rub bottoms with a porcupine'), a crocodile with fish ('do not insult the crocodile before you cross the river') or a tortoise ('if hair were easy to grow, would not the tortoise have some?').[41] Their sheer abundance suggests the scale of the West African gold trade. One British collector estimates he may have handled more than one million over the course of his life.[42]

Asante's artistic spirit is also displayed in the rich profusion of carved wooden stools, some decorated for royalty with sheets of patterned silver on their seats and legs. It is there, as well, in the carvings of the small female figures called *Akua'ba*, dolls carried by girls and women in days gone by and which symbolise fertility and the Asante ideal of beauty. It is also there in the varieties of *kente* cloth, often made from silk and cotton and woven on narrow strip looms, worn over one shoulder in the style of a toga and paraded at festivals and other social occasions, or used to clothe the dead.

By the end of the eighteenth century, Asante power and influence extended over three to five million people, from the Atlantic seaboard in the south, for some 600 kilometres inland and far into the savannah country to the north, dominating much of what is today Ghana.[43] The Asantehene had sophisticated administrative, judicial and tax systems at his disposal. Malcolm McLeod describes Asante at this time as 'one of Africa's most powerful, complex, and spectacular kingdoms, a state distinguished by its extremely hierarchical ethos, military might and vast wealth.'[44] It might be better understood as a confederation, dominated by the old kingdoms in and around Kumasi, and in which more distant ones had a vassal status, obliged to pay tribute and supply manpower. The Asantehene would consult the more powerful subsidiary kingdoms – such as Bekwai, Dwaben, Kokofu, Mampong and Nsuta – on decisions of diplomacy, war and peace, but the exact status of the tributary and satellite states was often fiercely contested. And as Asante sought to protect its coastal trade, its relations with the Fante to the south, fellow Akan people who had come to occupy a lucrative position as middlemen for the Europeans, grew increasingly fraught.

The forests, and the fear of fever, kept the Europeans largely confined to their Atlantic forts. In 1812, a British official on the Gold Coast wrote that his country 'could claim no right of conquest in Africa ... The people are regulated by their own laws and customs and will not submit to our's [sic] ... The forts have been maintained for the purposes of trade only.'[45] This arm's-length relationship was to Asante's advantage. In 1732, a London publisher released a book by Jean Barbot, a veteran French slave trader. Barbot wrote that West Africans he met on the coast 'had gold mines in their countries, and those not very remote from the coast: but would never tell where, nor how did they work them: so politick and discreet they are in that point, lest foreigners should know them, and be tempted to invade their country, for the sake of those subterraneous treasures.'[46] It was a telling observation. The kingdoms of the interior were wise to meet Europeans on their own terms and guard their secrets.

Asante: fierce pride and pageantry.

2

'KING OF KINGS'

In April of 1817, four British officials, accompanied by more than 100 African carriers and guides left Cape Coast Castle, and marched north, into the forest, in the direction of Kumasi. Their instructions from Governor John Hope Smith were clear: they should present themselves to the Asantehene, to 'conciliate so powerful a monarch, and to propitiate an extension of commerce.'[1] Hope Smith said they should try 'to ascertain where and how the natives collect the gold, and the extent to which trade in that article, and in ivory, might be carried on.'[2] The expedition included the governor's own nephew, a man called Thomas Bowdich, who had trained as a hatter in Bristol, but whose ambitions stretched much further. Natural history, travel and what today we might call anthropology; these were Bowdich's passions. Now in his mid-twenties, the mission to Asante was the opportunity he had been waiting for.

Their journey was not without danger. They passed desolate Fante towns and villages that had been laid waste to by the Asante army. They saw abandoned forest clearings and deserted homes. But the Asantehene, Osei Bonsu, was aware of their approach and 'sent down messages to order that these British visitors and everyone with them was to be treated with kindness and propriety.'[3]

As the British entered Kumasi, they were met by tens of thousands of people and the most terrible din: 'awful bursts of martial music, discordant only in its mixture; for horns, drums, rattles, and gong-gongs were all exerted with a zeal bordering on phrenzy.' The cacophony of instruments, the bangs of blunderbusses, the clouds of gunpowder smoke, the dancing of manic-like figures and the waving of flags – including Danish, Dutch and English – all left Bowdich overwhelmed.[4] Osei Bonsu had invited 'all his Provincial Chiefs and tributaries into Kumasi for the reception of the visitors' and Bowdich and his companions progressed slowly through the packed streets, 'our movement as gradual as if it had taken place in Cheapside'.[5]

Eventually they came to an assembly area 'of nearly a mile in circumference ... crowded with magnificence and novelty.' The Asantehene and his nobility sat before the British, shaded by at least 100 enormous scarlet and yellow umbrellas made from silk and topped with sculptures of pelicans and elephants. Each umbrella was large enough to protect thirty people from the sun. The Asantehene's messengers wore gold breast plates, while his chiefs – Bowdich calls them 'caboceers' – wore 'Roman Togas' and had 'massy gold necklaces, intricately wrought' and gold anklets. 'Gold and silver pipes, and canes dazzled the eye in every direction.' An estimated 30,000 soldiers carried gold-handled swords and muskets with golden rims, and guarded drums decorated with the bones and skulls of vanquished enemies.

As for Osei Bonsu himself, whom Bowdich judged to be in his late thirties, 'his manners were majestic, yet courteous' and his cloth was of dark green silk. He had 'a necklace of gold cockspur shells strung by their largest ends, and over his right shoulder a red silk cord, suspending three saphies [amulets] cased in gold', his bracelets were made from beads and gold, his fingers covered in rings and round his ankles were 'strings of gold ornament of the most delicate workmanship', while his sandals were of soft white leather and decorated with jewels. He held a 'pair of gold castanets on finger and thumb, which he clapped to enforce silence.' His low chair was richly ornamented with gold. His servants waved elephant tails spangled with gold before him, giving the effect of a small cloud. The Golden Stool itself had been placed to the side of him, under its own splendid umbrella.[6] Later, the British were taken to the royal palace, 'an immense building of a variety of oblong courts and regular squares, the former with arcades along the one side ... the entablatures exuberantly adorned with bold fan and trellis work of Egyptian character.' The rooms above had windows covered in wooden lattice, their frames cased in thin gold. The inner chambers had 'chairs and stools embossed with gold, and beds of silk, with scattered regalia'.[7]

'We have intruded this sketch' wrote Thomas Bowdich, 'to impress the power and resources of the monarch we are to conciliate', just as the Asantehene sought to impress his visitors with the splendour of their reception. But was this a meeting of friends? The British brought gifts – 'silks, velvets, glass ware, silver dishes and bowls, a telescope and many other beautiful articles' – which the Asantehene received with gratitude.[8] But he distrusted his visitors, whom he feared had grown too close to their Fante allies. 'I know the English come to spy the country: they come to cheat me; they want war ... They join the Fantees to put shame upon my face,' Bowdich quotes him as saying.[9] Bowdich replied this was not true and that the British had come for trade and friendship. Whereupon Osei Bonsu seemed to melt somewhat. And yet, as his words implied, Anglo-Asante relations were already clouded by suspicion.

The first confrontation had come more than a decade earlier, in 1806, when the Asantehene led his army down to the coast in pursuit of rebellious chiefs of the Asen people who had sought sanctuary with the Fante and the British. A brutal battle took place on the beach outside the small British fort at Anomabu, a few kilometres east of Cape Coast Castle. In *History of Ashanti*, Prempeh II describes the Asante victory: 'The King's army attacked and defeated the Fantis with a great slaughter and captured many prisoners and took much booty.'[10] A nineteenth-century British historian writes more graphically: 'Day dawned upon a horrible scene of bloodshed and devastation. Eight thousand Fantes had perished, most of them in the vicinity of the fort; heaps of dead encumbered the beach in every direction, or were washed hither and thither in the surf, and the sands were red with blood.'[11] Osei Bonsu – hitherto more widely known as Osei Tutu Kwame – takes his name from this victory. He marched over the sand, dipped his *Mpomponsuo* sword into the ocean and demanded the Fante chiefs hail him as a whale, the great animal which sinks ships. 'The King then said *"Efri nne yebefre me OSEI BONSU,"* meaning: "From today onwards I shall be called OSEI BONSU or Osei the Whale."'[12]

An ignoble British humiliation followed. The Governor of Cape Coast, Colonel George Torrane, met Osei Bonsu and recognised, at least verbally, his title to the British forts and castles and his authority over the Fante. Torrane arrested an Asen chief, Kwadwo Otibu, and handed him over to the Asante, to the indignation of those in Cape Coast who had naïvely trusted in British protection. Otibu was tortured and then beheaded by the Asante, his jawbone subsequently attached to Osei Bonsu's ceremonial horn.[13] Torrane also surrendered to the Asante half of the estimated 2,000 Fante refugees who had sheltered in Anomabu Fort. Many of these were sold into slavery.[14] Osei Bonsu returned in triumph to Kumasi. The Asante had shown they could dictate affairs right down to the Atlantic seaboard. Afterwards, Osei Bonsu is said to have reflected that he now took the British as friends 'because I saw their object was trade only and they did not care for the people.'[15] Perhaps, but it hardly seemed a basis for lasting trust. And unfortunately for Osei Bonsu, British trade policy was about to undergo a momentous change.

In the eighteenth century, British ships carried more than two and a half million enslaved Africans across the Atlantic, more than those of any other country.[16] But in 1807, the British parliament passed the Act for the Abolition of the Slave Trade. This reversal of policy made for some dizzying changes of circumstances, not least on the Gold Coast, where British interests were run by the private African Company of Merchants, managed by representatives from Bristol, Liverpool and London. 'On the Gold Coast the abolition of 1807 made illegal some nine-tenths by value of British commerce there,' writes Tom McCaskie. But for Asante too, for whom 'participation in the export-import cycle of the transatlantic slave trade had come to form the bedrock of its commercial economy,' British abolition signalled an unwelcome adjustment.[17] Albert Adu Boahen was an eminent Asante historian and politician of the late twentieth century and his writing suggests an enduring discomfort about the degree of complicity in one of the great European crimes of history: 'That the abolition and suppression of the slave trade came as a shock to many Africans and posed a great challenge to them cannot be denied.'[18]

★★★

Abolition threatened to overshadow Thomas Bowdich's mission to Kumasi in 1817; 'slaving', as he put it, 'being the most natural trade of the natives, because it is the most indolent and the most lucrative.'[19] He passed on letters from Governor Hope Smith at Cape Coast to the Asantehene, explaining that the African Company of Merchants was looking for alternative sources of trade. In one letter, the governor emphasised that 'it is the benevolent anxiety of the British Government to improve the condition of the people of Africa, through the legitimate medium of commerce', but in another he said 'the abolition of the slave trade was an act of the King and the Parliament in England, in which the government of this country had no concern.'[20] Hope Smith could unheroically distance himself from abolition, but no one on the Gold Coast could escape its consequences. Osei Bonsu hoped the British king would 'consider if he cannot renew the Slave Trade, which will be good for me.'[21] Bowdich worried that as long as other European countries persisted with their trade the Asante would 'view the English invidiously, as the enemies to what they conceive to be their only natural commerce.'[22]

Disagreements notwithstanding, by the time Thomas Bowdich left Kumasi, in September 1817, he had successfully convinced the Asantehene to sign a 'Treaty of Trade and Friendship.' This recognised the authority of the British Governor to mediate between the Asante and Fante people close to Cape Coast but also obliged the British to protect any Asante who travelled south into this area. Osei Bonsu provided Thomas Bowdich and his companions with 'Guides and Hammock-men' and ordered his musketeers to fire volleys in honour of their departure. He instructed his chiefs to study the treaty carefully and explain it to towns and villages across the Asante lands, as he 'had determined in his mind to become the friend of the English on the coast, as well as the King of England.'[23] He even entrusted Bowdich with four of his children, who were to enjoy the benefits of a British education at Cape Coast Castle.

Thomas Bowdich's eventful life ended only seven years later, in 1824, when he died of malaria on the River Gambia at Africa's western tip. He was thirty-three. He was travelling with his wife, Sarah, who was left destitute with three young children but would go on to build her own remarkable career as a zoologist and author.[24] Bowdich's posthumous fame had already been secured, for his account of his four months as a guest of Osei Bonsu, *Mission from Cape Coast to Ashantee*, had been published in London in 1819. His description and lavish illustrations of a wealthy African kingdom at the height of its powers (see plate section) were initially met with disbelief, but it soon established itself as a reference book for Asante and non-Asante historians alike and is still frequently quoted today.[25] Less enduring, though, was the Anglo-Asante friendship Bowdich had worked to secure.

The Asante historian Joseph Adjaye describes Osei Bonsu as a man with a strong faith in 'the sanctity of international agreements [and] zeal in seeking the external goals of his nation through peace and diplomacy.'[26] His British interlocutors were less consistent. In 1819, Asante tax collectors were attacked by Fante crowds at Cape Coast and nearby Komenda.[27] Osei Bonsu sent messengers urging Governor Hope Smith to enforce the terms of their treaty. When the messengers reported back to Kumasi that the British refused to help, an enraged Osei Bonsu had them clapped in irons.[28] Rivalries between British officials on the Gold Coast in the 1810s and 1820s were compounded by suspicion and frustrations in London, where abolitionists were dismayed at the African Company's failure to diversify away from slavery and a parliamentary committee picked over reports of mismanagement and corruption within its ranks.[29] Osei Bonsu, unaware of these distant machinations, veered between 'hope, puzzlement, disappointment and anger' in his dealings with the British.[30]

In February 1820, another British envoy arrived in Kumasi. Joseph Dupuis had been sent from London to, as he put it, 'cultivate the existing harmony with the king of Ashantee, and, upon the basis of a mutual confidence, to nurture the seeds of an accidental friendship.'[31] Dupuis agreed a new treaty with Osei Bonsu, which conceded Asante sovereignty over Fante territory to the south while also placing this same territory under British jurisdiction. It was a subtle distinction that was unlikely to survive the frequent misunderstandings between Britain and Asante. In any case, Governor Hope Smith, who had opposed Dupuis's mission from the start, refused to ratify his treaty. The governor told his superiors in London that Dupuis had gone too far to accommodate Asante; 'no individual, however imbecile, who has ever had influence over the affairs of Africa, has by his timidity and malignancy, (an expression as true as it is strong) so much reduced the influence of Europeans as Mr. Dupuis.'[32]

Joseph Dupuis returned to Britain in April 1820 a disappointed man. But like Thomas Bowdich before him, he left a revealing account of his stay in Kumasi. Osei Bonsu, according to Dupuis, understood the importance of an alliance with Britain. Here were two powers, unrivalled in their respective parts of the world, with mutual interests. 'He declared that he knew the English king to be king over all other white kings and that his subjects were the most powerful and warlike of the white nations; just as he was the black "king of kings, and his people the greatest black warriors."'[33] Osei Bonsu had still not forgiven the British for trying to end the slave trade. 'If they think it bad now,' Dupuis quotes him as saying, 'why did they think it good before…? If the great king would like to restore this trade, it would be good for the white men and for me too, because Ashantee is a country for war, and the people are strong.'[34] He offered 10,000 of his own slaves to the British king, 'And if he wants fine handsome girls and women to give his captains, I can send him great numbers.'[35]

In July 1821, the government in London dissolved the African Company of Merchants, which had 'connived at the maintenance of the slave trade' and assumed direct responsibility for the eight British forts and other possessions on the Gold Coast.[36] These came under the authority of Governor Sir Charles MacCarthy, who was based in Freetown, Sierra Leone, some 2,000 kilometres to the west of the Gold Coast. MacCarthy – a tall, bearded, Irish army officer, veteran of the Napoleonic Wars and fervent abolitionist – sailed to the Gold Coast and expressed delight with its 'beautiful appearance'.[37] Osei Bonsu initially took his appointment as 'welcome news ... for he hoped this new Governor would not treat him as badly and dishonestly as Hope Smith had done', according to Prempeh II's *History of Ashanti*.[38] But MacCarthy, or 'Mankata' as his name was pronounced on the Gold Coast, quickly decided that Britain's interests lay with the Fante, not the Asante.[39] 'Instead of hearing from both sides the new Governor formed the firm opinion that the Fantis were sadly oppressed and trodden down,' according to Prempeh II's *History of Ashanti*. Osei Bonsu waited for a formal greeting from MacCarthy, but when he learnt the governor was in fact enlisting soldiers for a war against Asante he 'was flabbergasted, for he truly could not understand the ways of the British and their Governors.'[40]

In Sir Charles MacCarthy's newspaper, the *Royal Gold Coast Gazette*, Osei Bonsu, assiduously courted by Thomas Bowdich and Joseph Dupuis only a few years earlier, was now denounced as 'the horrid monster of wickedness', 'the great barbarian [who] foamed at the mouth' and whose captains had vowed to 'cut the throats of all the whites ... [so that] their skulls and limbs might ornament the banqueting room.'[41] By the beginning of 1824, after a series of skirmishes, MacCarthy was leading an army, comprised of the recently formed Royal African Corps – West Indians brought from Sierra Leone – as well as a collection of local allies of varying degrees of commitment, into Asante territory where he hoped to inflict a decisive defeat on Osei Bonsu.

Sir Charles MacCarthy's hubris caught up with him at the Battle of Nsamankow on 22 January 1824. His men were already exhausted by the march through the forest, carrying heavy loads on muddy paths and were running short of food. His gunpowder and other supplies were soaked by rain and river crossings. His intelligence, too, was faulty; he had been led to believe the Asante army was poorly motivated and anyway still some way to the north. His problems were compounded by his decision to split off columns into diversionary forces, meaning that an army of a few thousand had dwindled to 500. He stumbled into his opponents, some 10,000 strong, and suffered a defeat which cost him his life.

One of MacCarthy's officers, and a successor as Gold Coast Governor, Major Henry John Ricketts, left an account of the battle. The Asante 'armed with muskets, and having a large description of knives stuck in their girdles ... were heard advancing through the woods with horns blowing and drums beating.' MacCarthy ordered the band of the Royal African Corps to respond with 'God Save the King,' but this had no impact on the Asante advance. 'Our gallant little force' in Major Ricketts's words, 'were completely overpowered by their myriads, who instantly beheaded nearly every one of those who unfortunately fell into their remorseless hands.'[42] Mr J. T. Williams, Colonial Secretary, was captured by the Asante in the battle and 'locked up at night in the same room with the heads of Sir Charles, Mr Buckle, and Ensign Wetherell, [another British official and a soldier], which, owing to some peculiar process, were in a perfect state of preservation. Sir Charles MacCarthy's presented nearly the same appearance as when he was alive.' Williams, in excruciating pain from a bullet wound in his thigh and tormented by the heads of his erstwhile companions, was forced to watch more beheadings and only given 'as much snail soup in the morning and evening as could be contained in the palm of his hand.' Two weeks later, naked and with his hands tied, he was released at Elmina.[43]

The news of the disaster at Nsamankow did not reach London until May, and only in a roundabout way when a ship from Barbados passed on the information from West Africa. This defeat, inflicted 'by a people only known to us as barbarians', said *The Times*, was cause for 'grief, shame, and apprehension'.[44] The Asante, according to their own accounts, had intended to capture Sir Charles MacCarthy, but after he and his companions killed several Asante soldiers with their guns, they shot him dead. 'He was divested of his uniform and his corpse was beheaded. His head was taken off to Kumasi,' according to Prempeh II's *History of Ashanti*. But this 'splendid victory' was overshadowed by tragic news from home. The Asante army would customarily have been led by its king in such an important engagement, but Osei Bonsu was gravely ill back in Kumasi. The news of his death reached Nsamankow just as the battle began and 'greatly infuriated the Ashanti troops who now fought like a lioness who had lost her cubs'.[45]

★★★

In 1830, a London publisher, Fisher, Son & Co., printed a series of guidebooks entitled, 'The Modern Voyager and Traveller.' It said these would be 'avoiding all dry and uninteresting details' and were 'peculiarly adapted for Youth, by whom books of Voyages and Travels are generally sought after with the greatest avidity'.[46] Today they provide valuable insights, not necessarily into how the world was in the early nineteenth century but into how the British thought it was.

Volume I of 'The Modern Voyager and Traveller' is devoted to Africa and has a lengthy chapter on Asante. The tone is surprisingly emollient. There is no mention of Sir Charles MacCarthy. Perhaps this is because, by the time the book was published, relations between Asante and Britain were on the mend. Although the First Anglo-Asante War had not yet reached a formal conclusion – a peace treaty between the British, the coastal kingdoms and the Asante was signed at Cape Coast Castle in April 1831 – hostilities had stopped. Asante would renounce territorial claims to the kingdoms to the south in return for respect and free passage for its traders. These terms reflect the crushing British victory that had taken place at the Battle of Katamanso (also called Dodowa), in August 1826, close to Accra on the coast. The Asantehene, Osei Yaw Akoto, successor to Osei Bonsu, had made the mistake of fighting on an open plain, terrain which favoured his enemies. The British, with the assistance of local allies including the Fante, the Ga, the Denkyira, the Akwamu and the Akyem, estimated they killed 5,000 Asante soldiers. In the heat of battle, just as it seemed the Asante would prevail, the British fired their Congreve rockets. These had a devastating effect as they 'occasioned the most dire terror and confusion; the hissing sound when thrown, the train of fire, the explosion and ghastly wounds they made, caused them to suppose they were thunder.'[47]

The wounded Osei Yaw Akoto escaped Katamanso with the Golden Stool itself, but the loss of other Asante regalia was 'immense', perhaps worth as much as half a million pounds according to contemporary reports.[48] British officials sent at least two captured objects back to England. One is a wooden drum, sixty centimetres high and perforated with musket shots. It was presented to George IV in October 1827 and has been on loan from the Royal Collection to the British Museum since 1938.

Two human jawbones that were once attached to it are now missing.[49]

The other object, intriguingly, is said to be Sir Charles MacCarthy's skull. *The Times*, in its report of the Battle of Katamanso, said it was amongst 'the sad trophies' of the day. The Asantehene had:

> carried it always with him as a powerful charm, and on the morning of the battle, he poured a libation of rum on it ... to cause all the heads of the whites on the field to lie beside it. The skull is enveloped in paper, covered with Arabic, and a silk handkerchief; over all is tiger-skin, the emblem of royalty, which shows the estimation in which he was held by them.[50]

The skull was delivered by ship to customs officials in Dartmouth, Devon in November 1826, in a package addressed to Earl Bathurst, Secretary of State for War and the Colonies.[51] It was then interred in St Saviour's Church in Dartmouth, where in the 1880s workmen renovating the chancel uncovered it in a wooden box.[52]

Despite these precise details, the fate of MacCarthy's skull remains an enduring mystery of Anglo-Asante historiography. In the mid-nineteenth century, two European missionaries in Kumasi separately reported that MacCarthy's skull was still with the Asante. One said it was 'preserved with great care', the other that it was 'kept in a brass basin, covered with a white cloth' in the royal mausoleum at Bantama, just outside Kumasi.[53] Moreover, an African man fighting for the British in the 1820s, John Duncan, who spent years as a prisoner in Kumasi, said the decorated skull carried off by the British at the Battle of Katamanso was not in fact MacCarthy's but belonged to the previous Asantehene Osei Bonsu, which Osei Yaw Akoto had taken to war for good fortune.[54] This, strangely, would mean that the skull in the Devon church does not belong to a British soldier but to one of Africa's mightiest kings, taken to England by mistake.

★★★

Three decades of peace between the British and the Asante followed the treaty of 1831 and 'The Modern Voyager and Traveller' reflects the optimism at the beginning of this peaceful hiatus. 'It is somewhat remarkable that we should just now, for the first time in the course of two hundred years, learn any thing certain of this rich and populous nation whose capital is not much more than 150 miles from the British factory.'[55] Friendship with the Asante, it argues, would unlock the wealth of the African interior: 'it will be a great mistake if the shortest and best road for Europeans to Timbuctoo, will not be found to be that from Coomassie.'[56] The book reaches back to the first years of the nineteenth century, to quote the then Governor George Torrane: 'all the principal Ashantees seem half a century advanced in civilization beyond the people on the waterside … an intercourse securely opened with Ashantee, offers prospects of the highest advantage, and the more so as the slave trade is now at an end. The Ashantees have ivory and gold in great abundance.'[57]

'The Modern Voyager and Traveller' leans heavily on Thomas Bowdich's account of 1819 for its descriptions of Asante culture but also for the spirit in which it is written. Bowdich did not romanticise the Asante. Indeed, he was often appalled by them. On his first day in Kumasi, he wrote, he saw a man being tormented prior to his sacrifice. He had a knife through his cheeks, one ear was cut off and the other hung by a thread, he had knives in his shoulder blades and was being led through the crowd by a cord that ran through his nose.[58] After Bowdich observed the annual Yam Festival, at the beginning of September, which involved a parade of more than 100 skulls of enemies of the Asante, he wrote, 'I never felt so grateful for being born in a civilized country.' He wrote about the sacrifices that accompanied this festival, as well as the funerals of prominent persons, when slaves would run from their houses and hide so as not to be selected for execution. Although typically, he 'observed apathy, more frequently than despair or emotion, in the looks of the victims.'[59]

And yet, Thomas Bowdich found much to admire as he came to know his hosts. He estimated that Kumasi was a city of some 100,000 people, with handsome architecture in which 'arcades and piazzas were common' and there were rigorous standards of domestic hygiene. He was impressed by the potters and goldsmiths, as well as the beautiful women of the 'higher orders' with their 'finest figures' and 'regular Grecian features with brilliant eyes set rather obliquely in the head'.[60] And, despite unfavourable initial impressions, he even learnt to enjoy Asante music: its flutes had 'a sweetness and animation beyond any barbarous compositions I ever heard'. In one memorable scene, he described being taken to a feast by the Asantehene in a garden square in a village outside Kumasi. They sat in the shade of four large scarlet umbrellas and dined on roast pigs and ducks, eaten with silver cutlery, and received gifts of gold. 'We never saw a dinner more handsomely served, and never ate a better,' wrote Bowdich.[61]

When Thomas Bowdich took Osei Bonsu's hand for the last time, after the signing of the treaty in September 1817, he 'reflected on the benevolence, the solicitude and the generosity I had experienced whilst my life was in his hand.'[62] The Asante king had enjoyed talking with Bowdich – albeit through interpreters – and especially questioning him about life in England. The Asantehene's curiosity had been piqued by one institution in particular, for Bowdich wrote that Osei Bonsu's parting gifts included for 'the British Museum, six specimens of the goldsmith's work. (I had interested the King, by my account of this national repository).'[63]

In 1818, back in England, Thomas Bowdich donated a collection of thirty-three Asante objects to the British Museum. He listed these carefully: 'Carpentry of Ashantee', 'Ashantee pottery', 'a child's umbrella (injured by damp)' and a dagger with a decorated brass hilt. He also listed the 'Goldsmith's work of the Ashantee': two circular pendants, a tiny golden drum and bell and a miniature lute-harp, barely four centimetres across, modelled on the full-size instrument said to have been played by the first Asantehene, Osei Tutu.[64] Bowdich complained that the goldsmith who had made these had been distracted by other commissions and had been sent to prison before he could complete them, and his modest donation to the British Museum barely hinted at the power and wealth of Asante.[65] And yet he had respected Osei Bonsu's wish that the national museum in London would include amongst its vast inventory objects which would serve as lasting ambassadors for his kingdom.

Inspiration flowed both ways. In 1820, Osei Bonsu took Joseph

Dupuis to a building site adjacent to his palace. He told the Englishman he wanted to build a fort 'like Cape Coast Castle', high enough to see the whole city. '"Do you know captain", said his majesty, "why I sent you? That building you see is to be made very grand. The inside shall be gold, ivory and brass pan."'[66] In May 1822, the *Royal Gold Coast Gazette* reported that the new building was complete: 'The house is built of stone, is two stories high, and the apartments are spacious ... the masons and other artificers were sent to him from Elmina, a few likewise were sent from Dutch and Danish Accra; lime and American boards were supplied from Elmina.' Osei Bonsu had searched far and paid 'liberally' in gold for the best materials and skilled labour.[67]

While the palace itself remained the heart of Asante political life, the new stone *Aban*, or Palace of Culture, projected the kingdom's grandeur to visitors. A Methodist missionary, Thomas Birch Freeman, the son of an African father and English mother, visited Kumasi in 1841 and was invited to see the *Aban* by the then Asantehene, Kwaku Dua. He paints an urbane scene:

> We entered a court yard, ascended a flight of stone steps, and passed through an ante-room into a small hall, in which were tastefully arranged on tables thirty-one gold-handled swords. In the same room were several of the King's calabashes [gourds used for storage], overlaid with gold, out of which he drinks palm-wine ... On tables in different parts of the room various articles manufactured in glass were arranged, such as candle-shades, beautifully cut glass tumblers, wine-glasses, &c., time-pieces, covered with glass-shades, &c.; and almost every piece was decorated with golden ornaments of various descriptions ... The weight of pure barbaric gold which we saw, would probably be from eight hundred to one thousand ounces. Two small boxes, about sixteen inches deep, were shown as specimens of native workmanship.[68]

Ivor Wilks says the *Aban* was 'one of the most cherished projects of

Osei Bonsu, who had been interested to learn of the functions of its distinguished and older counterpart, the British Museum.'[69] Was it really a 'museum' as we might understand the term? People could not just wander in off the streets of Kumasi to admire its treasures. And yet Freeman's description, of themed displays of local arts and crafts, as well as splendid objects from elsewhere, has many of the characteristics of what we call a museum today.

Sadly, the *Aban* would not survive the depredations of later British visitors and the spirit of cultural reciprocity that briefly flourished between Osei Bonsu and Thomas Bowdich would prove an aberration in the overwhelmingly unhappy story of nineteenth-century Anglo-Asante relations. And yet, a small part of that spirit has survived the history. In 2024, when Julie Hudson of the British Museum brought back to Kumasi some of the objects plundered by British soldiers in 1874 and 1896, she also carried with her the miniature golden lute-harp, *sika sankuo*, which Osei Bonsu gave to Bowdich (see plate section). It is now on display in the Manhyia Palace Museum. A delicate eight grams of gold, it is not the most extraordinary of the thirty-two objects the British returned to Ghana. But it is the only one that offers a tantalising glimpse of how Anglo-Asante history might have taken a different path.

Sir Garnet Wolseley said Asante was 'the most horrible war I ever took part in', but it made him a household name.

3

'AN END TO ALL THE PEACE AND QUIET'

'*Asante Kotoko, wokum apem a apem beba*', goes the Asante war cry. 'Porcupine Asante; if you kill a thousand, a thousand more will appear.' Peter King Appiah, a small thickset man with twinkling eyes, leans forward in his chair and says, 'I'm a full-blooded Asante,' and laughs loudly. Peter is Head of Research at Kumasi's Centre for National Culture and we are sitting in his dark office, sharing a breakfast of *fufu* – pounded cassava – and spicy stew. 'Sometimes people call us arrogant,' he says. 'But the Anglo-Asante Wars invoke a sense of pride and dignity. They are in our songs ... We were the tribe that withstood the British – not just once, but maybe in seven different wars.'[1]

The Asante are hardly unique in building an identity around great victories and valiant defeats. Indeed, they are not unlike their old foes the British in this respect. But their sense of pride can be overpowering for other ethnic groups in the modern state of Ghana. 'Japanese tourists tell me they've heard so much more about the Asante than the nation Ghana,' Peter says. 'They even asked me "Is Ghana part of Asante, or the other way round?" I had to correct them!' He laughed again, with pleasure.

Asante celebrates its prowess in war, but the Asantehene who steered his kingdom through the fraught decades of the mid-nineteenth century was a man of peace. Kwaku Dua was enstooled in 1834, ruled for more than thirty years and is remembered above all for his aversion to military adventurism. His outlook was shaped by his experiences as a young man at the Battle of Katamanso, where he witnessed the grievous losses suffered by the Asante against the British. In Asante folklore there is a story of the youthful Kwaku Dua meeting a destitute soldier, who is so hungry he is prepared to eat a bird's head. The soldier said it was war which had reduced him to this pitiful state, whereupon Kwaku Dua vowed to follow a peaceful path.[2] To achieve peace, he had to master rival factions and their competing agendas. Asante relied on trade but was landlocked and defended its interests through a combination of conquest and friendly alliances. But the end of the slave trade had exacerbated tensions between those Asante chiefs who favoured a strong military and aggressive foreign policy, as well as the enrichment that came with conquest, and a newer class of merchants who profited from the trade in gold and palm oil with Europeans on the coast, as well as gold and kola nuts with Muslim states to the north.

Kwaku Dua could do little about the gradual spread of British authority over the Gold Coast to the south. British exports from the Gold Coast, worth £131,000 in 1831, had risen to £325,000 by 1840.[3] The British established a more formal protectorate in 1844 in which 'protected tribes', such as the Denkyira and Asen, subscribed to a 'Bond' and recognised their jurisdiction.[4] Britain's European rivals were gradually being elbowed aside; in 1850, Britain purchased the Danish settlements for £10,000. In that same year, the British Gold Coast was separated administratively from Sierra Leone and would soon acquire its own supreme court and legislative assembly.[5]

By the early 1860s, Kwaku Dua's policy of realpolitik and peace was breaking down. In April 1863, he ordered an Asante army across the Pra River, the boundary of the still ill-defined British protectorate, in pursuit of a fugitive chief who had escaped with gold. The British governor, Richard Pine, wrote to London with a request for an army of sufficient size to defeat Asante and capture Kumasi. In this way, he argued, 'a final blow shall be struck at Ashanti power, and the question set at rest for ever, as to whether an arbitrary, cruel and sanguinary monarch shall be for ever permitted to insult the British flag and outrage the laws of civilisation.' Without this support, Pine wrote, 'the most I can hope is, to drive the Ashantis from the Protectorate ... and remain in constant dread of subsequent incursions of a powerful enemy.'[6]

Richard Pine's plea exposed a fundamental ambivalence in the British position in West Africa in the 1860s. Governors on the ground pushed for an extension of British control as a means to suppress the slave trade and increase trade, but governments in London – concerned about cost and the lives of white British soldiers – were still reluctant to move beyond the coastline. On this occasion London prevailed and Pine was turned down.

In December 1863, Asante troops crossed the Pra River again and Pine responded by sending as many soldiers as he could muster, mainly West Indians based on the coast, up to the frontier. They established quarters by the Pra, but with the onset of the rains in March 1864 dysentery and malaria swept through their ranks and they were withdrawn without firing a shot. Many men, too weak to carry their guns and ammunition, dropped them into the river or buried them in the forest before staggering back to the coast.[7] Kwaku Dua triumphantly observed: 'The white man may bring his cannon to the bush, but the bush is stronger than the cannon.'[8] And yet the apparent lesson for the Asante from this fiasco, that Britain lacked the resolve to fight another large-scale war against them, would prove dangerously misleading.

Ivor Wilks writes that following the death of Kwaku Dua in April 1867 it was a 'tragedy' that the war interests in both Asante and the Gold Coast Colony were in the ascendancy, drawing them into conflict.[9] Prempeh II's *History of Ashanti* explains the frustration of those who supported a more aggressive foreign policy:

> Kwaku Dua ruled peacefully. He never did lead the Ashanti army to invade or attack any other country. But as the Ashantis were warlike people, they thought this was not right at all. Many Chiefs and Kumasi Elders saw that Ashanti became powerful and feared because of its wars and so they wished

to continue with them and to gain riches and fame for themselves from them. After Kwaku Dua's Funeral Custom many chiefs ... said that they heartily longed for war and all of its benefits as in the past times of glory.[10]

The new Asantehene, Kofi Karikari, emerged weeks later out of a contested succession process. He lacked his predecessor's authority but also his cautious instincts. 'On the day he was sworn into office', according to Asante folklore, 'Kakari [sic] held a flint in his mouth to indicate to the people that they should prepare themselves for his objective was war.'[11]

The Dutch withdrawal from the Gold Coast during this period, culminating in their sale of Elmina to the British in 1871, made Karikari's prophecy all but inevitable. The Asante position was clear; Elmina was not for the Dutch to sell. Karikari wrote to the British administrator at Cape Coast Castle, Herbert Taylor Ussher, and explained that the Dutch had 'from time immemorial paid annual tribute to my ancestors by right of arms ... Elmina ... is mine by right.'[12] The Dutch informed the British that they had indeed paid an annual sum to Asante, not as rent or tribute, but rather out of friendship, a sort of gift to lubricate relationships and encourage trade. The core of the disagreement was about the exact obligations that came with the so-called 'notes' held by Asante not only for Elmina but a number of coastal settlements. Did these 'notes' confer a right to extract rent and did the payment of that rent imply a recognition of sovereignty? In earlier times, writes the historian Joseph Adjaye, 'as long as no attempt was made to give definition to what the notes represented, European officials were prepared to pay ... without question.'[13] But in the 1870s, as colonial ambitions began to harden, questions of sovereignty could not always be fudged. The British hesitated, but then took Dutch assurances at face value and pressed ahead with the Elmina purchase. For Asante, this was a loss of honour but also a strategic and economic setback. The Elmina people had traditionally allied with Asante in wars with the Fante and had protected Kumasi's imports of muskets and ammunition. Britain was now the sole European power on the Gold Coast. And Asante had lost its gateway to the Atlantic world.

Britain's interests were also growing in the eastern part of the Gold Coast, as officials and traders moved inland from the settlement at Accra and up the Volta River, historic lands of the Ewe people. Karikari had sent an army to re-establish Asante authority in this area, under the command of a ruthless young general, Adu 'Bofuo' – 'the hunter' – Bobi, 'nationalistic and committed to the ideology of an imperial Greater Asante.'[14] In June 1869, Bofuo's army seized Swiss and German missionaries, as well as a French trader, and marched them back to Kumasi, where they would spend the next four years. The Swiss missionary couple, the Ramseyers, lost their baby son on the march, but would have two more children in Kumasi. Initially chained at night, they and the other Europeans gradually came to be treated as special guests, with a monthly allowance of gold dust for shopping and servants to wait on them.[15] But they were hostages, at the centre of negotiations which pulled in the British and hastened the drift towards war.

Adu Bofuo took a hard line; the Europeans should only be released upon payment of a large ransom. He also wanted assurances that the British would put a stop to Fante attacks on Asante traders, release Asante captives held at Cape Coast Castle and offer better terms on trade. Prempeh II's *History of Ashanti* records the anger of Kumasi elders that 'Fante troublemakers', assisted by the kings of Denkyira, Asen and Akyem, were engaged in a 'disgraceful blockade', preventing Asante traders from reaching Elmina. All these people, 'former subjects and slaves', needed to be punished 'for their treacherous and insulting behaviour'.[16] The Fante could be easily defeated, and if the British stood in the way, they too must be confronted. 'I have been to war,' said Adu Bofuo, 'I have gained victories, and lost more than a thousand men, and now I am to give up all that has been gained? No! ... never, never will I let these prisoners go free! Never I say!'[17]

***

At the end of February 1873, the steamship *Bonny* arrived in Britain with dramatic news from West Africa: 'Ashantee Invasion'.[18] An Asante army, comprised of 12,000 fighting men, had taken five days to cross the Pra

River in late January. British officials reported that 'marauding parties ... have entered the protected territories and have plundered and burnt some villages'. The King of Elmina, still allied to Asante, was reported to have asked for their assistance 'to drive out the British Government'. The British, in turn, offered arms and ammunition to all 'loyal Kings and Chiefs' who resisted the invaders.[19] The Asante took the town of Dunkwa in April 1873 and were soon some thirty kilometres from Cape Coast. Refugees flooded south. Beleaguered British officers, in charge of a combined force of less than 1,000 men – West Indians, Hausas (Muslim soldiers, often from what is today northern Nigeria and used by the British across West Africa in this period), Fante policemen and local volunteers – warned it would be impossible to defend the coastal forts.[20]

The Asante invasion of the Gold Coast was a rude awakening for Britain. As recently as 1865, a parliamentary committee had examined whether it was worth Britain's trouble to stay in the Gold Coast at all and concluded that any 'further extension of territory or assumption of government would be inexpedient.' In the meantime, Britain should seek to transfer more administration to local chiefs, 'with a view to our ultimate withdrawal.'[21] And yet the subsequent purchase of Elmina had signalled a much deeper commitment. These contradictions had consequences, which the government in London would now have to confront.

On 10 May, John Wodehouse, the Earl of Kimberley, Colonial Secretary in William Gladstone's government, met with Edward Cardwell, Secretary of State for War, and decided to send more West Indian soldiers to the Gold Coast as well as some 100 Royal Marines. It was a holding measure, reflecting in part the government's lack of information, but also its inherent aversion to deeper involvement. When, later in May, Kimberley was presented with a proposal from the War Office to invade Asante, he was scornful: 'If we wish to weaken ourselves we cannot adopt a better course than to spend a few millions in conquering Ashantee, and establishing a West African Empire. It is to be hoped that no Govt. will be mad enough to embark on so extravagant an enterprise.'[22]

Many Asante soldiers had brought their wives and children on the invasion and their progress southwards was leisurely, and often delayed by pillaging.²³ But in early June, Amankwa Tia, commander of the main army, resumed his advance to Jukwa, just twenty kilometres to the north of Elmina and nearby Cape Coast, where a Fante force blocked his way. 'The battle was very severe,' *The Times* reported, but 'after a stubborn resistance the Fantee were driven from all their positions with great slaughter. The Fantees fled in great confusion to Cape Coast and were greatly harassed during their retreat.'²⁴ Some 30,000 refugees arrived in Cape Coast, looking for shelter, food and water.²⁵

The Asante were now free to move down to the coast itself. One hundred and nine British Royal Marines, who made a timely landing from HMS *Barracouta* on 9 June, were rushed to Elmina Castle, where the neighbouring town, of some 10,000 people, was already filling with Asante soldiers. 'The Elminas had continued actively to aid the Ashantees,' according to *The Times*, 'supplying them with arms and ammunition'. ²⁶ On 13 June, the British bombarded the town with rockets and artillery from the castle walls, as well as from boats offshore. The assault, according to Lieutenant Colonel Francis Festing of the Royal Marines, lasted only fifteen minutes, sufficient for the British to have 'destroyed the treacherous quarter' of Elmina.²⁷ 'Flames were soon issuing from every part of the town. Constant explosions were heard, as large quantities of gunpowder were concealed in the houses.'²⁸ The British advanced from the castle into the burning streets and onto the beaches and drove back the Asante soldiers.²⁹

It was a victory for the British, of sorts, but their overall situation remained dire. The Asante army, now estimated at 30,000, held the country between Elmina and Cape Coast and rumours of an imminent assault on the latter were rife.³⁰ The news from Elmina did not reach London until mid-July, in part because the captain of the mailboat *Calabar* had unvaliantly sailed off without waiting for the outcome of the battle.³¹ But when Kimberley learnt of what had happened, he wrote, 'An end to all the peace and quiet for the unlucky Colonial Office.'³²

★★★

In the 1980s, Albert Adu Boahen wrote eloquently of how African rulers at the end of the nineteenth century did not realise 'the Europe they were about to encounter was not the same Europe that they had been dealing with since the fifteenth century.' It was a Europe transformed by the Industrial Revolution, hungry for raw materials and markets. It wanted territorial control, not just informal influence. It was a Europe that had the steamship, the railway, the telegraph, all of which facilitated a dramatically faster movement of information and soldiers. It had new weapons, much more destructive than those available to Africans. It also had improved techniques to avoid and resist disease, especially malaria. 'Our forefathers', wrote Adu Boahen, 'miscalculated so gravely' in failing to understand this transformation of European power and ambition.[33]

Not all the changes described by Adu Boahen had taken effect by the 1870s. Communication between West Africa and Britain, for example, was still ponderous and erratic. The competition between European powers to claim the African interior – the 'Scramble for Africa' – had not yet begun in earnest. But in other respects, the new world he described was already taking shape and Britain, the pre-eminent global power, was at its vanguard.

The Asante soldiers who fought the British on and around the beaches of Elmina were amongst the first to confront this new reality. They came armed with 'Long Dane' muskets, down the barrels of which they poured gunpowder, followed by 'bullets' made of lumps of lead, scrap metal or stones. These weapons were inaccurate and unreliable, although the loud explosions and clouds of smoke, mixed with war cries and the beat of drums, could have a powerful psychological impact.[34] But the British responded with Sniders, their new breech-loading rifle, which gave them far greater speed and accuracy of fire. Lieutenant Colonel Festing reported that the Asante showed 'great dash', but 'staggered from the rapid fire pouring in from the Snider on all sides'. The British, outnumbered, killed more than 200 Asante soldiers and suffered only two deaths of their own. 'They have not been seen since, and I do not believe they will dare to face Englishmen again, at least in the plain,' wrote another British officer.[35]

In July and August of 1873, the Asante general Amankwa Tia pulled his men back from the coast amidst heavy rains and outbreaks of smallpox and dysentery amongst his men.[36] The fighting at Elmina, and subsequent skirmishes, had left him with a feeling of foreboding. He had learnt, according to Prempeh II's *History of Ashanti*, that the Asante 'could no longer withstand the British with their new and greatly superior weaponry.'[37] The Snider was not quite the Maxim gun, which would inflict terrible slaughter in the coming decades, but its arrival signalled the dawn of a new era in colonial warfare.

On 13 August 1873, British ministers and generals met at the War Office to discuss the Gold Coast. Kimberley and Cardwell's thinking had progressed. 'It is very provoking to have to spend such large sums of money on these savages,' wrote Kimberley, 'but we cannot leave the matter as it is.'[38] He and Cardwell had already approved a plan for Commander John Glover of the Royal Navy, along with a handful of officers, to raise support amongst Ewe people to the east of Asante and launch an attack from that direction. Now they considered a more ambitious project. 'Are we to contemplate an attack on Coomassie and could we assemble a force sufficient enough for the purpose?' Kimberley wrote to Cardwell in July.[39]

An army officer whom they had invited to their meeting, Sir Garnet Wolseley, had been pondering over Asante for months. In May 1873, a colleague, Evelyn Wood, walked into Wolseley's office and found him poring over Dutch maps of Asante. 'He told me, in reply to my questions, that there was a King there who required a lesson to bring him to a sense of the power of England,' wrote Wood.[40] By August, Wolseley thought that an attack on Kumasi was feasible and perhaps necessary and had privately submitted the outline of his plan to Cardwell. He would need British soldiers, he warned, because it was 'evident the Fantees would not face their old and dreaded enemies the Ashantees unless thus backed up.' Wolseley was prepared to march to Kumasi, and if the Asantehene would not make peace, he 'would destroy his palaces, burn his capital and lay waste his country as well as I could.'[41] Even at this early stage, there is an unmistakable impression; politicians prevaricated, but Wolseley knew what he wanted, and how to get it. At the War Office meeting, he was offered the position of Administrator and Commander-in-Chief of the

Gold Coast, with the understanding he would hold this position strictly for the duration of the forthcoming campaign. 'I at once assented – Heavens, with what internal joy I did so!', he wrote.[42]

Wolseley was from an Anglo-Irish military family and had just turned forty. He was a rising star. From Burma to the Crimea, to India and China, and most recently Canada, he had distinguished himself in battle. Seriously wounded in the first two of those campaigns, it was as if, wrote a biographer, he had decided the best way to get ahead was 'to try and get killed every time he had the chance. Daring and indifference to danger would attract his superior officers and lead to promotion and honours.'[43] But Wolseley was also a master of organisation and logistics, his reputation enhanced by his manual *The Soldier's Pocket-Book for Field Service*, published in 1869. He was a moderniser too, supporting Cardwell's hotly disputed reforms of the army, above all the 1871 abolition of 'purchase', the antiquated system whereby officer's commissions had been sold, typically to the socially well connected.

Wolseley made enemies throughout his career – and not only amongst the more snobbish and less competent officers – but he could also charm. William Winwood Reade, the writer and explorer who would accompany Wolseley to Asante as *The Times* correspondent, wrote that he 'had the talent of giving commands in such a way that they give a pleasure to those who received them, and his manner to young subalterns was inexpressibly gracious and kind.'[44] Benjamin Disraeli, who became Prime Minister while Wolseley was in the Gold Coast, judged him 'a most intelligent man ... and winning from his modesty ... a little man, but with a good presence, and a bright blue eye, holds his head well, and has a lithe figure.'[45]

Public opinion in Britain, meanwhile, was moving Wolseley's way, in the wake of further alarming news from the Gold Coast. On 14 August, the day after Wolseley took up his appointment in London, Commodore John Commerell of HMS *Rattlesnake*, Senior Officer for the Cape of Good Hope and West African squadrons and holder of the Victoria Cross, led a small boats reconnaissance up the Pra River from the Atlantic at Shama. He was in search of a rumoured Asante presence, some way to the west of their main forces. The British had travelled a short distance upriver when, they reported, 'a murderous fire was poured into them from a large body of Ashantees and Chamahs [the people of Shama] who were ambushed in great force on the thickly wooded banks.' Commerell, shot four times, was 'prostrated with loss of blood'. Two British captains were also wounded, one by a musket slug which 'ripped open all the top of his head'. Meanwhile, back at the beach, a boatload of Fante policemen and British sailors was attacked by the Shamas. 'Some of the police got ashore and instantly had their heads chopped off,' according to a British officer. 'One blue jacket, too, got ashore and they cut off his head and stuck it on a pole, and ran shouting about with it.' Commerell said the people of Shama were 'guilty of the grossest treachery' and ordered HMS *Rattlesnake* to bombard their town, which, 'in less than two hours' time … was a heap of burning ruins.'[46]

For British newspapers, the 'Disaster on the River Prah' was a barbarous attack on the venerated Royal Navy and the moment apathy turned to anger. *The Times* wrote 'Our forces have met with a serious disaster, and the Ashantees have gained a success which will be of enormous moral value.' Wolseley did not yet have *carte blanche* to invade; the paper still hoped that 'all that is necessary may be done more easily than by the burning of Coomassie, and more satisfactorily than by the destruction of the Ashantee kingdom.'[47] But the reaction from Wolseley's inner circle, his coterie of thirty-five trusted officers known as the 'Wolseley Ring', is telling. They were on the island of Madeira, already en route to the Gold Coast, when the news from Shama reached them in mid-September. Henry Brackenbury, Wolseley's military secretary, wrote, 'May it be confessed that, mingled with regret, was a dim belief that Providence had specially interfered to convince the authorities at home that the matter in hand was not that easy walk-over which … so many judged it to be.'[48] Another officer was more explicit: 'Most of us declared it was the reverse of a disaster for the expedition. Hitherto the British people had looked upon the war with languor and distrust … it would cost money; many fine young men would perish ignobly from the climate, and victories gained over naked savages could not be viewed with satisfaction … But the disaster on the Pra was a blow in the face for Europe, and it stirred the spirit of the Nation.'[49]

Commerell would recover and eventually become Admiral of the Fleet, although when Queen Victoria met him in March 1874 he still had a bullet in his lungs and, she wrote, looked 'desperately ill'.[50] Wolseley, meanwhile, sailed on to West Africa. And although he complained about the rat- and cockroach-infested mail ship which took him there – 'the dirtiest craft I have ever been on … the stewards of the lowest and dirtiest class of Irish Liverpool ruffians, whose filth and diseased appearance is very loathsome' – the political winds were blowing in his favour.[51]

Events at Elmina and Shama might have been cause for British introspection. Why were some Gold Coast chiefs allied with the Asante? And how would bombarding their towns change their minds? Instead, they strengthened an emerging British consensus for the use of force. 'There is no policy more merciful, in the case of such a Protectorate as ours over barbarous tribes, than a prompt and severe punishment of all armed resistance,' wrote *Spectator*.[52] That autumn the British newspapers were full of letters from self-proclaimed experts in warfare and Africa, speculating on the challenges ahead. In *The Times* one contributor warned the new Gatling machine gun would be as much use in the thick bush as 'a fire engine. But if by any chance Sir Garnet Wolseley manages to catch a good mob of savages in the open, he cannot do better than treat them to a little Gatling music,' which would rip apart their bodies at a distance of 400 to 600 yards.[53] The civilising mission was not for the squeamish.

Above all, the British honed in with horror and fascination on the issue of human sacrifice. This was not a new concern but one which had gradually gained in salience and which had come to define the extraordinary wickedness of Asante in British minds. The historian Ivor Wilks writes, 'Throughout the nineteenth century "Ashantee" and "human sacrifice" were virtually inseparable in the European imagination.'[54] The connection can be traced back to the accounts of Bowdich and Dupuis, but as the century wore on it impacted more and more on Anglo-Asante relations. In 1848, Governor William Winniett of the Gold Coast travelled to Kumasi and told Kwaku Dua of Queen Victoria's desire that 'sanguinary rites should be abolished.'[55] The Asantehene assured him the practice was much reduced. But Europeans and Africans were often talking at cross purposes. Joseph Adjaye writes, 'The Asante Government clearly distinguished between "sacrifice" and "executions", a distinction which the British administration apparently failed to draw.'[56] He argues that, wilfully or not, the British were misconstruing capital punishment as human sacrifice.

'When a great man dies he requires attendants in the place to which he is gone,' explained an Asante official to a visiting Methodist missionary in 1843.[57] A deceased Asantehene or prominent chief, destined for *Asaman*, the land of the ancestors, needed wives and servants to accompany him and indeed some would volunteer for this journey. Asante society depended on good relations with the ancestors for its well-being, and so funerals of royalty were often accompanied by killings. These could serve a dual purpose; appeasement of the gods and ancestors, but also, sometimes, punishment of wrongdoers. Ivor Wilks writes that 'in Asante, the taking of life was regarded with a certain indifference, a certain nonchalance (though no more than in most societies past and all too many present).' Perhaps it was not so much that life was cheap in nineteenth-century Asante, but that death was not to be feared.

In Britain, most government officials saw the issue in simpler terms: Asante practices were barbaric and cruel, and any war with them would therefore be built on firm moral foundations. Ironically, the prime minister himself, William Gladstone – otherwise curiously absent and inattentive in the looming crisis – was something of a dissenting voice, arguing with his ministers in September 1873 that human sacrifices were 'not *crimes* under the moral law as recognized in Africa', to which Kimberley replied that Queen Victoria looked on the matter with 'horror'.[58] The British historian Alan Lloyd puts it in colourful terms:

> If there was some doubt in British minds about the geographical location of Ashanti, there was no doubt that in spiritual terms it lay pretty close to Inferno and Gehenna. Stories of the unremitting ferocity of the Ashanti people, of a gigantic

golden cauldron at Kumasi filled to the brim with human blood, and so on, were used to cruel effect by the soldiery on susceptible kitchen-maids, while Kofi Karikari himself, the terrible 'King Coffee', reigned supreme for many a long month among the shadowy ogres lurking around night-lit nurseries, the ultimate deterrent to juvenile delinquency.[59]

★★★

Peter King Appiah is leading me out of his office and down towards the Prempeh II Jubilee Museum at the bottom of the hill in Kumasi's Centre of National Culture. He is a bit rueful about the small museum, a single-storey building arranged around a courtyard, with a modest collection of Asante stools, drums, historical photos, muskets and brassware. 'It opened in 1956,' he says, 'and hasn't changed much. Plans are in the pipeline for an update ... or should that be pipedream?' Peter laughs. To one side of the museum, parked under a porch, is a 1930s grey Plymouth car from the United States. 'It was Prempeh II's. We want the engine to be fixed, we want to drive people around in it.' Until then, it gathers dust, most of the windows cracked.

We walk back up the hill towards Peter's office. 'We must also tell the bad side of our history,' said Peter. 'Yes, human sacrifice. A man lives as a chief or a king and goes to the ancestral world. And he must live the life of a king over there. So the belief was that people must accompany him to the ancestral world.' Such practices were abolished, Peter said, before the end of the nineteenth century. 'The Asante king has demystified the fear around the palace – a place where you could lose your head. That fear persisted, but it has long gone. It wasn't the Europeans who made us stop human sacrifice, we were evolving anyway, and these things had to stop. The Europeans came with the Bible, but they also engaged in cruel and horrible treatment of our people. We are moving on.'

Of all the wars with the British, Peter said, 'the most devastating one was the Sagrenti War of 1874.' Sagrenti? Say it out loud. Sir Garnet Wolseley. How could the Asante forget him? The man who marched a British army right into Kumasi and laid waste to their city.

THE ASHANTEE WAR—A BUSH FIGHT

Wolseley complained that Britain's African allies were unreliable in battle. 'If I am to get to Coomassie, I must have Europeans,' he wrote.

4

'THE WHITE MEN HAVE GUNS WHICH HIT FIVE ASHANTEES AT ONCE'

'We were very much like drowned rats,' wrote Acting Corporal George Little in his diary on the evening of 21 November 1873.[1] It was his first night on board HMS *Himalaya*, en route to the Gold Coast with some 650 soldiers of 2nd Battalion, Rifle Brigade. They had sailed from Cork, southern Ireland, that afternoon, and it had been a miserable day. They had been roused in their barracks at 1.30 a.m., had endured a 'very long and tedious' train journey and then spent hours at the docks standing in heavy rain, punctuated by 'any amount of shouting' from the officers. A sympathetic captain bought them coffee, but they had to pay for their own bread and cheese. A band played on a nearby ship and crowds cheered and waved handkerchiefs, but the soldiers were subdued.

Things did not get much better the next day. The *Himalaya* ran into a heavy gale, and George Little wrote, 'mostly all hands are more or less sea sick … we are very much crowded and have scarcely room to move.'[2] There is a vast amount of British literature on the 1873–4 invasion of Asante, but Little's 'Diary of the Ashantee War by an Eye Witness', wonderfully eloquent, occasionally subversive and never hitherto used by any historian of the conflict, is an invaluable insight into the perspective of an ordinary soldier.

It was an inauspicious beginning, but Sir Garnet Wolseley had got his way. No army of white British, or indeed European, soldiers had ever been sent into the West African interior. Now three British battalions – the 2nd Battalion of the Rifle Brigade as well as the Royal Welch Fusiliers and the 42nd Royal Highland Regiment, known as the Black Watch – were on their way. *The Times* reported that the War Office had been inundated with officers volunteering to fight the Asante and that 'among all ranks there is expressed a willingness and even a desire' to take part.[3] And yet the cabinet only held its first detailed discussion about Wolseley's expedition in early October, two days after he had arrived at Cape Coast Castle.[4] It sent him instructions stressing its reluctance to send British troops into battle and saying it would accept an honourable peace if the Asante would withdraw from the protectorate.[5] William Gladstone was concerned about cost and sceptical of what Wolseley could hope to achieve. But the prime minister would soon discover that events were moving beyond his control; the tacit support of his ministers Kimberley and Cardwell for a more ambitious expedition, delays in communication between London and Cape Coast and the shift in British public opinion following the debacle at Shama, all gave Wolseley the leeway to jettison the caution which had characterised British policy on the West African coast for decades.

On 14 October, Wolseley led several hundred men – Royal Marines and sailors, as well as West Indians and Hausas – in an attack on villages near Elmina which were reportedly supplying the Asante army with food. When one of the village chiefs had been summoned to Elmina beforehand, he had insouciantly replied, 'Come and fetch me, white man no dare go bush.'[6] So the raid was intended to show the Asante that the new British commander meant business and to boost the morale of the British and their Fante allies. The British destroyed several villages, but Wolseley's chief of staff, Colonel John McNeill, was shot in the arm – his muscles and tendons standing out 'like strands of an unravelled rope's end' – and evacuated back to England.[7] Afterwards, Wolseley wrote in his journal that 'I have learnt a lesson that if I am to get to Coomassie, I must have Europeans ... The Houssas [Hausas] have heaps of pluck but they are wild to a degree and expend their ammunition in a way that is dreadful to contemplate, as for the W.I. [West Indian] troops they are of little use in the bush under the present organization.'[8] In fact, Wolseley had sent his request to London for more white British soldiers the day before the raid. In the words of one British historian, 'it is abundantly clear that he had made up his mind beforehand that the Africans would be useless.'[9]

Amankwa Tia's Asante army – hungry and depleted by disease after many months in the field – had begun its retreat back to the Pra River in October, but there were frequent clashes with Wolseley's reconnaissance forces. On 3 November, Lieutenant Frederick Eardley-Wilmot of the Royal Artillery was killed after local troops allied to the British, the so-called 'native levies', fled an Asante attack. Eardley-Wilmot came from a prominent political family and *The Times* reported 'the news of poor Wilmot's death cast quite a gloom over the place.'[10] His fellow officers buried him in the colonial cemetery at Cape Coast Castle. Wolseley wrote in his journal: 'I heard a young fellow say when they were filling in the grave *"that is the first for us."* Whose turn will it be next? ... It is hard that a fine young fellow should be sacrificed I may say by a cowardly lot of n******rs who won't fight for their own country.'[11]

Wolseley dwelled on this grievance over the following weeks. The Fante, Britain's supposed allies, were 'only fit to be slaves to the Ashantees', he wrote to an officer in November 'and it would be far better for us if the Ashantees had possession of this country – trade would increase 100 fold, and we should have to deal with a fine warlike race instead of with the Fantees who certainly are par excellence the cowards of the world.'[12] But what was more characteristic of Wolseley was an ugly contempt for all black people. Two months earlier, on 27 September, he sailed into Freetown, Sierra Leone, the final stopover before the Gold Coast. Freetown – its harbour set amidst a dramatic background of forested mountains – had been established by the British as a refuge for freed slaves. At the end of Wolseley's first day in West Africa he reflected in his journal on what he had seen:

> I have seen the slaves in the South [of the United States] before they were emancipated, and I have seen something of negroes in many parts of the world, and now that I have seen them en bloque, [sic] I feel convinced that to be in slavery until they can become profoundly educated in civilization is their true place: Slavery carried out under stringent laws to protect the slaves from cruelties or from the separation of domestic ties etc etc is the only position that the negro in his natural condition is fit to occupy. Here at Sierra Leone ... it is monstrous to think that such naturally productive localities should be given over to waste and idleness ... because the people who are supposed to own the soil are too lazy and worthless to till the soil, and I cannot believe that the Creator intended there should be races left on the face of the earth to vegetate in sensual idleness, without labouring for their daily bread.[13]

It is an extraordinary passage, not because it is so offensive – many of the values of the men who carved out the British Empire have not aged well – but because it is so at odds with contemporary British policy. Time and time again in the late nineteenth century the British justified military expeditions in West Africa through the necessity to stamp out slavery. And yet the man who led the largest such expedition privately believed that Africans were good for nothing else. Ironically, in his autobiography, published in 1903, Wolseley argued that British suppression of the slave trade was the root cause of the 1873–4 war: 'As the King of Ashantee's revenue, which had been considerable, was chiefly derived from the sale of slaves captured in his frequent wars, he was naturally furious with us for having thus deprived him of his market for them.'[14]

An earlier indication of Wolseley's thoughts had indeed come in the United States. In 1862 he was smuggled across the lines to meet the Confederate general, Robert E. Lee. Sympathy for Confederates was not unusual in the British establishment, but Wolseley was effusive. Lee 'seemed the greatest man I ever conversed with ... the majesty of his manly bearing, the genial winning grace, the sweetness of his smile and the impressive dignity of his old-fashioned style of address, come back to me amongst the most cherished of my recollections.'[15] In 1863 he argued for recognition of the Confederacy: 'the military despotism of one portion of the States under the dictatorship of an insignificant lawyer [Abraham Lincoln] attempts to crush out the freedom of the rest.'[16]

Wolseley's Asante journal was never intended for public consumption. He wrote to his mother, 'there is much in it that is very confidential, it must not therefore go out of your hand … nor is anything I say there about public affairs or individuals to be repeated beyond our family. Please be very careful about this.'[17] An astute political operator, he was probably concerned about the impact on his career of gossip or undiplomatic remarks about other soldiers or politicians. But if these seem relatively trivial today, other unguarded observations are more damning of his legacy.

★★★

The troopship HMS *Himalaya* carrying the Rifle Brigade anchored off Cape Coast on 10 December 1873. George Little could see a coastline of low, thick forest and make out figures on the beach. The journey from Cork had taken three weeks and the men's morale improved as they steamed south and the weather warmed. Five days after leaving Ireland they were off Madeira, which felt 'just like a summer day in Old England,' and the soldiers swapped tobacco for fruit and cheese with traders. The several Royal Navy ships in Funchal harbour gave the *Himalaya* a rousing send-off with lights on and sailors cheering. By now there was 'singing and dancing on deck every evening in which officers and men join most heartily.' The men were fitted with tropical helmets – 'very nice light kind of hats made of cork and covered with some light material' – and what Little calls 'Ashantee uniforms' of loose grey smock-frocks and trousers. Wolseley had sweltered through jungles in the Second Anglo-Burmese War of 1852–53 and was determined his men would not suffer in the same way. But when the *Himalaya*, as well as the *Tamar* and the *Sarmatian*, carrying the Royal Welch Fusiliers and the Black Watch respectively, arrived off Cape Coast, the soldiers were in for disappointment.

Wolseley, who had pleaded for British soldiers, was now dismayed by the timing of their arrival. 'They have arrived too late & too soon,' he complained in his journal. If they'd come a month earlier, he believed, he could have 'finished the war' by destroying the Asante army while it was still close to the coast.[18] But by mid-December, the Asante had retreated across the Pra and the British, struggling with the complex logistics of a march into enemy territory, were not yet in a position to pursue them. They needed to widen and improve the 100 kilometre narrow track which ran through forests, swamps and hills, from Cape Coast to a forward base at Prahsu on the south bank of the Pra and roughly half-way to Kumasi. The Royal Engineers were busy supervising the building of 237 bridges, as well as eight camps where soldiers could eat and rest, and two hospitals.[19]

There was, Wolseley feared, only a narrow window of opportunity. From December to February, the weather on the Gold Coast was dry and relatively cool, as winds blew down from the Sahara. Thereafter, rains made the forest tracks impassable and malaria, yellow fever and dysentery could overwhelm his men. The first two of these were particularly deadly. The British could to some extent treat malaria in the 1870s – quinine had been standard issue in the Royal Navy since the 1850s – but it wasn't until 1897 that a Scottish doctor in India discovered the disease is transmitted by mosquitoes. Some of Wolseley's officers believed fevers were caused by draughts and miasmas coming from the earth, so they wore a flannel tightly round their waist, known as a 'cholera belt', to keep their abdomen warm. Many drank generous amounts of champagne and claret, which they also believed would keep them healthy.[20]

Whatever Wolseley thought of such inventive solutions, he had already seen the impact of disease on white British soldiers. Most of the 100 Royal Marines who had fought at Elmina in June were now so sick they needed to be invalided home.[21] He didn't want to have his three battalions standing idly by at Cape Coast, also exposed to disease, as they waited for an unknown period of time for the order to advance. So he took what he decided was the least-worst option. Small numbers of soldiers – medics, logistics officers and engineers – were allowed to disembark. The remainder, Wolseley instructed, should stay onboard, their ships sent back out to sea on what he called 'a cruise', with instructions not to return until 31 December. 'It causes a great dissatisfaction amongst all hands as everybody is eager to land and get to work,' wrote Little.[22] So near, and yet so far.

The most acute problem Wolseley faced, and one which threatened to destroy all his plans, was a shortage of labour. More than one million rounds of Snider ammunition, 400 tons of food (equivalent to thirty days rations for 6,500 men), building supplies and machinery, tents and groundsheets – who was to carry this all the way to Kumasi? Not the British soldiers, whom Wolseley had restricted to a minimum load to avoid their collapse in the heat. He toyed with a railway and even shipped out track and equipment, but decided it was impractical. Donkeys were prone to sleeping sickness. Elephants from India (African ones were regarded as untrainable) were considered, but Wolseley's military secretary Henry Brackenbury wisely pointed out the 'great difficulty' of trying to land the enormous animals in the heavy Gold Coast surf.[23] That left local labour as the most realistic option. But the march into Asante territory was dangerous, food en route was scarce and the British did not pay especially well, even though Wolseley doubled the rate from 3 to 6 pence per day.[24] Not surprisingly, carriers melted away as fast as they were recruited. Wolseley's officers calculated they needed some 8,500 carriers to reach Kumasi, but by November they had barely 1,300 at their disposal.[25]

'The people are so naturally lazy,' Wolseley wrote in November to the Duke of Cambridge, Commander-in-Chief of the British army and Queen Victoria's cousin. 'I cannot afford to allow the Expedition to come to a stand still through a too rigid observance of English laws, laws that are in every way unsuited to these nations.'[26] It was a candid admission. 'Wolseley cast all forms of legality aside,' writes a biographer, 'Kidnapping began on a large scale.'[27] Villages were destroyed, women and children pressed into service. By early January 1874, Wolseley was at the forward base at Prahsu, frustrated he could not go further. He wrote to his deputy, Brigadier-General Sir Archibald Alison, back at Cape Coast Castle, 'Whatever measures you consider necessary to obtain

*Fante women; 'more useful and willing than men'
as carriers for Wolseley's army.*

carriers you may depend upon my supporting you in. You had better make a regular "drive" in Cape Coast and seize every man you can & march them … under a strong police escort, guarding them at night & if necessary shutting any of them who attempt to escape.'[28]

By mid-January, the crisis had eased. In part, this was achieved by British officers offering pardons for 'political offences' by the 'disaffected tribes of Elmina' and others. But primarily it was because they had resorted to brute force.

> I sent Colonel [George] Colley from Dunquah to the eastward of that place,' wrote Wolseley in his journal, 'giving him a carte blanche to use coercion to any extent he liked short of shooting and he has done capitally. He began by burning a village that had ill treated some police sent to arrest deserters: he surrounded villages at night, beat them up at unexpected

hours & the result has been most satisfactory. The men have now come forward in large numbers ... This makes my heart light again.[29]

The war against slavery, evidently, was not always pretty.

While Wolseley fretted about carriers, his army whiled away at sea. 'Yes cruising, everlasting cruising' wrote George Little laconically on the *Himalaya* on 14 December. There were distractions; flying fish tangled in the rigging, turtles swimming on the surface, the glow of phosphorescence at night and shark-fishing with pork bait. A lieutenant wrote that one shark 'caused some merriment by being drawn up and down the deck until it was quite exhausted.'[30] They slept on deck in the heat and kept busy sharpening their bayonets and practising packing tents and clothing 'into convenient bundles for the natives to carry.'[31] The various ships were often in sight of each other and would draw closer to exchange salutes and news. An 'Ashantee Band', very 'happy and jolly', tried valiantly to raise spirits on the *Himalaya*, but the men had been at sea for almost a month and Little wrote on 23 December that 'everybody seems to be downhearted.' On the 25th – 'Cruising And Christmas Day' – there was beef and extra plum pudding and an extra pint of stout, and the chaplain gave 'a very able discourse'.[32] The band played again and the men cheered their officers, but they were desperate to stretch their limbs. 'It will be a happy release to get off this ship' Little wrote on 30 December.[33]

Their wait was almost over. The ships were now back in view of Cape Coast Castle, and Wolseley had authorised the disembarkation. This began in the early hours of 1 January 1874. Cape Coast, battered by waves, has no natural harbour and so the soldiers were put on launches, which were towed by steamboat to within a few hundred metres of the shore where they transferred to 'Surf Boats' and were taken ashore through the waves by skilled Fante paddlers. The soldiers staggered on to the beach amidst the 'incessant yelling' of the crowd that had gathered to watch.[34] Wolseley was determined that his men, once ashore, would 'not be kept inactive for one single day' and so they had barely caught their breath when they were ordered to begin the march inland.[35] The

Black Watch and the Royal Welch Fusiliers were also ashore by 5 January, and they too were instantly on their way.

They walked in the mornings, covering some ten kilometres each day, and rested in the heat of the day. They carried their own rifles, bayonets and some ammunition. There was much to admire in Wolseley's preparations; the generous daily rations (1 pound of preserved beef, 1 pound of biscuit, tea, sugar and rice each day, with grog at night), the well-prepared sleeping stations with elevated beds and the sensible instructions not to expose the head to sun or drink unfiltered water.[36] The atmosphere, George Little wrote, was 'thick and sully, and the perspiration ran off us copiously'. He admired orange and cocoa trees and 'the continual song of the reptiles which made the whole jungle sing.' An officer wrote:

> The vegetation is more glorious than anything I have ever seen. As underwood there are groves of plantains with huge green leaves and flowers of the most brilliant scarlet, masses of convolvuli of all colours, and palm trees with their trunks covered with exquisite ferns. Shooting up here and there are bamboo plants looking like bunches of huge green ostrich feathers. Above all this tower the gigantic trees, their stems bare for the first 100 or 150 feet, then leaves spreading out above like clouds of bright emerald green.[37]

From the very first days of the march, Little reports the flogging of Fante carriers who refused to carry their seventy-pound loads (thirty-one kilograms). On 9 January, at the camp of Nyan Kumasi Assin, he writes: 'there is such a number deserting from us that we are obliged to place double sentries all around the camp and have orders to shoot them if they attempt to pass.' A deserter was shot that day, 'as an example to the others,' and when six more were brought in that night by a patrol, Little wrote, 'I suppose they will be flogged tomorrow.' A few days later a Fante chief was hanged for 'intimidating' the carriers. By now the British were employing many women, generally felt to be 'more useful and willing than the men', to carry supplies.[38]

'The White Men Have Guns Which Hit Five Ashantees At Once'   55

The handful of British journalists who accompanied Wolseley's expedition had some 100 servants and carriers to help them. Two of the press pack – Henry Morton Stanley, the famed discoverer of David Livingstone in 1871, and William Winwood Reade – were already experienced travellers of the African interior. In contrast, Melton Prior, artist with the *Illustrated London News*, was a greenhorn. Twenty-nine years old and newly married, Wolseley's war was the big break of Prior's career and he travelled to the Gold Coast in a state of high excitement. He marched inland with eighteen servants and wrote that one of his four female porters was 'carrying between fifty and sixty pounds' weight of whisky and claret on her head, besides the baby at her back'. When Stanley whipped a servant for 'insubordination', Prior couldn't bring himself to do the same to one of his own, so Stanley did it for him (the correspondents took this duty upon themselves, as the less humane alternative was for their servants to be dealt with by Royal Marines with cat-o'-nine-tails at the camp whipping post, an 'ordeal' which would have rendered them 'quite useless for a time').[39]

Wolseley had a complicated relationship with journalists; he damned them as 'those newly invented curses to armies … they eat the rations of fighting men and do no work at all,' and yet they played an essential role in his rise to fame.[40] One British historian writes that Wolseley's march on Kumasi came to be followed back home as 'one of the military dramas of the Victorian age' and he had the gentlemen of the press to thank for this.[41] Melton Prior, through the sheer volume and drama of his drawings in the *Illustrated London News*, was perhaps the most influential. 'Melton Prior's debut as a war artist in 1873 marks the beginning of the golden age of the British war "special"', according to a historian of the Victorian press.[42] Wolseley, however, had little respect for Prior. A letter to his wife, later heavily redacted by his daughter Frances, suggests his contempt: 'this correspondent is a [phrase erased by Frances] and has never been [passage erased by Frances] … this little [word erased by Frances].'[43] Wolseley also had unkind words for other journalists; William Winwood Reade of *The Times* was a 'wretched whist player' and 'a most cadaverous looking man … he reminds one of a debilitated mute', while George Henty of *The Standard* – who would go on to become a prolific author and passionate champion of the British Empire – was 'a fat jolly looking man without any pretence to being a gentleman ... he is very dirty.'[44]

On 10 January, George Little reported the death of a sailor from 'fever' and wrote that already 'a great many men' were falling sick each day.[45] When Little reached the base at Prahsu on 18 January, he 'saw lots of sailors in Hospital all bad with the fever.' On 19 January, Captain George Huyshe, a trusted member of Wolseley's staff, gravely ill with dysentery, became delirious and collapsed. 'Poor fellow he went to another & I trust a happier world at 7 p.m. It is a great blow to us all,' wrote Wolseley, who struggled to sleep that night as he listened to the carpenters assemble a coffin from the flooring of a hut. The next morning, Huyshe was buried with military honours on the banks of the Pra, his grave dug nine-feet deep, Little wrote, 'to prevent the natives or wild animals from molesting his remains'.[46]

There was gruesome evidence of fighting along the trail. On 7 January, Little had 'noticed a number of human heads lying about close besides of the Roads and the woods smell very offensive'. The following day he came across a dead man in the bush – apparently an Asante soldier – and 'drove away a number of birds of prey who were eating the entrails.' Many villages had been abandoned and apparently hurriedly so. But the Asante army itself was frustratingly elusive. British soldiers passed on rumours that the Asantehene, King Coffee as they called him, had withdrawn his forces all the way to Kumasi, where, Little wrote on 9 January, 'he evidently intends to make a stand.'

In fact, even at this late stage, Kofi Karikari was doing his best to keep his options open. Also on 9 January, he released the German hostage, Johannes Kühne, who was in his fifth year of captivity in Kumasi. The Asantehene, seated in his palace and surrounded by purring cats, told Kühne, 'Aburoni Tenteng (tall white man), you are now going to Amrado (the governor); tell him that I am his good friend.'[47] He gave Kühne parting gifts of beautiful cloth and a bag of gold dust. Kühne was accompanied to the advancing British army by an Asante negotiator,

Owuso Koko Kuma, who carried a white flag. Kühne, looking dreadfully ill, was ushered before Wolseley and told him the scattered Asante army was in no position to defend Kumasi.⁴⁸ Wolseley refused to meet Koko Kuma, but gave him a letter to take back to Kumasi, in which he insisted the Asantehene should comply with a set of demands he had presented some days earlier; that all European and African prisoners be released, that the Asantehene pay 50,000 ounces in gold as an indemnity, effectively a punishment, for having 'unjustly forced this war upon the Queen of England' and that a peace treaty be signed in Kumasi itself.⁴⁹ He told the Asantehene that 'you can no more prevent an army of white men marching into your territory … than you can stop the sun from rising every morning.'⁵⁰ The letter was written in English and was translated in Kumasi by a Fante interpreter, Joseph Dawson, who had been imprisoned there since 1872, when he was working on an earlier mission for the British.⁵¹

Fifty thousand ounces of gold. This demand would cause consternation in Kumasi. Wolseley, in a letter to Karikari just after his arrival on the Gold Coast back in October, had only written that the Asantehene should 'give guarantees for the payment of ample compensation to all whom you have ill-used'.⁵² Wolseley, and the War Office in London, estimated that 50,000 ounces of gold was equivalent to £200,000 (roughly £23,450,000 today).⁵³ Did he believe the Asantehene had all this treasure at his disposal or was he asking the impossible in order to justify his invasion? Historians estimate that in the mid-nineteenth century, the indigenous miners of the entire Gold Coast were producing some 30,000 ounces of gold per annum, but this had declined to only 5,000 ounces per annum in the final decades.⁵⁴ Maybe Wolseley was influenced by British accounts of the vast treasure taken from the Asante army at Katamanso all the way back in 1826. But on 23 January, Wolseley was told by another released hostage, the French trader Marie-Joseph Bonnat, that stories of Karikari's wealth were greatly exaggerated and that his regalia was worth, at most, a quarter of what Wolseley was demanding. Wolseley, who was at least generous in his prejudices, wrote that Bonnat was 'a Frenchman & I don't like men of that nation,' but conceded that he was also an intelligent and astute observer.⁵⁵ And yet he continued to insist on 50,000 ounces of gold. This British demand and the Asante failure to pay more than only a tiny portion of it, would bedevil Anglo-Asante relations for decades to come. More immediately, Wolseley's demands threatened to destroy Karikari's authority with his own people, as both men surely knew.

This authority was already under strain. In his *History of Ashanti*, Prempeh II writes disdainfully of Karikari as a man who was 'too fond of women', squandering public assets on gold for his concubines. 'The Kumasi Elders became appalled by the King's wasteful habits ... Nana Afua Kobiri, the Queen-Mother advised the King almost every day to stop wasting the money in the public treasury but all her words fell on deaf ears.'⁵⁶ Friedrich Ramseyer, the Swiss missionary who had also been held in Kumasi since 1869, wrote that the death of Karikari's brother in September 1873 was followed by a wave of public killings. 'It was really a reign of terror ... the king himself actually killed some members of the royal house, many slain corpses lay exposed and in forty days the same dreadful doings were to be repeated!'⁵⁷

Erratic and indecisive, Karikari increasingly relied on a group of trusted Muslim advisers for spiritual guidance through the gathering crisis.⁵⁸ But the mood in the city darkened as more information trickled in about the size of the approaching British army, its deadly weapons and its unexpected resolve. When Amankwa Tia and his generals asked for permission to bring the weakened Asante army back to Kumasi, Karikari's reply was unhelpful:

> You wished for war and you have it. You swore you would not return till you bring me the walls of Cape Coast, and now you want me to recall you because many chiefs have fallen, and you are suffering ... What can I do? I am drunk today and must play Kete [royal music and dance] with my wives. In due time I will send you an answer.⁵⁹

In the following weeks, Ramseyer writes, 'Soldiers came continually into the town, some of whom said plainly, "Even if the king send us forward again, we will not go unless he accompany; we are sick of it. The white men have guns which hit five Ashantees at once. Many great men and princes have fallen."'[60] On 18 December 1873, Amankwa Tia arrived back in Kumasi and revealed the full extent of Asante casualties from the Battle of Elmina and subsequent skirmishes, as well as from smallpox and dysentery. Some 280 Asante chiefs had died, their bones contained in seventy-nine boxes, according to one of the European captives.[61]

Friedrich Ramseyer paints a graphic picture of those fateful days as the British army drew near and fear and foreboding spread through Kumasi. 'Suddenly a cry of distress arose which rolled like a wave through the whole town … The sacrifices were then freed from their chains, and after being pierced through the cheek, beheaded amid the beating of drums. Almost despairing I cried out, "O God! how long shall these things be?"' But amidst such apparent depravity, Ramseyer also witnessed courage. The people of Kumasi were busy making bullets from lead and iron scraps and preparing and packing corn and cassava as provisions for the soldiers who had resolved to defend their city. 'The king would not humble himself to sue for pardon. Ashantee must show itself valiant!' wrote Ramseyer.[62]

Jungle fighting. 'Pouring a ceaseless fire into every bush…'

5

'EVERY DOCTOR LOOKED LIKE A BUTCHER'

On 23 January 1874, Wolseley camped at the foot of the Adanse hills, which were covered in dense forest and shrouded in mist. He was just thirty kilometres from Kumasi. The bulk of the British force was over the Pra – Lieutenant Joseph Thomas wrote in his diary that with a width of 250 feet it was by far the largest river they had crossed – and were closing in on the Asante capital.[1] That morning, five white people made their way slowly into Wolseley's camp: Friedrich Ramseyer, his wife Rosa and their two children (one only a few weeks old) and Marie-Joseph Bonnat. Lieutenant Thomas said, 'They were in a pitiable condition; and were quite overcome with their reception by Sir Garnet and his staff.'[2] George Little wrote that Rosa Ramseyer 'looked very delicate, her two little children, born in Commassie were nice looking, both very pale.' They were the last European hostages that had been held in Kumasi and they said that throughout their long captivity they had been well treated by 'King Coffee'.[3]

The Europeans carried a note from Karikari to Wolseley, in which he suggested that 'since I have no quarrel of any kind with your Excellency, you would stop the progress of the forces and let us go on with peaceful negotiations.'[4] Wolseley's reply to the Asantehene, on 24 January, was uncompromising: 'I intend to go to Coomassie. It is for your Majesty to decide whether I go there as your friend or as your enemy. If I go there as your enemy, I shall march at the head of an irresistible English force, and I must again remind you of the consequences that this may have upon your Majesty's dynasty and upon the Ashanti kingdom.'[5] He included new and even more humiliating demands: that the Asantehene hand over the Queen Mother or Asantehemaa, Afua Kobiri, as well as his brother and intended heir, Mensa Bonsu, and four other prominent Asante chiefs, all to be kept by the British as hostages, and also that half of the indemnity of 50,000 ounces of gold be paid straight away. If the Asantehene complied, Wolseley promised to hold back most of his army and march into Kumasi with only some 500 men to sign a peace treaty.

Wolseley had achieved his most important objectives – the European hostages were free and Asante troops had withdrawn from the Gold Coast Protectorate. But he, and his army, had come too far to stop now. In his correspondence with the Asantehene, he stressed he would prefer a peaceful outcome. But a military confrontation suited his ambitions, and, as he argued in his autobiography decades later, was also in Britain's interests. He had a 'conviction that until we had utterly defeated their army and taken Koomassee, we should never have any assured peace in our West African settlements … It is always a serious danger to have on your frontiers a fighting race of savages imbued with this firm belief in their own irresistible strength.'[6]

The day after Wolseley sent the Asantehene his latest demands, he wrote to the Duke of Cambridge that, 'Like all negroes, he is not to be depended upon.'[7] He did have more substantive grounds to suspect Karikari of duplicity, as the Fante interpreter in Kumasi, Joseph Dawson, had sent Wolseley a coded message with a Biblical reference – 'Lest Satan should get an advantage of us: for we are not ignorant of his devices' – which implied the Asantehene was preparing to fight.[8] The historian Joseph Adjaye argues that while Wolseley complained of a 'dilatory' response to his demands, he failed to appreciate the typically slow pace and dispersed nature of Asante diplomacy; any Asantehene, but especially a weak one such as Karikari, needed to confer with the subsidiary kingdoms within the Asante confederation before he could make extraordinary concessions.⁹ By now the Asante had an appellation for Wolseley – '*So wo be a ente*' ('If you tell him anything at all he does not listen or heed it').¹⁰

Ramseyer believed that despite all their losses of recent months, 'the Ashantees ... were determined to measure their strength with the white intruders.'¹¹ In early January, the Asantehene turned to two noblemen to lead the mobilisation and defence of Kumasi. The King of Mampong, or *Mamponhene*, Kwabena Dwumo, and Asamoa Nkwanta, a general known as *Skrafokra*, 'the soldier's guardian spirit'; both commanded respect, in part by having never belonged to the now discredited 'war party', which had advocated the ill-fated invasion of the Gold Coast Protectorate.¹² 'The troops who served under [Nkwanta] regarded him with devotion and affection,' writes an Asante military historian.¹³

The British crossed the Adanse hills, which rise some 500 metres above the coastal plain, and reached Fomena, the first substantial Asante settlement on their path. Henry Stanley noticed signs of hasty departure – scattered pottery in the courtyards – but also 'immaculate cleanliness' and the sophistication of the buildings, their ochre red and white walls covered in bas-relief decoration: 'Cornices are set off with many grooves, friezes with singularly bold diamond-shaped designs with embossed centres, pediments are something of the Ionic order, severely plain and square, the walls with intricate scroll-work relieved by corollas in alternate squares.' He admired the elegant household objects – furniture, soup ladles, sandals – all 'evince the taste and industry of the Ashantees'.¹⁴

Wolseley set up his headquarters in Fomena's deserted palace. That night, the British soldiers formed a circle under a huge tree and lit a fire, 'which was constantly kept up from the furniture of the surrounding houses.' The flames leapt high into the night and would have been an ominous sight for the Asante scouts to the north. The British were entertained by 'an odd little Fante boy' whom they dubbed 'mischief Pickles', who 'ran like a little imp to and from the men to the fire' to light their pipes.¹⁵ By now, George Little's Rifle Brigade had lost more than ten per cent of its men through what the soldiers described as fever and dysentery, including the captain of his own company.¹⁶ But if British soldiers worried about sickness, the greater fear for many was missing out on battle. The Black Watch was coming up behind the Rifle Brigade and one of its soldiers wrote in his diary, 'Met a good number of sick coming down country – mostly seamen and riflemen; many of them look very bad. Our men hanging out very well, but about 40 complaining. They are afraid of being left behind, and say they are better than they really are.'[17]

Wolseley received two more letters from the Asantehene in the final days of January – 'He begs me to halt, to halt, to halt, that is the burden of his song,' he wrote in his journal – but his heart was set on battle. 'We are now certainly in for a big fight, and I am glad that we now know that we are as this humbugging negociation [sic] on the part of the King complicated my position,' he wrote.[18] Wolseley had done his utmost to prepare his men for this moment, providing them with pamphlets on the nature of warfare in the forests the Asante knew so well. The British would be moving along narrow paths, 'surrounded', as he put it, 'by hordes of howling enemies'. They would need bugle calls to keep in contact and to take bold and decisive action in small groups or even as individuals, in a seemingly chaotic battlefield. And to Kwaku Dua's taunt of 1863 that 'the bush is stronger than the cannon', Wolseley's rejoinder was that the British enjoyed an inherent racial and technological superiority: 'It must never be forgotten by our soldiers that Providence has implemented in the heart of every native of Africa a superstitious awe and dread of the white man ... be cool; fire low; fire slow and charge home; the more numerous your enemy the greater the loss inflicted upon him, and the greater your honour in defeating him.'[19]

By 30 January scouts from both armies were reporting that the enemy was a short distance ahead. George Little wrote, 'everyone seems in high spirits and anxiously waiting' for the coming battle.[20] Wolseley wrote, 'We shall have our grand fight tomorrow so eagerly looked forward to by all here. I have left nothing undone to obtain a peaceable termination to this war, but Mr. Koffee in the folly of his barbarian pride has decided upon war. Upon his head be all the blood that may be spilt tomorrow.'[21]

The Asante selected a horseshoe-shaped ridge at the village of Amoafo, overlooking a swampy ravine. There, shortly before 8 a.m.

on 31 January, the Black Watch, led by Sir Archibald Alison, marched into a storm of Asante musket fire.[22] Wolseley had reservations about Alison – 'I don't care much for him & don't think he is the man I want ... I am very much annoyed,' he wrote of his second in command – but considered the Black Watch his best troops.[23] Robert Ferguson, a private with the Black Watch, describes the ensuing battle: 'Seldom we got a right shot at a black fellow, they kept so well under cover, but they did keep popping at us! And so close it was too! ... The most of our men were getting wounded ... Blood was running from nearly every man, and I was thinking myself lucky, that as we were driving them off I was always escaping.'[24]

The 2nd Rifle Brigade, and George Little, fortified by a breakfast of cocoa and biscuits, was bringing up the rear and could hear 'rattling musketry mixed with an occasional dull boom about a mile ahead.'[25] British soldiers stumbled through the jungle, shouting frantic requests for information and orders. The sound of rifles was 'interspersed with the noise of the little Mountings Guns the hissing of the Rockets and the resounding boom of the Enemy Guns all which mingled sounds increased by the echoes of the forests blending into a deafening roar which continued for 6 hours.' Little was overwhelmed by the deafening noise and terrified, both of the invisible enemy and of being accidentally shot by colleagues. He fired on one side then the other, but never even saw the Asante. Only when the gunfire subsided did he see 'a lot of Dead and wounded Ashantees lying on their faces like bronze figures.'

George Henty, correspondent for *The Standard*, wrote that the Battle of Amoafo 'consisted simply of five hours of lying down, of creeping through the bush, of gaining ground foot by foot, and of pouring a ceaseless fire into every bush in front which might contain an invisible foe.'[26] Wolseley was forced to revise his opinion of some of the journalists. William Winwood Reade of *The Times* was a 'very cool and daring man' and Henry Stanley was:

> the bravest of comrades ... Time after time as I turned in his direction I saw him go down to a kneeling position to steady

his rifle as he plied the most daring of the enemy with a never-failing aim ... the close-shut lips and determined expression of his manly face ... told plainly I had near me an Englishman [Stanley was in fact born in Wales and later took American citizenship] in plain clothes whom no danger could appal.[27]

Melton Prior of the *Illustrated London News* was also much more than an observer at Amoafo. 'I had reloaded, and with my right barrel shot one man full in the chest. The other turned to fly, but I got him in the back with my left and so killed them both.'[28] The war correspondent of the twenty-first century, typically taught to embrace an ethos of detachment and neutrality, can only marvel.

Prempeh II's *History of Ashanti*, so rich and detailed in its account of the rise of the Asante kingdom, passes over the Battle of Amoafo, a seminal moment in its decline, in terse prose: 'The Ashanti army fought with all the gallantry as it always was used to doing, but the superior arms of the British eventually drove them back when they could no longer hold their ground. Very heavy losses were sustained in this fight.'[29] Wolseley's army at Amoafo numbered some 2,200 men, (of whom 1,500 were white soldiers from Britain) while the Asante army was perhaps ten times larger.[30] The long list of chiefs who died included Amankwa Tia, who had led the Asante army to Elmina only six months previously, and who was shot through the back of his ceremonial chair, while Kwabena Dwumo was wounded.[31]

British weapons – not just the breech-loading Snider but also an artillery gun and rockets fired from less than fifty metres away – inflicted gruesome damage. One British sailor wrote that it was 'murder, not a fair fight'.[32] George Little wrote that most of the day after the battle 'was spent in burying the dead which was very great on the enemy side and the stench was horrible. In some of the places I saw women mixed with men lying dead they were all horribly disfigured some with the heads smashed where pieces of shell have struck them others that have been struck by rockets, more scorched and mangled so that you could not tell which they were.'[33] Stanley wrote of the 'important service' of the artillery, which produced 'ghastly heaps ... of rent bodies and disfigured dead.'³⁴ A British intelligence report said the enemy loss 'could not be ascertained as they took much trouble to carry off their dead, but it must have been very severe, as about 150 corpses were found near the road alone.'³⁵ The Royal Engineers reported burying 3,010 Asante corpses, although other British accounts estimate the number of Asante killed at between 800 and 1,600. Lieutenant Joseph Thomas of the Rifle Brigade passed through Amoafo on his return from Kumasi, a full ten days after the battle, and wrote 'the roadside to-day was found to be literally covered with the dead Ashantis, and we had great difficulty marching over them.'³⁶

The British, in contrast, suffered a mere four deaths.³⁷ And yet the battle was not as one-sided as these fatality figures suggest. Although Asante muskets were often ineffective beyond point-blank range, almost 200 hundred British soldiers were wounded, including a quarter of the Black Watch, who struggled for four hours to break the enemy lines.³⁸ Wolseley, who spent the battle trying to project calm by smoking cigars, whistling and singing snatches of songs at his command post, wrote to his wife Louisa, 'our loss was heavy and my heart was sick … Every doctor looked like a butcher his hands & clothes covered with blood.' In his journal he wrote that it was 'a hard fight that lasted all day, the enemy fought like men.'³⁹ Years later, in his autobiography, he wrote that if the Asante had had Sniders at Amoafo, the British would have been 'destroyed'.⁴⁰ Sir Archibald Alison wrote to his wife that the Asante flanking attacks were 'beautiful' and that he had never experienced such heavy fighting.⁴¹ Coming from a one-armed veteran of the Indian Uprising and Crimean War, this was not faint praise. A British naval officer wrote that amongst his wounded colleagues, 'many were the expressions of admiration of the undaunted courage and good fighting properties of the Ashantees.'⁴²

'At this imminently critical time', according to Prempeh II's *History of Ashanti*, 'King Kofi Karikari now moved from Kumasi to the front to take the supreme command'.⁴³ He was accompanied by his bodyguard and at the village of Odaso, some ten kilometres from Kumasi, he prepared a final defence of his capital. The British were a further ten kilometres to the south, running into frequent Asante ambushes, their supply lines coming under attack and with many of their Fante carriers refusing to carry on. A British intelligence report said the Asante had an enviable ability to 'slip through the untangled underwood here so plentiful with a wonderful quickness ... the country, nearly impenetrable to us, was almost open to the Ashantis.'[44] George Little wrote that British soldiers were vomiting after drinking contaminated water and that when he was sent into the bush to find a clean stream 'no one envied our duty as it was most dangerous.'[45] The following day, 3 February, he describes 'turning a bend in the path we received a volley almost point blank which wounded four men, we instantly returned their fire though we could not see them.'[46] It was nerve-shredding stuff.

That evening the British slept by the River Oda, on the opposite bank to the Asante army. 'We had our coats to lie down on', Little wrote, 'but it thundered lightened and rained pouring all the night long ... It was one of the most miserable nights I spent in the country but in spite of the wet and the noise of the huge trees swaying about and the thunder scaring I layed down and slept as sound as ever I did and did not awake until nearly choked by the water for it was very bad indeed.'[47]

It was what Wolseley had dreaded. Rain would make rivers impassable and turn forest paths into muddy quagmires. Running short of food and carriers, he had gambled on a lightning advance and had left his beleaguered supply convoys behind. Without tents, his men slept out in the open, consoled with a 3 a.m. distribution of rum.[48] There was a final, inconclusive exchange of letters between the Asantehene and Wolseley, who warned again that unless the Queen Mother and heir apparent Mensa Bonsu were surrendered immediately, he would advance to Kumasi.[49] Wolseley's officers supported his idea of a dash forward. 'It was as plucky a thing as has ever been done in the world,' wrote Colonel George Colley, 'but it was the right game – once you have licked a n****r keep him moving – any hesitation, or a day's halt, and I believe we should never have reached Coomassie.'[50]

On the morning of 4 February, the British crossed the Oda on a bridge heroically built by the Royal Engineers amidst the downpour and soon ran into the Asante army. At the Battle of Odaso, according to Prempeh II's *History of Ashanti*, the Asante 'fought to the point of exhaustion but they could not stand up against the British.' George Little wrote that 'again we poured volleys, rockets and shells into them but they would not give way for some time and the slaughter must have been fearful on their side as we passed a great number of dead lying in heaps shot down ... Still they advanced bravely ... and as one body was shot down another would take its place ... it seemed a pity to touch these brave fellows but they would not be taken prisoners and seemed to court the death they received.'[51]

Wolseley was knocked over when a lead slug from a musket smashed into the side of his helmet and, fortunately for him, hit the folds of his puggaree, a cloth wrapped around it. 'My helmet & Puggaree saved my old nut,' he wrote phlegmatically.[52] He got to his feet, suggested to an officer they find cover and suffered from a severe headache for the rest of the day.[53] After six hours of fighting, the Asante retreated. According to Prempeh II's *History*, 'seeing that it was quite useless to resist there any longer and to expose his men to the deadly new weapons of the British, which wreaked very many casualties of dead and badly wounded, Kofi Karikari widely ordered "Cease Fire" and fell back through the forest with his army.'[54]

'The road was strewn with war-horns, drums and fetishes,' wrote Lieutenant Thomas. 'The great war fetish, [perhaps some sort of shrine] about 7 feet high, was captured.'[55] Wolseley pushed the Black Watch forward for the final kilometres. They smashed their way through ambushes, 'with pipes playing, the men shooting everything before them, and cheering along the whole line.' They entered Kumasi at dusk, another soldier remembered, 'our pipes playing the "Highland Laddie." We gave three cheers for old Scotland after all was over.'[56] Kumasi had fallen.

George Little, and most of the other British troops, drenched in sweat, hungry and thirsty, lagged some way behind. On the outskirts of the city, they waded up to their knees through the stagnant and stinking waters of what they called the 'Fetish Pond' in which they were told the Asante threw their human sacrifices. When Little looked up, he saw Wolseley pass him, riding on a mule. Seeing how tired his men were, the British general tried to raise their spirits: 'Come on my lads you will have a house to sleep in tonight, perhaps a Palace.'[57]

The British capture Kumasi, 4 February 1874.

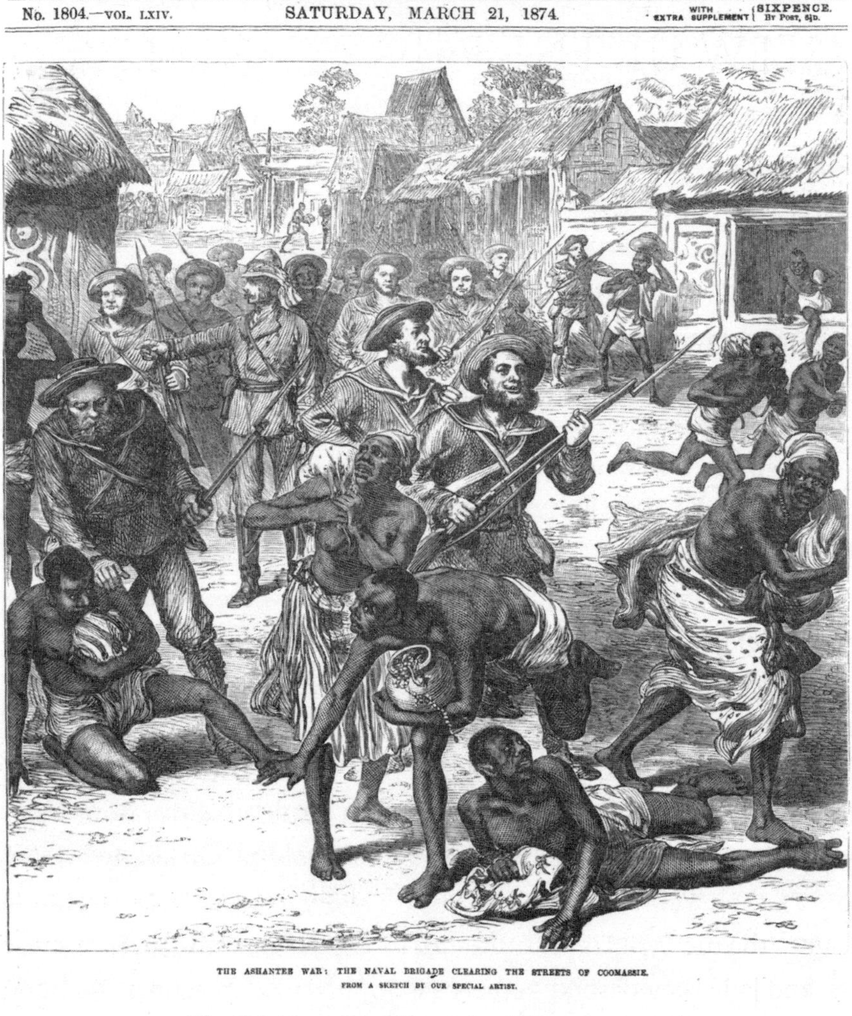

6

'BLEW UP THE PALACE AND LEFT COOMASSIE IN FLAMES'

Tristram Hunt, Director of the V&A, wrote that Sir Garnet Wolseley was 'the Kurtz of nineteenth-century British colonial violence, having seen action at Lucknow, the Summer Palace, the Zulu Wars and Khartoum.'[1] It is a memorable line, even if misrepresentative of both Joseph Conrad's morally corrupted river trader and Wolseley's long and varied career. 'Perhaps I should have called him the Forrest Gump of Empire,' Hunt told me, 'he simply got everywhere.'[2] Indeed, by the time Wolseley marched in to Kumasi he had already witnessed, and to an extent participated in, two of the most notorious episodes of nineteenth-century European imperial plunder.

After the fall of Lucknow, in March 1858, during the Indian Uprising, or Mutiny, a young Captain Wolseley watched as British soldiers rampaged through the Qaisarbagh Palace. 'The scene of plunder was indescribable,' wrote *The Times* correspondent William Howard Russell in an infamous account, 'the men wild with excitement, "drunk with plunder"... China, glass, and jade they dashed to pieces in pure wantonness: pictures they ripped up, or tossed on the flames; furniture shared the same fate.'[3] Wolseley did buy a few small objects from the British officers who belatedly attempted to control the pillage and his men gave him some silver bowls and a cashmere shawl, although, ironically, these were later stolen from him.[4]

In October 1860, Wolseley, by now a lieutenant-colonel, was in Peking, watching a procession of French soldiers 'struggling like ants under loads of jade, pearls, furs, clocks, and other art objects' as they made their way out of the Chinese emperor's Summer Palace.[5] Many donned outlandish outfits – women's richly embroidered gowns, Mandarin hats and so on – as was 'the practice usual with soldiers upon such occasions'. The French, Wolseley felt, 'seemed to have been seized with a temporary insanity; in body and soul they were absorbed in one pursuit, which was plunder, plunder.'[6] A French artilleryman, seeing Wolseley had taken nothing, gave him an enamel figurine: *'mon camarade, voici un petit cadeau pour vous'*. It was of a man with flowing locks and had itself apparently been a gift from Louis XIV to the Chinese Emperor. Wolseley thanked the soldier and pocketed the figurine. Some years later his wife identified it as the work of the seventeenth-century enamel painter Jean Petitot. In his old age Wolseley wrote, 'It is the only piece of loot I possess, but it is a valuable one.'[7]

Eventually, the British soldiers in Peking joined in the pillage. 'Those officers who were fortunate enough to have carts and time for amusement, brought into camp large collections of valuables,' wrote Wolseley. But the British commander, Sir Hope Grant, ordered officers to share their loot 'for the purpose of having it sold by public auction upon the spot and the proceeds distributed immediately amongst the army'. The auction lasted two days and was, according to Wolseley, 'the source of much amusement to all'. With the Chinese winter closing in, fur coats sold at a premium. The 'prize agents', meaning the men appointed by Grant to run the auction, ensured that the majority of money raised went to British soldiers, each of whom received the equivalent of £4. Wolseley approved: 'Prize money is a subject well understood but seldom received by our soldiers ... any reward or recognition of services is doubly prized if conferred upon the spot or at the time of their performance.'[8]

The distinction drawn by Wolseley, between frowned-on 'plunder' and the morally acceptable acquisition of 'prize', was not always as clear-cut as he and his fellow British officers liked to imagine. Wolseley's 1869 *The Soldier's Pocket-Book For Field Service,* his portable guide for soldiers throughout 'our great empire', was amended in later editions to include a specific section on 'prize money', in which he attempted to codify a hitherto ad-hoc series of traditions. 'All booty taken in war legally belongs to the Crown', he explained, and if sold off at auction the proceeds should be divided amongst the troops, with about one third going to officers and two-thirds to the remainder. 'I have felt it necessary to give these details because no orders on the subject are to be found in our regulations,' he admitted.[9]

From the perspective of the twenty-first century, Wolseley's attempts to define an acceptable type of looting reek of hypocrisy and self-justification. But Victorian military commanders saw the world differently and were anyway more concerned with the maintenance of discipline than the judgement of posterity. 'Throughout my soldiering career I have never been a looter,' Wolseley wrote at the end of his career, 'not from any squeamish notions as to the iniquity of the game, for I believe that, as a rule, to the victor should belong the spoils of war, but in the interests of order and of discipline.'[10] In Lucknow in 1858 he had recoiled at the sight of officers and privates looting side by side, but only because he worried they would argue over what they had taken. And yet he also believed that the tighter an army has been kept under orders, the more it was prone to moments of wild abandon. 'When looting is once commenced by an army,' he reflected, 'it is no easy matter to stop it ... Soldiers are nothing more than grown-up schoolboys. The wild moments of enjoyment passed in the pillage of a place live long in a soldier's memory.'[11]

★★★

The British were met with curious scenes in Kumasi on the evening of 4 February. The streets were full of Asante soldiers, many of whom they had just fought at Odaso. But hostilities appeared to be over; the soldiers were armed but made no attempt to resist the invaders and some even greeted them with the words, 'Thank you,' repeated again and again.[12] The men of the Black Watch reported that Asante women fetched water for them and 'could not have been kinder to us, if it had been Edinburgh we were marching in.'[13] In the central market place, the British soldiers lined up, Wolseley rode to the front and took their salute and ordered three cheers for the Queen.

The British looked for accommodation and oversaw the release of Fante prisoners. These, according to George Little, 'were in a pitiable state, some were chained to blocks of wood others have shackles of iron on their legs'.[14] He was told that while the battle raged at Odaso, the Asante had offered 'a great number of these poor wretches ... as sacrifices to their gods for success.'[15] He went to see what he called Kumasi's 'sacrificing ground' that was a:

> sickening sight, there was hundreds of human bodies laying about some with the flesh almost eaten off others quite fresh as if they had only been executed about a day some were bounded by their hands and legs ... the expression of agony on the features of the poor wretches ... cannot be described, we came away sick of the sight and thankful we belonged to a Christian country.[16]

Wolseley's military secretary, Henry Brackenbury, said he could not sleep for the excitement of what they had achieved but also the loathsome smell of decaying bodies which surrounded them.[17]

Wolseley said Asante politics were 'so based upon treachery that the king does not ... understand any other form of negotiation'.[18] And yet, now that he had taken Kumasi, he depended on the Asantehene's co-operation if his military victory were to be turned into something more durable. Wolseley was like Napoleon in Moscow, in possession of a capital but with no one to negotiate with. And in Kumasi too, time was not on the victor's side. Food supplies were low, more men were falling sick and the clouds threatened more rain. King Prempeh II's *History of Ashanti* records that the Asantehene had retreated to the village of Akwaboa, outside Kumasi. 'There he regrouped his army and sent messengers to fetch the Queen-Mother and the rest of the Royal Family.'[19] Wolseley sent him a letter, saying that now that he had demonstrated 'the power of England' he would be 'merciful' and would treat the Asantehene with 'royal dignity' should he return to Kumasi.[20]

Wolseley gave instructions that there should be no looting. George Little, in his diary, says these orders were specifically aimed at 'the blacktroops' in the British army and came with a warning that any Fante transgressors would be hanged. Robert Ferguson, with the Black Watch, wrote that in Kumasi 'our black fellows were always stealing, and we had often to lash them for their lazy ways.'[21] There were many fires in the city on the night of 4 February; the British blamed these on released Fante prisoners taking their revenge. British soldiers spent much of the night pulling down houses in the way of the flames to prevent their own ammunition supplies from catching fire.[22]

A young Fante policeman who was caught looting that night was indeed hanged from a tree in the middle of Kumasi, where Little wrote 'he made a dreadful noise supplicating mercy but in vain.'[23] His body was still there the following morning as an example to others. It is not clear whether discipline would have been enforced in the same way against a white British soldier. Brackenbury wrote that during the occupation of Kumasi 'the troops refrained, with the most admirable self-control, from spoliation or plunder.'[24] What is apparent, however, is that during the following day, 5 February, Wolseley came to the realisation that his wait for Kofi Karikari was in vain. His journal reflects his impatience. 'I sent messengers to the King last night and again this morning asking him to make peace and warning him of the consequences unless he did so. During the day very heavy rain fell. I began to feel nervous about the many streams to our rear.'[25]

Wolseley spent the morning with Brackenbury, receiving a tour from Joseph Dawson, the interpreter who must have been a canny operator just to have survived the tumultuous events of the past days, but whom Wolseley uncharitably dismissed as 'either a fool or a ruffian, perhaps a little of each.'[26] They walked through the now deserted streets of Kumasi and into the Asantehene's palace. They admired a great court that could hold 200 people, its supporting pillars 'highly ornamented with scroll-work in glazed red clay', many 'enormous umbrellas of various materials ... litters covered in silk and velvets' and in the rooms upstairs 'many other treasures of profusion'. They also saw drums surrounded by skulls and thigh bones, and stools covered in blood. Flies rose in clouds as they approached. In the royal chamber, its door decorated with 'many stamped placques of gold and silver', they found a 'gorgeous four-post bed covered with silk'. It was, Brackenbury thought, wonderful that all these things had not been taken away. Wolseley, he recounts, had seen enough and ordered that the palace be well guarded.

In his autobiography, Wolseley elaborates on his original ambitions in the war against the Asante: having 'taken the capital and its far-famed palace', he would 'make peace there. Should the king refuse my terms, I intended to burn both city and palace, and then to get the white troops back on board ship with the least possible delay. The deadliness of the climate forbade me to calculate upon any greater military results.'[27] In a letter to his wife, en route to Kumasi, he says he hoped to spend only one day there.[28] By the late afternoon of 5 February, Wolseley had concluded that the Asantehene was once again 'humbugging' or playing for time which the British did not have. Two envoys the Asantehene had sent to Kumasi were caught 'treacherously', as Wolseley put it, trying to take gold dust and ammunition out of the city.[29] Meanwhile, he received reports that rivers were rising over the improvised bridges he would need on the return journey to Cape Coast.[30]

The heroic Asante defence at Amoafo, but also Odaso – which resulted in a further two British deaths and sixty-six wounded – had perhaps not been in vain, as it may have strengthened Wolseley's conviction that he could not afford to wait.[31] His journal is direct and terse. 'I determined upon falling back tomorrow; gave orders to have the Kings palace ruined, and every arrangement made for burning the city. Prize agents appointed.'[32] In this way he would make sure 'to leave such a mark of our power to punish as should deter from future aggression a nation whom treaties do not bind.'[33] Brackenbury, his military secretary, explains the withdrawal; if the climate had been good, and all men in health, Wolseley would have pursued the Asantehene, but under the existing conditions, 'to chase the King from one place to another ... would but have been to add failure to what had hitherto been unbroken success.'[34]

It was an anti-climactic and inconclusive victory. The strongest criticism came from the journalists. Henry Stanley believed the downpours did not herald the beginning of the rainy season but were merely a 'freak in the weather' and 'the real-cause of our panic-like departure from Coomassie was want of food, which the General's inattention to the Transport and Control Department caused.'[35] He argued that the British should have disarmed Asante soldiers as soon as they arrived in Kumasi and proceeded the short distance to Bantama, the royal mausoleum and 'treasure-house' of the Asantehene and presumably have looted and destroyed it as well as the palace.[36] Instead, Stanley complained, Wolseley wasted the 5th of February 'listlessly wandering about the capital'.[37] William Winwood Reade of *The Times* was also critical of Wolseley's 'vacillation' at Kumasi and for generally being insufficiently severe on the Asante.[38] He blamed the Secretary of State for the Colonies, Kimberley, for tying Wolseley's hands with 'half-and-half' instructions:

> Lord Kimberley has been Viceroy of Ireland, and ought to know something about savages. They are not like civilised men. A hostile savage is like an ill-tempered dog: try to pat him and he bites you; give him a cut with your whip and he attacks you furiously; take him by the collar, thrash him within an inch of his life, and he will never try to bite you any more.[39]

Stanley describes Kumasi as an impressive town, with houses in the style he had admired at Fomena, their stuccoed facades embellished with what he took to be Moorish patterns. The 'streets were numerous, some half a dozen of them were broad and uniform ... By the general order and neatness ... I am compelled to say that in their domestic life they appear to me to be a very cleanly people.'[40] A British officer wrote that some of Kumasi's houses 'are a very good size, and the main street is quite as broad as Regent street.'[41] But much of what the British write about the Asante capital is damning. The journalists visited what was said to be the ritual killing ground, just as George Little had done. Stanley called it the 'Great Golgotha' and saw thirty to forty 'decapitated bodies in the last stages of corruption, and countless skulls',[42] George Henty of *The Standard* described 'the remains of some thousands of the victims of fetish. Five or six were only two or three days old, while of the great majority nothing but the skulls remained, and there were scores of bodies in various stages of putrefaction.' It was a 'horrible scene ... none of those who saw it will ever forget it.'[43] Frederick Boyle of the *Daily Telegraph* appeared to give his lurid imagination free rein. Kumasi is:

> the Metropolis of Murder ... where blood is plastered, like a pitch coating, over trees and floors and stools – blood of a thousand victims, yearly renewed; where headless bodies make common sport, where murder pure and simple, monotonous massacre of bound men, is the one employment of the king, and the one spectacle of the populace ... The sight they love is severed necks, and spouting blood ... Murder is their delight, their joy.[44]

The journalists also visited the Asantehene's palace. Winwood Reade counted ten or twelve courtyards, 'Moorish' in style and surrounded by alcoves and verandas. 'The rooms upstairs reminded me of Wardour Street. Each was a perfect Old Curiosity Shop. Books in many languages, Bohemian glass, clocks, silver plate, old furniture, Persian rugs, Kidderminster carpets, pictures and engravings, numberless chests and coffers.' There was an ivory-handled sword bearing the inscription 'From Her Majesty Queen Victoria to the King of Ashantee' (a gift to Kofi Karikari's predecessor Kwaku Dua), a copy of *The Times* from 17 October 1843, as well as gold-studded sandals, leopard-skin caps adorned with beaten gold and magnificent umbrellas of velvet and satin. Stanley wrote of 'war drums, stained with blood, and decorated with ghastly trophies of wars and triumphs, with human skulls'. His 'hastily written inventory' of the 'much valuable plunder' includes 'Regalia staffs, gold topped ... Royal stools, beautifully carved and ornamented with gold and silver ... Seven gold masks, each weighing several ounces ...' as well as more exotic items, such as 'A breakfast and dinner service of silver, with English cutlery, Bohemian vases ... An oil painting of a gentleman ... An old uniform of a West Indian soldier' and a copy of *The Bristol Courier*, also from 1843. 'And so on, *ad infinitum*, of valuable, curious and worthless things heaped together in every room'.[45]

The journalists had not just come to look. After the battle of Amoafo, Winwood Reade sent his assistant Edward Lake 'to "loot" for curiosities' and wrote that the taking of plunder was 'a harmless recreation, which it is mere pedantry to forbid'.[46] In Kumasi, Wolseley summoned them, and, according to Melton Prior, said 'Now gentlemen, I am very sorry to have to do so, but I have no doubt you will be paying a visit to the castle, and I must put you on your honour not to take anything from it.' The journalists, Prior writes, 'very reluctantly gave the necessary assurance'.

Prior neglected to tell Wolseley that by the time this conversation took place he had already visited the palace and helped himself to its treasure. 'By the side of [the Queen's] bed were a pair of slippers with beautiful gold buckles,' he wrote.

> I could not resist examining them; then an idea came into my head that one would make a handsome brooch for my wife in England, so it did not take me long to remove it from the slipper. Then I thought, if I take only one it will be missed, so I had better take the other, and nobody will know there were any at all. On visiting other rooms I found gold pipes, gold masks, and what appeared to be tea services. I am afraid that I must own to filling my pockets with the smallest things I could find.

Rather than surrender these items, Prior employed creative logic to justify keeping them: 'it occurred to me that as I had been placed on my honour after I had helped myself, I was not called upon to return those things which I had already taken.'[47]

Meanwhile, Wolseley proceeded with his own plans for a more systematic looting of the palace. His team of prize agents included Captain

Redvers Buller, an intelligence officer who would subsequently win the Victoria Cross in the Anglo-Zulu War of 1879 and rise to become Commander-in-Chief of the British army in the Boer War, Captain Henry Dugdale of the Rifle Brigade and Lieutenant Maclean of the Naval Brigade.[48] They were helped by Andooa, the King of Elmina, who had switched his allegiance to the British, and Marie-Joseph Bonnat, the former hostage who despite being French was judged useful by Wolseley. 'Mr Bonnât, the French prisoner, appears ... to have used his eyes and ears, whilst others sulked at being prisoners,' wrote Lieutenant Frederick Maurice, Wolseley's private secretary.[49] Bonnat had accepted Wolseley's offer of a guinea a day and officer's rations in return for his knowledge on the approach to Kumasi, but remained sympathetic to the Asante although he had been their prisoner for several years. He refused to carry a weapon and performed only medical duties at Amoafo. 'The King's kindness to me and my companions during our captivity had extinguished all rancour in my heart,' he wrote.[50]

The prize agents and thirty Fante carriers set off for the palace after dark amidst lashing rain with instructions from Wolseley to work until dawn. Brackenbury describes the scene inside the palace. By the light of two candles they 'worked with most ardent energy in despoiling King Koffee of his property.' They examined gold masks and gold 'faces of savage men, about half the size of life ... Box after box was opened and its contents hastily examined, the more valuable ones being kept, and the others left ... Silver-plate was carried off, and doubtless much left behind. Swords, gorgeous ammunition-belts, caps mounted in solid gold, knives set in gold and silver, bags of gold dust and nuggets; carved stools mounted in silver, calabashes worked in silver and in gold, silks embroidered and woven, were all passed in review. The sword presented by her Majesty to the king was found and carried off; and thousands of things were left behind that would be worth fabulous sums in cabinets at home ... Captain Buller and the other prize agents worked on through the night.'[51]

Marie-Joseph Bonnat judged that the Asante had already removed most of their treasure. This is consistent with Prempeh II's *History of*

Ashanti which records that the Asantehene's 'Elders came to join him in Akwaboa with as much of the royal regalia as they could save and carry.'⁵² And yet, Bonnat records, the British were still able to find much of value. 'Everything was packed up and sent to the general,' he wrote. He reflected on how easy it would have been to fill his own pockets, but his heart was not in it. 'I didn't want to take anything, and I left with my hands empty. This nocturnal pillage, to my eyes, was something repulsive and shameful. I did not want to be complicit.' British officers told him he was being foolish. Sickened at what was happening to the palace he knew so well, Bonnat eventually lay down and fell asleep on a mat. He was overcome with a feeling of melancholy.⁵³

The Royal Engineers were also working hard to mine the palace and set Kumasi alight, so as, in Wolseley's words, 'to ensure its total destruction'.⁵⁴ They were led by Captain Robert Home, whom Wolseley judged 'one of the most remarkable men I have ever known … This was his first campaign, and no one strove harder to make it a success.'⁵⁵ Home did not have all the explosives or fuses that he needed, as the Engineers' supplies had somehow become mixed up with the reserve ammunition of the Rifle Brigade and never reached Kumasi. The Engineers' report says, rather obliquely, that '160 lbs. of Ashantee powder were procured and some slow match made, also a number of palm leaf torches.' But Home still needed to improvise, for when the Engineers examined the palace they found it was a solid

> two stories and in part three stories high, with a strong stone staircase on the outside … it was apparent that what is termed a hasty demolition would be a failure, owing to the want of powder. The pillars were attacked with the pickaxes … large cuts were made in a similar way to the outer walls, and the powder divided into six charges, placed under the main supports left to the building.

And just like Brackenbury's prize agents, the Engineers 'worked all night'.⁵⁶

It was a Lieutenant Mark Sever Bell who was instructed to light the fuse. Bell had performed heroics at the Battle of Odaso, 'urging on and encouraging an unarmed working party of Fantee labourers, who were exposed not only to the fire of the Enemy, but to the wild and irregular fire of the Native Troops in the rear', for which he would receive the Victoria Cross.[57] Now he 'completed the mines, attached the slow match and fired them: two were seen to explode and a large mass of the Palace fell.' Henty of *The Standard* wrote there was no large blast, but the palace fell 'like a pack of cards' and a British officer would later report it as 'completely ruined'. Meanwhile, Lieutenant Hare 'fired the town' itself, starting from the north. 'To every quarter', Boyle of the *Telegraph* wrote, 'the torch-bearers rushed.'[58] The rain had fallen heavily throughout the night and the thatched roofs were soaking. But eventually the flames caught. At dawn on 6 February, Kumasi was ablaze. 'The fetish houses and temples were also burned', reported the Royal Engineers.[59] Henty watched on, 'The smoke of the burning town was dense in the extreme, and flames leapt up fiercely from time to time.'[60]

'I had done all I could to avoid the necessity, but it was forced upon me,' wrote Wolseley at the time.[61] Kumasi, he told his wife, 'has now ceased to exist as a city.'[62] Years later, he expressed no regrets. 'I believed that the absolute destruction of Koomassee and its great palace, the wonder of Western Africa, would be a much more striking and effective end to the war than any paper treaty ... that I might obtain from this brutal and deceitful monarch.'[63] At 9 a.m. on 6 February, according to the Engineers, 'the work of destruction was completed.' By then, almost all the British soldiers had left. George Little describes this momentous morning in the most perfunctory terms: 'Rouse sounded 4.30 a.m. We had breakfast and paraded at 5.30. Broke a lot of rifles, blew up the Palace and left Coomassie in flames ... and started on our way to "Old England."'[64]

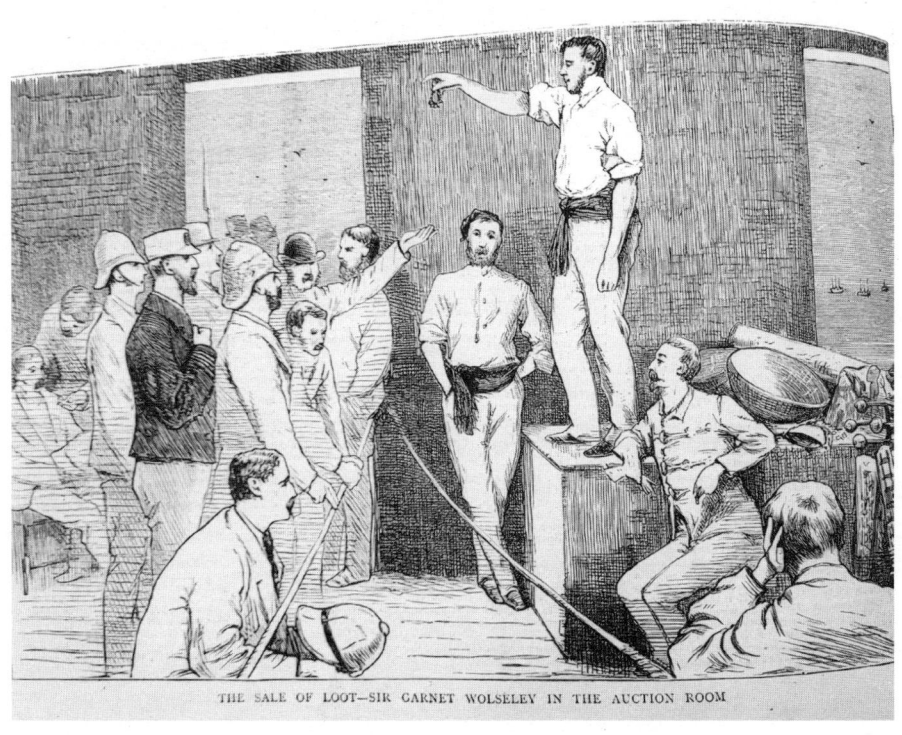

Auctioning the treasure; Cape Coast Castle, 23 February 1874.

7

'GOLD IS ALWAYS PRETTY'

Wolseley spent his second and final night in Kumasi huddled under an umbrella, kept awake by 'a succession of tornadoes … very very heavy rain.' He left the city on 6 February at 7 a.m. and 'found the road in a dreadful condition; one of the swamps was up to the men's armpits … The Ordah river was swollen and rising … a man of 5 ft. 6 inches in height could just ford it without his mouth being covered, and the current was very rapid.'[1] George Little wrote that water levels had risen three feet in two days, bridges built by the Royal Engineers were almost submerged and many men had to ford the rivers but could not dry out in the persistent rain.[2]

The British were victorious, but their return journey to Cape Coast was far from triumphant. They burned the Asante villages they marched through and counted their growing numbers of casualties. Of the roughly 2,500 British troops on the entire expedition, 71 died, 394 were wounded and more than 1,000 were invalided home with various sicknesses.[3] Officers suffered disproportionately; forty died, although only six from injuries in battle.[4] On 8 February, Lieutenant Joseph Thomas wrote that 'men who had landed six weeks previous, strong, robust and healthy, were reduced to mere skeletons.'[5] The following day George Little was distressed to learn that Corporal Church and Charles Penwell – 'fine young men and much loved in the company' – who had been left behind in a field hospital on the march up had died of dysentery. And when the rain eventually stopped, the scorching sun brought no respite. Little wrote that it 'would dazzle your eyes and cause a blind and burning sensation in the head and make you feel quite giddy ... I even saw men staggering about as if under the influence of licquer lots of men fell ill on this march and the exposures to the climate tells on them now and the hammocks are full.'[6]

Kofi Karikari had returned to Kumasi to find his palace in ruins and the city destroyed. He went to stay at his 'Country Retreat' at Manhyia village.[7] There he brooded over his fate. Perhaps the most alarming news was that another British-led army was approaching Kumasi from the east. This was the force led by John Glover of the Royal Navy, approved by the British government even before it had endorsed Wolseley's expedition. Glover's army was comprised of a handful of British officers, Hausa and Yoruba soldiers, brought from Lagos and elsewhere in what is today Nigeria, and whichever disaffected people he had managed to raise in the regions to the east of Kumasi.[8] Wolseley had insisted that Glover's army should be one of three diversionary forces which would assist his main thrust against Asante. The second, led by Captain William Dalrymple and supposedly comprised of soldiers from the Wassa kingdom to the south-west of Asante, never crossed the Pra and was abandoned in January 1874. The third, led by Captain William Butler, got closer to Kumasi but his reluctant Akyem soldiers deserted at the first threat of battle.[9] By early February, Glover was also facing difficulties. His army was subsisting on yams and plantain, he had only a few hundred reliable men, his officers were weak with dysentery and fever, and he had lost contact with Wolseley. He was, nonetheless, doggedly advancing on Kumasi, which he would eventually enter unopposed a week after Wolseley had left.

Some of the most important tributary kingdoms of Asante were now re-evaluating their loyalty to the Asantehene. Glover met the King of Dwaben, Asafo Agyei, on 8 February, while on 12 February, Wolseley, camped at Fomena beneath the Adanse hills, was visited by the King of Adanse, Kwabena Oben.[10] Both these men, former allies of the Asantehene, were seeking to make terms with the British. Kofi

Karikari's authority was draining away and so he too despatched his envoys to talk to Wolseley. 'The King', Wolseley wrote in his journal, was 'begging for peace'.[11]

Lieutenant Frederick Maurice, Wolseley's private secretary, describes the scene at Fomena on the morning of 13 February. Wolseley's officers, in their headquarters of huts thatched with palm and plantain leaves, watched a delegation of Asante noblemen approach, carrying a large white cloth. Other British officers looked on, surrounded by a cordon of Fante policemen and West Indian soldiers. 'Behind gathered on every little vantage ground of hillock or fallen hut as many natives as could get a chance of viewing the sight,' wrote Maurice. When the Asante emptied their cloth before Wolseley, it was found to be 'filled with gold plates and figures, nuggets, bracelets, knobs, masks, bells, jaw-bones, and fragments of skulls, plaques, bosses – all of the metal as pure as it can be, and an endless variety of shape and size.' This treasure, wrote Maurice, 'could hardly have been paid over at a spot more picturesque', its handover a 'sign patent to all men of the submission of the Ashantee King.'[12]

A less effusive witness to this surrender was the French former hostage Marie-Joseph Bonnat, who recognised many of the most sacred items from the Asantehene's court. He said that 'his heart hurt' to see a people whom he loved reduced to such misery and wondered why the Asantehene had given up his most precious objects just when the British were retreating.[13] The Gold Coast Protectorate's official gold tester, brought up from Cape Coast by Wolseley for just such an eventuality, inspected each item and identified some of the bags of supposed gold dust as mere brass. A few more pieces were found in the folds of the robes of the Asante noblemen, where they had been hidden, in the words of one British historian, perhaps 'in the hope of retaining them as a secret commission'.[14] Then the gold tester weighed everything: 1,040 ounces.

This was far short of the 50,000 ounces Wolseley demanded as the indemnity, or even the 5,000 he said he would accept as a short-term gesture of good faith. He wrote in his journal that although he was sure the Asante were lying about how much gold they could produce, 'I am too anxious to get a treaty to stick out for money.' Prempeh II's *History of Ashanti* suggests that Kofi Karikari scraped together as much treasure as he could find in a hurried attempt to placate Wolseley. 'The time for paying over the first instalment of the indemnity was so short that it was not even possible to call any of the Provincial Chiefs into Kumasi to contribute what they could. So King Kofi Karikari was obliged to bear the brunt of this payment alone. He took some of the regalia that had been rescued [from the palace] and added the available gold dust that he had to hand.'[15] In other words, if the British prize agents in the Kumasi palace had seized objects the Asantehene had chosen to leave behind, he was now reluctantly handing over his most precious treasure.

Wolseley was relieved the British journalists had already left for the coast, so he could conduct 'negociations [sic] freed from their accursed presence'.[16] This implies give and take with the Asantehene's envoys, but in reality he was dictating terms. The envoys – Kwaku Suo, Adu Yaw and Esen Kwaku – raised objections to the treaty laid before them, and in particular to the indemnity and the renunciation of any rights over the previously subservient kingdom of Adanse, but Wolseley would not compromise. 'The King's three envoys did not argue any further and they silently acquiesced to the other clauses in the draft treaty', according to Prempeh II's *History of Ashanti*.[17] The 'Treaty of Fommanah' (as the British called Fomena) also obliged the Asantehene to 'renounce for ever' rights over the port of Elmina, to withdraw troops from the coast, to abandon claims over other neighbouring kingdoms, to open his land to trade and to 'use his best endeavours to check the practice of human sacrifice … repugnant to the feelings of all Christian nations.' In return, the British assured the Asante of 'perpetual peace', in which 'Her Majesty's subjects and the people of Ashanti are henceforth friends for ever.'[18]

Wolseley told the Asantehene's envoys that he would wait at Cape Coast until 28 February for a copy of the treaty with Kofi Karikari's signature attached. After the envoys returned to Kumasi, he wrote to his military and political masters in London and summarised the achievements of his campaign. 'I think I may say that my mission here is now at an end,' he told the Duke of Cambridge, 'I have taken part in most of the wars that we have had for the last twenty-two years ... In none have I met with a braver enemy.' To Edward Cardwell he wrote, 'Success has attended my military mission ... [not only] having defeated the enemy's army, and occupied and destroyed his capital, but in our having thoroughly established in this kingdom a wholesome fear of the British power, and a knowledge of the advantages of Her Majesty.'[19]

The War Office in London did not receive this letter until 16 March, some five weeks later. By then, William Gladstone's Liberal government had left office, defeated by Benjamin Disraeli's Conservatives in the February general election. Wolseley's expedition occurred during the infancy of telegraphic communications and the result was a jarring delay between events on the ground and any knowledge or political impact of those events back in London. On 5 February, for example, Wolseley wrote a hurried note to the War Office, announcing his entry into Kumasi: 'Reached this place yesterday, after five day's hard fighting. Troops behaved admirably. All wounded doing well.' On the same day, *The Times* could only speculate on his progress towards the Asante capital and said there had been no fighting so far. The Asante War, *The Times* said, had been 'one of the central controversies' of the election campaign, as the Conservatives sought to blame the government for blundering into an expensive and pointless conflict, and Gladstone would have 'reason to regret' the poor communications with the Gold Coast: 'everybody knows that the news of a victory or a defeat coming at the crisis of a general election would turn to one side or the other thousands of votes.'[20] On 25 February, the new Conservative cabinet met and grumbled that news from Asante was still 'indecisive'.[21] It was only the following day that the new Secretary of State for War, Gathorne-Hardy, finally received Wolseley's Kumasi message and rushed to the Queen with the joyous news. 'Her Majesty expresses the greatest satisfaction at the intelligence sent ... I congratulate you on your success,' he replied.[22] Wolseley's march on Kumasi would eventually capture the British popular imagination, but long after the events on the ground had played themselves out.

These delays were not for lack of trying on Wolseley's behalf. He had asked the Royal Engineers to build a telegraph line using bamboo poles along the route from Cape Coast to Kumasi. Although this got off to an impressive start ('5 miles a day' George Little wrote in his diary), officers soon complained that it was 'unsatisfactory ... frequent as were the interruptions.' Trees fell on the line and operators suffered from quinine-induced deafness.[23] But the more insurmountable problem was that there was no connection from Cape Coast onwards. Although by the 1870s underwater cables were starting to connect London with distant parts of the empire, West Africa remained very much offline. This was acutely frustrating, not just for Wolseley and his officers but also for the British journalists. The Royal Navy positioned two paddle-wheel steamers, the *Enchantress* and the *Vigilant*, on Madeira, with instructions to intercept the West African mail boat coming from Cape Coast. Either steamer could make the subsequent journey to Lisbon – where there was a telegraph station – in just over forty hours. There, representatives of rival London newspapers hired oarsmen to rush out to meet the steamers and return to shore, where 'telegrams are put upon the wire without loss of time' and the Portuguese watched on in bemusement.[24]

★★★

On 14 March 1874, the *Illustrated London News* carried a striking double-page picture, 'The Burning of Coomassie', by its artist Melton Prior. 'Coomassie was burnt,' he explained, 'and therefore I think it would be more interesting to show it in flames.'[25] Prior didn't tell his readers, at least until he wrote his autobiography almost forty years later, of his determined efforts to cling on to the loot he had taken from the Asantehene's palace. Although Wolseley praised his soldiers for their discipline in Kumasi, 'from which they did not carry away a single thing of any worth', he apparently suspected that not everybody had behaved honourably, for at the bridge over the Pra River, he made a final attempt to ensure nobody left Asante territory with a private collection.[26] Prior wrote 'there were sentries put at the head of the bridge to examine everything that went across. I thought this was rather hard lines after having collected many interesting specimens of Ashanti art, to say nothing of the one or two little articles which I had taken out of the palace, so carefully thinking the matter over, I put everything I could into my hammock, covered my spoils, and then got in and affected illness.' His deceit worked. 'Not so with many other men: they told me with many lamentations afterwards that they had had to deliver up a lot of valuable and interesting curios.'[27]

This complaint – that British soldiers were being deprived of hard-won trophies – is repeated in the diary of Lieutenant Joseph Thomas, who returned through the battlefield at Amoafo on 9 February on his journey back to Cape Coast and wrote: 'The Prize Committee caused great ill-feeling and grumbling amongst the men, by taking even little brass ornaments, not worth two pence, and small strings of worthless beads ... but which possessed considerable value in the eyes of the men, from there having been taken from the bodies of the Ashantis whom they had killed.'[28]

Wolseley, of course, saw his own organised removal of treasures from the palace, not to mention the extortionate nature of the indemnity, as of a different and legitimate character. He reached Cape Coast on 19 February, where residents came out to salute the conqueror of the hated Asante. 'Was received by the whole population roaring and screaming, the women throwing themselves in heaps on the ground in front of me, triumphal arches, Guards of honour, the fleet dressed with flags, and a Royal Salute ... in honour of the fall of Coomassie.'[29] The celebrations were still going on two days later, when George Little and the Rifle Brigade arrived. 'All the natives rushed out to welcome us and the town was a proper babel of tongue,' he wrote. The soldiers were not able to savour the moment. More and more were falling sick and Wolseley wanted them embarked as quickly as possible. After a hurried cup of cocoa, the Rifle Brigade was put on surf boats and taken out to the *Himalaya*, where sailors gave the soldiers bread, mutton, steak and tea and were 'most kind'. When the *Himalaya* sailed for England two days later, Lieutenant Thomas wrote that his men were 'heartily glad to turn our backs on the West Coast of Africa'.[30]

Wolseley's own staff was severely depleted. Of the thirty-five officers of the so-called 'Wolseley Ring', seven were dead and only Henry

Brackenbury was well enough to march alongside his commander into Cape Coast.[31] 'All my staff are more or less sickly, and I want rest myself,' Wolseley wrote to the Duke of Cambridge on 22 February.[32] That evening he wandered over to Cape Coast Castle, where he walked up the broad stairs to the grand entrance of the 'Palaver Hall', a handsome room some fifteen metres long, with high ceilings and eight large windows and a veranda overlooking the British ships anchored below. He had come to examine the loot laid out by his prize agents, Captains Buller and Grosvenor, as well as Dr Henry Fegan of the Royal Navy, in anticipation of the auction to be held the following morning.[33]

Frederick Boyle, correspondent for the *Daily Telegraph*, paints the scene in the Palaver Hall at 10.30 a.m. on Monday 23 February:

> The long centre table was covered as thickly as it could bear with jewellery and gold. On a side table stood the king's plate. Against a broad screen hung swords and cartouche belts of leopard skin, and canes of huge silver heads, and calabashes bound in gold and silver, and embossed brass pans. Beneath lay the stools so placed that their fine silver bosses and adornments could be seen in one glittering display ... At the other end of the room cloths and silks were disposed, neatly wrapped and labelled, one on another, hundreds of them. The prize agents ... had shown considerable taste in the arrangement of their stores, but it is easy to make a fine display of things tastefully coloured. And gold is always pretty.[34]

These were the treasures taken from the Asantehene's palace on 5 February by the prize agents, as well as some pieces subsequently surrendered by British officers, and anything confiscated from Fante carriers and other African allies on the return march, 'no inconsiderable addition to the total' according to Maurice.[35] They did not include, however, the gold regalia which the Asantehene's envoys surrendered at Fomena, the so-called 'indemnity jewels', which were put aside to be sold in London. There had been a discussion amongst the officers about this, but the Fomena regalia was generally felt to be too fine to be auctioned amongst the soldiers. Boyle explained: 'London will enjoy its chance when the king's regalia are sold; his bracelets, a score of them, weighing four or five pounds, pure metal; his necklaces, fetishes, nondescript articles, all of gold. To offer such things to us here was obviously absurd. No soldier's purse could afford him a keepsake worth two or three hundred at the Mint.'[36]

Some British officers had misgivings that many soldiers had already embarked and so would miss the auction, leaving Wolseley's staff, Royal Navy officers and colonial officials to do much of the bidding. But if the British presence in Cape Coast was reduced, local Fante society was willing to step into the breach. 'The hall was crammed with natives, those of better class,' wrote Boyle. They were particularly interested in fabrics and the beautiful glass Aggrey beads, prized in Akan culture and which caused 'great excitement … for an Aggry bead is to a Fantee woman, or indeed to a Cape Coast lady, what a diamond is to us.' Boyle watched in admiration as women already dripping in gold bid for yet more jewellery: 'It did not appear to the observer that these dames could have need of more aggrys or more gold.'

Several gold items fetched more than £100 each (equivalent to about £11,730 today). These included a 23-ounce gold mask, 'a hideous object' according to Boyle, which sold for £102, as well as the 'King's bracelet', which went to the Black Watch's surgeon-major Dr James Clutterbuck, for £114 (about £13,370 today).[37] 'The most beautiful of all the stools discovered' was set aside as a present for the Prince of Wales and would 'not be out of place however magnificent its surroundings'.[38] The ghost of Sir Charles MacCarthy, so often lurking in the British imagination, also made an appearance with the sale of a covered tankard said to have belonged to the unfortunate governor of the 1820s.

Wolseley 'often looked in during the sale, and occasionally took part in the bidding', according to the *Daily Graphic*, which published a sketch of the scene (see page 84). It shows one prize agent holding up a piece for examination, another draped languidly over a table covered in loot and British officers, including Wolseley, held back by ropes as they make their bids. In the distance, through an open window, British war ships are dotted on the sea.³⁹ 'Everything fetched very high prices,' Wolseley wrote in his journal. British officers had put so much money into the local economy, he thought, 'that everyone, even the poorest looking n****r has plenty to spend.'⁴⁰ Boyle wrote that the 'proceeds of the sale will certainly reach £3560.'⁴¹

Wolseley informed his wife, Louisa, that he had been 'very proud' to buy the silver 'King Koffees Coffee-pot' of English design and which he attributed to the reign of George II and felt would provide conversation 'whenever we might have very stupid people with us'. He also bought a 'gold rattle taken from the King's nursery' as a present for his baby daughter Frances ('my runteefoozle'), wooden stools, Aggrey beads and a hat with gold and silver decoration said to have been worn by Kofi Karikari at the Battle of Odaso. Wolseley's staff pooled their resources to buy the sword which Queen Victoria had given to the previous Asantehene, Kwaku Dua, and presented it to him as a gift: 'very nice of them, is it not?'⁴² Many years later, after Wolseley's death, Louisa would give these objects to the Royal United Services Institution in Whitehall. In 1963, they were acquired by the National Army Museum now in Chelsea. In 2025, they were all being held in a warehouse outside London.⁴³

There was one more wonderful sculpture which Wolseley had set his 'heart upon'. He described it as 'a bronze group of about 50 little figures representing the King of Ashantee being carried in state'.⁴⁴ Each figure was about twenty centimetres high; they carried the King on their heads and held an umbrella over him. Maurice described it as 'perhaps the most valuable single item ... No one at Cape Coast knew how this somewhat exceptional piece of property came into the hands of the Ashantee monarch.'⁴⁵ Boyle agreed that it could not have been made by an African: 'It was indeed a most extraordinary moulding, full of spirit, and such as one cannot believe to have come from negro hands.'⁴⁶

Boyle and Maurice would not be the last Europeans to be caught off guard by the sophistication of West African brass and bronze casting. In 1897, the loot the British brought home from the kingdom of Benin – the Benin Bronzes – was received with surprise and admiration in London and beyond. The Akan people had developed similar skills

LONDON — KING COFFEE CALCALLI'S UMBRELLA AT THE SOUTH KENSINGTON MUSEUM

Victorian society admires the 'famous umbrella of King Koffee' at the South Kensington Museum.

8

'WORTHY TO FIND A RESTING PLACE IN THE BRITISH AND SOUTH KENSINGTON MUSEUMS'

'A bitterly cold morning', wrote Queen Victoria from Windsor Castle on 10 March 1874. She braved the gusts of chill wind and snow showers to watch the hounds chase a stag before retiring for lunch with the Prince of Wales and a small group of relatives. Then she received Lieutenant Henry Wood of the Royal Hussars, son of Lord Halifax and Wolseley's aide-de-camp, who had just arrived from the Gold Coast.[1] Wolseley had sent Wood ahead from his camp on 7 February carrying an urgent dispatch on the fall of Kumasi, some sketches by Melton Prior, as well as two trophies from the Asantehene's palace. Wood gave a wooden stool 'decorated profusely with embossed silver' to the Prince of Wales. The second trophy, an umbrella more than two metres in diameter and made of crimson and black velvet with gold trimming, was for the Queen.[2] The *Illustrated London News* described it as 'an emblem of pomp and dignity, held over the King's head on all ceremonial occasions'.[3] The *Daily Telegraph* proclaimed it the Asantehene's 'favourite' and said it was 'very capacious'.[4] Victoria passed on her thanks to Wolseley for 'the Royal State Umbrella ... which Her Majesty values highly as a symbol of the victorious termination of the campaign'. A British queen had vanquished an African king.[5]

Wolseley sailed from Cape Coast on 4 March – 'never did I leave any spot upon earth with such pleasure' – without waiting for the Asantehene's response to the Fomena treaty (a delegation of Asante noblemen eventually arrived from Kumasi on 13 March, carrying the treaty marked with two crosses at the bottom, signifying the Asantehene's assent).[6] He disembarked at Portsmouth on 21 March, where a reporter saw one of the now 'famous umbrellas', more than two metres tall, and several 'Ashantee military "standards"' (described as 'a long stick with a racquet-shaped head, on each side of which is strained a piece of leopard skin') being loaded into his luggage-cart. At Waterloo station, Wolseley could barely move through the enthusiastic crowd. 'As the General and his officers left their carriages they were received with deafening "Hurrahs" and "Welcomes."'[7] He had his own audience with Victoria at Windsor the next day.[8] They had a lively conversation; she thought he looked 'thin and grey but well … full of energy & calm & decided looking', while he wrote that he 'told her all sorts of amusing things about the Gold Coast that made her laugh'.[9] The day after that he was congratulated by Disraeli. A troop review at Windsor followed, as did a naval review on St George's Day at Gosport in weather 'more worthy of July than April', and a series of banquets.[10]

Wolseley's victory was no surprise – as early as November 1873 the Birmingham jewellers B. H. Joseph and Co had registered a design for the 'Ashantee earring' in anticipation of a glorious campaign – but he was nonetheless lavished with praise.[11] He was promoted to Major General, awarded by a unanimous vote of Parliament a grant of £25,000 (worth £2.9 million pounds today) and showered with medals and honorary degrees.[12] John Pridham, prolific composer of patriotic pieces celebrating imperial victories, released an 'Ashantee March' for the pianoforte, the cover of which depicts Wolseley on a white charger outside Cape Coast Castle, pointing the way to African chiefs and British officers.[13]

Wolseley would later reflect that Asante was 'the most horrible war I ever took part in'.[14] And yet it made him a household name. In the years that followed, 'All Sir Garnet' – the phrase means everything under control – entered popular usage, a tribute to his organisational skills. In

1880, when George Grossmith took to the London stage in Gilbert and Sullivan's comic opera *The Pirates of Penzance* and sang, 'I am the very model of a modern Major-General', he delighted the audience with his twirled moustache and haughty air, a winking allusion to Wolseley.[15]

The Asante expedition's perceived success was seen as vindication of the reforms Wolseley and Lord Cardwell had pursued and their vision of a more meritocratic, professional and modern army. Even the Treasury was impressed. The expedition came in on budget, at a cost of £815,000, according to the War Office (meaning the Asante indemnity, if it had been paid in full, would have covered a quarter of British costs).[16] By comparison, the British invasion of Abyssinia in 1868 had cost nearly £9 million, while the Second Anglo-Afghan War of 1878–80 would cost £23.4 million.[17]

On the *Himalaya*, the soldiers of the Rifle Brigade were subdued on the journey home. George Little wrote that many were unwell, and some had turned 'a nasty yellow colour' (presumably from yellow fever). The first funeral at sea, on 25 February, was a 'most solemn ceremony', as the enshrouded corpse was carried from hospital to bridge to gangway, and then lowered into the water. The Rifle Brigade held two more funerals before it reached the Cape Verde Islands, and some fifty sick men were taken off at Gibraltar. But at Portsmouth, on 26 March, 'the town was decorated in splendid style ... and we could hear nothing but cheering.' The crowds pressed beer, bread, cheese and tobacco into the hands of the soldiers, who struggled to make their way to the station. They eventually caught a train to their barracks at Winchester, where Lieutenant Joseph Thomas wrote, 'every available nook was secured by the inhabitants to catch the first glance of the "Ashanti heroes."' Bunting, arches and garlands decorated the streets, and the Rifle Brigade found it impossible to march through the throng. There were more crowds and pomp at Windsor a few days later when the soldiers were addressed by the Queen and the Prince of Wales, and after that another banquet in Winchester Guildhall, a 'magnificent spread ... Everyone seemed to enjoy himself. After the banquet grog was served *ab libitum* and cigars, ditto.'[18]

In the first weeks of 1874, British newspapers were dominated by news of the wedding of Queen Victoria's son Alfred to Czar Alexander

II of Russia's daughter, Maria (which Prince Leonid Vyazemsky had participated in) and the general election. But thereafter, the belated coverage of the Asante War took centre stage. As Wolseley's biographer wrote, 'The fall of Kumasi filled the penny papers with more print than a dozen Waterloos might have produced in an earlier age.'[19] There was humour too, of a sort, to be had from this triumph. The Moore and Burgess blackface minstrels, playing at St James's Hall on Piccadilly to 'crowded to overflowing' audiences with their 'great hit of the day', 'The Laughing N*****', added the 'Happy Ashantee' to their repertoire in April 1874, which, along with other comic sketches, 'kept the vast audience in roars of laughter'.[20] But victory also brought magnanimity. The Asante had been brave, wrote *The Graphic*, and 'we may fairly anticipate that in the future a nation who, in spite of their barbarism, possess many qualities superior to the cowardly Coastal tribes, may become our firm and faithful allies.'[21]

The journalists who had accompanied Wolseley rushed to take advantage of the popular interest; George Henty of *The Standard*, William Winwood Reade of *The Times*, Frederick Boyle of the *Telegraph* and Henry Stanley of the *New York Herald* all published Asante books within months of returning. Winwood Reade, who like Stanley had been an occasional critic of Wolseley in Asante, as well as British overall strategy in the Gold Coast, fell into line with the patriotic mood and concluded his book with a tribute to the soldiers he had marched alongside: 'I have learnt that the spirit which animated the bowmen of Agincourt and Cressy still lives, glowing and warm, in the ranks of an army which is drawn from the lowest classes of the people.'[22] But Asante, it seems, took its toll on Winwood Reade's health, for he returned from the Gold Coast 'a broken man ... and wasted away slowly but inevitably'. He died in April 1875, 'cut off in his prime' at the age of just thirty-seven.[23]

Stanley's efforts were especially impressive; he 'laboured night and day' over his 'literary work', which was completed within an incredible three weeks, and published on 25 April.[24] In *Coomassie and Magdala*, he compared the Asante expedition with the Abyssinia expedition of 1868, where the Emperor Tewodros killed himself as British soldiers stormed his mountain citadel, after which they ripped clothes and hair from his corpse.[25] Stanley, and several of Wolseley's officers, had taken part in both of these expeditions, and there are some uncomfortable similarities between them; the slaughter wrought by British soldiers against Africans trying to defend their homelands and the destruction and pillage with which they celebrated their victories.[26] But Stanley wrote that 'more brilliant successes than attended these two campaigns in hostile countries are not recorded in history'.[27]

While Britain basked in its triumph over African barbarism in the spring of 1874, it also mourned the death of David Livingstone, widely regarded as a saintly man who had toiled to lift up that benighted continent, and Stanley was determined to be at the centre of both stories. On the day he brought out *Coomassie and Magdala*, he somehow also released an 'entirely New and thoroughly Revised Edition' of *How I Found Livingstone*, updated to catch the drama, and opportunity, of the sad news which had reached him on his way home from Cape Coast: 'Livingstone was dead-… his body was on its way to England! Livingstone had then fallen! He was dead! He had died by the shores of Lake Bemba, on the threshold of the dark region he had wished to explore! The work he had promised me to perform was only begun when death overtook him!' On 18 April, 'the solemn day of the burial of my great friend', Stanley was a pallbearer at Westminster Abbey but was soon planning a return to Africa to discover its remaining secrets. By September he was in Zanzibar, about to begin another epic journey across 'the Dark Continent'.[28]

Melton Prior of the *Illustrated London News* was gravely ill on the journey back to England and Henty and Stanley feared for his life. But he survived, to the delight and astonishment of his wife, and was sent to Hastings to recuperate 'with a very handsome cheque to pay expenses'.[29] Over the next thirty years Prior would cover imperial wars in South Africa, Egypt, India, Sudan, Burma and Somaliland, as well as revolutions in South America, uprisings in Spain and Crete, several Balkan conflicts and the Russo-Japanese War. He was a 'light-hearted man, who found satisfaction in the romance of distant places, the excitement of battles, and the enjoyment of pursuing his craft under challenging conditions'.[30]

By the end of his career, the *Illustrated London News* would boast that he won 'an array of war medals ... which probably even few soldiers could match'.[31] He is one of a handful of journalists commemorated in the crypt of St Paul's, where his tablet was unveiled by a fellow Asante veteran, Sir Evelyn Wood.[32]

The *Illustrated London News* got its money's worth from Prior on Wolseley's expedition, publishing more than 100 of his sketches during the period from January to June 1874, with many used as covers or double-page spreads.[33] On 28 March it released a special supplement, 'From Cape Coast to Coomassie, An Illustrated Narrative of the Ashantee War', for one shilling, double the cost of the regular weekly edition.[34] It also commissioned the artist Louis Desanges – who specialised in depictions of Victorian military valour – to paint a battle scene, *Fighting in the Ashantee Forest*, on a canvas of more than four by three metres. Wolseley and a host of officers sat for Desanges, as did Prior, who is shown with pencil and sketchbook 'in diligent pursuit of his vocation' as the battle rages around him. In the background, an Asante soldier tumbles from a tree after being shot: 'strange fruit of the wild African forest!' wrote the *Illustrated London News*.[35] Desanges's painting, along with some 100 of Prior's sketches, was displayed in May 1874 at the Willis Rooms, on King Street in St James's, in London's most fashionable district.

The most tangible evidence of Britain's victory, however, were the trophies the army had brought home, and the Willis Rooms exhibition also included Asante ornaments, weapons and 'other curious objects'. Asante's finest treasures, however, went on display in April 1874, a few streets to the east of the Willis Rooms. Garrard, the Crown jeweller, was based in two Georgian mansions at 25 Haymarket where, it liked to boast, 'all London foregathered'.[36] Established in 1721, Garrard had displayed the Royal Arms on its ledgers since 1804.[37] Some of the British Empire's most precious jewels passed through its doors. In 1852, an elderly Duke of Wellington rode up Haymarket on his white charger. The hero of Waterloo was carrying the Koh-i-Noor diamond on behalf of Queen Victoria. Garrard brought diamond cutters from Holland to have it recut 'from its imperfect shape to that of an oval brilliant'.[38] In

1855, the Prince Consort asked Garrard to design a diamond pendant for the Queen to give to Florence Nightingale in gratitude for her services in Crimea.[39] In 1911, Garrard was commissioned to incorporate South Africa's Cullinan Diamond into the royal sceptre and crown for George V's coronation.[40]

On Saturday, 18 April 1874, *The Times* announced that the 'Golden Spoil from Ashantee' – meaning specifically the Asantehene's treasures Wolseley had received at Fomena – would go on display at Garrard the following Tuesday. The jewellers, the paper reported, had 'concluded an arrangement with the prize agents of the British force lately serving on the Gold Coast', paying more than £11,000 (worth about £1.29 million today) for the Asante gold.[41] This amount more or less matches the 'grant to the troops engaged, in Ashantee, value £12–13,000', which the incoming foreign secretary, the Earl of Derby, mentions in his diary on 25 April. Derby wrote, rather grudgingly, that the Cabinet felt the grant was 'not objected to on its own account, but there is a doubt as to the precedent which it will create: however, the troops are to have it'.[42]

Queen Victoria had already had first pick of this latest haul. On 31 March, her private secretary, General Sir Henry Ponsonby, wrote to her explaining that Wolseley's soldiers had carried home some 'curious specimens of rough working in gold of the Ashanti'. The officers 'consider it their duty as well as an honour to submit these articles to Your Majesty before publicly selling them'.[43] On 2 April, the Queen was at Osborne House on the Isle of Wight. After a walk in a 'dreadfully high wind', she wrote in her diary, she 'looked at some gold ornaments, huge gold masks, rings, bracelets & other ornaments brought from Coomassie, (all of pure gold) by officers & others, sent in as an indemnity. They are being sold for the benefit of the Army & I have bought some.'[44] Her purchases included an Asante gold head, while a history of Garrard records that she paid £125 (about £14,660 today) for a necklace, two bangles, two plaques, a bell, seven rings and some leopard or lion claws. Her daughter Princess Louise bought a knife handle for £15.[45] Her son, Alfred, Russian wedding out of the way, is reported to have bought 'a bracelet and two small lions; an amulet, representing the lower jaw pierced through to wear; and a bird, which has been mounted on a small pedestal for His Royal Highness'.[46]

Garrard's purchase of the Asante loot, according to the company history, was 'a bold, even foolhardy, undertaking, since the number of customers for these tribal ornaments might have been limited.'[47] But Garrard imposed a handsome mark-up; it bought the objects at £9 per ounce of gold and sold them at £15 per ounce.[48] When the first accounts of the Asantehene's palace reached Britain in March 1874, the *Daily Telegraph* expressed disappointment they did not match expectations. 'Where is the much-vaunted golden staircase? – where the Royal idols and fetishes twenty-two feet high, and overlaid with *laminae* of twenty-two carat gold? where the sacks of gold dust, the nuggets big as pumpkins, the armlets and bangles and necklaces and "round tires like the moon" of the African El Dorado?'[49] But now, displayed in central London, Asante loot enjoyed the lure of the exotic. *The Times* said the gold objects would 'be treasured in England as memorials of the recent struggle'. But they were more than souvenirs. The craftsmanship which had gone into these African treasures could not be dismissed, even in the England of 1874.

Many of the reports of the Garrard exhibition are tinged with an unexpected humility. The circular and individually patterned badges, the *akrafokonmu*, some worn round the neck by officials responsible for the ritual purification of the Asantehene's soul and hence often known as 'soul washer badges', were, according to *The Times*, 'wonderful ... it would be difficult for any skilled goldsmith in Western Europe not so much to surpass, but even to equal them.'[50] Other pieces also evoked praise: 'They must be seen to be understood and appreciated ... every object is beautiful in workmanship and, at the same time, different in design.'[51]

The Globe, reviewing the exhibition on 30 April, speculated luridly as to why one of the swords had a blunt blade: 'This bluntness, doubtless, added to the horrors of the constant executions, and, perhaps to the delight of the savage monarch who so continually revelled in them.' And yet it could not deny the skill of Asante goldsmiths: 'The most extraordinary fact is that, with one or two exceptions, the whole of these objects are cast, and not wrought or hammered… The English jewellers are not above owning that they may take some hints in casting from the Ashantee workmen, some of whose designs are, as they frankly admit, clever enough to baffle their conjectures as to how they were executed. *"Fas est et ab hoste doceri"*, but we hardly expected to gain by our expedition against King Coffee a lesson in the art of gold-casting.'[52] The specialist *Jeweller and Metalworker* speculated that much of the jewellery had originated in Birmingham, but conceded that some of the pieces 'bear the undoubted stamp of genius'.[53]

Britain's provincial newspapers – serious and wordy publications at the time – also wrote lengthy reviews. The *Nottinghamshire Guardian* said 'the craze of the season will be … the possession of an Ashantee ring, or shield, or necklace.'[54] The following week, the *Northampton Mercury* said there was indeed 'a craze for these Ashantee relics, and they are being bought up very quickly.' Society, always hungry for novelty, could not resist 'the most curious collection of jewellery ever got together in any country'.[55]

Garrard's viewing rooms were crowded, *The Globe* reported, and by the end of April many of the best pieces had been sold. The aristocratic Cecil family bought two of the largest soul washer badges, *akrafokonmu*, so admired by *The Times*. They chose to mount these in the centre of much larger contemporary English gilt-silver dishes.[56] On the back of one, William Cecil, the Marquess of Exeter, put his crest and coronet, and the following inscription: 'The gold ornament in the centre of this dish is a portion of the indemnity paid by the Ashanti King Coffee Calcalli to Her Majesty's Forces under the command of Major-General Sir Garnet J. Wolseley, January [sic] 1874.' The other dish also carried the family crest and the monogram of Cecil's son, Francis Horace Pierrepont Cecil. In this way, Asante religious pieces were both dwarfed and desecrated and turned into British military souvenirs.

In 2024, when the British-Guyanese artist Hew Locke included one of Cecil's dishes in an exhibition at the British Museum he wrote, 'The original Asante object, the aesthetic of it, has been ensnared within a European design. It ignores its function completely, it's just there as a trophy. It traps it and it kills it at the same time.'[57] And yet paradoxically both the original Asante *akrafokonmu*, with its intricate and apparently European rococo-like leaf pattern, and the Victorian dish, which in turn emulates the patterns of the inner badge, albeit with bombast and ostentation, suggest a more complex history, defined by the mutual willingness of two cultures to admire and borrow from each other.[58]

This characteristic of Asante art had already caused comment in Britain. *The Times* wrote that 'perhaps the most striking feature of the collection is the extraordinary imitative talent which it proves the Ashantee goldsmiths to possess. Whatever struck them as curious or strange in their intercourse with Europeans, and the outer world, they instantly copied and reproduced in gold.'[59] 'The Ashantees are great copyists,' wrote the *Northampton Mercury*, 'but it must be said that their plagiarism shows them to have been possessed of undeniable taste.'[60] But 'imitative talent' might just be another way of saying 'openness to new ideas', arguably the hallmark of any successful culture. In any case, as *The Times* conceded, 'It is scarcely possible to do justice to the variety and beauty of these specimens of Ashantee goldsmiths' work.' The finest pieces, the paper argued, 'would be well worthy to find a resting place in the British and South Kensington Museums'.

As it happened, both these institutions were following events closely. On the same day *The Times* review was published, the South Kensington Museum (which in 1899 became the Victoria and Albert Museum) bought thirteen of the finest Asante pieces from Garrard – a gold peace pipe, three gold soul washer badges, seven pieces of sheet-gold ornament, a silver straining spoon and a pair of silver anklets – for a combined price of £251 (about £29,430 today). Of these, the most expensive item, at £85, was the pipe, *abua*, a wonderfully slim and delicate object, and the very one that would go back to Kumasi in 2024.[61] (Wolseley's private secretary, Lieutenant Frederick Maurice, took another beautiful gold pipe in 1874: 'the pipe of Koffee Kalkali, King of Ashanti ... acquired at the capture of Coomassie.' His son bequeathed it to the British Museum in 1951.[62])

Robert Soden Smith was a giant figure in the early years of the South Kensington Museum, as it built its reputation in the decorative arts. Born into an Irish military family and originally destined for the church, he instead became a scholar and founder and Keeper of the museum's Art Library for more than thirty years, until his death in 1890.[63] In the spring of 1874, Smith recognised that the 'mass of treasure' recently arrived from Asante had an 'intrinsic importance', not only, as he put it, 'due to the circumstances of its acquisition' but also because it was 'the most striking illustration which has yet reached this country of the art of an ancient race hitherto imperfectly known to us'.

Smith's booklet, 'Notes on specimens of wrought gold, forming a portion of the Ashanti indemnity', written for the *Archaeological Journal*, is both admiring and dismissive, as he struggles to reconcile the beauty and sophistication of the pieces with his Victorian world view.[64] The Asante were 'little advanced in the scale of civilization', wrote Smith, and whereas more sophisticated people such as the Assyrians or Mexicans had perfected techniques to turn gold into objects of daily use, most of the pieces at Garrard were merely 'barbaric adornments' for personal decoration. The Asante castings 'evince undoubted skill'; some were 'splendid', others 'remarkable'. But he damned with faint praise. The Asante workman was largely copying 'elaborate foreign models' from Europe, often of objects that would be 'wholly strange to him'. Moreover, Smith argued that casting had gradually replaced an older and more intricate skill of coiling delicate threads of gold wire. This inspiration had originally come from elsewhere, perhaps Egypt or Abyssinia, but was now gradually fading away. 'The Ashantis are the inheritors of traditions,' he argued 'which in the lapse, perhaps of ages, have become partly obscured'. They were, as the British so often concluded of those whose treasures they had looted, a people in decline.[65]

On the other side of London, the curiosity of another eminent curator had been piqued. Augustus Wollaston Franks had joined the British Museum in 1851. Marjorie Caygill, chronicler of that institution, writes that although virtually unknown today, Franks was 'arguably the most important collector in the history of the British Museum'. He was 'a polymath', interested in 'a vast range of subjects – Japanese flint instruments, Cypriot Bronze Age Metalwork, Anglo-Saxon ivories, Irish trumpets, medieval drinking bowls, Indian sculpture, Mexican turquoise mosaics – to name but a few'. Franks himself wrote that 'collecting is a hereditary disease, and I fear uncurable.' He certainly indulged his passion, with the assistance of a large family fortune. When he died in 1897, he left tens of thousands of objects to the British Museum, valued at £50,000 (about £6.8 million today).[66]

By 1874 Franks was Keeper of the British Museum's sprawling department of British and Medieval Antiquities and Ethnography. On 13 March, as soon as the news from Kumasi and Fomena reached London, he wrote to the museum's trustees. He had 'noticed in the public papers that a portion of the indemnity to be paid to Great Britain by the King of Ashantee has been paid to Sir Garnet Wolseley in the form of gold ornaments'.[67] Franks had two worries – that others would take or buy objects before the British Museum had a chance to make its selection, and that the government would simply melt them down to realise their value as bullion. But the British Museum trustees, with little information about the Asante indemnity, delayed a decision on whether to ask the government for the right of first refusal. In May, Franks took up the matter again. He had been to Garrard to see the collection but grumbled that 'some of the more dramatic specimens have been secured by private individuals.' The trustees promptly gave him permission to spend 'a sum not exceeding £100' (worth about £11,730 today). On 21 May, Franks reported that he had spent £96, 17 shillings and 6 pence at Garrard. 'From the very large number of objects that had previously sold the choice was very limited,' he complained, but he had nonetheless managed to select ten objects at a good price, 'which to a certain extent illustrate the mode of working gold among the Ashantees'.[68]

On 28 May, James Morton Pask, a sailor on HMS *Druid* recently returned to London from the Gold Coast, offered the British Museum two more items which had come from the Asante War. 'Dear Sir, I send you two skulls,' his letter from Twickenham began, explaining they were taken by 'King Hamadikky (King of Dixcove)', an ally of the British, following the bombardment by HMS *Druid* of the coastal village of Akwidaa in August 1873, where the Royal Navy exacted revenge for the 'Disaster on the Prah'. Pask had married on 20 May and, perhaps not coincidentally, was now seeking to get rid of the skulls, which he described as 'cut as drinking vessels'. Franks acknowledged receipt of this macabre offer, describing the skulls as 'presents to the trustees'. They remain in the vaults of the British Museum.[69]

Meanwhile, also in May 1874, the British Museum wrote to the Treasury, asking for permission to examine any 'further portions of the Ashantee War indemnity, with a view to the acquisition direct from the Government'. Franks, it seems, had a hunch, or perhaps reliable intelligence, that not everything Wolseley had taken at Fomena had appeared at Garrard. Sure enough, two and a half years later, in January 1877, Franks wrote to the trustees with exciting news. The Crown Agents for the Colonies – based in Downing Street and responsible for colonial finances – were selling more ornaments from the Asante indemnity, 'at a much lower price' than Garrard had asked for back in 1874. This time Franks used money from the Christy Fund – an independent fund which contributed generously to the British Museum during this period and of which he was a trustee – to buy a further eighty-nine objects, all listed as 'From Ashantee, part of the King's indemnity', including gold badges, bracelets and staffs, and a twisted neck torc which weighed almost a kilogram. The Crown Agents charged the Christy Fund £371 and 4 pence for these (worth about £44,080 today).[70]

Belatedly, Franks had got his way and the British Museum had acquired a major collection of Asante gold. The Royal Scottish Museum in Edinburgh (today the National Museum of Scotland) also made important acquisitions, spending £100 (about £11,900 today) at Garrard in 1875 on six Asante pieces, including a soul washer's badge and dozens of smaller fragments.[71] However, both these museums, and the South Kensington Museum, had been comprehensively outspent. When Franks had complained of 'private individuals' buying 'dramatic specimens' of Asante gold, he would have had one man very much in mind: Richard Wallace, the illegitimate son of the 4th Marquess of Hertford, who in 1871 moved from Paris to London, to the red-brick mansion of Hertford House in Manchester Square. He brought with him a considerable fortune, inherited from the Marquess who had died the previous year, as well as a wonderful collection of fine and decorative arts which the two men had lovingly built up over previous decades. Wallace was made a baronet and continued to grow his collection in the 1870s, with record-breaking purchases of an eclectic range of objects and paintings, from richly decorated arms and armour, to an exquisite wine cooler from Renaissance Italy, to the works of the Dutch Masters. Xavier Bray, Director of the Wallace Collection, says, 'Wallace had an unbelievable eye for quality, and he was also opportunistic.'[72] His taste extended far beyond Europe. In 1872 he bought a pair of Chinese wine cups at auction in Paris, part of the vast loot taken from the emperor's Summer Palace in 1860. These lovely cups are made of gold, studded with pearls and gemstones and decorated with kingfisher feathers of iridescent blue in an ancient technique known as *tian tsui*, or 'dotting with kingfishers'.[73] In 1876, he bought a crystal statuette, 'The Good Shepherd', bedecked in gold, rubies, emeralds and sapphires, which came from Sri Lanka or perhaps Goa.[74]

Wallace worried that wealth and refined taste could only take him so far in British society; his illegitimacy and his marriage to a French woman, Amélie, also illegitimate and with poor English, were handicaps to the status he craved. The Asante gold sale at Garrard, which his biographer Suzanne Higgott describes as of 'exceptional, high status, intriguingly "Oriental" artefacts', was of obvious appeal.[75] On 1 May 1874, Wallace bought sixteen pieces of Asante loot, spending £1,256 (worth about £147,300 today).[76] Higgott says this 'ranked him alongside the Queen as a fellow purchaser of Asante artefacts [and] provided him with status as a collector at the highest level'.[77] By Wallace's extravagant standards, this was not an enormous purchase. The following month, for example, he spent £1,575 on a painting by Ferdinand Heilbuth and in 1878 he gave the Prince of Wales £6,300 for a painting by Sir Edwin Landseer.[78] But Wallace had, as Franks complained, bought many of the most impressive Asante objects. These included a pair of cast gold eagles, each more than seventeen centimetres tall, which were probably finials on the Asantehene's chair, for which he paid £350.

Wallace's largest Asante purchase, however, was a near life-size gold cast head, weighing just over 1.5 kg, for which he paid £500 (about £58,640 today).[79] It is arguably the most spectacular single treasure taken by Wolseley and perhaps the largest gold object to have come from Africa outside of ancient Egypt. It was distinctly more lifelike than the smaller one which Queen Victoria had bought and provoked widespread comment when it appeared at Garrard. *The Times* said it 'seems to represent the head of a victim gagged for sacrifice' and proclaimed it 'ghastly'.[80] The *Illustrated London News* agreed it was a 'hideous and horrible effigy.'[81] *The Globe* pronounced it 'of great antiquity'.[82] Robert Soden Smith called it 'a very remarkable work ... massive and cumbersome' which bore 'a certain resemblance to ancient Egyptian work'.[83] In 1974, writing on the centenary of Wolseley's expedition, the ethnographic curator of the British Museum, William Fagg, called it 'a masterpiece ... not only a masterly work of sculpture, but a technically excellent piece of lost-wax craftmanship'.[84] In 1959, Fagg had visited Kumasi. He asked the then Asantehene, Prempeh II, whether the gold head was, as British curators had speculated, a representation of one of his ancestors. Prempeh II was 'genuinely shocked' by this suggestion, which he considered sacrilegious.[85] More likely, Asante scholars say, it was a trophy head, attached to a ceremonial sword and depicting a vanquished foe, perhaps an eighteenth-century king of Banda to the north called Worosa.[86]

The 'Wallace Head' is far from perfect. Martha Ehrlich, an American scholar of Asante regalia, says its 'conception exceeds the execution'.[87] It has been repaired many times, especially around the left temple, and carries the dents and bruises of its eventful history. It conforms to the conventions of Asante tradition and yet its power also derives from its realism. In this way, it bears some similarity to the famous five Queen Idia ivory masks from the kingdom of Benin. All of these objects presented a challenge to the European sensibilities and aesthetics of the late nineteenth century, which were about to undergo a dramatic change. William Fagg speculated whether Wallace 'had some inkling of the revolution which was even then stirring in Europe and to which the Ashanti gold head would seem as relevant as a bomb'.[88] Wallace may not have thought in such prescient terms, but his gold head, like the Queen Idia masks for Benin, has become a potent and emotive symbol of the entire Asante loot.

In June 1874, the South Kensington Museum put on an exhibition: 'A Collection of Gold and other objects from Ashanti.' This was comprised of its own recently purchased objects as well as the Queen's, and Wallace's golden head, pair of eagles and three swords. This display, writes Suzanne Higgott, 'caught the imagination of the press and the public who attended in large numbers'.[89] In July 1874, *The Graphic* published a sketch from inside the entrance hall of the South Kensington Museum. There, on a platform in the middle, amidst statues of kings in medieval armour and old paintings, is the Asante umbrella which Lieutenant Wood had presented to Queen Victoria in Windsor on that snowy day back in March. She had instructed, only two weeks later, that it should be exhibited at South Kensington.[90] Gentlemen in top hats, and ladies in tight corsets and long skirts, are clustered around and underneath it (see page 98). 'King Coffee's umbrella', wrote *The Graphic*, 'would afford easy shelter for about a dozen persons.'[91] It seems to have stayed there for some time, as the American abolitionist Moncure Conway called it 'the famous umbrella of King Koffee' in his 1882 guide to the museum.[92]

The South Kensington display, according to Suzanne Higgott, was 'mounted on the crest of a wave of triumphant imperialism'. Of this, there was plenty. But there were other reactions. Conway, who had made Britain his adopted home and transferred his anti-slavery fervour to other progressive causes, complained that the looted Maqdala and Asante treasure in the South Kensington Museum 'marred' an otherwise 'happy' museum and were 'unpleasantly suggestive of the worst phase of British policy or impolicy'.[93] On 5 May 1874, the Commons held a long and heated debate on the Gold Coast. Several MPs bemoaned the cost of the war and doubted the prospects of lasting peace with the Asante. But one member, Henry Richard, the Liberal representative for Merthyr, went further and questioned the very morality of Britain's actions. What possible good, he asked, could come out of the destruction and suffering Wolseley's men had inflicted? They had marched into Asante with all the modern weaponry 'which perverted science had placed at their disposal, and ... easily conquered an army of brave and ill-armed savages. They had destroyed thousands of those savages, burnt down their principal city, together with the villages and towns on the line of march, and had come back bringing with them an old umbrella, £10,000 worth of old barbaric jewellery, and a treaty not worth the paper on which it was written.'

Richard then cast his net wider: 'There were some things they had done within the last twenty years, upon which He thought scarcely any Englishman could look back with pride. The bombardment, of Canton – the burning and looting of the Emperor of China's Summer Palace – the burning of Kagoshima [in Japan in 1863] – the demolition of Magdala – and now the destruction of Coomassie – those were things not worthy of a country which boasted that it stood at the head of Christian civilization. Those were not triumphs of Christian civilization, but of barbarism and brute force.'[94] Richard, known as the 'Apostle of Peace', was a maverick on the fringes of the Commons. But 150 years later, though his words are archaic, his values are more appealing than those of many of his parliamentary contemporaries.

Wallace's six Asante treasures would stay on display at the South Kensington Museum for three years, until 1877. In December 1881, he lent them out again, along with an Asante knife with a golden sheath and handle, to the 'Ryde Art Treasures Exhibition' at Ryde Town Hall on the Isle of Wight (Wallace's own collection was bequeathed to the nation after his death in 1890, but would not go on permanent display until 1900). Wallace also lent Ryde a pair of silver candlesticks taken from the Chinese emperor's Summer Palace and a sword with a jade hilt decorated with diamonds, rubies and gold which was said to have belonged to Tipu Sultan, the 'Tiger of Mysore', who was killed by British soldiers in 1799.

Wallace and his Asante treasures were again moving in the ambit of royalty. Ryde is a short distance from Osborne House, and the Queen also gave objects to the exhibition – her contribution included 'Tunisian guns and pistols' and a sword that belonged to Charles I – which was opened by her daughter, Princess Beatrice (a more mysterious Asante addition to this exhibition is described as 'the royal State robe of the King of Ashantee', supplied by a Mrs D. Chinery of Hampton Court). *The Times* complained that Ryde Town Hall was 'a somewhat pretentious and ornate pile' and the opening poorly organised. But the exhibition was popular and extended its run into February 1882, and despite its variety of exhibits, from Gainsborough to Japanese enamels, *The Times* reported that 'to the average spectator probably the most interesting objects' were Tipu Sultan's sword and the 'collection of Ashantee curiosities ... including the battered gold mask ... and the executioner's sword.'[95]

The traditional buildings of Kumasi, of 'admirable construction...'

9

'KUMASI WAS FALLING INTO A RUINOUS STATE'

On the dull and drizzly evening of Saturday, 25 June 1881, the Royal Mail steamer *Volta* chugged up the Mersey, the final stage of its journey from West Africa.[1] On board was a weary soldier, Captain Knapp Barrow, who had embarked at Cape Coast, carrying a wooden box addressed to Lord Kimberley (restored to the Colonial Office by William Gladstone after the Liberal victory in the 1880 election). When the *Volta* docked at Liverpool, newspapers reported, Barrow disembarked immediately and he and his box were rushed through customs 'without the usual examination' in time for him to catch the night train to London.[2] Inside his box was one of the most sacred of Asante objects, the Golden Axe.[3]

The Asante believe that the Golden Axe, *Sika Akuma*, came down from the sky, like the Golden Stool itself, and symbolises the power of the Asantehene to resolve disputes.[4] It is two-thirds of a metre long and has an iron blade and a wooden handle coated in leopard skin and gold leaf. According to Barrow, the Asantehene, Mensa Bonsu, who had assumed the Golden Stool from his elder brother Kofi Karikari in 1874, had not wanted to relinquish the Golden Axe and had only surrendered this 'emblem of high sovereignty' on the understanding it would be given to Queen Victoria herself. He had been 'led to believe that some such sacrifice was essential' to convince the British of his pacific intentions. Barrow kept his side of the bargain; a few days later he took his box to Windsor Castle and was ushered in to see the Queen. He was a heavyset and typically powerful looking man, but according to the Queen he 'has been very ill & is still very feeble.' She accepted the Golden Axe as 'an everlasting pledge of good will'.[5]

Confusingly, when this same axe had first been presented to a British official, the Gold Coast Governor William Brandford Griffith, at Cape Coast some six months earlier, it caused consternation and panic. It came from Mensa Bonsu in Kumasi with a demand that the British surrender an errant chief who had fled to them for protection. On 25 January 1881, the Reuters news agency reported 'great excitement' at Cape Coast: 'an attack on the town by the Ashantees is expected ... as "the gold axe" is tantamount to a declaration of war.'[6] Brandford Griffith requested reinforcements be sent from Sierra Leone and even Britain and prepared for an Asante invasion the British feared 'imminent'.[7]

The invasion never happened. In April 1881 a new governor, Sir Samuel Rowe, received envoys from the Asantehene, who said the 'warlike intention imputed to him are merely the slander of his enemies'. The Golden Axe, the envoys clarified, meant peace, not war, and they hugged the governor's knees in submission.[8] Later, the Asantehene volunteered a payment of 2,000 ounces of gold as 'proof of his friendship' and surrendered the Golden Axe.[9] Barrow then took it to England, as well as the first part of the payment, variously described as 1,200 and 1,400 ounces of gold dust but which was also said to include 'many personal ornaments formerly belonging to the King and his chiefs'.[10] Of these, the newspapers made particular mention of a 'unique gold ornament – the Royal Order of Ashantee – worn by the king on state occasions' and perhaps an *akrafokonmu* badge.[11]

In this curious story of mutual misunderstanding, two things are apparent. Firstly, despite Wolseley's victory in 1874, British officials in the Gold Coast in the 1880s lived in fear and ignorance of the Asante and panicked at the merest hint of another war. The British historian William Claridge, in his monumental 1915 *History of the Gold Coast*, writes, 'Their conduct was ridiculous and absurd to a degree, and was, in fact, little short of disgraceful. The natives alone kept their heads.'[12] But, secondly, and paradoxically, it also shows the lengths to which the Asante were prepared to go to avert another military confrontation with the British. They apparently gave up more gold, at least in weight, than they had given to Wolseley at Fomena in 1874, as well as one of their most valuable cultural objects. 'In sending this axe for ever away from our country, we are sending away that which is associated with all the greatest glories of the Ashanti kingdom', said Boakye Tenten, husband of the Asante Queen Mother Afua Kobiri, who led the negotiations with the British, 'but as this axe has been the cause of such serious troubles between the Ashanti kingdom and the Queen of England, the King begs Her Most Gracious Majesty to accept it.'[13]

In Cape Coast, and in London, there was relief. Captain Barrow was rewarded with a grand dinner in London and promotion into the colonial service where he would rise to become Administrator of Lagos.[14] The Golden Axe itself was dismissed by *The Times* as 'a hideous implement', apparently soiled by blood. But Queen Victoria considered it 'curious and handsome' and later in 1881 ordered that it be sent to the South Kensington Museum (it is today back in Windsor Castle).[15]

The Asantehene Mensa Bonsu, meanwhile, was widely resented back in Asante for what was perceived as a humiliating act of appeasement. He had little goodwill to fall back on; Prempeh II's *History of Ashanti* says he 'was the wrong person to rule over the Ashanti. He was selfish, greedy and known to be of bad character.'[16] In 1883, with many provinces in revolt, a crowd stormed and ransacked Kumasi's rebuilt royal palace and Mensa Bonsu was forced to abdicate.[17] After his eventual death, in 1911, there were protests at his funeral, and an African priest in Kumasi, Rev. N. V. Asare, wrote: 'This King was the most cruel among all the Asante sovereigns ... he beheaded plenty of people in his time. He was not only cruel, but very wicked, and vicious. He killed many noblemen privately, solely because he liked to own their fine looking wives and personal effects.'[18]

★★★

The British invasion of 1874 had left Asante weakened and fractured. 'Wolseley's expedition ... designed to make the Ashanti kingdom a respectful if still independent client of Britain, had only shattered its unity and turned it into a menacing disorder', write Ronald Robinson, John Gallagher and Alice Denny in their celebrated analysis of British imperialism, *Africa and the Victorians*.[19] Wolseley himself had anticipated the dangers of the crushing victory which he had craved. After he destroyed the Asantehene's palace, he wrote to Lord Kimberley, 'I believe the result will be such a diminution in the prestige and military power of the Ashantee Monarch, as may result in the break-up of the kingdom altogether.'[20] He worried that the 'feeble races' of the coast would struggle to fill the vacuum. Kofi Karikari had abdicated in October 1874, six months after the departure of Wolseley's army. According to some accounts, he had been caught in the sacrilegious act of taking gold regalia from the bodies buried in the royal mausoleum in a desperate attempt to restock his treasury.[21] The Kumasi Elders, the *History of Ashanti* recounts, told Kofi Karikari he had lost their confidence, and he agreed to step down in return for the Golden Stool going to a relative and guarantees of safety. 'The Kumasi Elders drank "Fetish" [took an oath] to fulfil these conditions, and once this was done Kofi Karikari ... abdicated quietly and handed over the Golden Stool into their care.'[22]

In May 1874, the new colonial secretary, Lord Carnarvon, told the House of Lords, 'A great nation like ours must be sometimes prepared to discharge disagreeable duties ... It is certainly not a desire of selfish interest or the ambition of larger empire which bids us remain on the West Coast of Africa; it is simply and solely a sense of obligations to be redeemed and of duties to be performed.'[23] In other words, Britain could not run away entirely from the consequences of its own victory, even if it was inclined to do so. In July 1874, the British government declared the Gold Coast forts a Crown Colony, and in August it increased British legislative power over the surrounding protectorate, up to the still ill-defined borders of Asante.[24] In 1877, the British moved the capital from crowded and unsanitary Cape Coast – 'one vast public privy and dunghill' according to a journalist on the *African Times* – to Accra, to the east, where the absence of swamps was thought to make a healthier climate for European administrators.²⁵

The British, says the historian Tom McCaskie, had 'embarked on an inexorable if still makeshift "forward policy" in the Gold Coast', marked by a growing capacity and willingness to meddle in Asante affairs.²⁶ But if this was practice on the ground, it was not yet policy from London. Formal annexation of Asante was not on the agenda. 'It was as if the Asante state existed on the sufferance of the British; defeated yet independent,' writes the historian Emmanuel Akyeampong.²⁷ And yet whatever the British inclination, the instability which they had themselves created now pulled them into Asante affairs, as rival factions sought their favour.

★★★

In January 1884, a young member of the Gold Coast Constabulary, Brandon Kirby, arrived in Kumasi. Kirby, born in Australia and a former London bank teller, had been sent by Governor Samuel Rowe as a special commissioner, to gain intelligence on what had deteriorated into an Asante civil war and to stress British neutrality. Kirby was already seen as something of an Asante expert, for in 1883 he and Captain Barrow (of Golden Axe fame), had spent five weeks in and around Kumasi, trying to assess the situation around the time of Mensa Bonsu's abdication.²⁸

Brandon Kirby stayed in Asante territory from January to April 1884. The Asante chiefs told him they had decided to place a young prince, Agyeman Kofi, on the Golden Stool as Asantehene Kwaku Dua II. On the evening of 23 June, back in London, Kirby recounted his experiences to the Royal Geographical Society, then at Savile Row, Piccadilly. He said Kwaku Dua II had assured him that, 'acting on the advice of the British Governor, and also the wish of the white Queen, he had stopped all human sacrifices.' Kirby believed this to be true, as he saw no vultures, whereas on his previous visit 'the place was literally swarming with these birds.' He said that Kumasi 'shows signs of again returning partly to its old prosperity. The streets and chief palaces ... are being rapidly rebuilt.'

Asante still controlled considerable wealth. In 1881, a Basel missionary in Kumasi, David Huppenbauer, had seen the Asantehene's treasures and wrote 'these small chests, of which five were carried past, should each contain roughly 200,000 francs in purest gold dust. They are so heavy (roughly 140 lbs.), that to each small chest is allotted a number of slaves, who take turns in carrying it.'[29]

In 1884, Brandon Kirby saw gold being traded in Kumasi and watched the royal goldsmith produce regalia for the Asantehene using the traditional lost wax method. He also described his journey beyond Kumasi – he claimed to be the first white man to travel in Asante territory significantly north of the city – where he reported the slave trade was still widespread. In Kintampo, some 100 kilometres north-east of Kumasi, he saw 'slaves, both male and female, chained together in batches of about a dozen.' They were bought by traders from the north, some from Timbuktu, who also bought kola nuts, and in turn sold cotton goods and knives.

There are two fascinating details from Brandon Kirby's journey to Asante which he omitted to mention to the Royal Geographical Society. The first is that he was accompanied by an accomplished African photographer, a man called Frederick Grant, 'a native of Accra', who took dozens of beautifully composed and historically significant pictures.[30] These include tantalising glimpses of Kumasi's handsome architecture and Kwaku Dua II surrounded by chiefs shortly before his enstoolment.[31] When Grant returned from Asante, *The Gold Coast Times* wrote that he was 'the first photographer who has visited, professionally, that country of unenviable reputation.' Grant, who ran a studio in Accra, was also an entrepreneur. On 28 June 1884, he was in London, taking the savvy step of registering the copyright of his Asante photos at the Stationers' Company, off Fleet Street. Presumably, he had been in the audience earlier that week when Kirby spoke to the Royal Geographical Society.[32]

Kirby also failed to mention that he had come away from Kumasi with two gold castings from the Asante royal regalia. One of these, striking and unique, is a dome-shaped spider, ten centimetres long, which would have been an ornament to decorate a sword, while the other is a T-shaped pendant, six centimetres long. Kwaku Dua II had originally attempted to give the spider, via an envoy, to Governor Samuel Rowe in Accra, as he sought British support in his bid for the Golden Stool. But Rowe, still cautious after the Golden Axe fiasco, rejected the gift and instructed Kirby to return it while he was in Kumasi. For whatever reason, this did not happen. By 1885, Kirby had retired from the colonial service and was buying cattle ranches in faraway New Mexico with a wealthy Scottish partner, James Cree. But Kirby, who had reinvented himself as an 'English gentleman' in tweeds and fur coats, soon made enemies on the American frontier and sold out to Cree in a hurry when he learnt that a lynching party was on its way to kill him (according to Cree family legend, he was 'smuggled out of the country in a pickle barrel'). He left behind a velvet-lined display box containing his Asante treasures, as well as an album of Frederick Grant's evocative photographs of Kumasi.

Brandon Kirby moved to Vancouver, Canada in 1891, then back to England before next appearing in Cape Town, South Africa, where he married in 1896 and became an engineer. Often in debt, and embroiled in legal difficulties, he died there in 1930.[33] In 2014, the Cree family presented his Asante gold and photographs to the Dallas Museum of Art, where they reside today.[34]

***

After Brandon Kirby spoke to the Royal Geographical Society in June 1884, its president, Lord Aberdare, said a few words. He was 'glad to hear that good results had followed [Wolseley's] expedition to Ashanti, for it was not always that invasions of barbarous countries produced good effects.'[35] He and Kirby presumably did not know that Kwaku Dua II had already died in early June, apparently of smallpox, after only six weeks on the Golden Stool. A fortnight later, Kofi Karikari, who harboured ambitions of a return, was also dead. Prempeh II, in the *History of Ashanti*, says Karikari died of dysentery, but many in Kumasi believe he was murdered, a victim of vicious infighting within Asante royalty.[36] From 1884 to 1888 Asante was engulfed in dynastic conflict, as a bewildering cast of factions contested the Golden Stool. 'The result of all these calamities was that Kumasi was losing its power and ... falling into a ruinous state,' writes Prempeh II. 'There was almost no food left in the capital,' and people 'perished from starvation' in the heart of the city.[37]

★★★

In the summer of 1886, Queen Victoria opened two exhibitions celebrating what *The Times* called the 'greatest colonial Empire on record'.[38] Liverpool's 'International Exhibition of Navigation, Commerce and Industry' featured reconstructions of buildings from around the world, including the 'Ashantee Palace ... a facsimile of the grass-thatched residence of Koffee Kalkalli, when he held autocratic sway in his capital, Coomassie.' The exhibition's catalogue says Wolseley himself provided 'valuable information' on this replica's courtyard, high pitched roof and veranda, all 'rather suggestive' of the Alhambra in Granada, albeit with 'Tudoresque' patterned decoration, but does not mention that he had destroyed the original palace in 1874. *The Times* reassured readers 'there are no ghastly fetishes hanging in front of the door.' The catalogue says that Wolseley and the Princess of Wales lent the exhibition, respectively, a richly wrought silver casket and stool, both taken from Kumasi. A Sierra Leonean lady was on hand to serve coffee, and four Mandinka boys 'Bocarry, Santiga, Kunardee and Baba' – shipped out from West Africa – performed hammock-carrying duties through the grounds.[39] In South Kensington, meanwhile (adjacent to the South Kensington Museum), the 'Colonial and Indian Exhibition' was visited by more than five million people over six months. *The Times* reported that amongst the West African exhibits, 'King Coffee's tent-like umbrella is one of the most prominent objects in the court' and that, once again, the 'public will be most interested' in seeing the gold ornaments from the Asante indemnity.[40]

The hubris of these exhibitions suggested the emergence of a new type of British imperialism, 'suffused with a vivid sense of superiority and self-righteousness'.[41] But despite this sentiment, and despite the carve-up of Africa by the European powers at the Berlin Conference of 1884–5 signalling a new and competitive era of colonial rivalry, Britain would hesitate over the expansion of its West African territories until the very last years of the nineteenth century. The white man, said *The Times* in its review of the 'Colonial and Indian Exhibition', was in West Africa 'mainly as a trader, and the influence which he has had on the native ... is neither wide nor deep.'[42] Indeed the emergence of a new Asantehene, in 1888, and the prospect of a return to stability, was initially marked by Anglo-Asante cordiality. Yaa Akyia, the sister of Kofi Karikari and Mensa Bonsu and a woman of 'steely determination' who had assumed the position of Asante Queen Mother earlier in the 1880s, brokered a consensus that her teenage son, Agyeman Prempeh, should be enstooled.[43] A British envoy, Captain E. A. Barnett, travelled to Kumasi, and urged chiefs to support Prempeh. He presented Prempeh with coronation gifts: £32, a case of gin and a silk cloth, and in return the new Asantehene passed on a message of thanks to Brandford Griffith, who had resumed the position of Governor of the Gold Coast in 1885.[44]

Later in 1888, according to British officials, the impoverished Prempeh privately requested they loan him £320 so he could hold the proper coronation ceremonies. Inspector H. B. Lethbridge travelled to Kumasi with this money. He was accompanied by a medical officer, Richard Austin Freeman, who says that when the tactless Lethbridge 'blurted out before the whole assembly of chiefs' that he had the money, the embarrassed Prempeh denied all knowledge and the loan fell through.[45] Freeman describes Prempeh as 'a fairly good-looking young man rather inclined to be stout, with a smooth, sleek, reddish-brown skin ... somewhat effeminate-looking ... I was at first a little uncertain about his sex until I was formally introduced to him.' Prempeh was bedecked in silks and gold, and Freeman, dazzled by the 'barbarous magnificence' of the Asante court, with its 'gorgeous colours of the garments, the gaudy umbrellas and the glitter of the massive gold ornaments' was 'irresistibly reminded ... of Ancient Egypt and Assyria.'[46]

Freeman was less complimentary about Kumasi. Unlike Brandon Kirby, he believed it had never recovered from Wolseley's invasion. 'So much had been destroyed ... The town was nothing more than a large clearing in the forest, over which were scattered, somewhat irregularly, groups of houses ... These houses once stood in wide and regular streets, but since the destruction of the city in 1874 the natives do not seem to have had the heart to rebuild them.' Thomas Bowdich's 1817 city of arcades and piazzas had fallen a long way. Freeman could 'not help reflect on the strange and regrettable fact that its ruin had been accomplished by a nation that yearly spends millions on the conversion of the heathen and diffusion of civilisation.' But although Kumasi was in a dismal state, Freeman was nonetheless impressed by 'the admirable construction, careful and artistic finish' of the better-class houses, decorated with fine ornamental patterns, several of which he sketched.[47]

In later years, Freeman became a writer of detective stories, which often include references to the Gold Coast. The plunder of Asante clearly left an impression on him; his 1927 short story 'The Trail of Behemoth' involves Kwaku Essien, a prince of Bekwai, one of the client kingdoms of Asante, who is a student in London and commits a murder in order to retrieve an elephant tail, part of the regalia which had been forcibly taken by a rapacious British colonial officer. In Freeman's sympathetic telling, Kwaku, the 'lawful owner' was 'morally entitled' to take back 'stolen property' and successfully evades the British police and returns to Bekwai with his elephant's tail.[48]

★★★

Back in Asante in the 1890s, the harmony between Britain and Prempeh was short-lived. Prempeh's ambitions, to reunite his shattered kingdom and control its economic reconstruction, did not match Governor Brandford Griffith's, or those of an increasingly assertive British commercial lobby. The palm oil merchants of Liverpool, Glasgow and London urged the British government to take control of the areas to the north of Asante, while the governor worried that the Gold Coast Colony would have no future unless it developed new cash crops: cotton, coffee and indigo. These in turn would require roads and railways, to connect the coast with the northern territories. But Asante lay inconveniently in between and, moreover, was trying to re-establish its own authority to the north. Meanwhile, France and Germany, whose presence was growing in the territories to the west and east respectively of the Gold Coast, were also seen by the British as potential threats in the north.

This situation was compounded by a large and vocal group of Asante exiles in the Gold Coast Colony, who campaigned for the extension of British rule and free enterprise. They saw the Asantehene as not just a commercial and political rival, but also an atavistic obstacle to a dawning new age of economic progress and law and order, which they were better placed to exploit. 'What is an African King?', one asked contemptuously. 'The poorest Englishman is wealthier than 1,000 of them; an Englishman's pair of trowsers is more valuable than their state appearance in full costume.'[49] Prempeh wanted Governor Brandford Griffith to repatriate these troublesome exiles, but the British were reluctant to do so without guarantees for their safety.

In March 1891 the governor proposed to Prempeh that Asante become a British protectorate. The Asantehene's reply was charmingly disingenuous yet unequivocal. That Asante should 'enjoy the protection of Her Majesty the Queen and Empress of India I may say is a matter of very serious consideration,' acknowledged Prempeh, but he concluded that 'my Kingdom of Asante will never commit itself to any such policy. Asante must remain as of old, at the same time to remain friendly with all white men. I thank Her Majesty's Government ... and appreciate to the fullest extent its kindness.'[50] In 1894, when Prempeh was finally able to afford a coronation ceremony and assume the Golden Stool, he wrote to the British in a similar vein: 'byegones will be byegones' and stating he would raise Asante 'to a prosperous, substantial, and steady position as a great farming and trading community... the trade between your Protectorate and my kingdom ... may increase daily to the benefit of all.'[51] Charm, however, would only take Prempeh so far. His vision, of a sovereign Asante, was no longer acceptable to Britain.

Prince Henry en route to Kumasi. Queen Victoria would bitterly regret allowing him to go.

10

'PREPARED TO SACRIFICE MYSELF TO SAVE THE LIVES OF MY PEOPLE'

In March 1895, seven Asante noblemen sailed from the Gold Coast to Britain on a mission to save their kingdom. The Asantehene, his relationship with the authorities of the Gold Coast Colony strained by his rejection of their renewed offers for Asante to come under British protection, had boldly decided to take his case directly to London.[1] The seven envoys included John Owusu Ansa and his younger brother Albert. John carried the title of 'ambassador extraordinary and minister plenipotentiary,' authorised by the Asantehene to conduct diplomatic and commercial negotiations with the Queen and her government.

John and Albert had grown up shaped by both Asante and British culture. Their father, Owusu Ansa, a son of the great Asantehene of the early nineteenth century, Osei Bonsu, had been given to the British in 1831 as surety for the treaty which ended the first Anglo-Asante War. He was baptised and educated in England, before returning to the Gold Coast where he married a Cape Coast woman, worked for Methodist missionaries and maintained links with his ancestral homeland.[2] Other Asante royal children would follow a similar path in the nineteenth century, as the kingdom sought to better understand, and build bridges to, the encroaching European powers. In 1837, Asantehene Kwaku Dua sent his son and nephew, both aged ten, to be educated in the Netherlands, to guarantee an Asante–Dutch treaty. 'Plucked up and carried off to Holland like exotic orchids', as one historian puts it, their journey ended in lonely cultural alienation.[3] The son, Kwasi Boakye, an engineer and coffee planter, died in the Dutch East Indies, while the nephew, Kwame Poku, returned to the Gold Coast, where, rejected by Dutch and Asante alike, he committed suicide.[4] In 1874, after the Treaty of Fomena, Kofi Karikari offered his son, Kofi Nti, to be educated in England. Kofi Nti went to school in Surrey – there is a photo of the newly arrived African prince standing beside a British major in London, looking stiff and awkward in a three-piece suit – and was later a civil servant in Trinidad but returned to West Africa by the late 1880s.[5]

John Owusu Ansa, educated in English in Cape Coast, had also been a civil servant but went to Asante in the 1880s to explore opportunities in gold mining and took charge of the rapidly expanding correspondence between the Asante and British authorities.[6] He walked the streets of Kumasi dressed as a London gentleman, according to Richard Austin Freeman, who met him there in 1889 and wrote, 'the most astonishing thing was that he wore his clothes and carried his cane with the unmistakable air of a man who was accustomed to them, and not the embarrassed manner of an occasionally dressed native.'[7] In theory, John Owusu Ansa was well qualified to bridge the gap between Asante and Britain. But even before he and his six companions had left West Africa, their mission ran into difficulties. They spent four months in discussions at Cape Coast and Accra, before Governor Brandford Griffith, unhappy at the prospect of being sidelined, grudgingly granted them permission to travel. In London, Sidney Buxton, Under Secretary of State for the Colonies in Lord Rosebery's Liberal government, told Parliament they would not be received. 'The King of Kumasi', as Buxton called Prempeh, signifying his diminished status in British eyes, was 'not a chief or ruler of sufficient importance to be allowed to send ambassadors to the Queen,' especially as he was suspected of allowing and countenancing human sacrifices.[8] The envoys therefore travelled in some trepidation, even making enquiries as to whether they would be tortured and killed upon arrival in

Britain.⁹ In the event, their personal safety was never threatened. Instead, these men, described in *The Times* as 'at best but intelligent savages and [who] therefore cannot be acquainted with the niceties of diplomatic procedure,' were treated with cool disdain.¹⁰

The Asante envoys hired lawyers in London and sought to make their case through sympathetic journalists. They said that Prempeh would open his country to British trade and accept a British resident in Kumasi, but this 'would not carry away the King's independence as a Sovereign.'¹¹ They denied, repeatedly, that he allowed human sacrifice or slavery. In October 1895, the Gold Coast Supreme Court in Accra heard testimony from several prominent Asante, who said they had witnessed ritual killings in Kumasi which were often ordered and attended by Prempeh himself.¹² Were these proceedings mere British propaganda, or were they indicative of a humane desire to end a cruel practice? Or perhaps a mixture of both? Britain's insistence on the abolition of 'inhuman customs' certainly seemed to get more strident as its territorial ambitions grew. The historian Ivor Wilks argues that human sacrifice 'provided a moral underpinning for what might otherwise be seen as naked aggression'.¹³

If the envoys' prospects of success were always small, they disappeared completely after the election that summer, which returned the Conservatives to power and brought Joseph Chamberlain to the Colonial Office. His appointment 'opened a new era in west African policy', said Robinson, Gallagher and Denny in *Africa and the Victorians*, 'a radical departure' from what had gone before. After decades of irresolution, Britain had a colonial secretary committed to developing tropical Africa as a state enterprise and to excluding European rivals. Chamberlain's policies, in short, put a new value on the explicit possession of territory.¹⁴

In the later months of 1895, officials in London and the Gold Coast Colony were alarmed at the news that Samori Toure, a Mandinka king who resisted French imperialism across the western Sahel for much of the 1880s and 1890s, was making friendly overtures towards Prempeh. In *History of Ashanti*, Prempeh II downplays this episode: 'It was not the intention of Agyeman Prempeh to befriend [Samori] but he accepted the presents out of courtesy. Some time later the King sent his own messengers with gifts for Samory.'[15] The British, however, were haunted 'by the spectre of an alliance between the forces of Samori and those of Asante', all the more so because of inaccurate speculation that Samori was by this stage manoeuvring on behalf of the French.[16]

The new governor of the Gold Coast, William Maxwell, who arrived a few days after the Asante envoys departed for Britain, presented the Asantehene with an ultimatum: accept the imposition of a British protectorate and a British resident and abolish human sacrifice, or prepare for an invasion. Prempeh would have to accept, as well, the right of any part of Asante to break away from Kumasi if it wished to have closer ties with the British. Moreover, Maxwell insisted Prempeh should come down to the Pra River himself to sign the treaty under a British flag. And the Asantehene should bring with him two of his sons, to be handed over to the British as a guarantee he would abide by the agreement.[17] Maxwell also suggested to London that the Asantehene's failure to pay the remainder of the 1874 indemnity – a grievance which had leapt back to the top of British priorities – justified military intervention. [18]

In October, Colonel Sir Francis Scott, the senior British soldier in the Gold Coast, was summoned back to England to discuss a new military expedition against Asante. Scott, 'a grey-haired hunch-shouldered man with a protruding jaw', born in India and a veteran of Sevastopol and Lucknow, had been a major with the Black Watch in Wolseley's 1873–4 expedition.[19] 'A force must be sent to Kumassi', he told Reuters News Agency. 'The matter must be settled thoroughly, and at once. Then we shall have peace, and trade will prosper.'[20] Scott was parroting his political masters. The Secretary of State for War, the Marquess of Lansdowne, wrote to him that the objective of the expedition was to 'enforce the acceptance by King Prempeh and the Ashantis of the terms demanded by the government' (which included, moreover, that Prempeh himself pay back the cost of the expedition).[21] Meanwhile, Chamberlain wrote to Maxwell. 'I have from the first refused to recognize the so-called Ambassadors', he told him. The British needed 'complete and efficient control' over Kumasi and if the Asantehene did not co-operate, 'recourse must be had to force'.²²

Word spread through the British army that another Asante expedition was imminent. Major Hugh Sinclair of the Royal Engineers wrote, 'Autumn came on and I was getting my horses fit for the hunting season when one day in October ... I received a telegram to proceed at once to the War Office ... an expedition to Ashanti had been decided on as the King, Prempeh, had been giving trouble ... I left with my head in a whirl. Active service *at last*'.²³ By the beginning of November the War Office had formulated staffing and logistical plans and officers and equipment embarked for the Gold Coast in the middle of that month.²⁴ On the 13th, *The Times* wrote that 'the obstinate folly and invincible ignorance of the King of Kumasi' had 'compelled the Government, with much reluctance' to prepare a punitive expedition. 'Coercive measures', it said, were 'inevitable'.²⁵

In Kumasi, writes Prempeh II in *History of Ashanti*, Maxwell's terms caused 'anguish'.²⁶ Some chiefs urged the Asantehene to prepare for war. But Prempeh spoke calmly and overruled them. He said the British had helped install him as Asantehene and so it would be dishonourable to fight them. Above all, he wanted peace and tranquillity for his countrymen.²⁷ 'Since the time of my accession to the Stool of my ancestors, it had been my chief aim', he said,

> that Ashanti might once more become a powerful nation as before ... I have asked for the return of the peoples of Adanse, Kokufu, Dadease, Manso-Nkwanta and Juabin, who had sought refuge in the Colony, and because of this they wish to take me away as a prisoner without any justification ... I am entirely prepared to sacrifice myself to save the lives of my people, and to avert the destruction of my country, rather than by allowing them to fight.²⁸

It was a statesmanlike declaration, evocative of Nelson Mandela at Rivonia in its subservience of personal welfare to a national cause. The historian Tom McCaskie describes it as 'the defining moment' of Prempeh's life, one which would ensure the remainder would be spent in peaceful resistance to British rule.[29]

On Saturday, 7 December 1895, the downcast Ansa brothers sailed from Liverpool back to the Gold Coast aboard the mail ship *Bokhara*. In the words of the Asante historian, Joseph Adjaye, their 'ill-fated mission to England … represented the climax of Asante diplomatic efforts to save a dying political independence.'[30] They had failed, and by way of cruel irony, the *Bokhara* carried 100 tons of ammunition and supplies for the new Asante expedition.[31]

On that same day, Field Marshal Sir Garnet Wolseley boarded a lunchtime train from Fenchurch Street to the Albert Docks to inspect the British soldiers about to board the troopship *Coromandel*, also destined for the Gold Coast. Wolseley had recently attained the pinnacle of his ambitions, at the end of October, when he had been appointed Commander-in-Chief of the entire British army and the subsequent weeks had been a whirl of banquets, speeches and troop reviews, as well as a dinner with the Queen. But he had also been closely involved in the preparations for the latest Asante expedition, presiding over a 'Confidential Mobilization Committee' and personally selecting some of the key appointments.[32] Now he, as well as several fellow veterans of 1874, cast eyes over the soldiers who would follow in his Asante footsteps. After an inspection of 'a most minute and practical description', Wolseley declared he'd 'never seen such a fine body of men'.[33]

His Royal Highness, Prince Henry of Battenberg, the husband of Princess Beatrice and son-in-law to Queen Victoria, was also at the Albert Docks, where he boarded the *Coromandel* as Colonel Scott's military secretary. Three weeks earlier, Henry, or Liko as the royal family called him, had broached the delicate subject of Asante with his mother-in-law. 'To my astonishment & concern Liko told me after breakfast,' wrote the Queen, 'that he seriously wished to go on the Ashanti Expedition, & I told him it would never do'.[34] She relented, a decision she would later bitterly regret.

Prince Henry's aide-de-camp was his nephew and a grandson of the Queen's, Prince Christian Victor of Schleswig-Holstein. This sprinkling of royalty, and the residual glory attached to Wolseley's expedition, gave the latest Asante campaign, the historian Alan Lloyd writes, 'a certain cachet of distinction ... One gets the distinct impression of a social occasion.'³⁵ Major Robert Baden-Powell, who would go on to become a national hero during the 1899–1900 siege of Mafeking, and later achieve worldwide fame as the founder of the Boy Scouts, recalls the excitement of being called up:

> The magic words 'You are selected to proceed on active service,' give to the recipient a gush of elation ... From that moment on he is a different being. He treads on air ... No sooner has his name appeared in the list, as published by the press, than circulars flow in upon him from outfitters, money-lenders, insurance agents and others ... Envious comrades congratulate him, while they beg his help to get them taken too ... Kind friends press on him presents of varied utility, from hip-baths to tea-coseys.³⁶

Scott's army of 1895–6 was smaller than Wolseley's of 1873–4 – some 2,000 men not including the irregular soldiers raised in the Gold Coast – but better armed. Military technology had moved on from the 1870s; Snider rifles and Gatling machine guns had been replaced by the more reliable Martini-Henrys and Maxims.³⁷ The battalion which sailed from England – the Special Service Corps – was composed of volunteers, including from prestigious regiments such as the Coldstream and Grenadier Guards. In the Gold Coast they would join West Indian and Hausa soldiers, both commanded by British officers, as well as the less formal force of several hundred 'native levies', whose various Gold Coast kings and chiefs had thrown in their lot with the British, and were led by Baden-Powell.

Finally, the War Office also instructed the 2nd Battalion of the West Yorkshire Regiment, returning through the Mediterranean from a seventeen-year posting in India, Burma and Aden, to divert towards the Gold Coast. Scott and his planners were torn between the perceived advantages of having more white British soldiers versus the well-known health risks. They hoped that the Yorkshire men, hardened by years in the tropics, would adapt to West Africa better than troops sent directly from Britain.[38] Other challenges for the British were much the same as in 1874 – not just the risk of sickness but also the logistics of marching an army along what was still a narrow pathway through forest towards Kumasi and the reliance on thousands of porters to carry supplies.

The Special Service Corps and the West Yorkshire Regiment arrived at Cape Coast at the end of December 1895 and set off straight away for Kumasi. Major Sinclair of the Royal Engineers wrote that they soon left open country and marched through the 'thickest and most impenetrable forest ... like walking in some vast giant hot-house ... the heat was appalling – 97–99 in the shade and so moist that the trees dripped all night and one was bathed in perspiration even sitting still ... I lost two stone during the expedition.'[39] Prince Henry rode a donkey and was protected by a small white umbrella, but other British soldiers, wearing traditional red tunics once again, did not fare so well. A corporal and a sergeant, both suffering from 'heat apoplexy', collapsed and died within a few kilometres of the coast and were buried in the bush, and dozens of men from the West Yorkshire Regiment, apparently not as habituated as the War Office had hoped, 'fell out like rotten sheep' in the first days of the march and were hospitalised. Some 250 men from the West Yorkshire Regiment, out of a total of 420, would eventually fall sick.[40]

Robert Baden-Powell had his own struggles. On 16 December, on a Cape Coast parade ground, he inspected the first 500 men to join his Native Levy. 'The stupid inertness of the puzzled negro is duller than that of an ox; a dog would grasp your meaning in one-half the time. Men and brothers! They may be brothers, but they certainly are not men.'[41] But, gradually, Baden-Powell writes, he imposed order. Kings and chiefs were installed as officers and each soldier given a red fez which 'gives as much satisfaction to the naked warrior as does his first tunic to the young hussar'. To a blast of elephant tusk horns, and the rumble of drums, they set off, 'a jabbering, laughing mob goes shambling through the streets, bound for the bush beyond.'[42]

The British soldiers' biggest worry was that the Asante would not fight. A newspaper correspondent who travelled by ship with senior officers wrote, 'fears were freely expressed that King Prempeh would tender his submission and that we might meet with telegraphic instructions at any port ordering our return to England.'[43] Once the march to Kumasi was underway, Baden-Powell wrote that a fight with the Asante 'was the great hope of those who toil through the long hot hours in this steaming, fetid atmosphere.'[44] On 3 January, Lieutenant Arthur Hood of the Grenadier Guards wrote in his diary that he had enjoyed 'a very jolly swim' in the Pra River. By the 8th, he admitted, 'the whole thing is more like a picnic than a campaign.'[45] As the British marched over the Adanse hills, tracing Wolseley's route of 1874, there was no sign of the Asante, and much less any resistance. Only false alarms and rumours, panicked defensive cordons, flank marches round imaginary enemy patrols, even an injury from friendly fire. 'Where Wolseley's expedition had walked a tightrope across disaster, Scott's Ashanti "war" wobbled perilously on the brink of burlesque,' writes the ever-sardonic Alan Lloyd.[46] On 15 January 1896, at Odaso, British officers met with an embassy from Prempeh. 'They offer his submission – complete and unconditional. Alas! This looks like a peaceful end of all our work,' despaired Baden-Powell.[47]

On 17 January 1896, after twenty days of marching and a final night under heavy rain, a British army entered the Asante capital for the second time. 'Kumassi at last! And what a disappointment!' wrote Baden-Powell.[48] The fabled city turned out to be no more than clusters of thatched huts, and as for the sound of the drums, 'it was getting louder and the roar of voices filled the air; but alas! It was peace drumming.'[49] The Hausa band, rather incongruously, replied with a rendition of 'Home Sweet Home'. Bennet Burleigh was the correspondent for the *Daily Telegraph* on Scott's expedition. He had fought as a pirate for the Confederates in the American Civil War and in his fifty-year newspaper career covered twenty-four wars on 'every continent'.[50] Burleigh dismissed Kumasi as 'more an accretion of West African villages than a town in any ordinary sense of the word'.[51] Moreover, the entire 'Ashantee Campaign was a cheat, for it had not even yielded a whiff of gun-powder smoke'.⁵²

Prempeh sat waiting for the British on a raised platform, sipping gin and munching biscuits according to Burleigh, surrounded by an 'awful barbaric din' and 'fools and misshapen dwarfs'.⁵³ Baden-Powell describes the Asantehene in more dignified terms: 'He looks a regal figure as he sits upon a lofty throne with a huge velvet umbrella standing over him, upon his head a black and gold tiara, and on his neck and arms large golden beads and nuggets.'⁵⁴ All this jewellery did not go unappreciated. 'Prempeh had on a beautiful crown and some capital gold ornaments, which we all longed for,' wrote Lieutenant Hood.⁵⁵

The Asante account of the British entry into their city, in Prempeh II's *History of Ashanti*, captures the humiliation of a fractured and fallen kingdom. For the British

> were accompanied by many Ashantis from Bekwai and other places, many of whom had been pressed into service as carriers. All of these Ashanti carriers from Bekwai, Asumenya, Amoafo, Pakyi, Asanso, Abodom and Esiankwanta were wearing white fillets or bands around their heads as a sign of their menial employment. The Adanse who came with the British from the Colony wore Fez caps while the Fantis and other of the coast peoples were actually wearing British medals. When the 'Kumasifoo' [people of Kumasi] saw all these people whom they had many, many times defeated in battle walking in triumph about their own town they became infuriated and resorted to 'hot drinks' (spiritous liquors) that inflamed their resentment and hatred even more.⁵⁶

Prempeh, seeing that his people were 'in a furious and dangerous mood', sought a meeting that afternoon with Colonel Scott to defuse the situation. The Asantehene was chewing a kola nut, which in Asante tradition symbolises an obligation to speak the truth. But Baden-Powell described 'his somewhat stupid expression rendered more idiotic by his sucking a large nut like a fat cigar'.⁵⁷ Scott, speaking via an interpreter, bluntly told Prempeh he would not have a political discussion, for this had to be conducted with Governor Maxwell who was expected in Kumasi imminently, and would 'arrange the day for your submission'. But he promised his army would keep the peace. 'I will be very particular, and not allow any of my people to plunder, any caught will be punished. Please understand that we will pay for everything we get,' he said. The two men shook hands.[58] The Queen Mother, the Asantehemaa, Yaa Akyia, was also present. Baden-Powell wrote 'she was a good natured, smiling little woman; but beneath that smile she is said, like others of her sex, to hide a store of villainy.'[59]

Governor Maxwell arrived in Kumasi on the morning of Saturday, 18 January. He thanked the British soldiers on behalf of the Queen and 'congratulated them on having annexed another country to our already great Empire'.[60] The soldiers paraded through the city, fired howitzers in the air and raised a Union Jack over the 'Palaver Ground', known to the Asante as *Annowo*, as the band played 'God Save the Queen'. On Sunday 19th, the British held a church parade, compulsory for all soldiers. They also ordered Prempeh to come and meet the governor the following morning.

The humiliation of Asante; Prempeh and the Queen Mother submit...

11

'I BEG THE GOVERNOR NOT TO TAKE MY PEOPLE AND MYSELF AWAY'

In a tattered War Office file in Britain's National Archives, there is a hand-written document entitled 'Report of Interview between Governor of Cape Coast Colony and King Prempeh at Kumassi, January 20th 1896.' There are many things this document does not tell us. It does not explain how British soldiers marched to the Asantehene's palace early that morning and pounded on the doors threatening to pull him out and of how he was carried out on his hammock through a side door rather than the main entrance as he had wished. It does not tell us how he was taken to the parade ground which was lined two abreast with British soldiers and was then deposited beneath a platform of biscuit and ammunition boxes on which sat Governor Maxwell, Colonel Scott and his second-in-command, Colonel Francis Kempster. And yet despite these omissions it still makes for uncomfortable reading.[1]

There were no diplomatic niceties. 'Twenty-five years ago', Maxwell said, his words translated for Prempeh by Albert Owusu Ansa, 'we believed in Ashanti promises, we made a treaty. None of the articles of that treaty have been observed ... This time I will not believe in words. It is no small matter to bring a large body of troops from Great Britain to this place, and those by whose fault this expedition has been necessary must pay the costs or suffer the consequences.' He demanded Prempeh's submission and the 50,000 ounces of gold from the 1874 treaty. 'There must be instant compliance,' he said. Prempeh removed his crown and slippers. He and the Queen Mother, Yaa Akyia, came forward, 'slowly and painfully' kissed the governor's booted feet and begged for forgiveness and peace under British protection. A British soldier wrote in his diary that Prempeh knelt down and kissed the ground three times between the governor's feet.[2] It was an unprecedented humiliation – 'a blow to the Ashanti pride and prestige such as they had never suffered before' according to Baden-Powell – but it wasn't enough for Maxwell. 'Now the question of money', he said.[3]

Prempeh had spent the previous day meeting his chiefs, seeking to raise the balance of the indemnity. They could not, or would not, lend Prempeh the gold he needed, but he had managed to scrape together several hundred ounces, worth £2,700 (about £375,500 today).[4] Prempeh explained to Maxwell, 'The Governor knows there is not much money in the country, but I offer 348 bendas (758 ounces) which I am prepared to pay, and the remainder I will pay by instalments.' Maxwell was not impressed: 'It is child's play to talk in this manner,' he said, and he could not believe 'the paltry sum' which Prempeh offered. Prempeh pleaded: 'I don't refuse to pay the amount demanded, but I beg that I may be allowed to pay some down and the rest to be paid by instalments.' Maxwell said the British had put up with Asante broken promises for twenty-five years. 'I must require King Prempeh to proceed to the coast with others I shall name,' he said, and he took a paper from his pocket. Prempeh again pleaded: 'I am willing to pay the money and beg you to take the instalment'. Maxwell ploughed on: 'You must be accompanied by the Queen Mother, your father and uncles, who are here, must also go, your brother and two war chiefs. There are other persons of minor importance whom I shall require to go down with me also.' The Queen Mother, the Asantehene's father Kwasi Gyambibi, his younger brother and heir apparent Barima Agyeman Badu and some fifteen others were ordered to one side and put under guard. Again, Prempeh pleaded: 'I beg the Governor not to take my people and myself away, all that we have we will pay down.' Again, Maxwell ignored his pleas.

'Had a thunderbolt burst in their midst, the Ashantis could not have been more amazed,' wrote the British journalist George Musgrave.[5] The chiefs and elders looked on in astonishment and then begged the Governor to reconsider. John and Albert Owusu Ansa tried to intervene with assurances that a French investor would guarantee the indemnity. This, perhaps unsurprisingly, did not go down well, and Maxwell also ordered their arrest. The brothers were handcuffed together and told they were to be taken to the coast as criminals, accused of forging their diplomatic credentials during their unauthorised visit to London.[6] 'The ceremony of submission was picturesque,' wrote Major Sinclair, whose men took Prempeh and the others away. The prisoners were instructed to remove crowns or other regalia and were then locked together in 'a small native hut'.[7] The Reuters correspondent wrote, 'The whole affair was splendidly arranged. British supremacy is secured in Ashanti.'[8]

With the Asantehene out of the way, the British proceeded to his palace. Baden-Powell was unimpressed. 'There is very little that is palatial about it. It consists of a collection of the usual wattle-and-daub huts, with high walls and enormous high-pitched thatched roofs; endless courts, big and little, succeed each other,' he wrote, although 'the foundations of the old palace, built on more substantial principles and destroyed in the last campaign, are still to be seen in the centre of the present place in a disused court.'[9] The West Yorkshire Regiment led the way, breaking down an inner door and disarming the palace guards, who offered no resistance.[10] The soldiers were ordered to collect all the valuables they could find. 'It was done most honestly and well,' wrote Baden-Powell. 'Here was a man with an armful of gold-hilted swords, there one with a box full of gold-trinkets and rings, another with a spirit-case full of bottles of brandy, yet in no instances was there any attempt at looting.'[11]

Prempeh's interpretation of British actions at this point is rather different. 'Orders were given to the soldiers to plunder,' he wrote many years later, 'and they plundered … all the properties in the King's palace and in the houses of the chiefs.'[12] But the haul, from the British point of view, was disappointing: 'not much better than a junk-shop collection' according to Burleigh.[13] 'Though a great many valuables were seized,' wrote Musgrave, 'there was no fabulous wealth discovered as in the palaces looted in India and China.' The 'seized spoil' nonetheless 'formed a pile of large dimensions ... Gorgeous State umbrellas ... enormous kinkassies or wardrums, brass-studded chairs, beautifully carved stools ... executioners' blades and torture instruments ... and so on *ad infinitum*.'[14] Baden-Powell complained the Asante had removed and hidden their most precious regalia, 'above all, the royal stool, the emblem *par excellence* of the King of Ashanti.'

The British soldiers then moved on to the royal mausoleum – what they called the 'Fetish Temple' – at Bantama, about a kilometre and a half away, where they hoped to find more treasure. Major Sinclair wrote that outside was 'a large bronze bowl with quaint figures on the edge and almost full of coagulated blood ... This bowl Baden-Powell, who had got there just before me, annexed and somehow got leave to carry off.'[15] The soldiers forced their way into the mausoleum but found only empty brass coffers. They set Bantama on fire 'and a splendid blaze it made.' They chopped down some of the 'gruesome fetish trees' and blasted others sky high with gunpowder. Burleigh says 'the natives gazed in awe' at this manifestation of British power, but Prempeh II, in *History of Ashanti*, says people 'were panic-stricken and began to flee from Kumasi with their property and belongings with an intention of going to the villages, but they were attacked and robbed by the soldiers on the paths.'[16] Lieutenant Arthur Hood wrote that as soon as 'our native allies and carriers heard that Prempeh was made prisoner, they started looting and burning the town and beating any Ashantis they could find; it was a disgraceful scene, as we had told the people they were British subjects that morning; they had not fired a shot against us.'[17]

The official British account of the expedition says that Bantama was destroyed 'in order to emphasize the final stamping out of human sacrifices'.[18] Major Sinclair said the grove surrounding Bantama was 'so strewn with skulls and bones that one could not avoid treading on them'. Baden-Powell believed these belonged to 'hundreds, and possibly of thousands of victims to the *regime* which ... has so dramatically been brought to a close'.[19] Other British soldiers strike a more sceptical note. Lieutenant Hood wrote that the ground of 'the Fetish Grove' was 'covered with skulls, bones and bone dust, but there were no signs of any recent sacrifices'.[20] Captain Thomas Berney, of the West Yorkshire Regiment, wrote that although he saw about sixty skulls at Bantama, they were all 'very old, none of them apparently more recent than 3 or 4 years ... I got one of the best of them and also some teeth from others, a morbid taste perhaps but still after all one has heard of the Ashantee slaughter house one feels a great interest in these things.'[21]

Communication with Britain had been transformed since 1874 – the Gold Coast was connected by submarine cable in 1886 and Royal Engineers laid a line to Kumasi as the British marched up – and so it was that also on 20 January, Colonel Scott had 'much pleasure' in delivering to his soldiers a message from Her Majesty. 'Delighted at good news, only just reached, congratulate you', said the Queen.[22] The following day, Scott was able to convey the congratulations of the Secretary of State for War for the 'successful and peaceful occupation of Kumassi.'[23]

The British meticulously recorded the removal from the palace of what they considered the most valuable items. On 21 January, Captain Oliver Sherwood of the Ordnance Store Department signed off on an 'Inventory of Specie. Gold Dust, ornaments etc from Palace of King Prempeh', which lists gold ornaments, swords and bracelets, as well as a helmet, scabbard and dagger all with gold plate, and so on, and estimated their value at several hundreds of pounds and their weight in gold at several hundred ounces. 'P.S', Sherwood wrote, '1 to 14 are in a tin case. The key with Sir F Scott.'[24] These were taken to the 'Headquarters Mess', where, at Maxwell's orders, an ad hoc board of officers was formed 'for the purpose of superintending the packing of gold and silver specie'. They put nine parcels – 'counted and recounted' to confirm their contents matched Captain Sherwood's inventory – into three boxes. The boxes were nailed down in the presence of the board and addressed to 'The Crown Agents for the Colonies, Downing Street, London, S.W.' Then the boxes were entrusted to the 'president' of the board, Major Charles

Barter of the King's Own Yorkshire Light Infantry and who served on the expedition with the Special Service Corps, who signed a receipt acknowledging possession.[25]

The British soldiers also held an auction, in the Kumasi marketplace, of some of the remaining plunder from the palace. It began on the evening of 20 January and resumed on the morning of the 21st, and one damaged photograph of this event survives, in which soldiers are clustered around piles of objects under a tree with the casual air of people sifting through bric-a-brac at a church fête.[26] Before the auction began, officers handed out certain prized objects as regimental souvenirs. Captain Walter Cayley of the West Yorkshire Regiment wrote in his diary, 'I got a big gun covered with leopard skin and 2 umbrellas for the regiment'. But when the bidding started, he complained that objects were sold 'at prohibitive prices – far beyond their value and it was impossible to pick up any small thing.' He had better luck the next morning. He bought 'a rather curious' drum with a skull on it, 'said to belong to the predecessor of the present chief who owned the drum. Paid 22/6 [about £156 today] ... very cheap compared to yesterday's prices. Got a second one to match it but without skull for 10/6.'[27] Burleigh wrote that 'big prices were given for war-drums, chairs, and other old rubbish, as souvenirs,' but that some loot simply slipped through the cracks. 'A few poor rascals of natives got flogged for not surrendering property when many whites – officers and civilians – escaped scot free.'[28] Governor Maxwell requested details of how much money was raised at the auction and William Brodrick, the Under Secretary of State for War, speaking some weeks later, gave the House of Commons a very precise figure: £150, 16 shillings and 9 pence (worth about £22,230 today). Brodrick said the 'articles ... were of little importance or value'.[29]

At dawn on 22 January, 'a chill, grey, vapourish mist and smoke hung over Coomassie' according to Burleigh and the bulk of the British force prepared to leave. Prempeh and his companions had spent a second night in captivity. He had been given a mattress, but the others had endured a 'wretched night, sleeping upon the earthen floors of their prison.'[30] When the British told Prempeh he was being taken to Elmina, he wept, but then brushed his tears aside and presented his robe, some gold dust and two small objects to 'his jailer for the night,' Captain Wilfred Davidson-Houston of the Gold Coast Hausas.[31] Governor Maxwell told the Asantehene and other noblemen they could take 'their wives, immediate relatives and servants with them to the coast and a number of these volunteered to go with them.'[32] The Governor also gave instructions that no prisoner should be allowed to escape alive and so the West Yorkshire soldiers took care to be seen loading their rifles.[33] Prempeh waited on his palanquin as the column slowly assembled around him, while the Queen Mother and other chiefs rested in hammocks. A couple of poor-quality photographs survive of this moment – 'King Prempeh, the Queen Mother & War Chiefs quitting Kumasi at dawn' – showing silhouettes being carried away on basket-like beds, the great cotton-wood trees towering above.[34] Many of the prisoners would never see Kumasi again.

★★★

On the first day of the march back to Cape Coast, the British officers received news which threw them into 'a gloom'.[35] Prince Henry of Battenberg, taken ill some ten days earlier and invalided home aboard the HMS *Blonde*, had died at sea, one of twenty-six British soldiers listed as dead from 'Fever or Heat Apoplexy' during the campaign.[36] 'Good Prince Henry! A martyr, if ever there was a martyr, to his sense of duty,' wrote Baden-Powell.[37] Even the small press corps had been fond of the prince. 'No man in the whole Expedition had been better or more deservedly esteemed by all,' wrote Burleigh. He 'sang for us German and Italian songs with a fair tenor voice' and had shared meals and 'after-dinner merry making'.[38]

The Queen and Princess Beatrice were on the Isle of Wight when they were told. 'Such an awful day that it is almost impossible to describe it,' wrote the Queen, 'my grief is great, & I am quite unnerved by the shock of this dreadful news.'[39] Prince Henry's coffin arrived at the Isle of Wight on 4 February and he was buried that day at the church at Whippingham, close to Osborne House. Wolseley, as well as Sir Evelyn

Wood and Sir Redvers Buller, joined the royal family for the funeral. The elderly Queen was able to walk in and out of the church 'but rested heavily upon the arm of one of her Indian attendants, whose Oriental attire contrasted with the sombre black worn by the mourners.'[40] (Her grandson, Prince Christian of Schleswig-Holstein, also fell severely ill during the Asante campaign. He recovered, only to die of malaria in South Africa in 1900 during the Anglo-Boer war).

The Asantehene, meanwhile, appeared to accept his fate with a degree of stoicism. A British journalist reported that he spoke little on the journey down, was 'quite reconciled to his position' and was looking forward to seeing Cape Coast Castle and the sea. On the first day, the Queen Mother was 'rather given to spit at any white men who approached' but later was said to be 'much more reserved ... always smoking, a pipe or a cigarette being scarcely out of her mouth.'[41] At daybreak on 4 February, the West Yorkshire Regiment and their prisoners arrived at Cape Coast. For many Fante and others in the town, it was a day to relish, the downfall of a feared enemy: 'a murmur of a thousand voices speaking in hushed tones, succeeded by one fearful yell of triumph and hate as the litters with prisoners came into sight'.[42] The crowd pressed in on Prempeh, and, according to Musgrave, 'had the wild passion of those frenzied people, kept back by the gleam of steel, been allowed full play, they would have wreaked a fearful vengeance.'[43]

The British marched the prisoners directly to the beach, where eight surf boats were waiting, as well as a 'dense throng of natives, who shouted and sang and altogether made a tremendous din'. Now Prempeh saw the sea, for the first time in his life, and his expression was 'one of blank astonishment, not unmixed with alarm, but he soon recovered himself'.[44] The British put soldiers on the surf boats, according to Baden-Powell, as they feared the boatmen 'might, in the excess of their hate, contrive to upset Prempeh in the surf, and hold him down till dead!' The boatmen paddled out to HMS *Racoon*, which waited in deeper water to take the prisoners west along the coast to Elmina. 'This was to them the climax of their troubles. Awed and nervous at their first sight of the ocean and their first experience of boats and ships, at the utter breaking up of all their royal prestige, and their ignorance of what it might portend, they huddled all together, chiefs and attendants, in one close, frightened group.'[45] The *Racoon* rolled in the heavy swell and many of the prisoners were sea sick. Their misery was complete.

The Asante Ewer; 'a remarkable survivor, a complete miracle.'

12

'SIMPLY A POLICY OF ROBBERY'

If you want to see the spoils of the most notorious British plunder of Africa, you must go to the British Museum's Sainsbury Gallery, beneath the Great Court, where the Benin Bronzes are displayed. A Nigerian friend told me that when he looked into the eyes of a Benin mask there, he felt he was 'visiting a relative behind bars'. But if you want to see the most mysterious object the British took from Africa in all their wars, you have to go upstairs in the museum, to the Medieval Europe Gallery. It is a large and dark bronze jug, weighing a hefty 18.3 kilograms and is some sixty centimetres tall. Lloyd de Beer, the British Museum's Curator for Medieval Britain and Europe, describes it as 'a virtuoso piece of metal casting, something that stops you in your tracks'. In truth, most visitors are more interested in the walrus ivory Lewis chessmen in the neighbouring display case and do not pay the jug much attention. For what makes this jug extraordinary is not its appearance but its history. Africans, we are sometimes told, are not able to look after cultural heritage as well as Europeans. And yet wonderfully this jug, the largest surviving bronze vessel from medieval England, was not found in an old English manor house or castle, but in the Asantehene's palace in Kumasi, 6,000 kilometres away, where it had been protected and preserved, probably for centuries. 'Because of its age, because of its origins, because of where it was looted, it is a remarkable survivor. It's just a complete miracle,' says de Beer.[1] The British Museum calls it 'the Asante Ewer'.

The jug's sides are engraved with falcons in roundels. Around its bulging belly is a relief inscription, in Middle English. It reads, 'HE THAT WYL NOT SPARE WHAN HE MAY HE SCHAL NOT SPEND WHEN HE WOLD DEME THE BEST IN EVERY DOWT TIL THE TROWTHE BE TRYID OWTE.' Or, in modern English, 'He that will not spare when he may, he shall not spend when he would. Deem the best in every doubt, till the truth be tried out.' I take that to mean use your money judiciously, but sometimes take a leap of faith and trust others. Beneath the jug's spout are the royal arms of England, as used between 1340 and 1405, supported by lions and topped with a crown. On each facet of its seven-sided lid is a royal lion, but also a stag, the personal emblem of Richard II, who ruled from 1377 to 1399. This jug, it seems, belonged to a medieval king of England, or at least somebody who displayed loyalty to that king.[2] So how on earth did it end up in faraway Asante?

The soldier who brought it back from Kumasi in January 1896 had his own theory. Major Charles Barter, the same officer who had been 'president' of the board appointed by Governor Maxwell to pack Prempeh's looted treasures, wrote to the British Museum after his return from the Gold Coast, from his barracks in Pontefract, Yorkshire. He said that he had a jug, which, in his 'humble opinion, is of some value', which he had had the good fortune to acquire 'at the public auction' in Kumasi. Barter recognised the 'arms of England' and old English characters and speculated it might have been taken by Crusaders to Palestine, then captured by Saracens and traded across Africa. The jug was sitting in his club in Pall Mall and he would be happy to take it round to the British Museum the next time he was in London (the jug was not Barter's only prize from Kumasi; he later donated an Asante drum to a regimental museum in Lancaster and other officers grumbled that the Special Service Corps had boarded the ship for home from the Gold Coast 'loaded with loot').[3]

From May to July 1896, Major Barter was in frequent correspondence with the British Museum's new ethnographic curator, Charles Hercules

Asantehene Osei Tutu II and the sacred Golden Stool.
'Respect for the past is the unbroken thread which keeps Asante together.'

'Crowded with magnificence and novelty.' Thomas Bowdich enters Kumasi in 1817: face-to-face with Asante opulence and power.

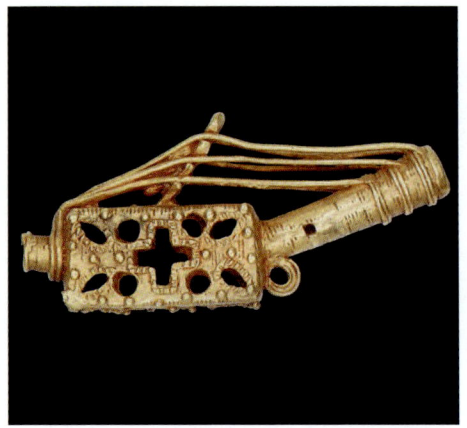 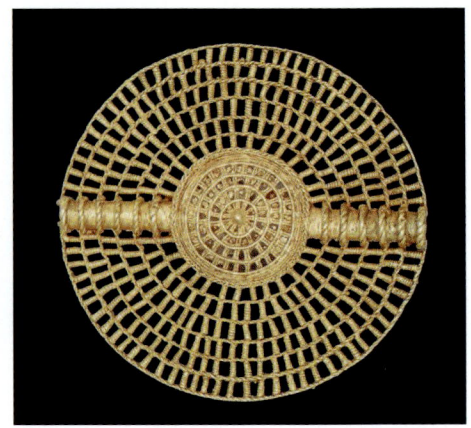

A miniature harp, *sika sankuo* (*left*), and 'soul washer badge', *akrafokonmu* (*right*). Donated to the British Museum in 1817 by the Asantehene during the honeymoon in Anglo-Asante relations.

Sir Garnet Wolseley called it the 'great palace, the wonder of Western Africa' – and yet he ordered its 'total destruction'.

Asante treasure on display in London in spring 1874. Queen Victoria, aristocrats and museums took their pick. One newspaper declared 'a craze for these Ashantee relics.'

Two spectacular objects taken by Wolseley's army. The trophy head (*left*) is on display at the Wallace Collection but the ram's head (*right*), is hidden from public view in the Royal Artillery officer's mess, where it is now held aloft by 'beautifully-moulded West African natives'.

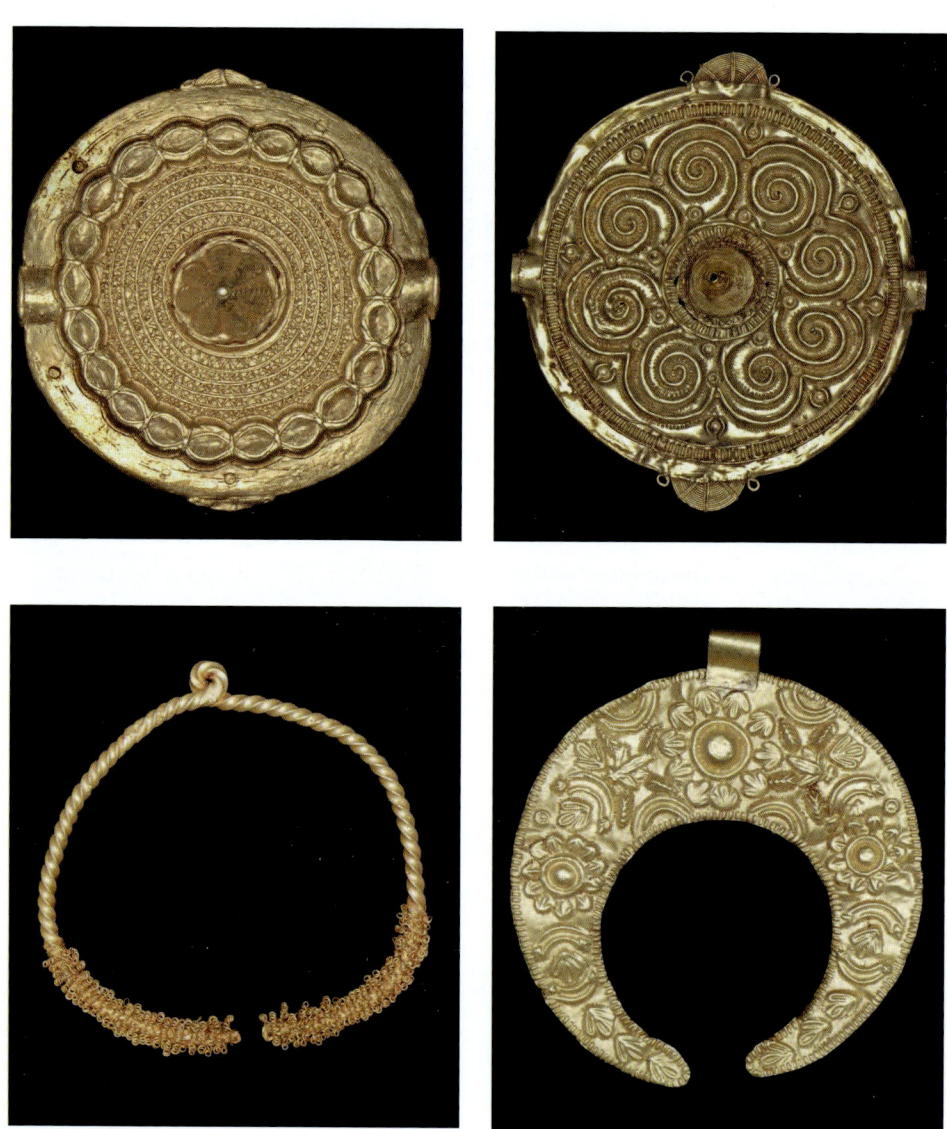

Regalia taken by Wolseley in 1874; a pair of *akrafokonmu* (*top row*), a necklace (*lower left*) and a pendant (*lower right*). The British Museum returned all four to Kumasi on a long-term loan in 2024.

Mpomponsuo, the 'greatest of the State Swords' (*above*), and the *Denkyemkye* helmet (*below*). Both looted by the British army in 1896 and returned to Kumasi in 2024.

Samori Toure's ring, a gift from Prempeh later presented to the British (*left*), and a gun-bearer's cap, *krobonkye*, decorated with strips of sheet gold and silver (*below*). Both now back in Kumasi.

Asante sacred objects become British souvenirs. In 1874 the Cecil family mounted two of the finest *akrafokonmu* on larger gilt-silver dishes. 'It's just there as a trophy. It traps it and it kills it' wrote the artist Hew Locke in his 2024 British Museum exhibition.

How did they get there? Medieval English jugs, photographed in the Asantehene's palace in Kumasi by Frederick Grant in 1884.

Queen Yaa Asantewaa II, descendant of the legendary warrior queen, with 'Prof' Malcolm McLeod. McLeod, with Ivor Agyeman-Duah (*right*), brokered the return of Asante treasure in 2024.

Read, who had taken over weeks before from Augustus Franks. The son of an army sergeant, Read had joined the British Museum as a teenager in 1874 and worked his way up. He was an astute man, gifted with charm and a remarkable visual memory. He would eventually acquire a knighthood (he liked to be known as 'Sir Hercules'), recognition as 'a famous antiquary' and by the time of his death in 1929, considerable wealth.[4] He was certainly too canny to let Major Barter's unusual offering slip through his hands. 'I should be glad to see your jug,' Read told Barter in an apparently off-hand tone. 'It is certainly a curiosity but scarcely as old as the Crusades, I fancy.'

Barter brought the jug to the British Museum in June 1896. Read told him that it had been valued by two dealers, at £25 and £40. Barter found these estimates 'v. disappointing' and threatened to take the jug to Berlin and Paris. But by July, Barter was prepared to sell for a 'reasonable' price of £60. Read, it seems, could sense that Barter had set his heart on the Asante Ewer ending up in the national museum. They settled on £50 (equivalent to £6,954 today).[5]

One evening in February 1898, in the elegant rooms of Burlington House on Piccadilly, Charles Read spoke to the Society of Antiquaries about the Asante Ewer. 'I was fortunate enough to secure it from the officer to whom it fell. He had the perspicacity to prefer the 'old jug' to the ordinary savage weapons and blood-stained sacrificial stools,' Read explained. He had two theories on 'its mysterious appearance among the paraphernalia of a negro king.' The first was that the Asante Ewer was carried on an English ship destined for a Mediterranean port, which was attacked by Moorish pirates or driven by storms to the North African coast. From there, it had been traded along the caravan routes of the Sahara, possibly through Timbuktu, before arriving in West Africa. His second and preferred theory was that it had been traded by Europeans along the West African coast, perhaps by the Portuguese prince, Henry the Navigator, in the mid-fifteenth century. 'What is more likely than that this enlightened and learned prince, the grandson of our John of Gaunt, should have included in one of his many cargoes assorted to please the eye of native potentates a selection of English goods?' Read grandly proposed. The English link is tantalising, for Prince Henry's mother – John of Gaunt's daughter – was Philippa of Lancaster, who became a Portuguese queen in 1387 and lived until 1415. Perhaps she took gifts to Lisbon from the royal household in England and these were later traded on to West Africa.[6]

This story is stranger, however, than Read knew. Charles Barter was not the only British soldier to bring a medieval English jug back from Kumasi. Also in 1896, the West Yorkshire Regiment came home with a smaller bronze jug. It is forty-nine centimetres high, with an ornate handle and decorated with a band at its widest point and stands on three legs which end in animal paws. It too is of distinctly northern European style and is thought to date from the late fourteenth century, or perhaps the fifteenth century. Just beneath its spout is a small metal plaque: 'Bronze Urn, Presented to the Officers 2nd Batt. P.O.W West Yorks. Regt. at Kumassi 17 Jan 1896 by the Governor of the Gold Coast.'[7] But the irrefutable proof that it and Charles Barter's Asante Ewer were together in Kumasi comes, astonishingly, from a photograph taken in 1884. This was by Frederick Grant, the Accra photographer who accompanied Brandon Kirby on his diplomatic mission. It shows a courtyard of the Asantehene's palace, with decorated walls and arcades, and Kirby can be seen in the background shadows, leaning insouciantly on his stick. In the foreground, under a sacred tree, are the two bronze jugs, their prominence suggesting their importance to the Asante (see plate section).[8]

The final plot twist came in 1933, when the British Museum acquired a third English bronze jug also taken from Asante. This had belonged to Sir Cecil Armitage, who died that year and had served as a soldier in Asante before becoming a senior colonial official. British Museum records, based on information from Armitage, say this 'medieval bronze jug' was one of two the Asante had taken in war from a rival kingdom to the west at an unspecified date, that it had remained in the Asantehene's palace until 1896 and that he acquired it in April 1900.[9] This jug bears a close resemblance to the one taken by the West Yorkshire Regiment and also stands on a tripod of legs and with a simple band round its middle, albeit with a height of only thirty-nine centimetres. It too is thought to be from the late medieval period.[10]

What to make of all this? The 'West Yorkshire Jug' and the 'Armitage Jug' are so similar, Malcolm McLeod writes, that they were 'quite clearly made by the same workshop ... Their overall shape and the details of the handles and feet all indicate they were cast in the same place, and possibly that the original waxes – for these are *cire-perdue* castings, were made by the same hand.'[11] And as these two ended up in Kumasi alongside a recognisably royal jug, it is tempting to speculate that all three came from the household of an English king and were taken to West Africa together. They might have been given by the English as diplomatic gifts. If so, an Asantehene was surely not their original intended recipient, as they are 300 years older than the Asante kingdom. Maybe Portuguese traders took them by ship to West Africa, where they were exchanged for gold or slaves with another kingdom which was later pillaged by Asante, as the note with the 'Armitage Jug' suggests. Or maybe, and this is to me an even more alluring possibility, challenging Eurocentric assumptions, they were given to a North African ruler, who then sold them to a kingdom to the south and they were carried over the desert, tied to the back of a camel.

If this book is in part a tale of how African objects became symbols of British power, the story of objects which made the reverse journey is especially fascinating. The Asantehenes of the eighteenth and nineteenth centuries accumulated European artefacts in the Kumasi palace, some in those piles of apparently discarded bric-a-brac, the 'Wardour Street' of random objects gleefully listed by the British journalists of 1874. But others – like the three jugs – had been incorporated into Asante customs and beliefs. In 1933, when the British Museum acquired the third jug from the collection of Sir Cecil Armitage, it also received a silver punch bowl he had likewise taken from Kumasi. Although extensively repaired by the Asante, its origins are unmistakable. On its base it carries a London hallmark, which reads '1764'.[12]

In 1979, the British Museum bought an oak and mahogany chair at an auction in Oxford which Major Hugh Sinclair had taken from Kumasi. According to Sinclair family tradition, on the morning of 20 January 1896, when he went to the palace to order Prempeh to hurry up for the impatient Governor Maxwell, he found the Asantehene sitting on this chair. The British Museum identified it, larger and with none of the decorative brass-work of the typical Asante *asipim* chairs, as coming from Spain or Portugal and probably dating from the late seventeenth century.[13] Also in 1896, Major Thomas Berney wrote in his diary that 'the real curiosity of the loot ... a small piece of silver plate with the arms of Henri IV of France on it' had been put aside, he believed, for Governor William Maxwell.[14] Berney also wrote that a fellow West Yorkshire officer, Captain Francis Pearce, ordered to 'clear out a fetish house,' made a 'very lucky' discovery: a European ship's bell, dated 1650 and with the Latin inscription 'Amor vincit omnia [Love Conquers All.]'[15] In 2010, Captain Pearce's great-nephew, David Pearce, said the bell was hanging in his Bristol hallway, where he used it to summon the family to meals.[16] And then there was the European eighteenth-century silver coffee pot taken from the palace in 1874 which Wolseley bought at the Cape Coast auction, and which curators at the National Army Museum now believe may be the work of the distinguished Norwegian silversmith, Emick Romer.[17] So many fragmentary histories, tying Asante to the world beyond.

Charles Barter died aged seventy-five, in Madrid in 1931, after falling ill on his way home from Lisbon. One of thirty-four British officers of the Asante expedition of 1895–6 who subsequently rose to the rank of General, the First World War was the pinnacle of his career.[18] But at the Somme, he was peremptorily dismissed 'with disgrace' for causing 'wanton waste of his men'. He rejected the charge with 'indignation' and his final years were consumed by unsuccessful appeals for an investigation to clear his name.[19] Today, the consensus amongst military historians is that whatever went wrong in September 1916 in High Wood, it was probably not Barter's fault.[20] But there is no resolution to the mystery of the 'old jug' he brought home from Africa. Should we regard the 'Asante Ewer', and for that matter the 'West Yorkshire Jug' and the 'Armitage Jug', as colonial loot or recovered heritage? They were pillaged by British soldiers, who had no interest in their significance to the Asante. But they were brought home to the country where they were made and today they are all in publicly owned museums. 'These jugs', says Lloyd de Beer, 'ask us to think about history'.

★★★

The sealed boxes of treasures taken from Prempeh's palace were opened in Joseph Chamberlain's rooms in the Colonial Office on the afternoon of 4 March 1896. Chamberlain, his civil servants and a select group of journalists pored over them. The Senior Crown Agent for the Colonies, Sir Montagu Ommanney told them that the 'intrinsic' value of the gold was only some £2,000 (worth about £278,200 today) and that whereas many of the ornaments brought back by Wolseley in 1874 were solid, these 'were mostly hollow and consequently much less valuable, although composed of the purest gold'. The *Daily Telegraph* blithely observed that 'since last we were in conflict with the Ashantees a spirit of economy appears to have pervaded the Court of that kingdom.'[21] But Sir Montagu hoped the objects would fetch good prices, because 'rare and curious examples of barbaric skill and splendour often had a value of their own far in excess of that indicated by the weight of the precious metals of which they were composed.' After Chamberlain and the other 'privileged persons' had had a good look, Prempeh's treasures were locked up again, pending a decision on their fate.[22]

The West Yorkshire Regiment, meanwhile, had arrived in Dover at the end of February with its own substantial haul of plunder – not just one of the three medieval jugs, but also any number of drums, shields, umbrellas, swords, wooden stools, muskets and so on, as well as several skulls and human bones. They triumphantly arranged many of these for a sinister photograph, taken in a Dover studio. Twenty-seven of the most precious objects taken by the West Yorkshire Regiment – including the wood and animal-hide bed in which Prempeh was carried into exile, a copper-covered chest lined with yellow silk that may have been a royal coffin or mortuary chest and a brass-decorated wooden chair or *asipim* with a plaque which reads 'King Prempeh's Chair, used by him when being escorted to the coast for exile' – found their way to the regimental museum in York, but are today in the Leeds City Museum, where they have been on loan since 1984.²³

There was also the impressive ornamental brass bowl, known as the *Aya Kese*, 120 centimetres in diameter which Major Hugh Sinclair complained that Robert Baden-Powell had 'annexed' at the Bantama royal mausoleum. Prempeh said the *Aya Kese* descended from the sky on a gold chain in a thunderstorm, along with an ancestress of the royal family, while in other Asante folklore it was said to have been taken from their original overlords, the Denkyira, and was therefore a symbol of independence, used by the great priest Okomfo Anokye to perform special rites.²⁴ (Lloyd de Beer and Julie Hudson at the British Museum believe that the *Aya Kese* is of European origin, possibly Dutch or Portuguese, from the seventeenth century, which would not be inconsistent with its seizure from the Denkyira.)²⁵ Baden-Powell assumed it was the same bowl seen by Thomas Bowdich back in 1817, who said it was used to collect slaves' blood, which was mixed with 'various vegetable and animal matter … to… produce invincible fetish.'²⁶ Baden-Powell wrote, 'It is ornamented with four small lions, and a number of round knobs, where there is a space for the victim's neck to rest on the edge.'²⁷ He explained, coyly, that it 'has now been brought to England'. He gave what *The Times* described as this 'very interesting, if rather gruesome relic' to the Royal United Services Institution (today Royal United Services Institute) in 1913, to which he also donated in 1919 an 'Ashanti war drum and sticks'.²⁸ (In 1963 the Royal United Services Institution passed on the *Aya Kese* to the National Army Museum in Chelsea).²⁹

The week after Chamberlain had examined King Prempeh's treasures in the Colonial Office, Parliament debated the latest Asante expedition, as the War Office had requested supplementary funds of £120,000 to cover the costs (this is roughly equivalent to £16,690,000 today, meaning it had been substantially cheaper than Wolseley's expedition). Chamberlain, the man who, in Winston Churchill's memorable phrase, 'made the political weather', delivered a long and confident address, punctuated by cheers from government MPs. Asante, he said, was 'rich in natural resources, probably rich in mineral resources', but had been destroyed by 'evil' rulers, who terrorised surrounding regions. It had become 'an intolerable nuisance ... in the way of civilization, of trade, of the interests of the people themselves.' He praised Governor Maxwell, who had behaved with 'discretion and foresight', but ridiculed Prempeh, by now in captivity in Elmina. The Asantehene 'appeared to enjoy his novel position very much indeed' and had expressed 'delight at the treatment which he has received'. To sustained laughter, Chamberlain told the MPs that Prempeh's only complaint was that he did not have enough spirits to drink.[30]

Sir Henry Havelock-Allan, holder of the Victoria Cross and from a celebrated military family, spoke for most MPs when he described the Asante expedition as 'a brilliant and complete success', even if the soldiers had suffered 'disappointment that they had not come into contact with the enemy'. But just as in 1874, there were dissenting voices, and the strongest criticism came from the Celtic fringes of the United Kingdom. Irish nationalist MPs, advocating at the time for Home Rule, were not surprisingly more finely attuned to the inequities of British imperialism. William Redmond, the member for East Clare, said he had 'feelings almost of disgust' when he read how Chamberlain had examined Prempeh's treasures in the Colonial Office: 'the plunder from this poor African king, who was not only taken prisoner, but plundered of all he had. Some men might call this a policy of expansion in Africa if they liked, but he called it simply a policy of robbery.' John Dillon, the member for East Mayo, condemned:

> the scandalous exhibition of sacks of gold dust and jewels which were robbed from the Queen [sic] of Ashanti. The loot collected by the Army should have been hidden away, and a more extraordinary occurrence than the exhibition of this plunder was never seen in the capital of a great nation like England. An expert valued the jewels at £3,000. If that was all they were worth, they should have been left behind.[31]

In April 1896, Prempeh's treasures were lent by the Colonial Office to the Royal United Services Institution in Whitehall, where they were put on display in Inigo Jones's Banqueting House, beneath Peter Paul Rubens' magnificent ceiling paintings, amidst medieval armour, model battle ships and tattered naval standards, and with a six-pence admission charge (waived for soldiers and sailors in uniform).[32] Across the road from Downing Street, and the Colonial, Indian and War Offices, the Asante loot was now a trophy 'at the nerve centre of the British Empire'.[33] In Parliament, another Irish nationalist MP, Daniel MacAleese, asked whether Joseph Chamberlain had been able to 'ascertain the approximate commercial value of the collection' and if the proceeds could go to the liquidation of the national debt. Chamberlain replied with a new and reduced valuation for the collection – a mere £400 – which, he drily observed, would therefore not cover the national debt.[34] But the issue did not go away; in 1897, and again in 1898, Chamberlain had to fend off more parliamentary criticism of the pillage of Kumasi, as yet another Irish nationalist MP, Michael Davitt, stuck to the matter doggedly. Why had the army, faced with no resistance, 'looted the King's house and dug up the graves of dead chiefs in search of treasure...?'[35] And how had 'avaricious officers' got away with 'looting, spoliation and desecration, more worthy of a ferocious and barbarous people, than of the subjects of a civilised and Christian Government'?[36]

The right of a conquering army to plunder – even a European one fighting in Africa – was under scrutiny as never before. In 1894, the British War Office's *Manual of Military Law* delivered a somewhat muddled message: 'The pillage of a town taken by assault is an act of barbarism excusable only by the difficulty of putting a stop to it ... English officers always endeavour to prevent it.' If, however, these officers failed, then the manual advised 'any property seized must be taken from the individual captors and distributed [amongst the soldiers] as booty of war.'[37] In other words, Wolseley's distinction between 'loot' (bad) and 'prize' (good) still just about held. But in 1899, fifty-one countries signed the Hague Convention, which prohibited all seizure, destruction or intentional damage to religious institutions, historical monuments and works of art.[38] The Hague Convention came too late for the Asante, or indeed for the Edo, whose Benin Bronzes had been taken by the British in 1897.

Nor did it prevent looting – in 1904, for example, from monasteries in Tibet, also by the British – but there was now at least a consensus that it was an embarrassment. In August 1914, Lord Kitchener wrote to the soldiers on their way to France. 'Never do anything likely to injure or destroy property,' he told them, 'and always look upon looting as a disgraceful act.'[39]

Chamberlain's reply to the Irish MP Davitt in 1897 was that 'articles found in the King's house … have been fully described and accounted for.'[40] This was to some extent true. The British officers who sent the boxes from Kumasi to the Crown Agents in 1896 had listed their contents with almost touching accuracy. The Colonial Office was also bureaucratically pedantic about the fate of the loot. Its files reveal that on 22 October 1896, an individual with unique access to Joseph Chamberlain made her own selection from Prempeh's treasures. Mrs Mary Endicott Chamberlain, his third wife and the beautiful and wealthy daughter of an American secretary of war, bought Asante 'ornaments' with a gold value of 21½ carats, to which 'a curio value of 15%' was added, meaning she spent £11, 19 shillings and 6 pence (worth about £1,666 today).[41] Mary, a hostess at the centre of British social and political life at the turn of the century, may have thought Asante gold had topical as well as aesthetic appeal, or perhaps she intended it as a gift for her parents in Massachusetts. (Mary lived until 1957, but unfortunately her correspondence makes no mention of this purchase.)[42]

At the British Museum, Charles Read followed the fate of Prempeh's treasures closely. The museum had fared comparatively poorly in 1874 and although Read considered the latest gold regalia from Asante inferior to that taken by Wolseley, he was nonetheless determined it should not miss out again.[43] He made his purchases from the Crown Agents in January and April of 1900, spending a total of almost £300 (worth about £41,000 today).[44] The objects he bought for the British Museum included the *denkyemkye*, the spectacular horned cap made of antelope hide, studded with gold ornaments and amulets, which the British press called 'King Prempeh's Crown', as well as the *Mpomponsuo* sword, decorated with gold ornaments and leopard skin (see plate section).[45] Read's purchase of the *Mpomponsuo* sword may have frustrated Robert Baden-Powell, who had unsuccessfully lobbied the Colonial Office, arguing that it in fact belonged to him as he had found it in the palace, 'hidden under some sacking'.[46] (In recent years the *denkyemkye* has been exhibited from Dallas to Tokyo and in 2024 both it and the *Mpomponsuo* were amongst the fifteen Asante treasures the British Museum returned to Kumasi).[47]

Charles Read wasn't only buying Asante gold for the British Museum but had also become a middleman for other interested parties. Although the Crown Agents had been able to sell some Asante pieces through the jewellers Watherston & Son of Pall Mall in 1896, Joseph Chamberlain accepted with gratitude in April 1900 Read's offer to 'arrange for the sale of objects from the remainder of the collection to institutions and private persons desiring them as curiosities'.[48] Read connected the Crown Agents with some of his important contacts, including Felix von Luschan of the Museum für Völkerkunde in Berlin, as well as the collector George William Neville, a former banker in West Africa. These two men had both been avid purchasers of Benin Bronzes and in late 1900 Read brokered a series of sales of Asante 'gold ornaments' to Neville and a friend, Mr Gordon, worth a total of £387 (equivalent to about £49,200 today).[49]

In January 1901 Read wrote to the British Museum trustees, explaining that the Colonial Office had offered him a ring which had been given to Governor William Maxwell back in 1896 by Samori Toure, the Mandinka king whose military prowess and rumoured friendship with the Asante had once caused the British such concern and who had died in exile in a French prison camp in central Africa in 1900. Read thought the ring 'not a very great one in itself' but argued that because it came from a 'notorious person ... [a] well known character in West Africa, who has been described as the Mahdi of that part of the continent', it was unusually interesting. Samori is remembered today as a hero of African resistance, and his ring is splendid; a delicate dome of swirling gold topped by a pointed cone (see plate section). British Museum curators were told by the Colonial Office that Prempeh may have originally given it to Samori, who then passed it on to the British. It seems fitting then, that this ring was also amongst the treasures which the British Museum returned to Kumasi in 2024.[50]

Charles Read stayed in close contact with the Crown Agents and Colonial Office throughout 1901 as they negotiated the fate of the last of Prempeh's treasures. There was one remaining piece of the 1896 loot which Read had resolved to acquire, an elegant gold vessel some seventeen centimetres high, apparently used as a sword ornament, which he told the trustees was 'of very considerable interest … it would not be wise to allow it to go either into private hands or into the melting pot.' In November of 1902, the Crown Agents were 'anxious to close this business' and the British Museum trustees approved its purchase for £62 (equivalent to about £8,055 today).[51]

This vessel, made in the style of a European eighteenth-century piece of silverware, is yet another example of what the British Museum curator William Fagg would describe in 1964 as 'derived rococo' in Asante gold craftsmanship.[52] Fagg delighted in other examples, such as a ring depicting three elephants with birds riding on their backs – 'an exquisite piece of rococo jewellery … a true marriage of European style with African subject matter', which Read bought for the British Museum from the Crown Agents in 1900.[53] But just as in 1874, the British in 1896 often reacted to this Asante incorporation of European designs with contempt. *The Queen* magazine wrote that 'unfortunately' the gold vessel was of an entirely Western design. 'It is most likely that the native jeweller on some visit to a more civilized country saw a vase which pleased his fancy, and he endeavoured to produce it in gold, from recollection, when he reached home.'[54] The *Illustrated London News* wrote that Prempeh's treasures were 'chiefly of interest for the close imitation of European models shown in their workmanship … the inventive faculty would seem to have little kinship with what counts for civilization in Ashanti.'[55]

A more generous interpretation is that the Asante were simply trying to adapt to a changing world. Malcolm McLeod writes that 'no study of Asante culture can be complete unless it takes into account the ways in which the Asante selectively adopted some of the European goods and ideas which were available to them.'[56] This process went way beyond matters of artistic style. In Prempeh's ambitious plan for national reconstruction in the early 1890s, for example, he envisaged British investors helping the Asante to build railways, waterworks, factories, schools and a mint, thus enabling his kingdom to develop economically without sacrificing its sovereignty or all its traditional beliefs. 'He wanted modernisation without Westernisation,' writes Emmanuel Akyeampong.[57] It was a forlorn appeal for partnership and co-operation in the age of rampant imperialism.

Sword ornament, looted in 1896. 'Derived rococo' in Asante gold craftsmanship.

The British fort in Kumasi, during construction in the late 1890s...

...And today, home to the Ghana Military Museum.

13

'WHY AM I NOT SITTING ON THE GOLDEN STOOL?'

The street leading up to the old British fort in the centre of Kumasi throbs with heat, cars and motorbikes and is lined with stalls selling t-shirts, wooden carvings and baskets for tourists. The fort itself is an indestructible-looking building: squat, with thick walls and hexagonal towers at each corner. It was built by the Resident Commissioner, Captain Donald Stewart, after the British took control of Kumasi in 1896 and it was from here that he, and a modest garrison of some 300 soldiers, tried to exert authority over the nominally annexed territories of Asante.

Today the fort serves as a military museum. Outside its ochre-red walls, a couple of ageing fighter aircraft, coated with dust, sit on a neatly clipped lawn. Inside, the museum tells a history full of contradictions and ironies. The inner rooms are decorated with faded black-and-white photographs of moustached and bemedalled British governors in plumed helmets and Gold Coast soldiers fighting against the Japanese in the jungles of Burma in loyal defence of King and Empire. Other historic photographs are stacked on the floor, apparently of little interest to staff or the modest number of visitors. But another room is captioned as a 'Hell Prison Cell', where the 'extremely cruel' British locked up those who fought for Asante freedom. 'Can you imagine the pain, the terror, the fear, the hell that they all passed though [sic] fighting for Africa & the Holy Golden Stool!' reads a notice. Irreconcilable histories, and the fort itself was once the fiercely contested prize in the struggle between them; in 1900 it was under siege for several months as a small group of British soldiers and their allies held out desperately against the surrounding Asante army. 'Africa is full of ghosts,' wrote a British historian who served with the Gold Coast Regiment in the 1940s, 'and nowhere in the Continent are they more likely to be found than in the old fort of Kumasi.'[1]

Governor William Maxwell ordered the construction of the fort after sending Prempeh into exile in January 1896. Captain Stewart instructed the people of Kumasi to carry stones from the 1874 ruins of the Asantehene's palace, and the British used hundreds of carriers to bring cement and building materials from the coast. Maxwell never saw the fort completed, for he died of malaria while travelling back to England at the end of 1897.[2] But the British transformation of Kumasi was well underway. In 1900, a British officer wrote that nothing remained of the once 'immense' palace of Kofi Karikari and that Kumasi was 'a shadow' of what it had been. The traditional 'steep-roofed, beautifully-built swish houses decorated with most grateful designs ... had also been destroyed to make way for the European buildings, the Hausa cantonments, and the parade ground.' Other traditional houses were pulled down for firewood.[3]

It was a bleak time in Asante history; people 'became all together angry, sorry and dejected', writes Prempeh II in *History of Ashanti*.[4] The British abolished slavery, demanded annual instalments towards the 1874 indemnity, imposed compulsory labour, established a magistrate's court which eroded the powers of Asante chiefs, encouraged the return of Christian missionaries and Fante traders and introduced a Hausa constabulary. 'All of these new colonial arrangements, which were rigidly enforced between 1896 and 1900, greatly infuriated and humiliated the Asante,' writes the historian and later politician Albert Adu Boahen.[5] But British rule also provided opportunities to those who made themselves useful to the invaders. The British-created 'Native Committee of Chiefs' was comprised, according to *History of Ashanti*, of men who 'began to molest and extort the people on their own behalf and by these means they got plenty of money and determined to keep that wealth at any cost.' There was 'great confusion and unease at this sudden and unwanted transition'.[6]

***

At long last the British were in a position to exploit the gold that lay beneath Asante land. Back in 1874, Stanley had written with disarming candour, 'King Coffee is too rich a neighbour to be left alone with his riches, with his tons of gold dust and accumulations of wealth to himself.'[7] Henry Brackenbury, Wolseley's military secretary, wrote 'Gold is there in profusion, and to be had for the seeking.' The Africans, Brackenbury thought, might not make sufficiently pliant miners, but 'Chinese coolies would be imported, who would breed in with the natives, and infuse some energy into the Fanti races ... By no other means but that strongest of all temptations, the acquisition of gold, can this country ever be opened up.'[8] Wynyard Hall, who served with the West Yorkshire Regiment in 1896, described Asante as 'the Eldorado of a thousand years, with its reputed millions and millions of tons of wonderful gold ore.'[9]

In 1895 Edwin Arthur Cade, son of an Ipswich watchmaker, a shortish, wiry man with red hair and beard, arrived in the Gold Coast to put such fantasies to the test. British geologists were particularly interested in exploring what are known as the Birimian rocks, which include quartz and sulphide reefs containing high-value gold ore, with some of the richest deposits to the south of Kumasi.[10] Asante miners appear to have already been exploiting these in the late nineteenth century, for when the British were taken to see 'King Prempe's Mine' at Ekwanta, near Kumasi, after they had forced the Asantehene into exile, they found timbered galleries leading almost 100 metres into the hillside.[11]

Cade hiked inland through forests and swamps to Obuasi, some sixty kilometres south of Kumasi, where three Fante entrepreneurs had bought a concession from the King of Bekwai. Cade was impressed by the miners he met there –'I have given the Ashantees every credit for their acuteness and skill in knowing where to work, and unstinted praise for the courage and patience of their endeavours'– but also by the concession's potential.

He somehow convinced the Fante entrepreneurs to sell to him, for an undisclosed price that was, he admitted, 'a very bitter disappointment to them all.' He signed treaties with local kings confirming his takeover and used their ignorance of maps to include extra mines in the concession.[12]

Cade was operating without Prempeh's consent, but the British annexation of Asante in January 1896 soon made this irrelevant. Instead, he had a ninety-year lease granted by the British government. In May 1897, the Ashanti Goldfields Corporation was launched in London, with the sale of 250,000 shares at £1 each. Cade returned to the Gold Coast with sixteen engineers and forty tons of mining equipment in November 1897 and began digging. The corporation produced its first gold in March 1898, employed more than 2,300 people by 1899 and paid its maiden dividend to shareholders in 1900.[13] 'The Ashanti Gold Corporation soon had in operation the most wonderful gold mine in the world,' wrote Wynyard Hall in 1939. 'It simply poured out gold in quantities far beyond the dreams of avarice. Nothing in the world has ever been seen like it. Forty years later it is still pouring out more and more gold, and paying higher and higher dividends. Eldorado indeed! Lucky Ashanti Goldfields! The very name quickens my pulse … at the thought of stirring events and happy endings.'[14]

Inevitably, the real story was less straightforward. Joseph Chamberlain had hoped that gold would drive the Gold Coast's economic development, but by 1910, cocoa exports were more valuable and would remain so for much of the twentieth century. The gold 'jungle boom' of the early twentieth century was followed by a slump in production during the First World War and Great Depression.[15] As for Edwin Cade, he found fortune, but not happiness. In December 1897, he wrote to his children in England from Obuasi: 'So lonely, and, often, so difficult and hopeless. Fancy living in a town without a single chimney to be seen. Where one drinks rain water – where horrid vultures live and are a necessity. Where all the people are black and talk a strange and unmusical speech; no shops; no drains; very few windows and where all the people are so unclean.'[16] In June 1903, while visiting a potential new site for gold production elsewhere in Asante, he died of malaria.[17]

Asante chiefs and landowners were 'alarmed and enraged' by the new gold-mining concessions, including that at Obuasi, according to Adu Boahen.[18] But they were powerless to prevent them or to help the exiled Prempeh. In November 1896, the British decided to move the Asantehene and almost thirty other prisoners – prominent Asante chiefs, wives, children and attendants – from Elmina to Freetown in Sierra Leone, to reduce further the risk of their interference in Kumasi politics. The British official who informed them of their fate described their reaction: 'They calmly received the news, but in spite of their self control, I could see that they were disconcerted by it, and Prempeh burst into perspiration.'[19] Prempeh begged to be allowed to stay at Elmina, saying he was a bad sailor – Freetown was five days away by boat – and professed obedience to the British, but in vain.

In Freetown Prempeh and the exiles lived in relative freedom. Their interpreter was Kofi Nti, Kofi Karikari's son who had been offered up for a British education after the 1874 Treaty of Fomena. Nti and the exiles had a difficult relationship. He said they only attended church so as 'to make the Government here consider that they had repented ... but their wickedness is s[t]ill as it is,' and he accused Prempeh of trying to prevent a son from going to school. Prempeh and his companions petitioned the British in 1897 and twice in 1898 to be allowed home and promised to pay the indemnity, but they were turned down each time. In Kumasi, in August 1898, the chiefs sent a plea of their own to the new British Governor of the Gold Coast, Sir Frederick Hodgson. They asked for Prempeh's return, said they regretted the past and were 'proud now to be under the power of the English Government'. Hodgson was unmoved.[20]

On 25 March 1900, Governor Hodgson paid his first visit to Kumasi.[21] He was accompanied on the twelve-day journey by foot and hammock from Accra by his wife, Lady Mary Hodgson, the first British woman to visit the Asante capital. The historian Alan Lloyd describes the Governor as 'a determined man with a square jaw, bull neck and well-cushioned torso.' As for Lady Hodgson: 'It would have been hard to find a more typical example of English beauty, with her soft, widely-set eyes, a fine sharp profile of the type that delighted Gainsborough, a girlish figure and fair tresses ... hung in gentle curves to the fashionable concavity of her waist.'[22] This might give the impression of a society debutante stranded in the African interior. In fact, Lady Hodgson had Gold Coast pedigree as her father had also been Governor in the early 1880s but died only a year after taking up the post.[23] She was devoted to both Empire and husband and would be a fierce defender of his reputation after the disastrous events which would soon unfold.

Even before Governor Hodgson stepped foot in Kumasi, he had managed to exacerbate its mood of simmering resentment.[24] In February 1900 he had sent Captain Cecil Armitage – later the Sir Cecil whose Asante objects would prove a significant addition to the British Museum's collection – to a village near Kumasi to find the Golden Stool, *Sika Dwa* itself, which the Asante had hidden after 1896 and whose capture, he believed, would consolidate Britain's authority. Captain Armitage did not find the Golden Stool – he was given false information by a defector – but even his failed mission caused consternation amongst the Asante. The British had already taken their king, but if they were to take the Golden Stool as well, Asante's soul, and what remained of its unity, would also disappear. 'In hearing that the Governor intended to seize the Golden Stool people all over Ashanti drank "Fetish" together to swear an Oath,' writes Prempeh II in *History of Ashanti*. 'Then they would rise up against the British oppressors and fight against them and throw them out of Ashanti.'[25] What more did they have to lose?

Superficially, all was well as the Hodgsons arrived in Kumasi. They were met by schoolchildren, who had been taught by the Ramseyers, the indefatigable Swiss missionaries who had been prisoners in Kumasi in the 1870s and had returned after 1896, still determined to save Asante souls. Mrs Ramseyer presented Lady Hodgson with a bouquet, the children sang 'God Save the Queen' and 'it was pleasant to hear our beautiful National Anthem sung at a place where only a few years before human sacrifice and every horror of savagery has been enacted.' Except, as Lady Hodgson would soon discover, things were not as they seemed, for 'alas! ... many of those who were present had in their hearts a detestation of the white man and all his ways.' The various kings and chiefs paraded before the governor. 'What a farce it all seems now to look back upon! ... this show of loyalty was in most cases a mere pretence.' Lady Hodgson admired the Asante gold regalia, abundant despite the pillage of recent years. There were gold crowns and swords, 'an impressive display of barbaric grandeur. The kings, dressed in multi-coloured and gaudy robes of silk or velvet, and decked with solid gold ornaments of native workmanship in such profusion as to excite one's envy.'[26]

Three days later, Governor Sir Frederick Hodgson, in military uniform and with Lady Hodgson by his side, spoke to the assembled Asante chiefs in the clearing by the fort. If some had hoped for a conciliatory message, they were soon disabused. Prempeh would never return to occupy the Golden Stool, Hodgson told them, as the British Resident Commissioner had taken his place and 'could order them to do any kind of work he wanted them to do'. Nor had Hodgson forgotten Wolseley's indemnity and he announced the Asante would pay annual interest of £16,000 on this, (equivalent to just over £2 million pounds today) although ten per cent would be returned to chiefs who helped collect the money. The Asante were also liable for expenses incurred by the 1895–6 expedition, Hodgson explained. Then, he delivered the shocking denouement: 'Where is the Golden Stool? Why am I not sitting on the Golden Stool at this moment?' he demanded. 'I am the representative of the paramount power; why have you relegated me to this chair? Why did you not take the opportunity of my coming to Kumasi to bring the Golden Stool and give it to me to sit upon?'[27]

'The Ashantis listened to this astonishing speech in deep and complete silence,' writes Prempeh II.[28] An Asantehene, much less a foreign overlord, has no right to sit on the Golden Stool, which is much more than a mere accoutrement of royalty. Hodgson had issued an 'arrogant and blasphemous demand' according to Adu Boahen.[29] In a subsequent letter to Joseph Chamberlain, Hodgson only says he 'referred' to the Golden Stool as he was 'certain that until the Government possesses this symbol of power ... it will not be wholly secure against intrigues and trouble.'[30] Later, amidst controversy as to what he had hoped to achieve, his wife defended him stoutly. His speech 'was in all respects careful and temperate' and had been misrepresented.³¹ It was 'absolutely untrue' that he demanded the Golden Stool, although he did say he hoped the Asante would produce it, 'not of course for him to sit upon' as calumnious accounts suggested, 'but to show their recognition of the Queen's position'.³² It is a subtle distinction, which suggests her husband was tactless, at best. But Chamberlain, when asked in Parliament, said the government's information was that Hodgson had indeed asked the Asante chiefs 'why they had not brought the golden stool to which [Queen Victoria] was entitled, and on which he should sit as the representative of the paramount power'.³³

Governor Hodgson's speech was the spark that ignited what Adu Boahen describes as 'the most protracted, bloody, and as it turned out, the last of the Anglo-Asante wars'.³⁴ Speaking in 1970, an old man called Kwabena Baako reminisced about how it started. 'The whites told the Asante they would bring Prempe back ... The Asante waited for three years. Prempe did not come back. After three years the whites came again for the Golden Stool. The war began.' He had been a 'sword bearer and war captain' in Ejisu, a town about twenty kilometres east of Kumasi.³⁵

Another Ejisu elder, Opanin Kwabena Boadu, had a more specific memory of the evening after the Governor's speech, as the shocked chiefs gathered to formulate their response. The Queen Mother of Ejisu, Yaa Asantewaa, about seventy years old, argued forcefully for war. Her cherished grandson Kofi Afrane, the King of Ejisu, was amongst the Asante leaders whom the British had taken into exile in 1896. 'How can a proud and brave people like the Asante sit back and look while white men take away their king and chiefs, and humiliate them with demands for the Golden Stool ... If you, the chiefs of Asante, are going to behave like cowards and not fight, you should exchange your loincloths for my undergarments, *Montu mo danta mma me na monye me tam*.' She leapt up and fired a gun and the chiefs, stirred – or shamed – into action, agreed to follow her and took oaths to fight the British.³⁶

Tom McCaskie, the British historian of Asante, says Yaa Asantewaa was motivated 'in part by patriotism (or a comprehensible xenophobia) and her embittered family feeling' but also by the specific interests of Ejisu itself, which had long nurtured a grievance over lost land and revenue within the Asante confederacy.[37] Today Yaa Asantewaa is revered not just in Asante and Ghana but across Africa and its diaspora, commemorated on banknotes, stamps and statues, and has schools and many little girls named after her. Margaret Busby, the Ghanaian-born British publisher, wrote that her courage in the face of 'foreign oppression' inspired activists and freedom fighters who followed in her wake: 'All Africans owe this heroic woman an incalculable debt.'[38] In Ghana the war which began in the days that followed Governor Hodgson's speech is often simply called 'the Yaa Asantewaa War'.

★★★

Governor Hodgson, seemingly unaware of the looming crisis, only poured oil on the fire when he despatched Captain Cecil Armitage and forty-five soldiers on another mission to find the Golden Stool, following a further tip-off. They marched with picks and shovels to the village of Bare, where Armitage wrote, 'everyone laboured amid great excitement to dig up the floor.' It took them an hour to dig a metre or so through the hard clay, but excitement turned to disappointment 'for there was no sign whatever of buried treasure.' On 2 April, on their return through Bare, they fell into an Asante ambush. 'A terrific fire was opened immediately all round the village, the slugs thudding on the walls and falling on the thatched roof like hail.'[39] They were the first shots fired between Asante and British soldiers since 1874. Armitage, shot in the neck and thigh, led a desperate return to Kumasi. 'This was merely a skirmish,' wrote Prempeh II in *History of Ashanti*, 'but it disclosed to everyone that war with the British was inevitable and now imminent.'[40]

On 5 April, the Reuters news agency reported from Accra that something had gone very wrong with Governor Hodgson's mission to Kumasi. 'The wires have been cut, communication has been stopped, and despatches have been destroyed. A force of Hausas is leaving here for the interior. The situation appears to be serious.'[41] From the British point of view yet another Asante war could not have come at a worse time. The army was stretched elsewhere, in the struggle to overcome the Boers in South Africa and reinforcements from Britain were not an option. Instead, Chamberlain ordered soldiers to be sent from Sierra Leone and the Nigerian protectorates, but it was not clear whether these would arrive in time to rescue the beleaguered force in Kumasi. The Asante chiefs presented their conditions: that Prempeh be released and returned, that Wolseley's indemnity be cancelled once and for all, that the Asante no longer work as carriers and labourers and that the British immediately stop their search for the Golden Stool. But Hodgson rejected all of these.[42] By 25 April, Asante soldiers had captured Kumasi's mission buildings, prison and hospital, and set the barracks on fire. Hodgson and his wife, the British officers and their Hausa soldiers, the Ramseyers and other missionaries, as well as several prominent Asante chiefs who had joined the British cause, had retreated to the fort. Lady Hodgson, with a keen sense of Victorian melodrama, wrote that they were 'hemmed in by savage hordes'.[43] The siege had begun.

The Asante blocked the roads leading to the fort with stockades, 'with the intention of starving the people inside', according to Prempeh II's *History of Ashanti*.[44] Fante traders, Christian converts, carriers and the families of Hausa soldiers all scrambled to climb the fort walls, but the British and their allies beat them back. 'I felt very much for these poor people,' wrote Lady Hodgson, 'but besides the fact that the fort would not have accommodated a third of them, the whole space was wanted for the troops and for defensive purposes.' She ran a soup kitchen for the children of these refugees, 'some hundred black mites', but had little to offer them except water thickened with crumbs, supplemented with the occasional crow shot by British officers. These were the only birds left in Kumasi, according to Captain Armitage, even 'the vultures and kites had long since left us to seek their food in the rebel camps.'[45]

The British slaughtered their five cows and two sheep at regular intervals, but 'poultry, eggs and fruit were not to be had for love or money' and they were running out of medicine. They tried to conserve their supplies on the basis of a military, and racial, hierarchy. Europeans were given a pound of tinned meat – 'often found to be enriched by a coating of green mould' – and four ounces of weevil-infested biscuits per day, while African soldiers received one third the European allocation of meat and fewer biscuits, and the carriers received only biscuits.[46] By mid-May, Lady Hodgson writes, 'things looked very black and dismal. The rains were in full force. Europeans and natives were constantly ill from the unwholesome and unnutritious food ... to add to our distress small-pox broke out among the natives.' By June, they had eaten their way further down the unappetising food chain; 'rats, lizards, parrots, dogs and pets of all kinds had long since disappeared,' some people were going mad from hunger and others were dying from eating poisonous roots which caused their faces to blow up like footballs.[47]

At night the British listened to the Asante drums and imagined they heard the gunfire of endlessly rumoured relief columns. Two small British forces did fight their way up from the coast, in late April and mid-May, but rather than 'relief' they brought more injured men and hungry mouths. Seven hundred and fifty people were now crowded into the fort.[48] And yet, even amidst these 'weary, weary days' there were almost surreal moments of levity and ceremony. Lady Hodgson hosted '"starvation" dinner parties' with make-believe food, as well as games of loo and solo-whist for the officers, the gramophone played an increasingly scratchy 'Rule Britannia' and on the Queen's birthday, 24 May, their cheers 'were certainly as heartfelt as any that were given elsewhere on that day.' (Cecil Armitage writes, with no attribution, that the Asante were especially interested in capturing Lady Hodgson as they believed she was Queen Victoria's niece and that he was Lady Hodgson's son and had prepared 'a small hut somewhere in the depths of the forest' to keep them before sending them as a 'present to the Great White Queen, against whom, they said, they had no quarrel.')[49] On 6 June the 'Inmates of the Fort of Kumasi' posed for a photograph in the courtyard, the ladies in elegant dresses and the men in bow ties and suits, looking as if they had gathered on the terrace for croquet at a Victorian house party.[50]

By mid-June the British and their soldiers inside the fort faced an unenviable dilemma. They could stay behind their walls with their Maxim guns and risk starving to death waiting for a rescue that might never come or, enfeebled as they were, they could make a break for freedom and hope to evade the Asante army and reach friendlier territory to the south. Governor Hodgson decided on the latter. He took about 600 soldiers with him. Most of the 100 who were left behind were sick or injured, under the care of a doctor almost too weak to stand. The Governor's parting words on the morning of 23 June would have brought them little comfort, 'Well, you have a supply of food for twenty-three days and are safe for that period, but we are going to die today.'[51]

'Inmates of the Fort of Kumasi', as if at a Victorian house party.

Yaa Asantewaa after her capture. 'The most amazing native woman…'

14

'GOLD WAS A PERFECT CURSE'

The bedraggled column assembled in the early hours under the fort walls, 'enveloped', wrote Lady Hodgson, 'in a blue-white mist, which hung like a death shadow over all'.[1] They took a westerly route out of Kumasi, to avoid the Asante army to the south, a secret deception planned by Governor Hodgson and a handful of officers. Lady Hodgson's description of the 'terrible march' that followed is one of sustained fear, frequent ambushes and incessant rain. Exhausted carriers drowned in muddy swamps or disappeared into the forest to forage for food and were never seen again, Lady Hodgson and the Ramseyers and other missionary wives ran for their lives along jungle paths and two British officers and dozens of soldiers were shot dead or went missing, with many others wounded. On the first night, huddled together in a muddy clearing, soaking and hungry, she writes, 'Sheer exhaustion gave me fitful doses but always with dreams that the Ashantis were pursuing me, and I woke up to know that they were not without foundation, for could I not hear the incessant beating of their drums.'[2] Fortunately for the escapees, the Asante soldiers were more intent on pillaging their supplies than pressing home their military advantage. 'The Ashantis captured many of the carriers and much booty,' wrote Prempeh II in *History of Ashanti*.[3] A British account – of the path littered with the headless corpses of the carriers and their women and children – is much more gruesome.[4]

On 25 June 1900, the British column had reached comparative safety. By now, the reinforcements from elsewhere in West Africa had arrived in the Gold Coast and were marching towards Kumasi. Colonel Charles Carter, who commanded some 200 men from the Southern Nigeria protectorate fell into an Asante ambush at a place called Dompoase and was shot in the eye.[5] Captain Ernest Roupell was shot through both arms and then the head in the same battle. Carter recovered to become a First World War brigadier-general, but Roupell was invalided out of the army soon afterwards. (Both men had earlier played prominent roles in the British sacking of Benin in 1897, and the Asante-Benin connection worked the other way as well. Bruce Meade Hamilton, a major on Colonel Sir Francis Scott's staff in the 1895–6 Asante expedition, later commanded the British soldiers in Benin.)

On 15 July Colonel James Willcocks fought his way into Kumasi. Willcocks had been summoned from the Northern Nigeria protectorate in early May and had travelled as fast as possible to board a ship at Lagos, overcoming bouts of blindness, food poisoning, blistered feet and a swollen knee.[6] In Kumasi he found a 'terrible scene (of) desolation and of horror; stench sickening; nothing but burnt down houses and putrid bodies to be seen, the latter right up to (the) fort. Garrison delighted beyond words. Native soldiers most of them too weak to stand. British officers thanked God for relief, as a few days more would have seen the last of the defence.' He paid tribute to his African soldiers, who had driven the Asante army out of the city. 'I am proud of Yoruba native soldiers, West African Frontier Force, who formed bulk of charging force … Their gallant conduct is the admiration of every officer present.'[7]

The most senior British officer left behind by Hodgson, Captain Frederick Bishop, had resolved with a colleague that they would kill themselves with poison if too weak to resist the Asante. Instead, he celebrated Willcocks's arrival by opening 'a pint bottle of champagne – one of our few remaining medical comforts', and shared it with his liberators.[8] In 2023 an art dealer friend in London showed me a handsome coiled gold disc, wrapped in a scrap of paper, which he keeps in a drawer in his Marylebone office. The faded handwriting read, 'This piece of gold was given to Captain F Bishop, in exchange for a biscuit full of weevils, in the Siege of Kumasi in 1900.' A poignant souvenir, procured by Bishop in the midst of an ordeal he doubted he would survive.

I found the well-preserved graves – marble headstones amid beds of gravel – of the handful of British officers who died in the Siege of Kumasi Fort in what is today the car park of the adjacent High Court building. They are individually named too, in a plaque above the fort entrance, as is one African soldier, 'Native Officer Akkere', whereas the remainder of the Africans who fought and died for the British are only referred to as 'seventy-nine non commissioned officers and men'. The Asante soldiers who fought against the British are denied even this cursory dignity. The fort curator, Emmanuel Quainoo, told me that, in 1983, an archaeologist found a mass grave below the walls, containing the bones of about 100 people, buried with muskets. They were assumed to be Asante soldiers, buried by the British during the siege to prevent disease. Emmanuel suspected there were other mass graves nearby, beneath the tarmac of the High Court car park. He showed me a small wooden box containing a few bone fragments, all that remains in the fort of this 1983 discovery.[9]

Recovering in genteel Surbiton, Lady Hodgson penned her Kumasi memoirs. 'So ended one of the five historic sieges of 1900,' she wrote (presumably referring to those which also took place that year in Kimberley, Ladysmith, Mafeking and Peking), 'in one of the worst climates in the world. The enemy was a savage and bloodthirsty one, and our only defenders were black troops, many of whom were recruits and inexperienced.'[10]

Savage and bloodthirsty? The Asante had no monopoly on cruelty in this war. In Willcocks's first report to London, he said his 75-millimetre artillery guns had caused 'terrible havoc' on the Asante defending the stockades who had 'left behind a great many mangled dead'.[11] From the relief of the fort onwards, the war followed a more familiar pattern, in which the British, with their superior weapons, wrested the advantage. Willcocks sent his soldiers, as he put it, to 'criss-cross the Kumasi district burning villages and chopping down anything that still grew in the field'.[12] In August 1900, he described a 'loot-laden Column' of soldiers from the

Nigerian protectorates marching into Bekwai to the delight of the local king, an ally of the British. The soldiers had 'captured articles of every conceivable description; foremost were several gold ornaments, some small bags of gold dust, about £100 in cash, flags, chairs, state umbrellas, clothing, books ... distributed amongst the troops who had helped to capture them'. Willcocks described his West African soldiers and local allies, or levies, as 'locusts ... devouring the farm produce and making themselves as unpleasant as possible ... The Ashantis have a habit of burying their treasure and ornaments, and I cannot but think that the many thousand Levies which eventually joined us must have searched out some of these hidden treasures.'[13]

The divisions within the Asante grew more acute as their situation worsened. Tom McCaskie describes this war 'as a nationalist uprising, but hardly a national one *en masse*,' as 'most Asante villagers remained prudently or fearfully inactive when it came to taking up arms.'[14] By September 1900 even Yaa Asantewaa was flirting with surrender but changed her mind due to 'the rough treatment' her envoys received at the hands of local levies.[15] She then sent a defiant message to the British to the effect that she would rather die than hand herself in and warned that her soldiers would 'surround any columns sent out against them, shoot down the white officers and slaughter the black soldiers'.[16] But in that same month, the British routed the Asante at Biemso (also called Obassa) to the north-west of Kumasi, where Colonel Willcocks reported 'their flight was a panic: they left guns, ammunition and everything they owned ... no attempt was made to remove their belongings nor even their dead. Sixty-two bodies lay in our direct front ... and I afterwards found we had killed one hundred and fifty.'[17] On 24 November Joseph Chamberlain in London received the good news from Willcocks: 'The campaign is at an end.'

On the following day, Asantewaa's most senior commander, Kwabena Kyere – 'a cruel murderer who had tortured to death many British subjects' according to Willcocks – was marched in chains to the Kumasi marketplace by the fort and hanged.[18] He and other Asante leaders had been hiding in the forests of Ahafo, but were betrayed by a local chief. Asante elders interviewed in the early twentieth century remembered how Kyere 'hated the British. Once in Kumasi after Prempeh was taken away he was beaten by Hausa soldiers who dragged him before a British judge. He was put into jail for a short time and gold dust that was on his person was taken away and he never could forget this and wanted a revenge.'[19] A British historian, a former military officer who had served with the Gold Coast regiment, wrote that Kyere's 'crimes had been numerous and unpleasant ... among other things he had a playful habit of cutting off the hands of his victims and otherwise mutilating them before turning them into the forest to die.'[20] A British officer wrote in 1901 that Kyere 'marched to the scaffold with the utmost sang-froid, with a look of contemptuous and undying hate upon his face ... his bearing was so manly that an involuntary murmur of admiration rose from the crowd of onlookers.'[21] Kyere spat and insulted his executioners as they put the noose around his neck. An Asante legend says that as he swung from the scaffold, a dark cloud covered the sun, but then cleared away. 'People took this as an omen that the British were like the clouds in as much as they too would pass.'[22]

Yaa Asantewaa did not surrender until 3 March 1901, many months after the fighting was over. In February 1935, Lieutenant-Colonel Samuel Hingley wrote to *The Times* from retirement in Somerset with his 'fairly vivid recollection' of that day. He had been the chief staff officer of the Ashanti Field Force and received Yaa Asantewaa outside the fort just after dawn. She was 'an old, shrivelled, ferocious, and extremely angry, tiny woman' who spat at him as he forcibly removed her symbol of royalty, 'a string of remarkable native beads'. In the days that followed, the relationship between Yaa Asantewaa and Hingley thawed somewhat. They spoke twice a day through an interpreter and 'we became quite friendly and even chatty!' wrote Hingley, for she was 'a wonderful old woman' even if her reign had been one of 'cruelty and blood'. A simple truth dawned on him, she was 'a patriot none the less, with no use for the white man'.[23] In 1937 Hingley said on BBC radio that Yaa Asantewaa was simply 'the most amazing native woman who ever lived in Africa'.[24]

★★★

Colonel James Willcocks led the West African Colonial Contingent at Queen Victoria's funeral in February 1901 and attended Edward VII's inaugural opening of Parliament, where the King 'expressed his high appreciation of the work of the Ashanti Field Force'.[25] Willcocks was feted in Liverpool and Manchester, and in London the Ashanti Goldfields Corporation gave a dinner for him at the Metropole Hotel, where Edwin Arthur Cade spoke in his honour.[26] Joseph Chamberlain also hosted a dinner to celebrate the end of what he called 'undoubtedly, the most serious rebellion with which we have ever had to deal in that part of the world'. Addressing Willcocks, Chamberlain said the British had fought 'a great, a dominant, a courageous tribe of savages to whose gallantry you have done full justice on many occasions ... I believe you and the Ashanti Field Force have shown these great characteristics of a great governing race.'[27]

Once again, just as in 1874 and 1896, the jingoism does not tell the whole story and in Parliament there was an undercurrent of unease. Had Governor Hodgson been acting under government instructions when he demanded the Golden Stool? In August 1900 Chamberlain blandly told MPs he did not know why the Asante had risen up, while in December he said he was 'not aware' of any government insistence that the Golden Stool be surrendered.[28] Hodgson, it seems, was being hung out to dry. Parliament debated Asante in March 1901 and William Redmond spoke powerfully, just as he had in 1896. 'Almost simultaneously with this expensive and sanguinary military expedition', he said, 'there were floated in the City limited liability companies for the exploration and exploitation of the gold-fields of Ashanti. There never was a case in which it was more clearly proved that gold was a perfect curse to the people of the country in which it might be discovered.' C. P. Scott, Boer War critic and later owner of the *Manchester Guardian*, was scathing of Hodgson. If the Asante had 'surrendered the Golden Stool it meant they ceased to be a nation,' he said, 'and became a scattered number of tribes ... The expedition was undertaken without any knowledge of the feelings of the Ashantis.' David Lloyd George, the future prime minister, said 'the quest of the Golden Stool was something like the quest of the Holy

Grail.' Swatting the young Winston Churchill's objections aside, he said Hodgson had been hypocritical to demand the Asante work as carriers and road-builders: 'The Ashantis might be savages, but at any rate they were a very intelligent race, and they could see the utter hollowness of the demand made by us for the suppression of slavery when we were forcing slavery upon them.'[29]

Colonel Willcocks described the campaign to a Reuters journalist. 'The Ashanti power is absolutely smashed,' he explained. 'Every one of their towns and villages has been thoroughly searched and their farms and fetish groves destroyed ... hundreds of fetish groves, with their sacrificial houses, were razed to the ground. Moreover, every chief who took part in the rebellion has either been killed in action or is a prisoner.'[30] If the army had been comprised only of white British soldiers, Willcocks argued, it could never have fought in such arduous conditions, whereas the African soldiers had done 'splendid work ... there were many instances of valour which would have earned white soldiers the Victoria Cross.' In July 1901 he was presented with the Freedom of the City of London at the Guildhall and dedicated the honour to 'all the officers, British non-commissioned officers, Sikhs, and African soldiers who so faithfully, loyally, and ungrudgingly had given their strength, health and lives in the service of the Sovereign'.[31]

Willcocks's words might have rung hollow to anyone who had paid close attention to the situation in the Gold Coast. The British triumph had come at a high cost, and not only to the Asante. The official report into the campaign reveals the plight of African carriers, some 10,000 of whom had been hurriedly shipped to the Gold Coast from East and other parts of West Africa because of what the British said was the refusal of the 'coast tribes' to serve in Asante territory ('lazy and indolent, thorough cowards, they preferred to risk a flogging rather than do a day's work'). The contingent from Central Africa suffered 'an outbreak of pneumonia' at sea which resulted in dozens of deaths en route and 'arrived in a most pitiful condition'. But the health of all the carriers in the campaign 'was undoubtedly poor; small-pox, phthisis [tuberculosis] and dysentery causing great ravages amongst them'. The army says that 3,581 were admitted to hospital, while its suspiciously round total of '400' deaths implies that nobody had taken too much trouble to count.[32]

In December 1900, when Colonel Willcocks was leaving Kumasi, he had told the 450 Sierra Leonean soldiers of the West Africa Regiment that they too would soon return home. But three months later, the Sierra Leoneans were still there. Their pay was in arrears, barracks uncomfortable, food inedible and equipment in poor condition. They were led by Colonel Charles Burroughs, who attracted mixed reviews from his British colleagues: 'very keen ... always anxious and ready for hard work', wrote Willcocks, whereas another officer described him as 'an extraordinary little colonel ... who has gout and can't wear a boot and has never been on service on his life.' His soldiers seemed to resent him; one said that 'he punish too much and flog plenty.'[33] The final straw came on 18 March, when Colonel Burroughs announced he was going on leave to Britain the next day, eleven days early.

Some 400 Sierra Leoneans marched down to Cape Coast in a disciplined fashion but in defiance of their officers. At Cape Coast, they 'encamped on the parade ground, behaving in a most orderly manner', according to a British officer.[34] Their leader, Private Morlai Mandingo – 'a very brave man who had been injured three times' fighting the Asante according to another officer – was arrested, pulled inside Cape Coast Castle, tied to a ladder and shot: 'a gruesome duty.'[35] Most of the Sierra Leoneans then surrendered, were disarmed and put on a ship to Freetown. But about 160, 'the worst of the mutineers' according to a Gold Coast newspaper, instead started to march westwards, apparently hoping to make the journey home, some 2,000 kilometres, by foot. By now their discipline had broken down and they pillaged villages on their way. The British were concerned, above all, that the mutiny would provoke renewed unrest in Asante and hurriedly sent troops back to Kumasi. 'I was not a little disturbed,' wrote an officer. 'It was just a year previously that the Ashantis seized the opportunity to rise. Would they use this regrettable incident to do so again?'[36] HMS *Forte* was sent in pursuit and caught up with the Sierra Leoneans at the village of Atuarbo. There, Colonel Herbert Brake of the Central African Rifles ordered his men to open fire on their former comrades with a Maxim gun and rifles, while the *Forte* shelled them from the sea. The Sierra Leoneans, hemmed in by swamps, had nowhere to hide. Twelve were killed and twenty wounded. 'Great credit' was due to Colonel Brake, according to *The Times*.[37] 'Poor brutes', said Matthew Nathan, who had taken over from Frederick Hodgson as Governor of the Gold Coast.[38]

A court of enquiry was set up in Freetown. Colonel Burroughs was rebuked and retired on half-pay. His disgrace was lamented in the *Army and Navy Gazette*, which described him as 'the bright, genial, and warm-hearted "little Charles Burroughs" who was such a familiar figure in all regimental gatherings.'[39] Six mutineers were given death sentences, later commuted to life imprisonment. Others received prison sentences. Most were fined and retained in the regiment. In Parliament, Thomas Lough, the MP for Islington West and a critic of the war, asked William Brodrick, by now Secretary of State for War, 'whether any care had been taken to make these troops understand the crime they committed?' MPs laughed and the Speaker did not allow the question.[40]

Prempeh sails into exile. Twenty-eight years passed before he was allowed to go home.

15

'CONSIDER HOW WRETCHED I AM'

Princess Molly Prempeh, a handsome and animated woman in her eighties, was waiting for me outside her house, at the bottom of a bumpy road in a village one hour's drive south through the sprawl which stretches out of Kumasi. Molly, a retired teacher, is Asantehene Prempeh's great-granddaughter and she likes to wear gold earrings and *kente* cloth. She has lived most of her life in and around Kumasi, but she was born on an island thousands of miles away, in the middle of the Indian Ocean. 'I'm the only remaining person here who was born in Seychelles,' she says. 'I'm Seychellois and Ghanaian, I was five years old when I came back. But I travel back to see my cousins.'

Molly uses the word 'back', I realised, to describe a journey to Kumasi just as she does for one to the Seychelles. In her old age, she has reconnected with the beautiful island nation of her birth and has made two visits in recent years and was busy planning a third. 'Sesel! I speak "Old Creole,"' she explained, 'they don't speak that there now, but they understand me. They are happy and astonished. "You can speak Old Creole! This woman!"' She laughed. 'They love me, they adore me, they cherish me. When I walk down the streets they shout "Heh Princess, how are you?!" "*Princess, vini, vini, tou i byen?*" They are lovely people. They love the

Prempehs in Sesel.' But her visits are tinged with sadness and memories of her mother, Hugette, who brought Molly as a young girl to the Gold Coast in 1948. When Molly was growing up in Kumasi, Hugette told her to never forget her native language, her Creole. But when Hugette returned to the Seychelles in 1969, the story goes, she in turn clung to her Twi, the language passed on to her as a little girl by Prempeh himself. Hugette, whom Molly never saw again, died in the Seychelles in 2005. She is buried in the Mont Fleuri cemetery on the Seychelles' largest island Mahé, where Molly goes to pray and weep. One family's extraordinary story, of loss and exile, but also endurance and cultural enrichment, all the legacy of Britain's determination to crush Asante independence.[1]

Sir Frederick Hodgson returned to Accra in July 1900, having survived the Siege of Kumasi, and telegrammed the Colonial Office in London the following day. Prempeh, he warned, was still able to influence events in Asante from Sierra Leone. The Asantehene had already been in exile for more than four years and was in his own words 'quite ignorant' of

Princess Molly Prempeh, proudly Asante, Ghanaian and Seychellois.

the latest outbreak of war, but the British now decided to remove him from West Africa altogether.² Joseph Chamberlain chose the Seychelles, a British possession since the beginning of the nineteenth century, as a suitably remote location. The Asante party of exiles, by now grown to more than fifty, sailed out of Freetown harbour on board the transport ship *Dwarka* on 19 August and arrived in the Seychelles almost a month later.³

They were taken to an old French sugar estate at Le Rocher, near Victoria, the Seychelles' capital on Mahé, overlooking the ocean and surrounded by coconut, mango, breadfruit, orange and jackfruit trees. Prempeh was given the estate's two-storey villa, while the British built sixteen wooden houses with corrugated metal roofs for his chiefs and their dependents.⁴ The estate was kept in good order and Prempeh and the chiefs awarded monthly allowances and free healthcare.⁵ In 1901, his little community grew, as Yaa Asantewaa and some twenty chiefs and attendants were also sent to the Seychelles following their surrender. Prempeh had 'a striking and marvellous personality', wrote a British official, and 'amongst his own entourage his word was law.'⁶ The initial

Prempeh with family, followers and British officials, Mahé, Seychelles.

restrictions on 'Ashanti Camp' – everyone home by 6.30 p.m., written permission for visitors – were soon lifted.[7] After all, the Asante were prisoners of geography, with no escape from their tropical paradise.

In November 1900, Archdeacon Henry Buswell of the Church Mission Society wrote that he was impressed by Prempeh's desire to embrace Christianity. 'One day, when I was trying as simply as possible to illustrate the teaching of the Lord's Prayer, he said, as it seemed to me, very feelingly, "I should like to give my heart to God."'[8] Both Anglican and Catholic priests on the Seychelles were keen to convert him. 'What religion is the King of England?' Prempeh is said to have asked, and upon being told, took a decidedly pragmatic decision: 'I am of opinion that all kings should have the same religion, therefore I accept the Church of England.'[9] In May 1904 Prempeh and the Queen Mother, Yaa Akyia, were baptised as Edward and Elizabeth. 'That is a doubtful thing which no one or many expected it will be one day, that King of Ashanti will be a Christian,' wrote Timothy Korsah, a Fante interpreter who had accompanied Prempeh from Sierra Leone.[10] Prempeh, argues Albert Adu Boahen, was not only determined 'to become a good and dedicated Christian' but also 'rigidly and uncompromisingly imposed that religion on his fellow political prisoners and their children'.[11]

In the Anglican Church of St Paul's, every Sunday, the Asante mixed with the descendants of African slaves, as well as the Indians, British officials and French settlers of Seychellois society. They were not the only exiles in the congregation, however, for they often sat next to King Mwanga of Buganda and King Kabalega of Bunyoro. Both these men, from what is today Uganda, had also resisted British rule and were taken to the Seychelles in 1899. Mwanga would die there in 1903, while Kabalega was allowed to leave the Seychelles as an old man in 1923, only to die en route to his home.[12] To see these displaced African kings side by side in church, wrote a British official, was 'a spectacle ... not devoid of interest'.[13]

Timothy Korsah wrote in 1904: 'Ex-King Prempeh now read and write fair well and sign over his own voucher of payment. And so do by some of the chiefs also.'[14] Prempeh's sons and nephews went to fee-paying schools in Victoria. In December 1900 a British official wrote that 'the recitation by the son of Prempeh of a short piece of English poetry was very creditable considering that the lad had only been learning English for some five weeks.' In 1908 we learn that another son's 'homework is consistently bad and caning seems to affect him little.' But in 1909 the Gold Coast government provided funds for the establishment of an 'Ashanti Camp School', which typically had some thirty children in attendance and was regularly visited by an Anglican chaplain.[15]

Prempeh's state of mind and motives, in his apparent transformation from 'barbarian king' to 'loyal' and 'civilised' British subject, are fascinating to interpret. Was his conversion strategic? His fate was in his captors' hands, and so his only chance of repatriation lay in appeasing them.[16] But his journey across two oceans, exposure to new learning and religion, not to mention the relentless passing of years, would surely have shaped and changed his outlook, no matter how determined he had been to resist. Perhaps the pain of exile drove him to seek spiritual solace wherever he could find it. In the Seychelles he also wrote, or in fact dictated through his son Frederick, a history of Asante and its customs, the wonderfully titled *The History of Ashanti Kings and the Whole Country Itself*.[17] This is not as comprehensive as Prempeh II's *History of Ashanti* but is still a valuable riposte to a vast British historiography. Prempeh did not know whether he would ever return to Asante, but he could at least record for posterity what his kingdom had been before it fell to the British.[18]

Some elders clung to the old ways. Kwadwo Appia, who had the title *Offinsohene*, was in his sixties when he arrived in the Seychelles and, according to a grandson, 'did not like the new religion … he had to force himself to attend church service. He was said to be complaining that he was likely to die soon because his soul was against it.'[19] Another chief, Kwabena Nkwantabisa, the *Adansehene*, built a traditional Asante house of mortar and mud in the camp. In the early days of Ashanti Camp, some of the elders, including Yaa Asantewaa, vowed never to speak Creole – 'Asante is the pure language we prefer' – but inevitably the new language crept in, whether it was through children, market traders or servants.[20] So too did Seychelles food – *la dobe* made with breadfruit, coconut and fish – and ways of dressing: trousers, shirts and coats for the men and long dresses and hats for the women. Even Yaa Asantewaa, the very last to yield to the British, was eventually converted to Christianity.[21]

The most poignant act of resistance came from a younger exile. In December 1905, a confused British consul general in Zanzibar, John Houston Sinclair, reported that an Asante boy – 'Petit Coffee' – had turned up in his office, presumably a stowaway from the Seychelles, and was asking to be sent home to Kumasi. This may have been Kofi, a son of Boakye Atonsa, the *Akomforehene*.[22] The dream of return was an enduring theme of the Seychelles years. As early as 1901, Prempeh and his chiefs wrote to the British authorities. They denounced the 'evil life' they had once led and 'therefore beg you most humbly to have pity on us and send us back to Ashanti.' More petitions followed, in 1902 and 1904.[23] In 1913, Prempeh wrote again, now in grovelling terms; the Asante had 'allowed ourselves to be deceived by our own mischieviousness [sic]', their faults had been 'too numerous to procure' and they humbly asked for the 'kind consideration' of the Governor of the Seychelles.[24]

Perhaps their greatest hope lay in the changes Asante society was undergoing back home. In September 1901, Asante – under British rule since 1896 – was formally annexed, put under the direct control of the Gold Coast Colony and divided into four provinces so as to dilute Kumasi's power over the subordinate kingdoms.[25] In October 1903, Joseph Chamberlain's ambition of a railway connecting Kumasi to the coast was finally realised. This was built with 'feverish energy', and along with the bicycle, the motor lorry and an ever-expanding network of roads, pulled Asante into the twentieth century.[26] Many of these changes were driven by the Ashanti Goldfields Corporation and its thousands of employees, 'a civilizing factor in the country' according to a British official, but also the growth of rubber, kola nut and, above all, cocoa exports, which brought prosperity to thousands of Asante farmers.[27] 'It was capitalism – expressed in the rapid spread of cocoa as a cash crop – that reconciled Asante to British colonial overrule,' according to Tom McCaskie.[28]

Sir Francis Fuller, Chief Commissioner of Asante from 1905 to 1920, wrote that he and his British colleagues had been able to 'convert a sullen and suspicious race, still smarting from defeat, into a contented and prosperous people'.[29] Amongst his achievements, Fuller included the delicate dismantling of traditional Asante slavery; slave families could no longer be separated without their consent, an enslaved woman who gave birth through her master became free and slaves had the right to buy their own freedom.[30] Christianity, and Western education, met with a receptive audience. But in *History of Ashanti*, Prempeh II records the changes in this period in less flattering terms; British-appointed chiefs, he writes, 'terrorised their subjects', extorted money from them and coerced them into supplying labour for road-building and other projects, or into sending their children to school.[31]

The ultimate test, from the British point of view, came in the First World War. The Gold Coast Regiment, now based in Kumasi and including many Asante, promptly invaded German Togoland and later fought in the Cameroonian and East Africa campaigns. Asante, according to Fuller, showed 'steadfast loyalty', despite the much-reduced military presence at home. He considered the Asante a 'valiant, clever and lovable people, of whom it is no exaggeration to say that they bear no malice and nurse no grievance … their many fine qualities have gained them the respect and admiration of all who have been fortunate enough to labour with and for them.'[32] In May 1919 a group of Asante political prisoners who had been held in Elmina and Accra since 1900 were allowed to return home and were met by cheering crowds in Kumasi. A British official who accompanied them said they were 'lost in wonderment of the whiteman's transformation of their once war-like country into a peaceful, loyal and industrial, and picturesque part of the Empire'.[33]

Prempeh followed the changes in Asante to the best of his ability, through newspapers and official reports. In letters home, he urged his family to convert to Christianity and go to school. He warned his fellow exiles in the Seychelles that change was inevitable and they needed to adapt. In 1912 he asked the Governor of the Seychelles to send him a magic lantern with pictures of the British Isles that he could share with his people. Some years later, he asked for football and cricket pitches at Ashanti Camp.[34] 'He kept telling us', one said, 'that there will be Christianity, education … on a large scale. And then the people will be much wiser than they were, and so we should get ourselves prepared for it before coming.'[35]

The years went by and the oldest exiles in the Seychelles passed on. Prempeh's father Kwasi Gyambibi died in 1903. In 1917 Prempeh lost his mother Yaa Akyia, the Queen Mother, with whom he enjoyed 'the most enduringly important relationship' of his life, as well as his brother Agyeman Badu. He suffered a 'palpable sense of disorientated loss' but was given permission to keep his relative's remains in a vault, with a view to their eventual repatriation.[36] News of these deaths, conveyed to the chiefs in Kumasi by Sir Francis Fuller, 'greatly grieved the Royal Family and the Chiefs', writes Prempeh II in *History of Ashanti*, and 'played a big part in stirring them' to campaign once more for Prempeh's return.[37] In October 1921, Yaa Asantewaa died, at the age of about ninety. British policy was that when a chief died, his family and followers were to be repatriated and so several groups did return from the Seychelles to Kumasi between 1907 and 1923. Prempeh's pleas to join them became increasingly desperate. In January 1918, he begged King George V to:

> cast a glance over his captives and by His Majesty's great mercy send us word to release us to our native land ... consider how wretched I am for I was being taken prisoner together with father, mother, brother and chiefs for now twenty-two years, and now how miserable to see that father, mother, brother and nearly three quarters of the chiefs are dead. The remaining quarter, some are blind, some worn out with old age and the rest being attacked of diverse diseases. And now I do not find where to glance and where to go to comfort myself.[38]

In September 1921, writes Prempeh II in *History of Ashanti*, 'the whole of Kumasi was thrown into a very great confusion.' People poured into the city from across Asante and 'all of them were wailing and crying and some of them ... voluntarily drank themselves to death in an angry despair. Every person, both old and young, put on mourning cloth and besmeared him or her self with red clay.' This 'unprecedented national sorrow' had been caused by the news of the 'wanton desecration of the Golden Stool'.[39] The Stool, carefully hidden by Asante elders during the two decades of British rule, had been accidentally discovered by a group of road workers digging their way through a forest in August 1920. Initially terrified, some connived with an Asante chief and a goldsmith to melt down and sell artefacts attached to the Stool. This was, Prempeh II writes, 'a national tragedy' and the Asante were 'perturbed and furious at the evil perpetrators'. For the British, the crisis was evidence that Asante nationalism was very much intact, and even raised fears of another uprising. But, on this occasion at least, they handled it with tact and sensitivity.

The British Chief Commissioner for Asante, Charles Harper, expressed his sympathy, but stressed this was an internal Asante matter, to be resolved by the Kumasi chiefs. 'I am not going to call upon you to show to me the Golden Stool or any part of its insignia', he told the chiefs. 'There is wild talk among some that I am going to ask now for the Golden Stool. That is false. I am not going to ask for the Golden Stool.'[40] This letter 'greatly cooled down the furious anger' of the Asante and enabled the British to sidestep demands for the execution of those involved in the theft, who instead were banished or imprisoned. Harper's approach had been encouraged by Captain Robert Rattray, whose appointment in 1921 as Head of an 'Anthropological Department in Ashanti' signalled a belated desire from the British to better understand Asante beliefs and customs. 'I do not think we realize what a power, working for us, this Stool has been, hidden away as it was,' wrote Rattray. 'I believe that it will be found to be the case that all the obedience, the respect and great loyalty we have been given by the Ashanti is given through and by reason of the Golden Stool. I believe that, so far from benefitting, had we ever taken this Stool – which would have been little more than a 'trophy' to us – that its power would have worked against us.'[41]

Six months after the 'affair of the Golden Stool', the Governor of the Gold Coast, Sir Gordon Guggisberg, visited Kumasi, congratulated the chiefs on the wise manner in which they had dealt with it and assured them again the British had no interest in the Stool and 'would help them to preserve the reverence and respect in which the nation held it'.[42]

Guggisberg was sympathetic to the idea of Prempeh's return. If the recent crisis had suggested this would bring risks for the British, it also raised the uncomfortable question of how the Asante would react to his death in exile. By now, moreover, the campaign for Prempeh's return was being championed by prominent figures in the Gold Coast's legislature and newspapers, such as Joseph Casely Hayford and Nana Ofori Atta, the King of Akyem Abuakwa. Slowly, the political calculation for the British was changing, to the point where they had more to lose from prolonging Prempeh's exile than they did from allowing him to return home.

In February 1924, the Liberal MP Dr William Chapple asked James Henry Thomas, the Colonial Secretary in Britain's first Labour government, whether he was aware that Prempeh had now been held on the Seychelles 'over 25 years [sic] without any charge or trial' and whether this 'ruler of a friendly State' should not finally be allowed to return to his country and people. Thomas replied that he 'had not yet been able to acquaint myself with the circumstances of Prempeh's deportation'. Thomas deserves some leeway – he was new in the job – but his answer reveals the gulf between the imperial government with its many and varied commitments and the people of far-flung lands who lived under it.[43] How many British politicians, let alone ordinary people, had followed the fate of the Asante or indeed the Ugandan exiles? (For that matter, how many know today that the British also used the Seychelles, at various times, to exile 'illustrious native kings and princes, troublesome political agitators, and deposed native chiefs' from such diverse lands as Aden, Egypt, Malaysia, the Maldives, Nyasaland, Palestine, Somaliland, Zanzibar and, most recently, Cyprus?)[44] In December 1923, 'all the Paramount and Head Chiefs of Ashanti' had presented yet another petition, stating that Prempeh's return was a matter of 'great urgency' for 'the entire Ashanti nation'.[45] And yet here was the British Colonial Secretary, admitting he knew almost nothing about the case.

Chapple's question, as it happened, was well timed, for in the spring of 1924 the colonies, and even Asante itself, would become untypically prominent in British popular consciousness. On St George's Day, King George V opened the British Empire Exhibition at Wembley, which would attract millions of people over the following two years. The Gold Coast pavilion was, like much of the exhibition, a celebration of wealth the Empire brought to the mother country. Visitors saw a large sign which said the Gold Coast produced almost half the world's cocoa and were presented with medals inscribed 'Gold Coast' and 'Drink More Cocoa'. They walked through an 'Ashanti Village', populated by real Asante people. On 14 April *The Times* reported that the Asante were initially 'lost and forlorn' in a London boarding house, but that once they were able to move into their 'homelike and familiar' village, they were 'vastly happier, and in yesterday's sunshine were all smiles'.[46]

Robert Rattray had recruited these Asante ambassadors, whose job was to drum, dance, weave, carve, cast brass objects and make clay pots and answer questions about their homeland. Today, the whole concept feels grotesquely outdated. And yet, as Malcolm McLeod writes, 'the Asante village and its people was an enormous success, and they became a favourite of the tens of thousands of visitors who flocked to Wembley daily throughout 1924 and 1925.'[47] When George V inspected the village, he was greeted by 'natives ... in magnificent silk togas', went into a straw-roofed hut and was 'quite at home'. He chatted with a weaver, said to be none other than a son of Prempeh, the lonely king the British had sent across the water.[48] We can only wonder what thoughts lay behind the Asante smiles. But did these ambassadors strengthen the case for Prempeh's return, even unwittingly, by simply demonstrating their common humanity with those who met them? Colonial Secretary Thomas had promised Parliament to make enquiries, and he was good to his word. In May 1924 the Chief Commissioner in Kumasi conveyed London's decision: Prempeh could come home.

★★★

On 11 November 1924, the Royal Mail Steamer *Abinsi* anchored off the Gold Coast port of Sekondi. Prempeh and his fifty or so Asante companions – most of whom had actually been born in the Seychelles – had been at sea for two months, travelling via Bombay and Liverpool. One old Asante chief, Kwame Gyansah, weak and blind, had died in the Seychelles just days before the departure. He had been due to travel on an earlier ship in 1922 but had been too frightened of the sea to make the journey.[49]

Prempeh was wearing a European suit and hat. 'We who do not know him are more than anxious to see his face,' wrote the *Gold Coast Leader*. He boarded a train for Kumasi 'amid great cheers and waving of hats', arriving at six o'clock the following morning; many people had slept at the station to greet him. 'The scene presented by the huge assembly of Ashantis with their white head bands signifying rejoicing or victory, some laughing and cheering, while others wept with emotion, was a most moving and never-to-be-forgotten sight,' wrote a British official.[50] It had been twenty-eight years.

In theory, 'Mr Edward Prempeh' was a private citizen, but his chiefs and people still revered him and presented him with regalia, including the Golden Stool. He was initially given a job working on a municipal sanitary committee, but in 1926 the British, sufficiently confident that his authority over his people also served their own purposes, installed him as King of Kumasi, the Kumasihene.[51] He selected Manhyia – 'all nations should come together' – as the site of a new two-storey home, paid for by public subscription. It is a house that even today retains a disconcerting feel of inter-war British suburbia. When the author Elspeth Huxley visited in the 1950s, she sat in 'a stiff English arm-chair under two life-size photographs of English royalty, wearing crowns. Everything is tidy, clean, and without taste, good or bad – perhaps no one has cared enough to impart it.'[52]

This was where Prempeh, straddling two worlds, reinstalled the royal harem and successfully lobbied for the reconstruction of the royal mausoleum at Bantama. He organised the exhumation and repatriation of the exiles' bones from the Seychelles and in January 1930, four packing cases containing the bones of twenty-nine people, 'their remains and relics carefully bagged and named' according to Prempeh II, arrived from Mahé. Yaa Asantewaa's remains were amongst them and she was buried in the royal cemetery at Ejisu.[53] In March 1931, a great funeral was held for all those who died abroad, as well as for Asante royalty who had died at home during Prempeh's exile.

Prempeh died on 12 May 1931. There were no ghastly rites, wrote a British veteran of 1896 and 1900, but instead a Christian burial.[54] In fact, Prempeh's funeral celebrated the blend of tradition and modernity which he, and Asante itself, had sought to achieve throughout his eventful reign. The historian Emmanuel Akyeampong writes that Prempeh had shown how 'the Asantehene could be a Christian and also remain loyal to his traditions. He was comfortable in cloth or in a suit, at a garden tea party or at a durbar of chiefs and people.' In this way, he was 'the last traditional king of Asante as well as its first modern one'.[55]

In January 1935, Prempeh's successor, his nephew Nana Osei Tutu Agyeman Prempeh II, was allowed by the British to assume the restored position of Asantehene, king once more of the entire Asante confederacy. *The Times* sent a correspondent to cover the celebrations in Kumasi, a city transformed from 'savagery to civilization'. Train whistles and cathedral bells merged with the sounds of traditional drums and Governor Sir Arnold Hodson's car entered the parade ground surrounded by mounted lancers to the tune of 'God Save the King'. Prempeh II, parading with the Golden Stool, was 'magnificently arrayed and his golden ornaments were so heavy that he had to be helped up on to the steps to shake hands with the Governor.' Drummers, horn-blowers and courtiers with dozens

Monarchy restored. Asantehene Prempeh II in 1936.

of enormous umbrellas marched behind him. 'The whole open space as far as the eye could see was now filled with leaping half-naked figures,' reported *The Times*, 'shouting their war cries and blowing horns, some turning complete somersaults, others throwing shields high in the air with a twirling turn of the wrist, catching them again by the handle before they reached the ground ... It was a scene unparalleled in Ashanti history.'[56] Unparalleled? What strikes me is how similar this description is to Thomas Bowdich's account of his own reception back in 1817, when the whole Anglo-Asante story began, in all its tragedy and folly. *The Times* correspondent was not witnessing the subjugation of a culture, but the assertion of it. In spite of everything, Asante had survived.

Asantehene Opoku Ware II at the British Museum exhibition, 1981.

16

'RETURN ALL STOLEN PROPERTY TO THE PEOPLE OF ASHANTI!'

The glass display case had been smashed open with a cobblestone and the piece of Asante gold within dislodged, but not damaged or removed. An attempted robbery, or some sort of a protest? It was hard to say, as none of the warders saw it happen. The man on duty hadn't even heard anything because, he said, the breakage had rather miraculously 'coincided with a clap of thunder'. It happened on 18 March 1974, in the Museum of Mankind, off Regent Street in London's West End (where the British Museum's ethnographic collection was displayed between 1970 and 1997, after which it returned to the main building in Bloomsbury). When the British Museum trustees were informed of this disturbing breach of security, they were told 'the case had been deliberately selected and the incident might have been connected with recent suggestions that the Ashanti gold objects should be returned to Ghana.'[1]

British Museum trustees can hardly be expected to know each of the millions of objects under their purview, but in 1974 they would probably have remembered this particular Asante piece, for they had authorised its purchase only the previous year. It was one of the two magnificent soul washer badges, or *akrafokonmu*, bought by the aristocratic Cecil family at Garrard in 1874 and subsequently mounted on larger gilt-silver dishes (see Chapter 8). William Cecil, the Marquess of Exeter and an aide-de-camp to Queen Victoria, died in 1895.[2] This particular badge and dish passed on to Major-General Lord Cheylesmore, Chairman of the National Rifle Association and a well-known face in London's gentlemen's clubs, as well as reputedly the first British peer to die in a motor accident after a collision with a telegraph post in 1925.[3] It was Lord Cheylesmore's step-granddaughter, Mrs J. Coram Wright, who sold the piece in 1973. She initially approached Christie's, where Hermione Waterfield of what was then the 'Tribal Art' department remembers her as 'a very nice, very wealthy woman in a mink coat'. But to Hermione's disappointment, William Fagg, the British Museum curator, 'intense and engaging' when he had his eye on an object, intervened, and ensured it went there instead.[4] The British Museum paid Mrs Coram Wright £4,600 (worth about £59,200 today).[5] Fagg was delighted with his acquisition; he said the badge in the middle of the dish was 'one of the two or three finest works of Ashanti art in this country … a fitting centre-piece for the British Museum's collection of Ashanti art.'[6]

By the time of the mysterious assault on the glass case, Asante loot in Britain had indeed begun bubbling up as a diplomatic issue. The Foreign Office, in the light of the imminent centenary of the 1874 war, had asked the British High Commission in Accra in February 1973 for its assessment of the likelihood of a return campaign 'blowing up'.[7] That same month the Foreign Office wrote – in a letter which rather undermines the notion of the British establishment as one cosy club working to protect mutually understood interests – to the British Museum, to ask whether it had any Asante gold, as 'we have hitherto not been aware of any'.[8] In November 1973 its concerns were vindicated when the Asantehene Otumfuo Opoku Ware II, who had succeeded his uncle Prempeh II in 1970, met his senior chiefs in the Kumasi Traditional Council, which resolved to use the centenary as 'a felicitous and auspicious occasion on which to press for the return of objects of the deepest significance to the cultural life of the people of Ashanti'. The council's petition, in elegant and restrained language, and with some input from the British historian Ivor Wilks, highlighted the most important objects taken by

Wolseley, as well as those of 1896, and argued that Kumasi had facilities to display them, both at the Prempeh II Jubilee Museum, which had opened in 1956, and at the Manhyia Palace itself, which was then in the process of being rebuilt.

The Kumasi Traditional Council presented its petition to the British High Commission in Accra in January 1974 and the issue was taken up, with gusto, in the local press. The Gold Coast had become the independent country of Ghana in 1957 and almost every other African state had achieved independence during the 1960s. According to *The Palaver*, Wolseley had been 'an arch-colonialist [who] in typical jungle style forcibly took away the regalia ... white vagabonds parading on the continent in the name of religion, plundered the treasures of the helpless Africans and carried the proceeds to display in their native homes.' It was high time that Britain bowed to the winds of change. 'Surely the era in which British Governors roamed about in the African forest with knickerbockers and khaki helmets being borne aloft in palanquins by overwearied natives has given way to a new era of African cultural supremacy ... *The Palaver* urges the British government to return all stolen property belonging to the people of Ashanti without delay!'[9,10]

British diplomats in Ghana enjoyed close ties with Asantehene Opoku Ware II, who had trained as a barrister at London's Lincoln's Inn. He and his wife, Madam Victoria, an influential politician in her own right and described in Foreign Office correspondence as 'a large, sentimental, affectionate and regal figure', were regular guests at the High Commissioner's residence in Accra, where they were invariably served the 'customary champagne and jam tarts'.[11] The High Commission warned London in November 1973 that 'we shall have to tread very carefully not to upset the presently excellent relations we enjoy with the Asantehene', while by January 1974 it had concluded it 'would be a very useful gesture to return at least something from the Regalia'.[12]

There was a precedent. In November 1961 Queen Elizabeth II visited Ghana, her first journey to an independent African country and a seminal moment in Britain's relationship with its former colonies. British politicians and officials often regarded Ghana's first president Kwame

Nkrumah, Pan-African hero and socialist, with suspicion, but the timing of this visit was particularly fraught. In September, Nkrumah – 'greatly disturbed' by differences with Britain over the crisis in the Congo – fired 230 British officers from the Ghanaian army, including the Chief of Defence Staff, Major-General Henry Alexander. 'It is politically imperative that ... direct command of the Ghana Armed Services should be held by Ghanaians,' he wrote in Alexander's letter of dismissal.[13] But if British officials anticipated the Queen's meeting with Nkrumah with some trepidation, her scheduled stopover in Kumasi – this too the first by a British monarch – threatened further complications. This was not so much because of any memories of the Anglo-Asante Wars, but because of tensions within Ghana, and specifically, differences between Nkrumah's government and the economically powerful and socially conservative Asante. 'De-colonisation in the 1940s and 1950s was a painful experience for the Ashanti', writes Tom McCaskie, and 'many wanted a restored sovereignty or at the least an autonomous position within a federal, independent Gold Coast.'[14] By 1961 Ghana was beset by strikes, inflation and anti-Nkrumah plots.[15]

In the event the visit was a triumph, still remembered in Ghana today for Nkrumah and the Queen – 'looking radiant and happy' in the words of Ghana's *Daily Graphic* – dancing highlife together at a State House ball.[16] Given past enmities, the Queen could not have expected a warmer reception, not only from Nkrumah but from the Asante as well. Tens of thousands of people lined Kumasi's streets and clambered on top of buildings and cars for views of the Queen. 'Kumasi goes wild with joy,' wrote *The Graphic*.[17] 'An epoch-making moment', said the *Ashanti Pioneer*.[18] The durbar, according to the *Daily Telegraph*, 'had all the savage pageantry of a dying African era ... drums throbbed and tribesmen blew weird music.'[19] The aged Prempeh II was not able to carry the weight of his full regalia, and yet 'there was little of him that was not glinting with gold' while other chiefs 'were decked and weighed down with clumps of gold ornaments'.[20] The Queen even saw the Golden Stool itself – as close as any British royal has ever got to it – and was presented with a contemporary wooden stool decorated with gold leaf.[21] In fact, wherever she went she was showered with gifts from what she called 'the gay and warm-hearted people of Ghana'; on one stop alone she received 'stools, dolls, bows and arrows, an elephant tusk, riding boots, juju walking sticks and carved wooden spoons'.[22] But much more significant, and certainly more surprising from our perspective more than sixty years later, are the gifts the Queen took to Ghana. For amongst these were an important group of Asante objects belonging to the Royal Collection, which the British had looted in 1874 and 1896.

In February 1961, the maverick Labour MP Tom Driberg, recently returned from Ghana, had written to the government recommending the Queen take on her forthcoming visit 'appropriate and interesting presents' for the new national museum in Accra which would 'build up good will'. But Driberg's suggested gifts – the Asante Ewer from the reign of Richard II, along with a selection of colonial-era stamps – were ill-conceived and quickly shot down by the Foreign Office.[23] The Royal Collection says that instead the Queen took two stools and two chairs to Ghana, all with plaques which connected them to the British military expeditions.[24]

These returns, by a successor British Queen, would appear to be an act of extraordinary symbolism, almost a tacit acknowledgement of past wrongs. The Royal Collection says they were presented to President Nkrumah 'as gifts and signs of friendship (rather than returned on request)'.[25] Oddly, they attracted little comment from British and Ghanaian journalists at the time. *The Times* wrote that the Queen gave Nkrumah 'four captured pieces of Ashanti furniture which have been displayed at Windsor Castle since the nineteenth century', while the *Daily Express* said Nkrumah 'warmly thanked the Queen for returning the golden stools [sic] of Ashanti'. In 1970 the distinguished Asante historian Alexander Kyerematen wrote that the Queen gave the stools and chairs directly to Prempeh II in 1961, who in turn passed them on to the recently opened Prempeh II Jubilee Museum in Kumasi.[26]

When I visited that museum in 2024, a guide showed me the stools and chairs returned by the Queen and later I was able to match these with historic photographs from the Royal Collection. One of these photographs shows the stool which Lieutenant Wood presented to the Prince of Wales at Windsor Castle in March 1874 (see Chapter 8). It is taken in the 1890s in the Prince's London residence of Marlborough House and shows the stool surrounded by palms and heavy Victorian furniture and beneath a huge tapestry of a battle in India. Today the stool is back in Kumasi, lying on its side in a glass case. The contexts are very different, and yet the stool, with its distinctive curved legs and lavish silver metalwork, is indisputably the same.[27]

★★★

From early 1974 until the end of 1976, Asantehene Opoku Ware II, the British Museum and Foreign Office diplomats were in regular contact, discussing the possible return of Asante loot to Kumasi. The Asantehene's petition had been addressed to the British government, on the premise that it could make decisions on behalf of any museum in Britain. This is true, to the extent that all these museums are ultimately subject to parliamentary legislation, but within their respective legal frameworks each of them, and perhaps especially the British Museum itself, has tended to jealously guard its autonomy. Of course, this was convenient for Foreign Office diplomats, most of whom were anyway fundamentally unsympathetic to the idea that Britain should return objects looted in colonial times. 'Where on earth would we draw the line if we did?' one argued.[28] There was no need, he said, for the Foreign Office to become involved 'in an emotional and moral argument over an issue which as much as anything turns on the concept of property and institutional rights under English law ... a separate question, though not perhaps one that is readily comprehensible to the Ghanaians.'[29] Ultimately, the Foreign Office in London believed, the Asantehene's request would have to be turned down, so it was 'all the more important that it should be the museums, rather than HMG, who should be seen to be doing so'.[30]

Some in the British High Commission in Accra took a less jaundiced view. On 4 February 1974, the Asante held a durbar to mark the centenary of Wolseley's invasion. A British diplomat who attended, Willy Turner, marvelled at 'the fact that the Asantehene and, apparently, the people of Kumasi could celebrate a disastrous war in which they lost their highly valued regalia without showing any hostility to the current representative of the country which had been the cause of this bitter historical memory.'[31] Opoku Ware II spoke with dignity of 'his fervent hope' that Britain would 'respond favourably' to his appeal for the return of regalia.[32] Turner warned his colleagues not to doubt the Asantehene's determination.[33]

In May 1974 the British High Commissioner in Accra, Harry Stanley, wrote to London with his concerns. He was not, he emphasised, advocating return. Apart from anything else, given Ghana's economic woes, he was 'very doubtful whether a mass of intrinsically valuable golden articles would stay very long in any museum'. But he did feel the Asante should be offered a 'token article', perhaps something of ceremonial significance. He had seen several Asante swords at the British Museum, surely it could be prevailed upon to surrender one? Above all, said Stanley, the British needed to be seen to be taking this 'with the utmost seriousness' (his underline).[34]

Foreign Office colleagues in London worried that the High Commissioner was 'making a considerable meal of this affair'. In what could pass for a *Yes, Minister* script, one wrote that the High Commissioner's preoccupation 'with the Regalia question may have the effect of stirring up local interest instead of damping it down. Asking people's opinions (as we know he has been doing) is apt to give the impression we have uneasy consciences. I do not think we need have.'[35] Stanley's subsequent suggestion also reads in the best tradition of Sir Humphrey. If the Foreign Office could only send a reply to Opoku Ware II with 'an authoritative, impressive and fully researched appearance,' this would help 'deflect attention from its inevitable lack of substance. If it has the effect of encouraging the Ghanaians to chase around themselves after institutions and individuals who held parts of the Regalia, this might also serve your purpose of extricating HMG from the front line.'[36] In August 1974, Stanley travelled to Kumasi and presented the Asantehene with just such a letter from the Foreign Office, which regretfully explained that much of the important regalia was in the British Museum and the

Wallace Collection, 'autonomous institutions over which Her Majesty's Government have no control'. The Asantehene, to Stanley's relief, 'was extremely friendly, showed no sign of personal resentment and indeed took his medicine quite admirably'.[37]

In December 1974, a Conservative peer, Lord Montagu of Beaulieu, asked in the House of Lords whether the Labour government, 'with a view to fostering Commonwealth relations ... would facilitate the early return of Ashanti Regalia to the Ghana nation'. Montagu argued that the Asante 'have very deep feelings about the return of these sacrosanct objects which are supposed to contain the soul of the Ashanti people'. Baron Goronwy-Roberts, the Foreign Office minister who replied for the government, disputed Montagu's characterisation of the regalia as 'war booty'. Rather, he said, they were 'part of an indemnity agreed by the former King of Ashanti, the proceeds of which were devoted to compensation for dependants of British troops killed in horrific conditions'. None of the peers disputed this grossly misleading historical summary of the events of 1874. Baroness Jennie Lee, a former Labour minister with impeccable progressive credentials as a founder of the Open University and the widow of Aneurin Bevan, joked that, 'when it comes to returning booty from this country we should tread warily because it may turn into a striptease.' Baron Gisborough, a Conservative, asked, 'would it be possible to keep the booty and return the soul?' The peers laughed, and the debate was concluded.[38]

If anything was to happen, then, it was up to the museums. In the spring of 1974, the British Museum had a new director, John Pope-Hennessy, determined to transform what he called 'an inbred institution where staff problems were of notorious difficulty'.[39] A decade earlier, the eminent historian of Africa, Basil Davidson, had written an excoriating article for *West Africa Magazine*. 'The British Museum, let us say it frankly,' wrote Davidson,

> is a national disgrace. Fabulous objects clutter its cellars and store rooms. The number of treasures that can never be shown – or shown briefly and rarely – is enormous. Even

'Return All Stolen Property to The People of Ashanti!' 217

those that may be seen by the ordinary visitor are crushed and cluttered together as though the greater part were on offer in a second-hand warehouse. Walk through the famous Ethnographical Gallery and you will find yourself engulfed in an overwhelming bargain-basement jumble of the arts and artefacts of many lands.

Meanwhile out of sight, down below, 'the cellars are stuffed to the ceiling.' Its curators know 'their Museum is like an iceberg whose true bulk is always out of sight ... But their task is almost hopeless. They have pitifully small financial resources. Worse still, they have far too little space.'[40]

The British Museum's ethnographic collection problems were meant to have been mitigated by the 1970 move to the Museum of Mankind, but Pope-Hennessy – 'the Pope' to his staff – worried that its new home was attracting few visitors and had 'never succeeded in getting off the ground'.[41] In May 1974, he tried to set a new course. The British Museum's trustees agreed that William Fagg, sixty years old and the doyen of Western curators of ethnography and African art, needed to be retired.[42] Fagg had long neglected administrative duties, but Pope-Hennessy had more ideological reasons for wanting him gone. He thought it 'essential' that a new head of ethnography should 'be free of the least taint of colonialism'.[43] He ruffled some colleagues by choosing Malcolm McLeod, a young anthropologist from the Cambridge Museum of Archaeology and Anthropology.

'It was an interesting appointment,' reflected Malcolm half a century later, speaking to me in his house on the Scottish borders, where he lives alone with a dog, surrounded by beautiful countryside and friendly neighbours. He generously drove more than thirty miles to pick me up from the nearest train station. I was torn between wanting to spend more time rummaging through his sprawling library, which meant braving a series of frigid rooms, and the comforts of coffee and his entertaining memories by the stove in his kitchen. 'It was the first time they'd appointed someone to be Head of department from outside for centuries,' Malcolm said, 'and I was only thirty-three. I was brought in as a new breed. I liked

John Pope-Hennessy enormously, he was intensely stimulating ... But if you got on the wrong side of him it was sudden death.'[44]

It helped that Ghana was a shared interest. Malcolm had worked at the University of Ghana in the 1960s, while Pope-Hennessy's grandfather, John Pope Hennessy (without the hyphen), had been Governor of the Gold Coast in the tumultuous early 1870s, when he was widely pilloried for misreading Asante intentions prior to their invasion of the protectorate.[45] In 1974 Ghana was back on the agenda, for amongst the 'boxes of unopened letters' which Malcolm discovered on William Fagg's desk was the petition from the Asantehene. 'It had been ignored ... it was scandalous,' he recalls. 'I went to see John Pope-Hennessy and told him, "This is rather important, and the BM has not responded, I've worked in Ghana and know the people involved." So the Pope said "you'd better get yourself out to Kumasi and see about this."'[46]

★★★

In 2022 the Franco-German academic Bénédicte Savoy wrote a compelling book, *Africa's Struggle For Its Art*, which argued that the 'twenty-first century idea to return cultural goods that were taken *en masse* to fill European museums during colonialism ... is anything but radical or groundbreaking.'[47] It turns out that restitution – so topical in the era of Black Lives Matter and Rhodes Must Fall – is not so new. 'Nearly every conversation today about the restitution of cultural property to Africa already happened forty years ago,' says Savoy.[48] Specifically, from the mid-1960s to the early 1980s, when Africa, in the flush of post-independence optimism, campaigned for the return of its lost heritage. But at that time European museum curators lied, dissembled and obstructed, and generally 'played for time in bad faith'. Many even refused to divulge what they had in their collections. They won, at least temporarily, but their victory, she says, was 'shameful'.[49]

Savoy's focus was primarily on Germany, but a reading of the British Museum's trustees' minutes from the 1970s provides plenty of material to support her thesis. The trustees – 'all white men except for Dame Kathleen Kenyon who dug up Jericho, she was splendid and actually born in the BM because her father was director,' as Malcolm McLeod remembers – generally do their best to resist and deflect demands for the return of looted artefacts. In July 1974, as the Asantehene's petition finally reaches them, they 'felt strongly that they should avoid encouraging demands ... for the return of objects'. They ask 'to be provided with lists of other similar materials which might be considered to have been seized', so they can prepare their defence.[50] In September 1974, they slapped down a request from Nigeria for the loan of one of the famous Queen Idia masks from Benin. 'The agitation for its return was artificial,' they grandly proclaimed.[51]

There is a timelessness, too, to the arguments put forward by Asantehene Opoku Ware II in 1974. His booklet, 'Centenary of the Sagrenti War – The Call for the Return of the Asante Regalia', reads like it was written by somebody making the pro-restitution case in the 2020s. 'The invasion had a profound psychological effect on the Asante,' it says, and the looted objects 'are much more than regalia or art pieces. They ... represent together with the bronzes of Benin and Ife the peak of our West African cultural heritage ... while to their admirers abroad they may be at best of exotic, artistic and romantic value, to us they hold the key to the wisdom and even the history of our ancestors.'[52]

On 11 October 1974, the Asantehene, visiting London, inspected the British Museum's collection of Asante regalia, accompanied by a number of chiefs.[53] John Pope-Hennessy told the Asantehene that the British Museum Act of 1963 made it impossible to accede to his request that objects be returned to Kumasi (the Act forbids the Museum from de-accessioning objects, with a few exceptions, such as when an object is a duplicate or so damaged it is deemed 'unfit to be retained'). He explained that the regalia had been bought with public money and was in no way the property of the British government. The Asantehene also visited the Wallace Collection on the same day, where he was particularly interested in the famous gold head but asked not to be photographed with it or any other objects as this could have been 'embarrassing' for him back home. In both museums, he expressed his appreciation for the good care taken of Asante objects.

What is not clear, however, is whether the Asantehene was told how little of the regalia he yearned for was even on display at either of these museums. At the British Museum, John Pope-Hennessy informed the trustees in September 1974, only a single piece was in the public galleries.[54] (The situation is not much better today; in 2024 according to the British Museum website, it displayed fifteen Asante pieces, of which six were gold, meaning that approximately 99.5 per cent of its Asante pieces were not on display.) At the Wallace, rather incredibly, records suggest the entire collection of Asante gold was hidden in storage for decades, from at least the 1950s to the 1980s. Basil Davidson, in his 1963 article which lambasted the British Museum, did not spare the Wallace: 'Consider the case of the splendid gold head ... A wonderful and unique object, but permanently out of sight ... Why not give this head back to Ghana?'[55] In 1981 the American scholar Martha Ehrlich wrote that the gold head was 'not exhibited for security reasons'.[56] The Wallace Collection today cannot explain why its Asante gold objects were hidden away for so long, whether it really was to do with security or whether curators felt they were an odd fit (one wrote 'we have perhaps been a little bit embarrassed by them') or were simply indifferent.[57] Nor can it even say precisely when the Asante gold did go back on display, although it believes 'it was at some point in the early 1980s'.[58]

In November 1974 Malcolm McLeod met the Asantehene in Kumasi. He reiterated John Pope-Hennessy's message: 'I had to explain to them ... that it's impossible for us to take things from the BM ... I'm sorry, but it would be illegal for us to comply with your request.' It had the potential to be a frosty meeting, but Opoku Ware II displayed his customary good grace: 'the king was very measured and intelligent. And understanding ... He was a lovely man,' recalls Malcolm.[59]

That the British Museum disappointed the Asantehene in 1974 is no surprise. What is surprising, however, is to discover how close the two subsequently came to a major agreement that some of the most important Asante regalia should at least be loaned back to Kumasi, and some objects even exchanged. John Pope-Hennessy was prepared to be flexible on these points and implied that his conscience was indeed pricked by the fact that almost all the regalia was in storage.⁶⁰ He told the trustees that it was 'difficult to defend a totally negative stance and there was widely conceded to be some moral weight behind the Asantehene's request.'⁶¹

Malcolm McLeod took up the negotiations, on that first visit to Kumasi in 1974 and, again in 1976, and developed a close relationship with the Asantehene's private secretary, Yao Andoh. The Asantehene and his advisers submitted a list of 'original pieces of regalia made in the time of the famous Okomfo Anokye ... of sacred and historical importance'. These included the *Mpomponsuo* sword, which they described as 'the greatest of the State Swords, originally made for Opoku Ware 1720–1750', the *bosumuru boaman* or 'greatest of the State Umbrellas, made by Nana Osei Bonsu', a dagger with a gold sheath, hilt and ornaments, a golden neck torc and some of the *akrafokonmu* golden soul washer badges.⁶² In July 1976 Malcolm urged the trustees to be sympathetic and his recommendations included that they agree to exchange their *Mpomponsuo* sword for another sword in the Asantehene's collection, to dispose of the dagger as a duplicate and to offer him six of the twenty-three *akrafokonmu* owned by the British Museum, as well as two gold wristlets.

The trustees were happy to proceed on this basis, provided they had legal advice that they were not contravening the British Museum Act, only to be told that the Treasury Solicitor, Mrs E. Mitchell, advised their powers 'did not extend to the exchanges proposed'.⁶³ Nonetheless, most trustees were still happy to back Malcolm McLeod's revised idea of a series of loans, with the Asantehene in turn loaning the British Museum some pieces of his own. 'On balance, as an experiment and in the interests of good relations, the risk was worth taking', they decided in September 1976. ⁶⁴ John Pope-Hennessy explained that objects being sent to Kumasi would be put on display, although he also wrote, 'we should be justified in turning a blind eye to the occasional withdrawal of individual objects from public display for ritual or other use.'⁶⁵ Malcolm said 'the Asantehene could be relied upon to treat these items with care.'⁶⁶ In November 1976, buoyed by congratulations from the trustees, he told the Asantehene that the British Museum was happy to loan items for a year at a time and offer training and support for a new museum in Kumasi.⁶⁷

So why did none of this happen? After all, it sounds remarkably similar to the agreement the British Museum eventually reached almost fifty years later, in 2023, with Opoku Ware II's successor, Osei Tutu II, when Malcolm McLeod was called out of retirement in his eighties and was once again in the thick of the negotiations. The issue of the Asante regalia disappears from British Museum and Foreign Office files from 1977 onwards. Almost all of the key players from that period, in both Ghana and Britain, are dead. Nonetheless, the documents are full of clues. The Asantehene and his advisers entered negotiations with the British with high expectations in 1974. But, for all the mutual politeness, they were surely disappointed and worn down by the obstructionism of both the Foreign Office and British Museum and the dawning realisation that the best they could hope to achieve was much less than they had originally hoped for. Was the unsatisfactory prize on offer even worth the bother? After the Asantehene saw the British Museum's Asante regalia, he confided to his private secretary Yao Andoh that he already possessed a very similar collection and there were only seven or eight objects he was really interested in. These included, above all, the *Mpomponsuo* sword, but when he learnt that the British Museum would not exchange this, he may have lost heart.

Politics in Ghana would also have been a factor. The 1970s was a decade of economic decline and political instability, in which the Asantehene needed to tread carefully, especially in his dealings with the military governments then in power. The return of regalia – which could have been interpreted as a statement of Asante nationalism – brought potential risks within Ghana's fragile polity. The Asantehene also wanted a new museum, but could it be that when faced with the economic and political practicalities of building and financing one, his interest waned? In October 1976 McLeod told the British Museum trustees that the 'King was in no hurry to conclude the matter and the public display area for the regalia had still to be built.'[68]

When I spoke to Julie Hudson of the British Museum, also closely involved in the 2023 deal, as to why nothing had happened in 1976 or indeed in any of the long decades since, she took a broader view. 'What happens so often', she said, is that 'there is no follow through, letters are not replied to, personnel change, people lose interest, and things die a natural death.' Bureaucratic inertia is not unique to West Africa, or the British Museum for that matter, and her diagnosis sounds familiar to what many people experience in institutions and governments over time. What seemed of pressing importance in the 1970s, and again in the 2020s, may not have seemed so important in all the decades in-between. 'We hear nothing, and so we don't follow up, interest ebbs and flows, and museums and cultural heritage are held victim to the political whims and interests of individuals who come and go.'[69]

There was also a more specific reason why the British Museum's and Asantehene's attention strayed away from a loan deal in the late 1970s, and that was the major exhibition which the museum opened in London in spring of 1981: 'Asante, Kingdom of Gold'. Malcolm McLeod's ambition had always been to showcase Asante culture on the global stage and he spent many months engrossed in preparations: 'what should go into it and whether or not the Asantehene should visit London to open it, how this trip was to be financed and how he should be accommodated'.[70] Behind the scenes the Foreign Office and British Museum squabbled over who would pay for the Asantehene's entourage of twenty people, including two ceremonial gun bearers, to fly first class from Accra.[71]

The exhibition in the Museum of Mankind – which featured a walk through a West African rainforest and displays of hundreds of items of gold, textiles, brass weights and wood carving – was opened by the Asantehene in February 1981. Sir Richard Thompson, a British Museum trustee, paid tribute to the 'pageantry and magnificence' of the Asantehene and his chiefs, bedecked in gold and robes: 'it puts us town sparrows in the shade.'[72] Richard Luce, a Foreign Office minister, said that 'out of the bloodshed of the nineteenth century has emerged the magnificent friendship of the twentieth century.' The exhibition was hailed by *The Times* as an 'eye-opener'.[73] The Asantehene told the BBC he 'was very proud, the exhibition ... shows the glory and the skill of the Asante ... The British Museum has been very kind, very fair.' But did his coming here, asked the reporter, mean he no longer wanted anything back? The Asantehene paused. 'This is a very difficult question. I wish I could get them all back.' He laughed. 'Yes, there are some things I'd be grateful if we had them back.'[74] In his own diplomatic way, he tried to keep the matter alive. In July 1981 he wrote to the British government, informing it of his continued desire that he be given 'certain items by the British Museum, possibly on permanent loan'. He received a polite acknowledgement of his letter, but no more.[75]

'Asante, Kingdom of Gold' is still remembered fondly in Kumasi today, where one company, Speedway Travel, put on special group flights to London. 'Asante delegations came every week,' Malcolm McLeod says, 'and I'd take them round. Sometimes they'd pray and pour libations; the carpet started to smell of gin. They were very pleased their culture was being exposed in London, even if they disagreed with some of what it said about Asante history.' In 1984 the exhibition moved to New York, where it was hosted by the American Museum of Natural History. Malcolm helped take the exhibits across the Atlantic. 'We reserved PANAM business class seats to take the gold. Passengers kept on asking me what was in the crates. I said, "Dinosaur bones, that's why they need all the security". It seemed a better answer than "Lots of gold"'.[76]

The Asantehene opened the New York exhibition as well, and in a heady celebration of Asante and Ghanaian culture, held a royal procession up Central Park West. He walked under an umbrella of gold and orange silk, led by a guard who carried a ceremonial musket and five gold daggers. Madam Victoria was close behind, with a retinue of royal shield bearers. Thousands of people, lined nine or ten deep, watched and cheered, and many reached out to touch the Asantehene. Mayor Ed Koch was by his side. 'I say to you Otumfuo, the city is yours,' he told the Asantehene, who acknowledged the cheers with an upraised arm. '"Our King, Our King is here," said Oheneba Asiedu, a 41-year-old welder from the Bronx who left Ghana nearly a dozen years ago,' reported the *New York Times*.[77] Alexandra Davis, a student from North Carolina, stumbled across the procession. 'I just walked through the neighbourhood and there he was … The King of Ghana, just walking down the street like that. Where else but New York?'[78] Malcolm also remembers those days with affection. 'We had a good time,' he said. 'The Museum gave the King a limo to go around in, and Yao Andoh and I drove around New York in this very long car drinking whisky. It was a lot of fun.'[79]

'The largest and... heaviest pendant from 1874', now in a private collection.

17

'THE MOST MARVELLOUS EXPERIENCE OF OUR LIVES'

In 1981, Martha Judith Ehrlich completed her PhD at Indiana University, entitled 'A Catalogue of Ashanti Art taken from Kumasi in the Anglo-Ashanti War of 1874'. It is a prodigious effort, more than 500 pages long and compiled in an era long before email, the internet and WhatsApp. But as Ehrlich ploughed through thirteen months of research in Britain, Ghana and the United States, she came to a bleak conclusion. 'It became increasingly clear', she wrote, 'that there is a vast difference in the number of objects mentioned in the reports of those who were with Wolseley in Kumasi and Cape Coast, and the number of objects I was able to locate.'[1]

Whole categories of objects, and notably cloths and beads, had simply been 'lost'. The bulk of these, Ehrlich concluded, had been sold at Cape Coast to local buyers, for 'far higher prices than could be had in Britain. They were valued by Africans as precious objects ... whereas the Europeans saw them only as trinkets or souvenirs.' But Ehrlich also noticed 'an obvious discrepancy in the case of the gold objects', many of which, of course, did go to Britain. Some of these, she conceded, were probably hidden in private collections. But the gold dust and nuggets that were in the Fomena indemnity, and many other pieces from that payment, appear to have disappeared. Citing a letter she received from

William Fagg in 1971, she concluded that 'much of the indemnity gold and perhaps many undamaged pieces as well, were probably sold for bullion value and melted down.'[2]

I too had wondered where all that gold went and what I was missing. There is a big gap, for example, between the £11,000 reportedly paid by Garrard for Asante treasure and the sums it subsequently received for that treasure from Richard Wallace, the British Museum, the South Kensington Museum and a handful of others. I dug out Garrard's 'Gentleman's Ledger' for 1874, 600 pages of cursive handwriting with a cast straight out of *Burke's Peerage*: princes, princesses, dukes, duchesses, lords and ladies listed along with their balances, credits and debits.[3] But the ledger, frustratingly, does not specify what objects they were actually spending their money on. In some cases, only it is impossible to say how many, the answer will be 'Asante gold'. William Fagg's explanation also makes sense. Gold will always have what the Victorians called an 'intrinsic value'. Gold dust and nuggets, and many Asante pieces judged as 'scrap', were surely melted down and are today in very different forms, their origins untraceable.

To try and track down all the loot the British took from Asante – not just in 1874, but also in 1896 and 1900 – has felt like a Sisyphean task, overwhelming at times, but with just enough encouragement to keep me going. The auction rooms give tantalising hints. In May 1946, Sotheby's sold an 'Ashanti Gold Badge' – *akrafokonmu* – shield-shaped, fifteen centimetres in diameter and the property of the late Lord Wantage.[4] It was mounted on a stand, with a plaque that read: 'Ransom Gold, Coomassie, 1874'.[5] In February 1957, Christie's put an even more impressive *akrafokonmu* on its catalogue cover: property of a Mrs J. Dix, seventeen centimetres in diameter and weighing more than half a kilogram, which Ehrlich describes as 'the largest and probably the heaviest known soul priest's pendant from the 1874 collection ... with carefully-executed foliate ornamentation of a pronounced European character.'[6] It was bought by Ernest Ohly, a renowned London dealer in ethnographic art, who paid £340 for it, equivalent to about £10,350 today.[7] This was the second *akrafokonmu* which the Cecil family bought at Garrard in 1874 and mounted on a larger English gilt-silver dish (the dish, also belonging to Mrs J. Dix, and by now detached from the *akrafokonmu*, was sold separately at the same 1957 Christie's auction, where it fetched £62).[8]

I've tracked the subsequent ownership of this particular *akrafokonmu* through three collectors in the United States, until, in August 1990, a canny Bond Street dealer, Lance Entwistle, brought it back to Britain.[9] Asante gold does not usually attract the huge prices that Benin Bronzes do – in part because the pieces are smaller and are not figurative sculptures – but Entwistle quickly sold his badge on for 'a low six-figure number'. This makes it, as far as I can tell, the most expensive single object the British took from Kumasi.[10] It was bought by the Dapper Foundation in Paris, which until 2017 ran a museum dedicated primarily to African art. Although the Dapper Foundation says its mission is 'to give more visibility to the cultures of Africa and of its diasporas', it would not answer my questions as to the whereabouts of the *akrafokonmu*.[11] Lance Entwistle would only say 'he'd be very surprised if it's in France.'[12]

In November 1961, *Country Life* magazine reported, 'two gold ornaments from once savage and blood-stained Ashanti made a great deal of money at Sotheby's'. These were a pair of golden lions, each about six centimetres long, 'savage, dignified and very rare', and sold to an American buyer for £980 (about £24,400 today). At the same auction, a golden Asante necklace 'with a heavy circular pendant in the form of a crab', which had belonged to the recently deceased Lady Phyllis Corydon, widow of a former British governor of Kenya, was sold for £480 (£11,950). These sales did not go unnoticed back in Kumasi, where they made the front page of the *Ashanti Pioneer* newspaper.[13] In October 1965, Christie's sold an Asante gold mask for 105 guineas.[14] In November 1967 Sotheby's sold 'an Ashanti gold-ring in the form of a frog, a fine Ashanti gold necklace and an important large Ashanti gold soul-bearer disc'.[15]

And so it goes on, through the decades and into our own century. In 2003, Christie's in Paris announced the upcoming sale of a leopard-skin hat decorated with prancing golden leopards and a pair of slippers, also generously decorated with gold. They came in a glass vitrine with a brass plaque that read in gothic script: 'Cap and slippers worn by the Ashanti King Coffee CalCalli. Taken from the Palace of Coomassie.'[16] These splendid objects had been taken by Lieutenant Lord Edric Gifford, one of Wolseley's most trusted officers, who was awarded the Victoria Cross for the courage with which he led local scouts on the approach to Kumasi.[17] They feature prominently in a May 1874 *Illustrated London News* sketch of the Asante loot (see plate section).[18] Christie's put them on the cover of its catalogue for its sale on 10 December 2003 with an estimated price of 40–60,000 euros.[19] It also displayed them in the window of its Paris offices, just off the Champs-Élysées. That was a fateful mistake.

A few days before the sale, the Asante hat and slippers disappeared. 'They were asking for it to be taken, putting it behind the curtain in the window with only a bored security guard', said an informed source. 'The police were useless, and Christie's did its best to stop it being publicised.'[20] Someone who worked at Christie's in Paris at the time told me the robbery was 'very embarrassing … I fear the gold was melted down'.[21] In response to my enquiries, the French police confirmed the theft and said those responsible were never identified.[22] In 2025, Christie's told me that 'given the passage of time, we don't have anything we can share.'[23] Many

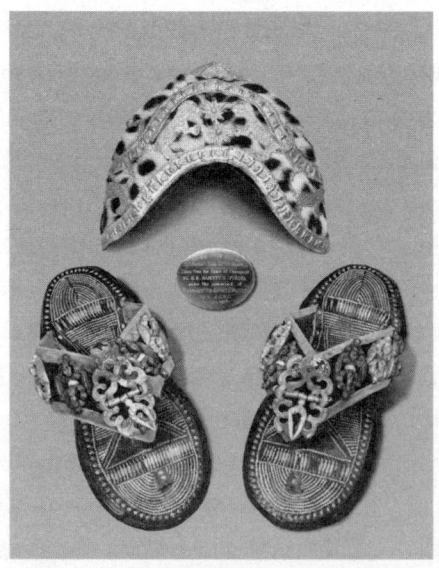

Lost treasure. Asante cap and slippers, stolen from Paris, 2003.

hats and slippers were taken from the Asantehene's palace in 1874, but sadly these, the finest of all, will probably never be seen again.

In December 2005, embarrassing mishaps notwithstanding, Christie's in Paris were given another opportunity to sell a handsome collection of Asante gold objects: a necklace, a ten-centimetre diameter gold badge and fifteen other gold ornaments, which all together fetched just under 30,000 euros. They had belonged to Sir Mark Wilks Collet, Governor of the Bank of England in the 1880s, and therefore presumably had also been taken by Wolseley's army in 1874. They had remained under rarefied ownership in the twentieth century, for they had subsequently belonged to Lady Norman, wife of Baron Montagu Norman, who was himself Governor of the Bank of England (1922–44), as well as being Sir Mark Wilks Collet's grandson.[24] In 2006, meanwhile, in New York, Sotheby's sold yet another gold badge, *akrafokonmu*, which had belonged to the famous sculptor Sir Jacob Epstein, whom, according to William Fagg, owned 'the finest … private collection in Great Britain' of 'tribal and other exotic sculpture', including many objects looted by the British from Kumasi and Benin.[25] There will surely be more sales of Asante loot. In 2024, a senior source at Christie's in London told me he personally knew of 'works of Ashanti gold work which remain in country house collections.'[26]

The sheer abundance of what the British took from Kumasi has produced plenty of confusion and dealers and museums have often struggled to identify and catalogue what they possess. In 1891 Augustus Franks at the British Museum asked the trustees for permission to spend £16 (about £2,200 today) on an Asante gun bearer's cap – *krobonkye* – decorated with gold and silver wreaths, and gold and glass beads, on sale at Phillips Brothers of Cockspur Street. They were 'stated to be from Abyssinia', wrote Franks, but in his opinion were clearly Asante. Curators today concur, for the cap was amongst the fifteen objects the British Museum returned on loan to Kumasi in 2024.[27] In 1918 the Cambridge Museum of Archaeology and Ethnography (which later became the Museum of Archaeology and Anthropology) acquired what it called 'a heavy gold necklace with moulded shell pendants taken from King Prempeh's treasure house at Kumassi in 1896'. The necklace is magnificent – it has sixty ornate discs and thirteen pendants in the shape of turritella shells – but an accompanying letter, from a Mrs Helen Taylor, explains it came into her late daughter Mabel's 'possession after the Ashanti war when our government sold King Coffee's personal jewellery', which suggests the British army in fact took it in 1874 and not 1896. Perhaps Mabel, of 98 Cheyne Walk, Chelsea, and formerly of Girton College, bought it at Garrard herself or maybe an ardent suitor presented it as a gift.[28] We are unlikely to ever find out.

In the files at the Wallace Collection, I came across a series of 1935 letters from a Miss L. Peacey of Highgate. She sent in a piece of gold leaf, with a note that said it came off a sword 'found in King Coffee's palace by Captain Graves' of the Royal Welch Fusiliers in 1874. Her mother and Captain Graves had been courting at the time, before she eventually decided to marry someone else and 'settled into a very different life & Captain Graves "faded out"'. The mother had nonetheless kept the gold for sentimental reasons. Now Miss Peacey was offering it to the Wallace. The curator did not reply with any enthusiasm. I read the back and forth of this obscure correspondence in the Wallace library with a degree of detachment, until I received a sudden surprise: the relevant piece of gold leaf had fallen from the letters and landed on the floor by my feet. With an embarrassed look around me, I hurriedly returned it to the file.

The Wallace Collection received another letter in 1935, from a Mr G. M. C. Luard near Bath, who wrote to say that he possessed 'a very fine gold necklace' and 'earrings' from Asante. His father had bought them at Garrard in April 1874 for £25 (almost £3,000 today). Would the Wallace like to see them? Startlingly, the curator's response to this flurry of Asante correspondence was to write to Garrard himself, to enquire what exactly Richard Wallace had bought sixty-one years earlier and how much he had paid. The Wallace Collection, evidently, knew very little about its own Asante objects. Fortunately, Garrard obliged with a helpful list of Wallace's purchases.[29]

★★★

If you mix gold's enduring value with the cachet of a dramatic backstory and add wealthy collectors on the hunt for rare objects, it is little wonder that the story of Asante loot is entwined with deception and fraud. Hermione Waterfield of Christie's recounts that Charles Ratton, a prominent Parisian dealer in African art, said that in the 1960s and 1970s in Côte d'Ivoire, Ghana's neighbour to the west, 'they were selling "gold" heads with the cabbages in Abidjan market. If you rub them with lime juice, the gold comes to the fore.'[30] Some of these dubious heads appear to have reached Paris. In February 1960, Cécile de Rothschild, heiress, professional golfer, connoisseur and confidante of Greta Garbo, wrote to the Wallace Collection. She had been offered an allegedly Asante gold mask, valued at £7,500 (about £194,000 today), which weighed about one kilogram. She doubted its authenticity and sought advice. Sir Francis Watson, curator and later Director at the Wallace, advised her to come and compare it with their own Asante collection: 'Why don't you come over to London to look at these objects? There is nothing like handling these things to give one the feeling of whether an offered piece is genuine or not.'[31]

The Wallace Collection files do not say whether Cécile de Rothschild did visit, or what happened to the gold mask she had been offered. Watson's description of it suggests it was not Asante: 'very different from ours ... the stylisation much more linear ... like an "Indian Picasso."' But at Christmas 1974, Watson, who by then had retired from the Wallace, sent his former colleagues a postcard – 'with affectionate memories' – of yet another purportedly Asante head, which seemed to be of significance, and which he recommended they keep on file. The postcard was made by the Princeton University Art Museum, in the United States, and shows a photograph of a 'Head of a King, Ashanti, Ghana ca. 1750', which it had 'on anonymous long-term loan'. I was intrigued. The head, based on the photograph, was in very good condition. If the British had seen it, in 1874 or 1896, they surely would have taken it and probably written about it. Why had this wonderful object not cropped up in all my research? And, moreover, given that the Princeton University Art Museum had once made a postcard of it, why was it now conspicuously absent from that museum's otherwise informative website?

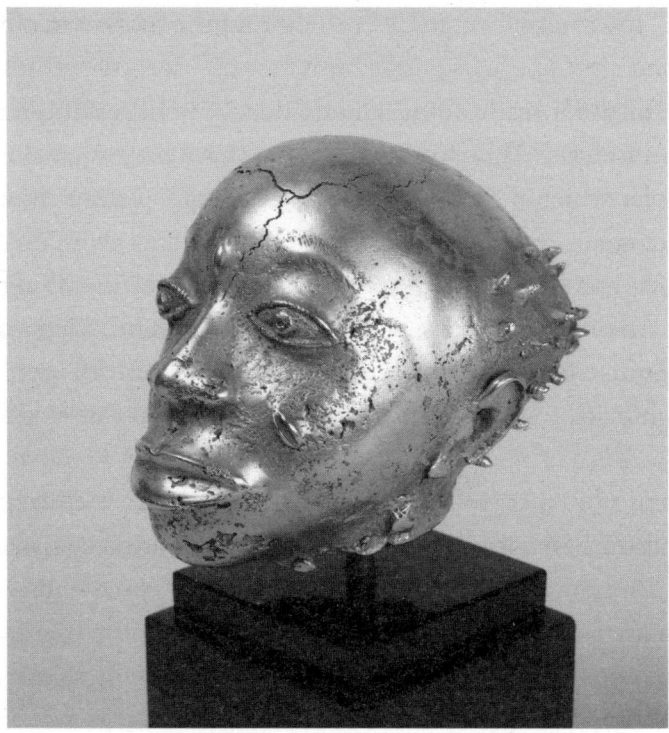

Fake treasure. The Princeton Head, posing as eighteenth-century Asante gold.

The awkward truth is that the Princeton University Art Museum still has the head but has long since concluded it is not as old or valuable as it once thought. 'It's been determined that this head was made in the twentieth century, and it's actually gold-plated copper alloy', Perrin Lathrop, the museum's African art curator, told me.[32] The museum had received it on loan in about 1970, from John Elliott, a Princeton graduate, Wall Street banker and 'outstanding collector of Asian art ... a true Renaissance man'.[33] Elliott, according to Lathrop, worked primarily through New York dealers. 'Clearly he bought the head in good faith,' she said. In February 1971, 'the rare Ashanti head' was part of a special exhibition of African sculpture, which the museum extended by a fortnight because of the 'unusual amount of interest that it has excited amongst Princetonians'.[34] In 1998, after Elliott's death, the museum acquired the head by bequest. By then, however, curators had grown suspicious. Today, it languishes in storage. As to why it was made in the first place, well, as Lathrop drily observed, 'It was likely created in response to the market in objects that were looted'.

Some of the Asante loot has found its way into Britain's regimental military museums. The Royal Green Jackets Museum in Winchester, for example, which is responsible for the history of the Rifle Brigade, has Asante chairs, stools, swords, clay pipes, as well as a large plate of 'gold alloy', and even part of a jewelled necklace 'belonging to King Coffee'.[35] All of these, it says, were 'removed from the King's palace' in 1874. The museum only received them in 1963, when they were donated by a daughter of Richard Frederick Meysey-Thompson, who had been a young lieutenant with Wolseley, was a 'keen rider and … writer of repute', and who died in 1926.[36] The Royal Signals Museum in Dorset has a handsome Asante chair, apparently taken from the palace by the British in 1896 and given to the Royal Engineers in recognition of their success in laying a telegraph line up to Kumasi.[37]

Of course, there are huge numbers of Asante objects not made of gold, or not judged to be particularly valuable in financial terms, which British soldiers and sailors brought home with them. One summer morning, I travelled to the London suburb of Chiswick and a cottage by the Thames which belongs to a well-known dealer in African art. He took me down to his basement and showed me an Asante 'talking drum', *atumpan*, used to convey messages, a single mighty piece of wood as high as my waist, hollowed and decorated with vertical lines and with elephant hide stretched tight over its head. Together, we managed to heave it off the shelf – it weighed about fifty kilograms – and with silver polish, wiped a shield-shaped plaque on its front. The words slowly emerged from the dark metal: '3rd Batt: W.I Regt. Captured At Djachi. Ashanti. 24th August 1900. Presented by Captain H A Thorne.'[38] A souvenir from the final weeks of Asante resistance.

Chasing another lead, I went to visit John Ryle, an anthropologist and writer, in his house in Notting Hill. John is an erudite man; *The London Review of Books* once wrote that 'he knows as much about eastern Africa as anyone in Britain.'[39] I was surprised to find myself having breakfast with another guest, the distinguished Somali novelist, Nuruddin Farah, who happened to be staying for a few days. We discussed Africa, colonialism and museums; our conversation frequently interrupted as John leapt up and pulled a tangentially related book from his shelves. Eventually, he led me and Nuruddin downstairs, past a bust of his great-grandfather, a man called Walter Claude Johnson, as finely moustached and confident-looking as any of the British officers who sacked Kumasi. Johnson, however, was not a soldier but a brilliant engineer, who made a fortune as a pioneer of transoceanic telegraph cables and was also a talented artist and founder of *The Connoisseur* art magazine.[40] Somewhere along this journey, he had picked up an Asante stool, which John keeps on a shelf in his basement study in the midst of his vast collection of books and files.

We took the stool upstairs, into the light of John's living room. It was handsome, but the wood was cracked and the thin story of its provenance derived from one yellowing piece of card with an inscription from 1904 in elegant cursive writing: 'This Stool Which Constitutes a throne, was looted by the British troops during the Ashanti War, from the Royal Palace of Coomassie after the Deposition of King Bomban.' Who on earth was Bomban? 'The Deposition' suggests this refers to Prempeh, and not Karikari, and hence the stool probably dates from 1896. But yet again British documents betray a woeful carelessness about what had been taken, when and from whom. John's great-grandfather may have revelled in his stool's status as a 'throne', but it is decorated with none of the gold or silver plate typical of those of high Asante aristocracy, so it seems more likely that it belonged to a less important courtier or village chief.

Thirty years ago, John wrote that this stool's 'presence in my house is a memento ... of the violent colonial appropriation of African ritual objects and *objets de vertu*, and the enduring misunderstanding of indigenous cultural practice on the part of the imperial power.'[41] Today, he says he is 'ambivalent about whether I should have this stool or not'. Swimming against a tide of shrill certainties, he says 'it is terribly important not to have simplistic notions of capitalism, empire and conquest ... the ethics of possession are not simple.' Although, as he ruefully observed, 'if you say it is complicated you are seen as apologizing for not returning.' He paused. 'I don't feel guilty,' he said, 'but if I knew the specific family to whom it belonged and they wanted to reconnect with their ancestors, of course that would be different.' Otherwise, he felt, 'there are many stools to go round and what I would like to see is Ghana having access to the art world. Really we should be giving them Michelangelos and Picassos.'[42]

★★★

Over the decades, and in a piecemeal and haphazard fashion, some individuals have taken it upon themselves to return looted objects to the Asante, not in an official capacity as the Queen did in 1961, but as private acts of conscience. In the mid-1950s the South African novelist Stuart Cloete visited Kumasi. He describes a dinner where he was shown ornaments which Robert Baden-Powell had looted in 1896 and which Lady Olave Baden-Powell, more than thirty years younger than her husband and a widow since 1941, had recently returned to the Asantehene. 'The collection consisted of rings, gold necklaces, gold weights ... General Baden-Powell had given them to his wife as a wedding present – they must have been his finest trophies, fitted into green leather velvet-lined cases.' It is not clear whether Baden-Powell consented to their return before his death, but Cloete thought it 'creditable' that Lady Baden-Powell had given them back 'to their rightful owners – the Royal House of the Ashanti Nation'.[43]

In October 1974, when Asantehene Opoku Ware visited the British Museum, Malcolm McLeod showed him an Asante green leather hat, with gold plate depicting five pairs of crocodiles wrapped around each other. According to Asante folklore, it was made for Asantehene Osei Kwadwo, who ruled in the mid-eighteenth century, to celebrate victory over the Banda king Worasa, who is said to be depicted in the famous gold head in the Wallace Collection.[44] Christie's, who were about to sell the hat at auction, said it had been taken by Lieutenant F. Cowan of the Royal Welch Fusiliers from 'the dressing room' of Kofi Karikari in 1874 and was now 'the property of a lady', a descendant of the lieutenant who was also selling an elephant tail flywhisk, likewise taken from the royal chamber.[45] Malcolm McLeod said the British Museum considered bidding for the hat but decided to refrain as a gesture of goodwill towards the

Asantehene, should he wish to buy it instead.⁴⁶ Opoku Ware II declined and the hat, prominently advertised in *The Times*, was bought by Charles Ratton in December 1974 for £2,520 (about £28,000 today).⁴⁷ Ratton, according to Hermione Waterfield, had 'fallen in love with it'. But, she recalls with some pleasure, 'Bill Fagg introduced Charles Ratton to the Asantehene and Charles agreed to sell it to the Asantehene for no profit. He asked only that he be given a few minutes alone with the hat first. "I would only do this for Bill", Charles said. People said Charles was a tough old nut, bloodless, but he wasn't.'⁴⁸ Fifty years later, I was thrilled to be shown this same hat in Kumasi, in a backroom of the Manhyia Palace, where it sat oddly beside a photo of Prince Edward, the Duke of Edinburgh, a wooden ship from the Freemasons Lodge of Mauritius and all sorts of other random gifts which are sent to the Asantehene. At least the hat still comes out for major Asante festivals, when it is worn by the royal gun bearers.⁴⁹

In 1950, Edward Hulme, of Reigate Hill, in Surrey, looking round a house to buy for his son, found an old stool at the back of a broom cupboard. It had a metal plaque saying it had been taken from 'the palace of Queen Ashantuad at Ojesu' (Yaa Asantewaa of Ejisu) in August 1900. Hulme had survived what he called 'the holocaust of Loos' as a teenager and had devoted his life to helping fellow First World War veterans.⁵⁰ He bought the stool for £4 and 10 shillings but soon felt uncomfortable about his acquisition. 'I believe all looted stuff should be returned, it's half the cause of wars,' he told the *Daily Mirror*, which described Yaa Asantewaa as 'the Joan of Arc of Africa'. Hulme was encouraged by the Labour government's Colonial Secretary, James Griffiths, who said the return of the stool would 'promote good understanding' between the Gold Coast and Britain. A Surrey newspaper reported that one of 'Yaa Asantewaa's grateful descendants, accompanied by countrymen wearing traditional West African dress of ceremony, came to receive the precious relic from its finder, for return to its country of origin.' Hulme's generous act, the newspaper said, 'was entirely characteristic'.⁵¹

In fact, Yaa Asantewaa's many stools, rather like Charles MacCarthy's missing skull, are a recurrent feature of the Anglo-Asante story. In 2011 the

British artist Angela Palmer bought a stool at an auction in Oxfordshire, which also had a plaque saying it had been taken from Yaa Asantewaa, with the more specific information that it had been removed from her compound on 30 August 1900 by Henry Russell, an English Cape Coast trader who was Private Secretary to Colonel James Willcocks. Russell brought back several items of Asante loot to Britain but died near Chester in 1912 when his car collided with a pony trap driven by a drunken man.[52] Angela says that as soon as she saw the stool at the auction she 'felt a strong urge to return it to the Ghanaians; it had no purpose or meaning in the UK.' She was connected through her Oxford University college, Exeter, to fellow alumnus John Kufuor, the former president of Ghana (who would in 2024 also assist in the return of the British Museum and V&A's gold regalia), who agreed to take the stool back to Kumasi.[53]

In November 2024, I drove from Kumasi to Ejisu with Malcolm McLeod and Gordon Frimpong of the Manhyia Palace Museum, to find out what had happened to Angela Palmer's stool. We had been told that, with the Asantehene's help, it had been returned to the Ejisu royal family. We were warmly received by Yaa Asantewaa II, the current Queen Mother, a direct descendant of the legendary warrior-queen and a formidable woman in her own right. She sat on a gilded throne, surrounded by chiefs in robes and facing an enormous television, her walls adorned with photographs of herself, in some of which she was waving a rifle in the air. She graciously allowed us into her bedroom, where she dismantled a wall of boxes of schnapps and lifted a cloth to reveal the stool we had come to see. It was covered in plantains and other food, offerings to the ancestors, but still bore the plaque confirming it had been seized from this same compound 124 years earlier. Yaa Asantewaa II took one of the bottles of schnapps and doused the stool as she said a prayer to bless us for our journey. 'This stool,' she said, 'has enhanced my dignity. As soon as it came back, I felt stronger, and I could feel the strength of Yaa Asantewaa herself.' Then she covered it up again. Its long sojourn in England seemed to have in no way diminished its spiritual power.[54]

In 1985, a seventy-two-year-old widow and horse-racing devotee from Cirencester in Gloucestershire, Diana Jackson, flew to Ghana to return yet another Yaa Asantewaa stool, also with a rich and unusual backstory. Her father, Samuel Hingley, was the officer who took the Queen's surrender in 1901 and, he says, subsequently formed a friendship of sorts with her (see Chapter 14). Hingley, writing in 1935, said that the night before Yaa Asantewaa was sent into exile she presented him with what she called the 'Interpreters Stool' or the Stool of N'cheti.[55] This is a plain wooden stool, with a lovely smooth curved seat, much simpler, according to Hingley than three other gold decorated stools which were forcibly taken from Yaa Asantewaa and handed to an unnamed British official.

Samuel Hingley had led a colourful life; before Asante he had been a rare British participant in the Spanish-American War of 1898, and afterwards served in India and was wounded at Ypres, before becoming a minor radio personality. He kept his stool – somehow, in the retelling, it had been elevated to the one Sir Charles MacCarthy was sitting on when his head was chopped off – and resisted a 'huge sum' from 'a big American collector' for it. After his death in 1939 it passed on to his

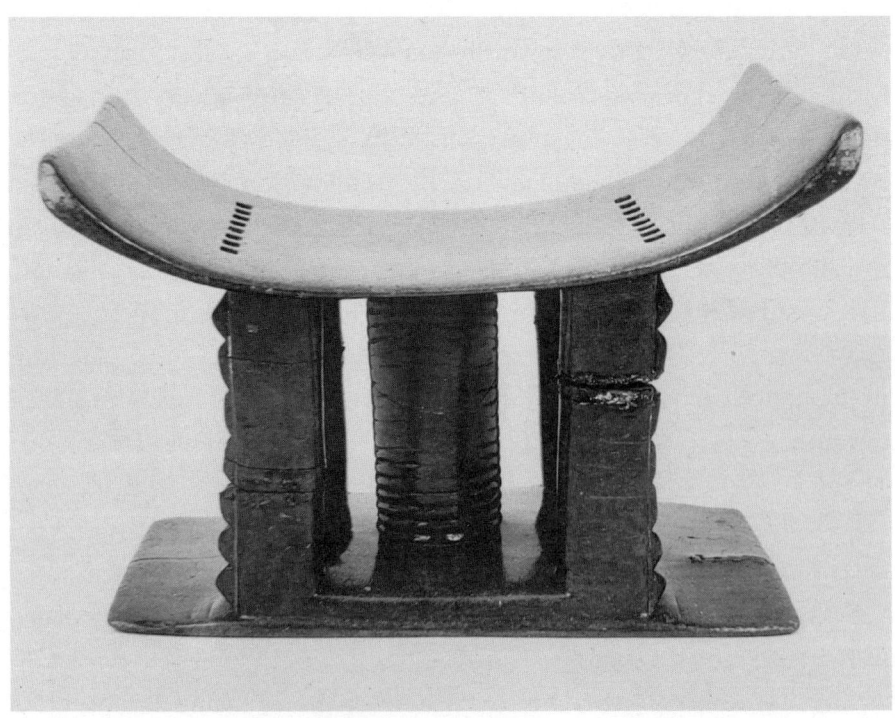

Returned treasure. 'We knew it came from an African queen.'

son Anthony, a colonial civil servant.⁵⁶ Anthony's sons remember the stool – 'beautiful in its simplicity of polished wood,' 'I loved sitting on it, we knew it came from an African queen' – as it was carted around homes in Ceylon, Kenya and Rhodesia in the dying days of Empire.⁵⁷ After Anthony died in the 1970s, and not without a family controversy and some bitterness, the stool passed on to his sister, Diana Jackson. 'My beloved Ashanti stool', she called it.⁵⁸

In 1984, Diana, widowed and writing her will, was 'foxed' as to what to do with the stool. One option was to send it to Jamaica, as Samuel Hingley had led West Indian troops in Asante. But their small regimental museum already had Asante memorabilia. And besides, Jamaica was 'so communistic'. She could have given it to her daughter, Deirdre, only she was married to an Italian and Diana 'did not want it to end up in Italy'. Instead, she was 'inspired' to think of the Asante themselves.⁵⁹ The British High Commission in Ghana was roped in and a message passed on to Asantehene Opoku Ware II. He replied that he was 'very keen' and offered to fly Diana to Kumasi as a special guest and incorporate a handover ceremony into the 'Golden Jubilee Durbar' he had scheduled for November 1985, which celebrated the fiftieth anniversary of the restoration of Prempeh II to the Golden Stool.⁶⁰ 'The question of the stool has been a potential irritant in UK/Ghana relations for some time, and it is good to see that it will be resolved so satisfactorily,' wrote a relieved British diplomat.⁶¹

Diana Jackson had not had an easy life. Her marriage, to an army officer and Olympic oarsman, was not happy, and her son died in tragic circumstances. A nephew says 'she had a Boris Johnsonian relationship to the truth; everything was either wonderful or terrible.'⁶² Her journal of her journey to Ghana should perhaps be taken with a pinch of salt and is certainly peppered with prejudices. The Asante and other Ghanaians, she pronounces, 'dislike and mistrust each other intensely'. Ghana's head of state, Flight Lieutenant Jerry Rawlings (who first came to power in a coup in 1979 and then ruled the country from 1981 to 2001) was a 'half-caste … communist', whereas the Asante were 'extremely pro-British, unwesternised, tribal and much the stronger morally'.⁶³ They 'are a very hospitable people, but they used to be the most terrifying tribe in the world, more so than the Zulus.'[64] And yet her journal also conveys the impression of a spirited woman, on the adventure of a lifetime, confronting her own prejudices.

She and Deirdre, 'the Marchesa', spent eight days being wined and dined by Opoku Ware II, his courtiers and British diplomats. 'The most amazing thing of the whole trip', she writes, 'was to find how exactly – and I mean exactly – the Ashantis are like us … their outlook on life as a whole, plus a very wide and shrewd perception of world politics'.[65] The Marchesa was certainly impressed. 'My dear daughter said to me when we had been there for two or three days, "Mummy, any young woman coming out here for over a month and stays a virgin, wants her head examined", I quite agreed!'[66] The highlight was the handover of the stool at the durbar in Kumasi stadium. Diana curtseyed before Opoku Ware II and said '"I have much honour in returning this stool to its rightful owners." The King took it, placed it on his knees, thanked me, beaming all over his face, in fact the whole arena were laughing and clapping and going back we were greeted the whole way.'[67] Opoku Ware II, so painfully thwarted by the British government and museums in the 1970s, now expressed 'the gratitude of a Nation, of all Asante, and indeed Ghana' towards this individual woman and hoped 'this generous act by the Jackson family will be the first step in a movement towards the return and restitution of regalia and other items of immense spiritual value which are locked away in private homes and museums.'[68]

Back home in Cirencester, Diana Jackson reflected on what she and her daughter had been through and typed up her sixty-page journal. 'I can genuinely say we both had the most marvellous experience of our lives – I have a very hard problem getting it out of my head even now.'[69] She died in 2004. A nephew, Christopher Hingley, speaking from his home in Bulawayo, Zimbabwe, said 'It was a good and brave thing which she did, I'm proud of her. And it must have been fun – who wouldn't want to do this?'[70] On her return, Diana had been asked by her local newspaper what had motivated her. 'I thought I would do my bit,' she said, 'but there is a lot still in the British Museum.'[71]

General Sir William George Knox, who looted at Maqdala and Kumasi.

18

'YOU EXPRESS THE VIEWS OF A CIVILIAN'

The letter from the Royal Artillery's regimental secretary was curt and categorical. The regiment was 'unable to agree' to my request to see its Asante gold ram's head, held in the officer's mess room at their barracks in Larkhill, a garrison town near Stonehenge. 'It has long been our policy, primarily on security grounds, not to allow public access to items held in the Regiment's private collection,' wrote the secretary. So we will have to make do with William Fagg's description instead. 'A marvel of ethereal eggshell-thin lightness, seeming to take off into the air like a wisp of smoke,' he wrote, a 'tour de main' of the lost wax method, 'among the most striking examples of West African metallurgy'.[1] The ram's head has spiralling horns, is some nineteen centimetres in width and weighs 1.2 kilograms (see plate section).[2] Fagg suggested it was probably made in the mid-nineteenth century as it was too fragile – in places only one-millimetre thick – to have survived intact for much longer. Alexander Kyerematen, the Asante historian, said it would originally have been made as an ornament to decorate a sword.[3]

In 1905 General Sir William George Knox wrote a candid account of how he had taken this glorious object from Kumasi. Back in 1874 he had been a young lieutenant, one of five Royal Artillery officers in charge of the 'Native Houssa Artillery', the African Hausa soldiers who carried and fired the big guns Wolseley used with devastating effect at the Battle of Amoafo. 'The night we entered the town', wrote Knox,

> two subalterns R. A (I was one) broke into the Palace and began to collect trophies. We had put by the Ram's head and a gold woman's breast (now in Officer's Mess Rifle Brigade) both of beaten gold and a good many other things when we were surprised by a visit from official searchers from head quarters. Next morning an order appeared directing all loot to be given up. We disgorged our treasure and they were handed over to the Prize Committee. Amongst other things I remember handing over the British flag that had been captured from Sir Charles MacCarthy (his skull was on the King's war-drum) and also a sword presented by Queen Victoria to King Coffee.[4]

Fortunately for Knox, he had friends in the right places. All the Royal Artillery officers had travelled out to the Gold Coast with Wolseley, and some were in his inner circle. They included Captain Henry Brackenbury, Wolseley's military secretary (who mentions seeing the ram's head by candlelight in the palace) and Lieutenant John Maurice, Wolseley's personal secretary. The ram's head was due to be sold at the auction at Cape Coast Castle, along with the other palace loot (although what became of yet another manifestation of Sir Charles MacCarthy's skull is not clear), but instead Brackenbury was given permission to buy it for its weight in gold on behalf of the Royal Artillery. 'The Artillery officers serving in the campaign bought it amongst them,' wrote Knox, 'paying about £135 (if I remember rightly)', or about £15,800 today.[5] When the Royal Artillery officers returned to England, on 20 March 1874, word soon reached the newspapers that they had 'the best trophy … very valuable' and 'one of the most remarkable trophies of the late war'.[6] On 13 April, Brackenbury presented the ram's head to the Royal Artillery Mess at Woolwich, where Major-General Sir David Wood gratefully received it on behalf of the regiment.[7]

The Royal Artillery Mess in Woolwich, in an imposing Georgian building with a great arch connecting the parade ground to the barrack squares behind, was no ordinary mess. 'Approached by a staircase of magnificent proportions', wrote the historian William Thomas Vincent, 'everywhere renowned for its wealth and grandeur and princely hospitality. Its store of plate is exceedingly rich, and comprises gifts from kings and emperors, souvenirs from other regiments, and spoils taken from the enemy.' The most recently acquired of these, Vincent wrote in 1875, was the 'massive ram's head of unalloyed gold, captured at the palace of the barbarous Ashantee King'.[8] In May 1874 the Czar of Russia, Alexander II, lunched in the Woolwich Mess along with the Prince of Wales while 'Mr Smyth's renowned band' played on the lawn outside.[9] Presumably the new acquisition from Kumasi took pride of place.

The ram's head was also exhibited at the South Kensington Museum soon after its arrival in Britain. In 1875 the Royal Artillery decided its 'rather primitive and fragile head' needed better protection and at 'immense trouble ... and considerable expense' commissioned various designs before instructing a London firm, Messrs. Lambert, to seal it in a glass dome and mount it on a tripod stand which is carried, Atlas-style, on the backs of what a regimental history describes as 'three bowed figures of beautifully-moulded West African natives', who are dressed only in loincloths.[10] On the base of this stand are engraved the words 'Amoaful Ordahsu Coomassie', commemorating the battles and capture of the city. The stand transformed the ram's head into a trophy and cemented its ceremonial role in the officer's mess. It is also, from the perspective of the twenty-first century, in shockingly bad taste.

William Knox was, according to a Royal Artillery officer, 'very much a soldier', from an aristocratic family and the son of a general, his career defined by the imperial wars of the late nineteenth century.[11] The ram's head was not the only trophy Knox brought back from Asante, for the Royal Collection at Windsor has an iron knife with a decorated wooden handle which he presented to Queen Victoria's third son Prince Arthur, and which is 'said to have belonged to King Kofi Karikari'.[12] A few years earlier, in 1868, Knox had taken part in the Abyssinian expedition, where he said 'the guns were carried on elephants for the greater part of 400 miles ... over most atrocious roads.' When the British army entered Maqdala, the stronghold of Emperor Tewodros, it 'was levelled to the ground and burnt', but Knox and a group of fellow Royal Artillery officers came away with a silver cross plundered from a church, which they later presented to their colleagues back in Woolwich.[13] This makes Knox, in the words of a regimental history, 'part donor of two of the most remarkable trophies in the Mess'.[14]

In 1890, the Maqdala cross and Asante ram's head were displayed together at the Royal Military Exhibition in Chelsea, along with several other objects looted from Abyssinia and Asante, 'specially selected on account of their connection with some deed of British valour' and where they formed 'a most attractive feature'.[15] In 1905 the Royal Artillery, presumably out of deference to Christian sensibilities, said the Maqdala cross was 'never used as a "table decoration" in the Mess, but generally put on the mantel-piece on guest nights'.[16] Royal Artillery officers speculate that its pear-shaped bosses contain rare jewels or even the ashes of an empress of Abyssinia. According to regimental legend, when the Emperor Haile Selassie dined at the Woolwich Mess – the date is variously given as just before or after the Second World War – he asked for it to be returned, 'to the consternation of all', only to promptly hand it back to the officers as a gift from the people of Abyssinia, amidst much relief.[17]

I pursued the path of William Knox's career in the years after Asante, through battles against the Zulus, the Afghans and the Boers, punctuated by spells at home, much of which seem to have been devoted to fox-hunting.[18] He was a brave man, from a different time. In 1877 he volunteered with two fellow officers to join the Red Crescent Society during the Russo-Turkish War – 'we decided one night at dinner in our club to go see the *vrai chose*' – where he distributed food and clothing to 'wretched refugees' fleeing the Russian army in the Bulgarian mountains and worked in a crude field hospital, assisting in operations performed by candlelight. He describes the Turkish soldiers he meets on the front line: 'Tall, fine, lithe, keen men – I never saw such stuff. Without any vice – except perhaps cruelty, which in a soldier may be excusable.'[19] In retirement he became a military pundit and commentator, with opinions so blimpish they are almost beyond parody. If only, he fulminates in 1909, there was less pheasant shooting and more fox-hunting in East Anglia, the British army would acquire the horse-riding skills to equip it for the coming European war. Never underestimate the value in battle of the 'cheer', he advises that same year, drawing on his experience of fighting the Asante. It is 'worth more than a million cartridges. To the cheering line it inspires the waverers, fortifies the funkers, and galvanizes the attack ... To the foe it causes them first to think, then to tremble, then to travel.'[20]

On a gloomy day in March 1913, Knox was amongst dozens and dozens of elderly generals at Wolseley's funeral at St Paul's Cathedral. By then many of the Asante generation of 1874 had already gone, and Wolseley himself had lived a reclusive and diminished final decade, much of it on the French Riviera. His coffin was carried through the fog, from the War Office along the Embankment, to the wailing lament of pipes and the muffled beat of drums, under street lamps 'that looked like the sentinel candles of some ghostly requiem', past an enormous crowd, the silence only broken by 'the slow and measured tramp of the infantry, the metallic ring of the hoofs of the cavalry-men's horses, the rattle of the artillery, and the low tones of the officers as they issued their orders'. Sir Evelyn Wood, old companion and sometime rival and irritant, was amongst the pall bearers, while veterans of more recent Asante campaigns, including Robert Baden-Powell and Bruce Hamilton, were in the congregation. Wolseley, a man 'whose great campaigns were fought under the brilliant skies and amid the rich colours of Africa and the East' was laid to rest in the crypt next to Nelson and Wellington, as 'London, the city of grey, wrapped another of the nation's heroes in her homely pall.'[21]

When the European war did come, in all its horror, Knox became a columnist for the *Pall Mall Gazette*, where his influential but anonymous 'Letters from Mars' berated his compatriots for having gone soft: 'War is the supreme test of national virtue ... You, my dear Great Britain, entered upon this strife with a heavy handicap ... Your ministers for a century or more have been wanting in moral courage', 'You, my dear Great Britain, cannot complain of insufficient warning of a coming danger' and so on.[22] If only there had been more hunting, he wrote in *The Times* in May 1916, as the fox and the hounds had done more than any person to equip the army with 'the cult of character, quick decision and nerve so necessary for leadership in war.' He quotes a general who has written to him from the front, warning that the end of fox-hunting would be 'a great victory for the Boche'.[23]

Sir William Knox died in December 1916, aged sixty-nine, and his coffin, topped with Union Jack, hat and sword, was brought on a gun carriage from his home in Portman Square, through Mayfair to St Mark's Church on Audley Street, where Scots Guards lined the steps.[24] I happen to know St Mark's, it is no longer a church, but an upmarket food hall, where I've eaten pizza with friends. It is hard to imagine what William Knox would make of that or the cosmopolitan crowds on the London streets outside.

In May 2007, the Royal Artillery left Woolwich for its new home in Larkhill, almost 150 kilometres to the west. The Victorian period, according to regimental historian Brigadier Ken Timbers, had been 'the zenith of Woolwich and the Royal Artillery Mess as well as the beginning of the decline of their status'. If so it was a gentle decline, for in 1936 *Tatler* magazine said the Woolwich Mess was still 'without a rival in this or any other country' and evoked glorious evenings in its dining room when 'the port had gone round for the second or third time' and the trophies were put out to be admired.[25] Every British sovereign from George III to Elizabeth II was entertained at the Woolwich Mess, where they were fussed over by waiters in eighteenth-century uniforms and the regiment's treasures and silver plate – 'the mess silver' – glittered in the light of chandeliers and candelabras.[26] In 2000, intriguingly, Jerry Rawlings, then in his final year as President of Ghana, also dined there.[27] But in the second part of the twentieth century the nearby Royal Dockyards were gradually scaled down and then closed, while the army's centre of gravity moved west of London, towards Aldershot. The Mess's collection of treasures was moved to Larkhill 'amid great security' in August 2007 after the completion of a new silver room to house them. The Queen saw them there in 2008.[28]

I had been warned that my efforts to visit the Larkhill Mess were likely to be in vain. 'These are much cherished items, the regiment is prickly and there may be a sucking of teeth and certain prejudices,' according to one retired Royal Artillery officer closely involved in mess affairs. The 'mess silver', technically, is the private property of a charity called the Royal Artillery Institution, to which all Royal Artillery officers belong. A general boasted that it is 'the most remarkable catalogue of military memorabilia that exists anywhere outside our national museums'.[29] My officer said, 'I've never known a piece to be sold, we're terribly acquisitive.' And, if for example, the Ministry of Defence instructed you to surrender a piece? 'We'd say no,' he told me, without hesitation.[30]

I've not been alone in my frustrations. I struck up an online friendship with Jarat Chopra, a lawyer who lives in Kenya and is a descendant of Diwan Mulraj Chopra of Multan, a Sikh governor in the Punjab who surrendered to the British army in 1849 and died in British custody in 1851. Jarat has waged an unsuccessful campaign for the return of Mulraj's sword – a curved blade with a handle covered in gold leaf and scabbard of dark green velvet with gold cap – which is also in the Larkhill Mess. He says the return of the sword, by purchase if necessary, would be of 'tremendous transcendental significance' to his family, in helping them lay to rest an ancestor with the proper rites. In 2019 he asked the Royal Artillery to show magnitude, and bring honour on itself, 'in keeping with the times'. In 2020 he too received an uncompromising letter from the Royal Artillery. The assistant regimental secretary, a retired major, said the sword had been 'formally bequeathed to the Regiment … This is now irreversible, and it cannot now be sold or otherwise disposed of.' The regiment would never consider returning military trophies, just as it would never seek the return of trophies captured from it in past conflicts. And as for Jarat's suggestion of moving with the times, the Major said, 'you express the view of a civilian, who misunderstands one of the main purposes of a military trophy, and that is to maintain the memory of past conflicts and of our forebears who fought and died in it.'[31]

Would the Asantehene get a more sympathetic hearing if he asked to see the ram's head? I suspect he would at least be treated more diplomatically. But for now, the Asante ram's head, the Maqdala cross and Mulraj's sword can only be seen by a select few. A director of a major national museum told me he had been allowed to visit them at Larkhill. He is a temperamentally conservative man, not instinctively sympathetic to the restitution cause. What did he think when he saw the treasures? 'When you see those things, and you realise no one else can see them, and they will never leave this place, it's like a punch in the stomach.'[32]

Osei Tutu II, Asantehene since 1999.

19

'THE PAST SHOULD NOT DICTATE THE PRESENT'

In May 2023, the Asantehene, Osei Tutu II, in London for the coronation of Charles III, also paid a visit to the British Museum. He met the museum's director, Dr Hartwig Fischer, in the Sloane Room, overlooking the columned entrance. It was a discreet, business-like affair; the Asantehene was in a dark check suit rather than robes and regalia. Malcolm McLeod – now working as an adviser to the Asantehene – was amongst the handful of people in the room. They sat beneath a painting by the artist Atta Kwami, who spent much of his life in Kumasi and whose abstract rectangles merge European modernism with the warm colours of Ghana. 'It was rather suitable,' Malcolm remembers. He spoke at the meeting of the history between the British Museum and the Asante, of the negotiations of the 1970s, the exhibitions in London and New York in the 1980s, of how he had helped establish a Manhyia Palace Museum in Kumasi in 1995 and of how the British Museum had trained its curators. 'I was trying to present the idea of treasures going back as a natural development, not a sudden new development,' he says.[1]

Asantehene Osei Tutu II spoke next, of how important the missing regalia was to his people and of how a series of upcoming anniversaries would provide the perfect context for at least some to be returned; 2024, he explained, would be the 150th anniversary of Wolseley's sacking of the palace, as well as the 100th anniversary of Prempeh's return from the Seychelles. It would also mark his own Silver Jubilee, as he had become the sixteenth Asantehene when he was enstooled in 1999 following the death of Opoku Ware II. According to Malcolm, the Asantehene 'made it clear he was not demanding return, but was up for some sort of arrangement. The word "restitution" was never mentioned. Hartwig Fischer listened, paused and then replied "this all seems perfectly reasonable." The King and I looked at each other as if to say "Did we really just hear that?"'[2] Formal consent to a loan did not come from the British Museum trustees until January 2024, but somehow, in one amicable and straightforward meeting, all the obstacles the museum had presented over decades were swept aside.[3]

The Asantehene's emollient approach was very much in character. Osei Tutu II is a diplomatic man who knows Britain well. He was a student in London and later worked, rather incongruously, for Brent Council as a personnel manager. He owns a large house in Henley-on-Thames, which he visits often. He would go and take tea with Queen Elizabeth II at nearby Windsor, and counted her, as he does Charles III, as a friend. He too, after all, is a hereditary king, leading a people who are in many ways profoundly conservative. 'I have over the years cultivated great friendships in high circles within the upper class,' he explained to me, somewhat disarmingly.[4] In a very non-threatening way, he has unique credentials to make the case to British institutions for the return of looted artefacts. 'There's always been a steady "we'd like it back,"' is how Malcolm characterises the Asantehene's approach, 'but it hasn't been a strident, table-thumping demand. Anyway, the King and his chiefs often have much more urgent things to deal with ... I went out to Kumasi with Andrew Burnett [a former deputy director of the British Museum] a few years ago. The King lent us a house and car, and looked after us very well. He said "you've got my stuff", but we were his guests and he behaved very properly.'[5]

The Asante scholar Ivor Agyeman-Duah, whom the Asantehene had appointed alongside Malcolm to negotiate for the return of regalia, was also at the meeting. While discussions carried on in the following months, Ivor selected the objects which would go back to Kumasi with the help of the British Museum's Africa curator Julie Hudson. 'Drawer after drawer, with Julie, I pointed out the ones of interest to us. Then I showed the photo images to the Asantehene. "These are the objects we are targeting." He said "Good, you made the right choices, I would also have chosen these ones." He approved.'[6]

Ivor is a short, intense and persuasive man, with a solemn manner. Only occasionally does he break into a warm smile. He has a multitude of roles, as an author, historian, diplomat and also as Director of the Manhyia Palace Museum. In Kumasi, he is a whirl of distracted activity, conducting multiple conversations, in person and on the phone, at any one time. Visitors who come to the city, depending on his time and connections, have to be patient. Just when you think you've got his attention, he disappears. The Asante, typically, opt for traditional one-shouldered robes for public events. To 'wear cloth', as it is called, bestows dignity, but it does involve much hitching and rearranging. I was intrigued that Ivor is invariably in a suit and tie. 'Why didn't you dress up today?' I asked after a ceremony at the palace. 'I'm too busy to wear cloth,' he said matter-of-factly. 'I always need to run around, and that is not easy in robes.'

In 1895, when the Owusu Ansa brothers travelled to London on their failed mission to avert a British invasion, Ivor's great-grandfather, Kwame Boatin, of Asante aristocracy with the title *Kyidomhene*, was one of the chiefs who accompanied them. When Boatin returned to Cape Coast, he met Governor William Maxwell and tried to convince him of Prempeh's good intentions – 'If the King means anything wrong he would not have sent us to England … the King sent us to say what is true' – but was brusquely brushed aside.[7] After Prempeh was captured in Kumasi and imprisoned in Elmina in 1896, Boatin raised money to pay for Cape Coast lawyers who drew up a petition calling for the release of the Asantehene and accused the British of acting in bad faith. For these efforts the British arrested him and sent him into exile with Prempeh, first to Sierra Leone and later to the Seychelles.[8] Kwame's son, Thomas Boatin (Ivor's great-uncle) who was born in the Seychelles, recalls his father was one of the elders who resolutely refused to learn the local Creole. They said, 'We will never speak this adulterated language, Asante is the pure language we prefer.' Kwame, who was eventually christened 'Henry', died in the Seychelles.[9]

Given this history, Ivor could have been forgiven for entering negotiations with the British with some scepticism. In fact, just like the Asantehene, he is something of an Anglophile, with a respect and affection for the ways of the British establishment. Anyway, the Asantehene's instructions were clear. 'He wasn't in the mood for antagonism,' Ivor told me. 'He wanted diplomacy, and our guiding line was that what went on in the past should not dictate the present.'[10] Ivor's own instincts were also non-confrontational. Exile brought suffering and loneliness to his family, he explained, but also opportunities. 'Those that went were exposed,' he explains, 'and had something to contribute when they came back'. Kwame Boatin had seven children in exile, including Ivor's grandfather Paul, who would all become members of the Gold Coast educated elite. They spoke French, as well as English, and took up senior positions in the Asantehene's palace, in the civil service, academia and later as diplomats for independent Ghana. 'We inherited so much from them, in terms of scholarship and public service,' Ivor says.[11]

The biggest point of contention, of course, was that the British Museum would only loan back its Asante objects for an initial three years. When news broke in early 2024 that the Asantehene had accepted these terms, Ivor found himself at the centre of the storm. 'A disgrace to us as a people', 'unacceptable', 'sad', 'pure skullduggery', were some of the online responses.[12] It wasn't just digital rage. 'Many people found it offensive,' Ivor concedes. 'It was very difficult, I was on about fifteen radio stations in Accra and Kumasi when the story broke.' Calmly, he made the case. 'It's not just a matter of desire on our part, those who have the objects also have their own laws. If we can't find a middle way, we'd continue to have this stalemate ... At first people were attacking me, but I think they started to understand.' Ivor had no time for suggestions that the Asantehene should accept the deal and then simply renege on it and keep the objects. 'We've signed an agreement and we will keep our word. Otherwise what kind of signal does it send? The test for us is to show that Africans can maintain standards, and that we can sign a loan agreement and stick to it.'[13]

★★★

In the era of Black Lives Matter and the withering reassessment of colonial legacies, Ivor's arguments are distinctly unfashionable. At the heart of the debate around restitution is the meaning of looted artefacts themselves. The Asante regalia, like the Benin Bronzes, and so many other pieces ripped from shrines and palaces across Africa by Europeans or their agents, had a religious significance. On the leafy campus of the University of Ghana, on the edge of Accra, I met Kodzo Gavua, a professor of archaeology and one of the country's leading thinkers on these issues. 'When these objects were taken, they were given a different meaning. They became "objects," but originally they were "entities," and some were the very souls of the communities they served,' he told me.[14] Professor Kwasi Ampene, an expert on Asante culture at Tufts University in Boston who travels frequently back to his homeland of Ghana, made a related but slightly different point to me. 'Besides their philosophic and spiritual essence, they also contain an oral narrative within them. People see them in the procession, and are able to infer the history they encapsulate. They are like mnemonic devices ... It is a big vacuum when you take these things away and put them in a vault somewhere.'[15]

I thought of what these professors had said when I visited the National Army Museum's storage facility in Stevenage, outside London. It is in an industrial park, next to the A1 express road.[16] The curator, Terri Dendy, brought out some of the museum's Asante objects, including all of Wolseley's purchases from the Cape Coast Castle auction and the 'Royal State Umbrella' which Lieutenant Henry Wood had presented to Queen Victoria – no longer scarlet, black and gold, but sad and faded.[17] Then Terri led me into a warehouse, through canyons of military memorabilia – 'All these spears! Baden-Powell says they're Zulu, but lots come from Sudan' – until we came to the right spot. At the top of a ladder, standing on tiptoes, I peered across shelves and into the Asante *Aya Kese* itself, the great brass bowl decorated with lions on its rim, which Robert

Baden-Powell had taken from the Bantama Mausoleum in Kumasi in 1896 (see Chapter 12). In 1931, shortly before his death, Prempeh had pleaded with the British authorities for this object's return. 'All souls of Ashantis are within it,' he wrote, and 'the Brass Pan is needful to those who dwell forever in the Mausoleum and if not they will keenly feel its loss to them.'[18] The authorities were unmoved. Those who have followed me this far will know I see the issues around restitution as complex. But at that moment, perched on top of a ladder in a chilly warehouse next to the A1, I was struck by an overwhelming sense of absurdity. What on earth was the *Aya Kese* doing here? It meant so much to the Asante, and so little to Britain, hidden away by a museum that had no plans to put it, or any of its other Asante objects, back on display.

Asantehene Opoku Ware II had tried to present similar arguments – that what are mere exotic trophies to one group of people are of sacred importance to another – to the British in 1974. He too had been disappointed. When I had visited the palace in Ejisu, I had seen how Yaa Asantewaa's wooden stool, dripping with schnapps in the corner of the Queen Mother's bedroom, had retained its religious significance despite having spent more than one hundred years in England. And yet I had also seen, in the Prempeh II Jubilee Museum in Kumasi, that the stools and chairs returned by Queen Elizabeth in 1961 now look forlorn in their aged glass cases, gathering dust and attracting few visitors. Maybe – sacrilegious thought – they had enjoyed more status in Britain as military trophies than they did now that they had come home, where the nature of their display almost seemed to imprison them. In 2024 some of the terms imposed by the British Museum, as well as the V&A – that gold regalia sent back to Kumasi would stay in high-security display cases, in air-conditioned rooms, protected by alarms – seemed to carry the risk of a similar diminution in value. It was a risk Ivor Agyeman-Duah was happy to take. 'They will remain as objects on display, there is no intention to use them for ceremonies, we now consider them as art works, and they have been replaced,' he said, in his straightforward way.[19]

Replaced? I had noticed, at festivals in Kumasi, that the Asantehene's attendants were carrying objects that looked remarkably like the specific ones the British had looted. For example, the sacred *Mpomponsuo* sword which they waved in the air looked just like the one the British had taken in 1896. According to Ivor, this second *Mpomponsuo* sword was made in about 1900. Likewise, Kwasi Ampene of Tufts told me that after the restoration of the Asantehene in 1935, the Asante had made 'a conscious effort to correct, to recreate artistically what they had lost. All these artefacts are part of rituals. They are known. In restoring the kingdom, there was a need for this particular ritual.' Ivor argues that this process, of renewal and replacement of the Asante gold regalia, would have happened anyway, regardless of British pillage. 'Some of these were made as functional palace objects, with low preservation methods and once they faded, and the gold elements declined, they would re-melt them and turn them into something else ... If the *Mpomponsuo* sword had not been taken away, it would have undergone its own regeneration.'[20]

That fits with what Thomas Bowdich wrote back in 1819: 'The royal gold ornaments are melted down every Yam Custom, and fashioned into new patterns as novel as possible.'[21] Martha Ehrlich, in her 1974 survey, writes that Asante jewellery 'has traditionally been made of very pure gold: by virtue of the softness of the material and the delicacy of workmanship it is highly vulnerable to damage when worn. Most of it is therefore impermanent and the rate of attrition must always have been high.'[22] In other words, the British had, albeit with the worst of intentions, ensured the preservation of pieces of Asante regalia that would otherwise have been melted down and recast. 'These objects are universal for humanity,' said Ivor, sounding more like a Western museum curator than an African scholar. 'They've been kept well over the years.'[23]

Kwasi Ampene at Tufts has spent years documenting the cultural and historic significance of Asante cultural objects. He writes, 'While the royal arts of many West African traditional states have been dispersed to museums and collectors around the world, the regalia of the Asantehene are among the very few that remain intact.'[24] It is a startling statement, apparently at odds with the story I have tried to tell in this book. What did he mean by 'intact'? He said that although the British pillage of 1874 in particular had left 'major gaps', it had not been as destructive as their looting of the Royal Palace of Benin in 1897. Asante, after all, is a confederation of kingdoms and chieftaincies. 'Asante artefacts are not just in one place,' he explained. 'They are not 100 percent in the palace, even to this day. They are with custodians, families tasked with looking after them and who bring them from the villages for special events. They are scattered all over the place.' This dispersal of Asante cultural wealth had protected it from the depredations of the British and their local allies.[25]

In the final decades of the twentieth century, many West African countries went through an economic downturn, with dire consequences for their material heritage. In Nigeria, for example, archaeological sites were pillaged and its underfunded museums were attacked by robbers.[26] Ghana also suffered. 'In several Akan kingdoms, people stole artefacts and sold them to tourists,' said Kwasi Ampene. 'People hardly talk about it but it happened. People went to the stool rooms and stole gold.' Asante was not immune from these violations, but according to Kwasi, the Manhyia Palace itself remained secure. 'People did not steal from them as they did from other places. Opoku Ware II, Osei Tutu II, kept adding even more objects ... In Kumasi objects were well protected.'[27]

* * *

All of these factors, messy and complicated, help explain why Asantehene Osei Tutu II and Ivor Agyeman-Duah were prepared to accept a loan deal. But the British Museum had its own reasons to be more co-operative than in previous decades, and meet the Asante halfway. Although the British Museum's ownership of the Parthenon, or Elgin Marbles, has been a point of contention for more than two hundred years – 'a boil that needs to be lanced' one trustee told me – the intensity of the more recent debate around colonial looted objects had left it hesitant and isolated. George Osborne, the chairman of the trustees, speaking at their annual dinner in 2022 said: 'We hear the voices calling for restitution. But creating this global British Museum was the dedicated work of many generations. Dismantling it must not become the careless act of a single generation.'[28] This was at least a decisive message. All too often the British Museum refused to enter the debate at all, apparently hoping it would go away. Director Hartwig Fischer was a respected scholar but not a confident politician or communicator. The Asante loan agreement at least signalled the museum's willingness to engage with one of the communities which had suffered at the sharp end of colonial conquest.

In August 2023 the British Museum admitted that some two thousand pieces of jewellery, gold and ancient gemstones had gone missing, apparently stolen over many years. It sacked a curator for Greece and Rome, Dr Peter Higgs, and launched a civil case against him. A colleague told me Higgs had been motivated by a 'mixture of money, deliberate thrill seeking and strange resentments built up over the years'.[29] Higgs denied any theft. From the perspective of Greece, or Ghana, or for that matter many other parts of the world, the word 'irony' hardly did justice to this story. A museum whose detractors say is full of looted objects had itself been looted. Moreover, a museum which once brushed away restitution claims on the basis that it was the best custodian of the world's treasures was shown to be not just incompetent, but also hypocritical. The British Museum owns some 8 million artefacts, but, as it now acknowledged, some 2.4 million of these were not individually catalogued. The museum could not be sure what had been stolen from it, because it did not know what it had. Hartwig Fischer resigned, as did his deputy Jonathan Williams, for failing to act on the warnings of a diligent dealer who first alerted them of his suspicions back in 2021.[30] During this debacle, a curator at the British Museum told me morale was very low and there was 'no openness, no discussions, no communications with staff … There is an overwhelming array of different issues and the museum needs a complete reset. The thefts have been a huge shock to the majority of us, and opened up the floodgates to all the day-to-day inadequacies.'[31]

The British Museum has suffered thefts before, of course, including an ancient Greek statue in 2002 and fifteen 'historically important' Chinese artefacts in 2004.[32] In 1991, I discovered, it also lost an important piece of Asante gold which it would only retrieve under fortuitous circumstances many years later. At lunchtime on 3 October, a warder in the Museum of Mankind was horrified to discover a wooden display case had been prised open, apparently by a thief using a screwdriver which had been discarded nearby. The museum was instantly closed and everyone within it searched, but to no avail. Three objects had been taken, with a combined value of £95,000 (about £198,600 today); two pre-Colombian vases made of a copper-gold alloy and the largest of the museum's Asante soul discs, or *akrafokonmu*, with a diameter of 21.5 centimetres.[33] The British Museum had been given this disc in 1925 by Sir Bignell Elliott, a timber merchant from Kentish Town in north London, when the acquisition of such an 'exceptionally large specimen' merited a special mention in *The Times*. The disc is unusual not only for its size but because of the regularity of its pointed sun pattern and surrounding decoration[34] (Malcolm McLeod speculates that it may have been made by Europeans in the early twentieth century on a machine press, perhaps as a sweetener gift to a chief whose land was rich in timber).[35]

John Mack, Keeper of Ethnography in 1991, recalls the theft was 'opportunistic' and there was no suspicion of an 'inside job'.[36] Within a few weeks, the two pre-Colombian vases turned up in Brussels where, according to Mack, they had 'come into the hands of M Emile Deletaille, a reputable Belgian art dealer, who had contacted the Department and subsequently passed the vases to the Belgian police.'[37] The British

Asante disc stolen in 1991, recovered in 2002.

Museum sent a curator to retrieve them in 1992, but would not recover the Asante disc for another decade. This is despite the fact that it was, in the rueful words of a British Museum curator, 'hiding in plain sight'. If anything, that is an understatement. By 1994 the Asante disc was in the possession of perhaps the foremost German collector of traditional African art, Karl-Ferdinand Schaedler, who included photographs of it in his glossy publications and loaned it to at least two museums for exhibitions, including Vienna's renowned Museum für Völkerkunde.[38] Schaedler sold part of his collection at Sotheby's in New York in May 1999, where a photograph of the stolen disc features in the auction catalogue.[39] It was bought for $9,200 by the Indianapolis Museum of Art. In 2002 this museum, delighted by its acquisition, made it the logo of its annual festival of African art, 'Africa Fest', and celebrated by printing special t-shirts of the disc. Only then did Doran Ross, a respected scholar of Ghanaian art at the Fowler Museum in California, happen to notice the similarity between this disc and the one missing from the British Museum and tip off his counterparts in London.

'It was very embarrassing how it just turned up,' remembers Nigel Barley, a British Museum Africa curator at the time.[40] It is difficult to say who comes out of this story the worst: Karl-Ferdinand Schaedler, Sotheby's or the British Museum. Did Schaedler investigate the provenance of the disc he mysteriously acquired in the early 1990s? He died in 2024 and I was not able to ask him ('He was a lovely person, completely honest and would have been horrified if he'd known it was stolen,' according to Hermione Waterfield of Christie's, who was a friend).[41] What diligence did Sotheby's do on the collection it sold in 1999? The person who was in charge of the New York auction would not answer my enquiries, and neither would the PR department. As for the British Museum, although its curators reported the theft to the police, they had no idea the disc was being paraded around the museums of Europe and the United States and had been sold by a famous auction house until the attentive Doran Ross alerted them as to its whereabouts.

Maybe, to be fair, we simply forget how unconnected we all were in the pre-internet age. In March 2002, this awkward business was settled as quietly and diplomatically as possible. British Museum trustees, informed that the Indianapolis Museum had purchased the disc at Sotheby's in good faith, agreed to loan it for the duration of 'Africa Fest'. The disc was returned to the British Museum in September 2002, whose webpage was disingenuously updated in 2025 to include the Indianapolis and European museum 'loans' but makes no mention of the theft.[42]

While I was investigating this robbery, I was surprised to come across several others from the British Museum, all of which occurred within a few years at the end of the 1980s and the beginning of the 1990s. Some of these had been publicised at the time – the theft of a Japanese vase worth £100,000 in 1990 (about £223,000 today) and two night-time break-ins in July 1993 when thieves prised open glass panels in the roof and made off with Roman jewellery and coins worth £250,000 (about £449,000 today) – but others had never been reported.[43] In May 1992, the police tipped off the British Museum that a pair of its ancient Greek earrings were being offered for sale; they were thought to have been stolen by a cleaner in the late 1980s.[44] The following month, the British Museum reported to the police that it had suffered 'a series of unsuccessful attacks on display cases containing gold coins'. These were carried out by people who seemed familiar with the museum, as 'the attacks had been surreptitious, had escaped the notice of warders and had not activated alarms.'[45]

The most eyebrow-raising thefts of this period, however, involved a former British Museum employee, who took hundreds of antique prints, mostly from the eighteenth century and British, apparently over the course of several years.[46] In April 1992, Nigel Peverett, an antique dealer who had worked in the museum's Department of Prints and Drawings in the 1970s, was caught trying to leave the building with thirty-five prints worth an estimated £5,000. When the police searched his cottage in Kent they discovered 169 more prints, worth an estimated £27,000. Mr Peverett then admitted to stealing a further 150 prints, which he had already sold to a friend, Anthony Guyan, who ran a stall at London's Portobello Road antique market. 'It was clear', according to the trustee's minutes, 'that Mr Peverett's thefts had been on a large scale and had taken place over a considerable period of time and there was some concern that many more than the 300 or so prints to the theft of which he had confessed had been stolen.'⁴⁷ Did he get away with it, the trustees wanted to know, because he had once been museum staff? No, according to Antony Griffiths, the Keeper of the Department of Prints and Drawings, it was more a matter of him having 'become accepted as a constant visitor'.⁴⁸

By November 1992, the British Museum had recovered fifty-five stolen prints from Anthony Guyan and other dealers. But Guyan typically sold goods for cash, often to customers he did not know. In 2025 he told me he had been unaware of the dodgy provenance of the prints and could never forgive Peverett. 'I trusted him, I was very angry. When I found out, I gave everything I had back to the British Museum. It cost me a fortune. It left a very nasty taste in the mouth.'⁴⁹ (Guyan abandoned his antique stall soon afterwards and enjoyed a successful career in television production, although he still dabbles in the occasional sale).

On the basis of Nigel Peverett's figures, 'not necessarily reliable' as the trustee's minutes put it, ninety-five of the museum's prints were still missing by late 1992, but the exact number will never be known. Many of the recovered prints were badly damaged, as Peverett had scraped off their museum registration with a razor blade or cut them down crudely

Nigel Peverett, prolific thief from the British Museum in the early 1990s.

in size. A fellow Kent antique dealer, Richard Luck of Hastings, told me that Nigel Peverett would boast to him of 'going into the British Museum with one bag and coming out with four. It was all before computers, he said the place was a shambles.'[50]

Nigel Peverett died in August 2023. One summer morning in 2025 I drove down to Kent to meet his family, in the midst of the Weald countryside of green hills, windmills and medieval churches. They painted a picture of a charming but feckless man. 'He loved antiques, beauty, classical music, the British Museum and the V&A', they told me. But he was 'totally irresponsible and hopeless with money', stole food from supermarkets even as he bought his children expensive gifts from Harrod's and set fire to his Porsche in an insurance scam. In 1992, his house repossessed and his marriage having collapsed, Nigel had been at a low ebb. When the police came knocking for the British Museum's prints, he suffered a nervous breakdown, tried to kill himself and spent six weeks in a psychiatric hospital. Afterwards, he received a suspended sentence. The British Museum hoped the whole business would never see the light of day. Incredibly, his family say, Nigel Peverett was allowed to keep his British Museum pension. 'Dad was such a storyteller,' his daughter Chloe told me, 'but this was one story he never told.' After he died, they found a quote from Shakespeare written again and again in his notebooks: 'O time, thou must untangle this, not I. Tis too hard a knot for me to untie.' Each of his three children now has it tattooed on their arms.[51]

★★★

These thefts are embarrassing, but perhaps not central to the restitution debate. Greece argues that the Parthenon Marbles should be returned to Athens because Lord Elgin had no right to take them, just as the Asante argue the gold regalia should come back to Kumasi because British soldiers stole it. The same goes for Nigeria and the Benin Bronzes, and Ethiopia and the Maqdala treasures. Their arguments, whatever their respective merits, are moral at their core and not based on comparative standards of custodianship or curatorship. Indeed, the Asantehene himself once suffered an embarrassing robbery of his own regalia, on a visit to Norway in 2012 when, in an Oslo hotel lobby, thieves made off with a case containing four to five kilograms worth of gold rings, bracelets and headgear. A former BBC colleague, Mark Eddo, happened to be in the hotel at the time, attending a meeting of the Norwegian–African Business Forum. 'I saw dozens of suitcases, so many people with the Asantehene,' he remembers 'and suddenly I heard a commotion – one of the suitcases had disappeared! The organisers of the event were panicking.'[52] The thieves, who were Peruvian, were eventually caught and sentenced to prison in Norway, but had already sold the gold – estimated to be worth more than £40,000 – to a jeweller in Sweden and much of it was melted down and never recovered.[53]

When the British Museum trustees were informed of the repeated thefts in the early 1990s, they responded with 'concern and regret'. In October 1991 the director, David Wilson, apologised to them that the Asante and pre-Colombian gold pieces had been in a wooden-framed case; given its 'comparative fragility' it 'should not have been used' to display gold objects.[54] In May 1992, the incoming director, Robert Anderson, spoke of 'very disturbing thefts'.[55] Security in the Department of Prints, Antony Griffiths admitted in October 1992, 'is now known to be inadequate'.[56] Eventually, in September 1993, Robert Anderson ordered a thorough review of the museum's entire security.[57]

The frustration felt by these British Museum curators and trustees, compounded by a sense of betrayal that someone who had worked at the museum had been stealing from it, was hidden from the public at the time, but is strongly reminiscent of the sentiments many would express thirty years later when the jewellery thefts brought down Hartwig Fischer. What had eroded in the meantime, however, was the British Museum's sense of confidence about its own mission. In 1981, David Wilson, when pressed in the same BBC documentary which featured Asantehene Opoku Ware II, imperiously dismissed requests from the Asante and others that treasures be returned. 'The material we have in the British Museum is better looked after than in practically any other museum in the world,' he said. 'We must continue to hold these things, we do know our stuff, we are very trustworthy … let's hold on to them for God's sake.'[58]

Honoured to return your treasures. Julie Hudson of the British Museum and Osei Tutu II at the Manhyia Palace Museum, 1 May 2024.

20

'A HAPPY DAY FOR ASANTE, FOR THE BLACK AFRICAN CONTINENT'

When I think of the Manhyia Palace Museum, I think of the plaintive meows of the peacocks which roam its lawns and cluster in the shade of the Indian rubber trees. The birds were a gift, palace courtiers say, from the Shah of Iran.[1] As for the enormous rubber trees, some are more than one hundred years old, their tendrils hanging down like lank spaghetti. In the 1950s the Polish journalist Ryszard Kapuściński wrote that Kumasi 'was like a giant botanical garden'.[2] In the same decade Elspeth Huxley wrote, 'the scarlet of poinsettia and hibiscus is everywhere; so is a profusion of hydrangeas, the ostentatious, waxy trumpets of the frangipani, the blare of bougainvilleas.'[3] Kumasi was known as 'The Garden City'. Today, that sobriquet is in danger of sounding like a cruel joke. Kumasi has a population perhaps thirty times larger, choking traffic jams and rubbish-strewn fetid rivers. But, on a quiet day in the museum gardens, it is just possible to imagine the old Kumasi.

This is where several hundred people – Asante chiefs and courtiers, businessmen and diplomats – took their seats on 1 May 2024. The museum is the two-storey house the British built for Prempeh in the 1920s when he returned from the Seychelles. It has Doric columns, balustrades and wide verandas on the outside, while inside, even today, it retains that incongruous mock Tudor semi-detached feel, with mid-twentieth-century furniture and a bookshelf lined with biographies of Sir Francis Drake and George VI and novels by Charles Dickens. It became a museum in 1995, when Asantehene Opoku Ware II moved the palace to an adjacent and grander residence.

Asantehene Osei Tutu II's entrance into the forecourt was announced by the shouts of praise singers and the beating of drums. He wore green robes and a gold headdress, had a gold bracelet on his arm and a gold staff in his hand. His entourage hovered busily around him, ensuring he never emerged from the shade of four enormous umbrellas. He sat down on a throne opposite our podium and one courtier waved a fly whisk to cool him while another dabbed the sweat from his face. We also sweated in our seats, sipped from plastic bottles of water and fanned ourselves with programmes. 'Homecoming; Adversity and Commemoration', said the banners across the museum balcony.

It had been three weeks since Ivor Agyeman-Duah, Julie Hudson and Malcolm McLeod had driven to Kumasi in their convoy with the thirty-two pieces of treasure returned by the British Museum and the V&A. Three weeks of busy preparations, often running late into the night, getting the Manhyia Palace Museum ready for this day. Tristram Hunt, the director of the V&A, bowed low before the Asantehene and addressed the crowd. 'We acknowledge the very painful history surrounding the acquisition of these objects, a history tainted by the scars of imperial conquest and colonialism.' It was right, he said, that the treasures had been returned. Only words, perhaps, but not ones the director of a major British museum would have used anywhere, let alone in this context, just a few years ago. Next, Malcolm McLeod walked slowly to the podium, helped by Julie Hudson. He said 'I did not imagine we'd be here today celebrating the return of these looted objects ... what seems inconceivable only two years ago has now happened.' Then it was Ivor Agyeman-Duah's turn. He was in a sombre dark olive suit, once again incongruous amidst the resplendent Asante robes. Ivor said the Asante had been asking for their treasure to be returned for many decades. He spoke about how his great-grandfather, Kwame Boatin, was 'bundled up' and sent into exile with Prempeh to the Seychelles, where he died. The final speaker was the Asantehene himself, from the steps of the museum. He said the British had only returned a small part of what they had taken: 'not all of them have come back but what we have here embodies the soul of Asante. Today is a happy day for Asante, for the black African continent.' People cheered and filed excitedly into the museum.[4]

'Priceless treasures from leading museums now languish in a remote local gallery in Ghana,' wrote the *Daily Mail* unkindly.[5] But for the British curators who helped bring the Asante gold back to Kumasi, the return was a moving, even cathartic process. Julie Hudson, who has spent her career in the British Museum's Africa collection and is usually a rather restrained person, broke down in tears when the objects she had carefully shepherded all the way from Bloomsbury and South Kensington finally reached the Manhyia Palace Museum. 'Goodness gracious, we've actually brought them home,' she later reflected; 'this was the most meaningful thing I've ever been involved in, absolutely.'[6] Angus Patterson, the V&A's senior curator of metalwork, who helped prepare the displays, wrote: 'The memory of proud Asante colleagues visibly moved on first seeing the gold as we unpacked it will stay with me forever.'[7]

If that Asante pride was hurt by the loan terms of the agreement, it was not immediately obvious. The excitement in Kumasi that the return had actually happened, and the deep deference for the Asantehene who had made the compromise, meant that criticism tended to be muted. Peter King Appiah, at Kumasi's Centre for National Culture, said, 'These were eminent people who sat down for a long period before they arrived at that position. We shall accept it and move on.' But as I probed, his frustration came out. 'It's quite a blow, quite a blow. It does go to assert this notion of the African still playing second fiddle to the European. Why this clause? Why us? Would they treat other advanced countries the same? Let's see how it pans out. After three or six years, we will stand up and say "No! We want our things back."'[8]

Also in the crowd at the Manhyia Palace Museum that day was Nii Kwate Owoo, the celebrated Ghanaian filmmaker who had told me the loan agreement turned his stomach. Nii's drive and energy belie his eighty years. He made his name in 1970 with a documentary called *You Hide Me*. A student in London at the time, Nii gained extraordinary access to the basement, or 'stores', of the British Museum, where he filmed some of the thousands of African objects, including from Asante, which the museum owns but rarely displays. He was followed closely by security guards 'to make sure that we didn't steal any of the things that they had stolen from us'.[9] Nii felt 'overwhelmed ... It smelt ancient. These artefacts, their wood, had their own scent. I felt the presence of my ancestors. As I was there, opening boxes and plastic bags, I was writing the commentary in my mind.' Shot in black and white, accompanied by Nii's unflinching narration – 'We the people of Africa ... demand that our works of art, which embodies our history, our civilization, our culture, should immediately and unconditionally be returned to us' – *You Hide Me* is a striking film, which has been rediscovered by the restitution campaigners of the twenty-first century and acquired cult status. 'I realised I'm an ancestral messenger,' said Nii with a hint of bombast, as he reflected on its revived impact all these decades later; 'there's something very powerful in this film that is going to wake up the entire world.'[10]

One of Nii's first memories, aged about four, was being lifted onto his father's shoulders at rallies for Kwame Nkrumah's Convention People's Party before independence. 'Shouting for "freedom, freedom!", I used to raise my hands like my father ... The seed of political resistance was planted in me as a child.' There was a gymnastics display in the stadium at Ghana's independence in 1957, where the children wore different colours to make up a giant version of their new country's flag; 'Girls in black formed the star. I wore red. School children! The feeling of patriotism!', he growls with slow delight over that last word. Memories infused with heady optimism but an ultimate sense of betrayal. Because in 1966 came the day when Nii heard that Nkrumah had been toppled in a coup. By then Nii was living in London. 'Nkrumah despot, blah, blah, blah, overthrown by his own people, blah, blah', he says, still seething at how the BBC reported the event. 'Nkrumah was ahead of his time, a visionary ... I was traumatised.'[11]

After the coup, Nii was angry and became 'even more radical' in his involvement in British politics. He joined the Black Unity and Freedom Party and the struggle against 'police brutality against the black community ... We distinguished ourselves by wearing black all the time, black turtle necks, black berets, black overcoats, whenever I stepped out of my digs.' Today, back home in Ghana, Nii still fights the good fight. 'The way forward now', he says, 'is to decolonise *You Hide Me*. It is in a colonial language, English, an elitist language ... It will not make any impact in this country unless it is indigenised into local languages. Then it can be shown at the village level. I decided to start with the Twi version ... which has to be launched here, in Kumasi.'[12]

Nii said that when he went into the Manhyia Palace Museum to see the returned treasure, 'I was pissed off, because some of the items I had seen in the British Museum which I thought would be there, were missing! I was like, "wait a minute", what's all this about. I was not happy.' But he had also felt 'very emotional, very moved' to see what had come back. Nii is a radical, and he is not Asante but has ancestry from the Akwamu and Ga ethnic groups, but even he defers to the Asantehene. He was disgusted with the loan but was careful to say it was 'entirely the prerogative of his royal majesty, Otumfuo Osei Tutu II, the Asantehene, because they received the terms and conditions. If I had my way I would demand the return of every single looted artefact. That's my personal feeling.'[13]

In 2022, Ghana's government set up a 'Focal Team on Reparation and Restitution', which included academics, civil servants, chiefs and museum curators and whose task, according to Ghana's then President, Nana Akufo-Addo, was to 'provide advice on international best practices and guidelines to support the country in the restitution process.'[14] In other words, speed up Ghana's recovery of looted cultural treasures. Nii Kwate Owoo is a member of the Focal Team, but in 2024 he told me it was 'completely moribund' and had been established by the government as a 'propaganda gimmick'.[15] Apparently, the government wanted to be seen to be doing something about an issue it was meant to care about.

Ghana, like almost every African state, is a colonial creation, its borders drawn to European priorities, often regardless of ethnic and religious differences. The chiefs and kings of old must coexist with the elected politicians of today, and the boundaries of their respective authority are not always neatly defined. The decades of peace Ghana has enjoyed since independence, and the robust democracy of recent decades, are testimony to the relative success with which it has navigated its complicated inheritance. 'The reconciliation of Ashanti people to Ghanaian citizenship has now been effected', wrote Tom McCaskie in 2000, 'in no small measure due to good sense and statesmanship in Kumasi and Accra'.[16] But when the British Museum and the V&A returned the Asantehene's regalia, they reached an agreement directly with him and not with the Ghanaian government. All the objects have gone back to Kumasi, and none to the national museum in Ghana's capital, Accra.

Tristram Hunt of the V&A, on a visit to Ghana in 2022, had initially tried to go through the government, but, in his words, 'hit a brick wall'.[17] This wasn't only because of the ponderous pace of state bureaucracy, but also because a loan was unacceptable to the Ghanaian government. Nana Oforiatta Ayim, a Ghanaian writer and art historian who helped broker the talks with the V&A, said the contract it offered was in 'patronising, ownership mode' and Ghana's Attorney General agreed it needed to be rewritten to respect the country's sovereignty.[18] At this point, Ivor Agyeman-Duah and Malcolm McLeod stepped in, with the Asantehene's support, and their more pragmatic approach offered a way forward. 'We spoke to the V&A and British Museum and what they needed from us was a guarantee there wouldn't be any government interference', Ivor told me. 'We told them the government would not, and the government never did. The government was copied into the correspondence, out of courtesy.' Ivor had to repeatedly reassure the two British museums that his approach would work; 'Tristram Hunt said "please run this by the President", I said, "I don't need to speak to the President. These items were taken from Asante before it was a part of Ghana. They belong to us" and no one in government has ever objected.'[19]

It was a delicate process, with many moving parts and everything could easily have fallen apart. In Nigeria, for example, for all the interest and favourable publicity around the return of the Benin Bronzes, discussions between the national and state governments and the traditional king, or Oba, over what should be done with returned artefacts have been so muddled and at times acrimonious that they have struggled to put any on display and some Western museums paused plans to give them back. But the Asantehene in Ghana is, relative to the rest of the country, a more powerful figure than the Oba of Benin is within the Nigerian polity. He is also wealthier – able to pay for flights, hotels, display cases and all the other lubricants of museum diplomacy. Once Osei Tutu II had decided how he wanted to proceed, he got his way. Naturally, the Asante celebrate this. Peter King Appiah, at the government-funded Centre for National Culture in Kumasi, said, 'I'm happy [the regalia] is coming back to the king. If it was the state, the government, I'd have a lot of issues with it. But if it's held privately by the King, it will be well maintained. Go to government institutions … they are not in good shape.'[20]

Professor Kodzo Gavua of the University of Ghana, who had told me how colonial looting had left communities spiritually impoverished, is the chairman of the national Focal Team on Reparation and Restitution, which Nii Kwate Owo had complained was 'moribund'. Kodzo admitted, coyly, that the Focal Team 'rarely meets. The state has provided no budget.' To his credit, he has kept busy anyway, travelling around Ghana and using his own research grants to hold meetings on restitution. When I visited the university, he was lecturing a group of young museum practitioners from across Africa and beyond. There was a buzz in the room and Kodzo spoke eloquently. 'Africa's entities and souls were taken away, and reclassified as "objects", without our interpretation,' he said. The audience hummed in appreciation.[21]

Kodzo is reluctant to define his own ethnicity. He is an Ewe speaker, from the east of the country but has Asante ancestors through his mother. 'But what is Asante anyway?' he asked dismissively; 'just a conflation of a group of people who came together at a point in time to pursue a certain project.'[22] I wanted to know what he, a Ghanaian intellectual deeply involved in the restitution debate, made of the returns of the Asante regalia. He was blunt. The agreement between the museums in Britain and the Asantehene 'undermines the sovereignty of the state of

Ghana ... Nobody would dispute they are Asante items. But today Asante is part of the republic of Ghana.' If museums in Britain were interested in 'true restitution', he argued, they would 'show some respect to the Republic of Ghana.' Instead, 'they recognise Asante. It's a neo-colonial type of thing.' Several members of the national Focal Team had urged him to publicly denounce it, he said, but he had decided on a more conciliatory approach. 'The items, whether we protest or not, are back, it's a beginning. Maybe it can be a test case, to see whether or not we can keep them safely.'[23]

Kodzo Gavua raised another, more abstract, concern. The Asantehene had been eager for the treasures to be returned in time to mark the various anniversaries of 2024. 'Is that all?', asked Kodzo. 'If we just bring them back to celebrate the war and the King's anniversary, it is not properly contextualised. We just rehash those memories of the Asante-British Wars, Asante power, Asante hegemony and so on ... We had a common heritage until the British came, so what about the rest of us?' He was not just raising a familiar Ghanaian grumble about the supposedly domineering Asante. He was asking a more profound question; what is restitution actually for? 'Restitution is to restore and repair the damage that has been done, an opportunity to build new relationships between coloniser and colonised, and alternative knowledge about who we are and our past,' Kodzo argued.[24] He worried that if Asante history was reduced to a series of wars against the British, an opportunity would be missed, for Asante and Ghana as a whole. And Africa's vast ignorance of its own past would endure.

★★★

The British Museum and the V&A were not the only museums to return Asante regalia in 2024. The Fowler Museum, of the University of California in Los Angeles, had returned seven objects at the beginning of the year, all of which had been looted by the British in 1874. There was, however, a crucial difference. The Fowler simply transferred ownership of its objects. Or, to quote its pointed press release, 'The Fowler's unconditional ethical return contrasts with the British Museum and Victoria and Albert Museum's six-year loan of looted objects.'[25]

These seven objects included a golden-handled fly whisk made from an elephant tail – *sika mena* – a symbol of kingship believed to date back to the first Asantehene, Osei Tutu, as well as a royal golden necklace, pieces of decorative repoussé (hammered or pressed on the reverse side) gold and a handsome ornamental chair – *asipim* – decorated with brass studs and bosses. The Fowler Museum had acquired them in 1965, as part of a huge gift from the Wellcome Trust, which manages the fortune of Sir Henry Wellcome, the British–American pharmaceutical entrepreneur who died in 1936 and who built up a collection of more than one million scientific, artistic and archaeological objects, 'the privilege of a wealthy white man in the Victorian era', as the Fowler puts it. 'We were a couple of basement rooms and all of a sudden we received 30,000 objects,' says Erica Jones, Africa curator at the Fowler.[26]

Henry Wellcome had bought the seven objects at Glendining & Co, an auction house in London's West End, well known for sales of the spoils of Empire. He paid £120 for six of them in November 1928 (about £9,100 today).[27] These had all belonged to the Peek family of Devon, who made their money in tea and biscuits (the company Peek Frean introduced the Garibaldi and Bourbon to Britain). Sir Henry Peek, a Conservative MP who died in 1898, had built a huge brooding house at Rousdon above the cliffs west of Lyme Regis, where he and later his son and grandson, Cuthbert and Wilfred, kept a museum of ethnographic objects and stuffed birds.[28] Cuthbert did the collecting, while Wilfred, perhaps significantly, was a friend of Robert Baden-Powell.[29] But when and how the Peeks acquired their Asante treasure is not clear. Three of their six objects were looted from the palace by Captain John Audley Harvey of the Black Watch, while the other three came from the indemnity and were sold by Garrard in 1874.[30]

Henry Wellcome bought the seventh piece at Glendining's in 1934. This was the chair, for which he paid a modest £5 (about £450 today). 'The King's State Seat', in Glendining's words, had been 'collected' from Kumasi by General Sir Arthur Paget, who was a young lieutenant with Wolseley in 1874 and later rose to become Commander-in-Chief of British forces in Ireland (where his handling of the 1914 Curragh Incident arguably emboldened both unionists and nationalists to arm for civil war) and died in Cannes in 1927. A steeplechaser, yachtsman and botanist, as well as an occasional novelist, Paget was, in his own words, 'a man who lived history rather than read it'.[31] Carpe diem was certainly his philosophy in Kumasi in 1874, for Glendining's also sold other parts of his Asante collection which included 'The King's ... cap of leather decorated with gold ... His State Sandals mounted in gold and silver ... His knife, the handle overlaid with gold', while the Nelson-Atkins Museum in Kansas City has a stool lavishly decorated with silver and a plaque which reads 'King Koffee's State Chair from his Palace at Comassie brought home by Arthur Paget, February 1873 [sic]'.[32]

It was not until 2019 that the Fowler set about researching the African objects it had received from Wellcome – 'We don't know what we don't know if we don't know what we have', as Erica Jones put it, a familiar lament amongst museum curators – and connected the seven Asante pieces with the Anglo-Asante Wars. From that point, Erica had no hesitation. 'The decision to return them was a no-brainer', she said. 'We know these are looted, they're not ours, they shouldn't be in our collection ... this was straightforward.'[33]

Kwasi Ampene, of Tufts University, acted as the go-between for the Fowler and the Asantehene. 'It was humbling, the opportunity to help,' he said, 'beyond anything I could imagine as a kid growing up in a village in Ghana. After 150 years – they came with guns, houses were burnt, lives were destroyed – but now kids in Africa could learn their history and this level of creativity.'[34] The Fowler curators flew with the seven pieces to Ghana in February 2024. They were discreetly stored at former President John Kufuor's house outside Accra for a couple of nights – just as those returned from Britain would be weeks later – before being taken to Kumasi. On 5 February 2024, 150 years to the day after Wolseley blew up the palace, Erica Jones and her colleagues presented them to Osei Tutu II. 'I have no reservations that we did the right thing', Erica said afterwards. 'People were moved, and saw it as a recognition not just of the past but of an ongoing vibrant culture.'[35] The Fowler had no business, she insisted, in what happened to the objects next. 'These aren't ours to begin with, it is not for us to determine where they go or how they are used. The palace takes things out of the museum all the time. The elephant whisk, I hope it gets used. It would be really interesting for people to see it.'[36]

The Fowler's returns were reported favourably across the world. The *Los Angeles Times* described them as 'a highly unusual if very welcome move'.[37] What was not publicised was that the museum has two more Asante objects which it did not give back to the Asantehene because they carry a more complex morality. These are an elephant tusk and a drum, both with human skulls attached. They also came from the Wellcome Trust, which bought them in London in 1928 and 1931 and they had also apparently been looted by British troops.[38] Kwasi Ampene explained, 'the Akan and Asante people, if they defeated another powerful people, they will capture the powerful commander, they will slay that person, they will decapitate that person and put their head on a drum. It was their idea of a humiliation, that they were able to defeat you.'[39] One of the skulls, of a young man, has signs of fatal injuries from blunt and sharp weapons.

How much more comfortable we all feel in addressing the injustices of a colonial war than in picking through the bones, in this case literally, of an intra-African one. 'It would be inappropriate to return remains to the people who probably killed them,' Erica said. 'These were victims of the Asante.' She believed it would be 'most appropriate to return them to the national government who can honour them as Ghanaian citizens in their homeland'. But does Ghana have any appetite to examine this awkward history? Even now, many decades after independence, trawling through the legacies of pre-colonial wars still feels like a luxury that African countries can ill afford. Erica says that when she approached the Ghanaian government on the issue, 'it didn't get traction.'[40]

In my conversations with British and American museums I often felt that the latter navigated the colonial past with a greater degree of certainty. Perhaps this is because, at least when it comes to Africa, they are one stage removed from the original colonial sin. In July 2024, when the University of Iowa Stanley Museum of Art returned two Benin objects looted by the British in 1897 – a plaque and a wooden altar piece – directly to the Oba in Nigeria, its curator Cory Gundlach even apologised to him for having used them to teach Benin history without his permission. Does an academic really need the Oba's permission to teach Benin history, I asked. 'I need the Oba's permission to use these objects to teach the history, because they were stolen,' replied Cory emphatically.[41]

Kwasi Ampene, at Tufts University, argues that young people across Africa itself are also radically reassessing the past. 'These days', he says, 'with social media, people are being informed and stories which were not being told are now being told. The British; they need to work fast … give it back in an organised way, before there's an uprising!'[42] But in Africa, just as in the West, different generations don't always see things the same way. At the 'Homecoming' ceremony at the Manhyia Palace Museum, I met Peter Osei-Bonsu Safo Kantanka, a warm and engaging seventy-year-old who works as a historian at the palace. He was philosophical about the ebbs and flows of history. 'War is war, the stronger took the booty. And the Asante themselves are guilty of this. We fought many wars, are we saying we have to return all the objects we took? I don't like the term "stolen items". These words are too strong. Some of us are too mature to be sentimental about this.'[43]

Guest of Honour. The Asantehene arrives at the British Museum, 19 July 2024.

21

'WHICH HISTORY WE REMEMBER'

One evening in 2024, Malcolm McLeod hosted a dinner in London's Athenaeum Club for a dozen people closely involved in the saga of the return of the Asante regalia. They ate in the club's North Library, an exquisite room which overlooks Pall Mall, lined with antique books on all four sides, crowned by a high gallery. The guests included Asantehene Osei Tutu II, the former Ghanaian president John Kufuor, as well as the V&A's Tristram Hunt and the newly appointed director of the British Museum, Nicholas Cullinan, who had only been in the job a matter of days. 'I was not nervous, or worried', Cullinan told me. 'I definitely didn't go into it thinking, "I'm in a difficult situation here."'[1] At the dinner, he spoke of his desire for the British Museum to be more open and generous.[2]

I met Nicholas Cullinan at the British Museum a few months later. It was a dismal winter day, but beneath his window visitors streamed through the security checks. 'I'm thrilled … you see people queuing up round the block in the rain, and packed galleries today. It gives me faith in humanity,' he said. A slim, dynamic man in his late forties, Cullinan came to the museum with a reputation as a reformer after his successful revamp of the National Portrait Gallery. But the challenges he faced in his new job were far greater, from raising an estimated £1 billion for an overhaul of the old Bloomsbury building, to giving the museum a renewed sense of purpose and confidence as it navigated between demands for decolonisation from the left and critics on the right quick to pounce on any hint of wokeism.

The 2024 ceremony in Kumasi marked the very first time the British Museum had ever loaned objects back to those from whom they were forcibly taken in a colonial war. And yet it marked this significant moment in its own history with diffidence. The V&A handled almost all the publicity and media, even though, as Tristram Hunt put it, 'the quality of our material – it's wonderful, but the BM material is of a different order.'[3] The British Museum trustee who went to Kumasi, Professor Chris Gosden, a well-respected archaeologist, was drafted in late and was making his first-ever trip to West Africa. Everything was a bit underplayed, Gosden conceded, but that was because 'the museum was in a state of flux' following Hartwig Fischer's departure.[4]

Tristram Hunt has long argued that the 1983 National Heritage Act needs to be rewritten so that the V&A can permanently return – 'deaccession' in museum speak – items from its collection. 'It's out of date and infantilizing and I think trustees should have responsibility for their collections', Hunt told me. And if the law did change, what would he advise his trustees to do with their Asante regalia? 'I would certainly make a strong case as Director that these were collections that should be considered for restitution.' In the meantime, he would be happy for the three-year loan of gold objects to Kumasi to be extended twice, the maximum allowed. 'We have no need to see them back in South Kensington for nine years,' he said.[5]

Nicholas Cullinan is similarly constrained by the British Museum Act of 1963, which likewise prevents him from offering anything more than long-term loans. But he does not seem unhappy about this. 'Tristram comes at it from a political perspective,' he told me, 'but I'm a museum person, and most museum people I think feel very nervous about deaccessioning, it is something that is in conflict with the idea that we're passing these on to other people.'[6]

So where does that leave the British Museum's Asante collection, and specifically the gold regalia which has already gone to Kumasi? A commentator in the *Daily Telegraph* fumed, 'Is what is happening a "loan" in any meaningful sense? Does anyone think these gorgeous, precious baubles will ever return to South Kensington and Bloomsbury?'[7] Talking to curators and trustees at the British Museum, he would appear to have a point. No one involved with the Kumasi returns wanted to be the person who had to go back and collect the regalia when the loan expired.

The issue troubled the British Museum; when it held interviews for a new head of the Africa, Oceania and the Americas department in 2025, the first question for applicants was how they would handle the expiry of the Kumasi loan. The museum offered this highly sensitive position to Chris Wingfield, a curator and academic at the University of East Anglia, who accepted only to change his mind two months later. He told me this was for personal reasons and because he enjoyed his current position at UEA's Sainsbury Research Unit. But he also said the application process had taught him that the British Museum is 'essentially an extension of the British state ... a place where it is difficult to get things done'.[8]

'I don't think we've thought ahead to the end of the Kumasi loan,' a trustee admitted, 'but it wouldn't be a good look turning up there with a suitcase.'[9] Intriguingly, Nicholas Cullinan said, 'I don't know that someone will have to do that ... I think it is undecided ... it might be that we both decide we'd like to rotate the objects, it would be more interesting to see a new set of objects.' The important point was, he said, 'I really don't want to have things in storage that could be shown elsewhere.'

There are signs of a new approach from the old institution. In 2024 the British Museum hosted an exhibition by the artist Hew Locke (who had been so damning of how William Cecil, the Marquess of Exeter, had mounted an Asante *akrafokonomu* in a gilt dish, see Chapter 8). It was an excoriating examination of Britain's imperial legacy, but also the museum's role 'at the cultural heart' of Empire. The objects he had selected from the collection told the story of the eradication of pre-Columbian societies, transatlantic slavery, exploitation in India and the pillaging of Maqdala, Asante and Benin in Africa. Locke's pithy thoughts were interspersed on Post-it notes around these – 'Is there a problem at the Museum? Well, obviously there is a problem' – as well as pieces of his own work, often ironic observations on imperial grandeur and cruelty.

Beneath a bust of Queen Victoria, decorated with absurd replica medals and baubles, he wrote 'she supported a lot of things that happened under her watch, she's not innocent.'[10]

Hew Locke's call for 'dialogue, serious dialogue' appeared to have been heeded by the British Museum, through the very act of hosting his exhibition. But the museum had already changed the language on panels around permanent displays in other parts of the building: 'The Looting of Maqdala', 'Benin: Colonial Conquest and Military Looting', 'Repression, Rebellion And Exile: The Anglo-Asante Wars'. In 2024 it made a symbolic change to its African display; a large portrait of none other than the Asante queen, Yaa Asantewaa, by the British–Ghanaian artist Kimathi Donkor, mimicking the pose of a plantation heiress in a John Singer Sargent painting, was positioned immediately beside the Benin Bronze plaques. According to the accompanying panel, Yaa Asantewaa's 'status as an anti-colonial heroine continues to resonate'.[11]

Nicholas Cullinan argues that in an era of 'echo chambers and nationalism', the British Museum can be a force for good. 'Share the collection, share the knowledge ... as widely as possible, in the building, outside the building, nationally, internationally, digitally, it's there for a public good, not just a Bloomsbury public, but a global public.'[12] In other words, the now often derided concept of a 'universal museum' or 'museum for the world' has been updated into something more generous and more open. He had never been to Africa at the time we spoke, but his vision was certainly not parochial. And yet, and here's the rub, the museum is still not prepared to cede ownership of its many contentious treasures.

Other British institutions are comfortable with the status quo. The Wallace Collection is forbidden by the 1992 Museums and Galleries Act of disposing of, or even adding to, any part of its collection. It only began to lend and borrow objects in 2019 and has been more cautious in its discussions with the Asante than the British Museum or V&A.[13] One morning, when I visited its Oriental Armoury, where the Asante gold is displayed, a primary school class from east London happened to pass through. Most of the children, and the teacher, appeared to be of South

Asian origin. 'The armour in this room comes from Ghana, China, India and so on', said the teacher, who paused before adding in a weary voice, 'and how it got here is a whole other story'. She pointed to a fabulous jewelled dagger once owned by the Mughal emperor Shah Jahan. 'How do you think this got here?' she asked the children. 'The British owned India and took lots of stuff', one boy volunteered. 'Yes, basically lots of our museums are full of stuff which the British stole when they had an empire', said the teacher bluntly.[14]

For that teacher, and many others, only radical change can make our museums relevant to the Britain of the 2020s, and certainly to the youthful, multicultural fusion of London. But the Wallace Collection's director, Dr Xavier Bray, a specialist on Francisco Goya, is an unapologetic defender of the universal museum. 'All works of art have journeys', he told me, 'but if you can present the Asante objects in a free museum, where they can tell stories in their complexity, well, that's enlightenment.' His ambition is an Asante exhibition at the Wallace, which tells the whole Anglo-Asante story, warts and all. What about at least lending some stuff back to Kumasi in the meantime, I asked. 'When we lend we expect to borrow something back,' he said.[15]

Then there is the Royal Collection. It is not owned, as many might assume, by the King as a private individual, but mysteriously 'held in trust by the Sovereign for his successors and the nation.' Despite this, the King and the trustees are not constrained by law in the same way as those who run the British Museum, the V&A, the Wallace or other national collections. They could give back all sorts of objects from the colonial period if they wanted to.

Remarkably, this is what used to happen. There were not only those barely reported returns of Asante stools and chairs by Queen Elizabeth II to Ghana in 1961 (see Chapter 16). In 1965, she visited Ethiopia. At her farewell banquet in Asmara, she gave Emperor Haile Selassie the crown and seal of Emperor Tewodros, looted by British soldiers at Maqdala in 1868. 'A token of our gratitude and esteem', she told him, taken at a time 'when the relations between our two countries were far different from those which so happily unite us now'.[16] British newspapers reported that 'tremendous applause greeted her statement' and the Queen was 'visibly moved'.[17] In her long and complex relationship with Africa, I can think of few moments as poignant as this one. And yet it is all but forgotten today. In 1966, the Royal Collection returned an arguably even more sensitive object: an Irish republican flag which flew above the Dublin General Post Office during the 1916 Easter Uprising, to commemorate the fiftieth anniversary of that seismic event. That was the last item the Royal Collection has ever deaccessioned.[18] If such boldness and generosity in the 1960s, why not now? The Royal Collection told me it would not speculate on future returns and that the King took advice from trustees and 'a range of internal and external stakeholders'. I take this to mean he will do what the government of the day asks him to.

In which case, His Majesty may be waiting for some time. Bell Ribeiro-Addy, the Labour MP for Brixton, has Ghanaian roots and is a campaigner for restitution, as well as reparations for slavery and colonialism. 'This is about diplomacy and Britain's place in the world,' she says. 'We left our largest trading partner and we're not doing very well. People don't like us, we have a very chequered past ... we need to make friends.' Restitution, she argues, is 'the softest form of diplomacy ever – say you're sorry and give something back.' If Ribeiro-Addy's analysis is sure to raise the hackles of British conservatives, they can console themselves that she still feels far from power, despite Labour's victory in 2024. Her campaign to be deputy leader in 2025 attracted little support, and she complained that the 'government is talking about changing laws, but only in relation to the Elgin Marbles, these discussions are shrouded in racism... The moment anyone rears their head from the right-wing the government backs off.'[19] At the V&A, Tristram Hunt, himself a former Labour MP, concurred that Keir Starmer's government had no interest in changing the laws. 'I can see no energy there at all,' he said. 'I can see no political will, or policy engagement in that sense. They frame it simply in terms of the Parthenon sculptures ... It's disappointing and I don't see much appetite for it.'[20]

Two nights after that Athenaeum dinner, the Asantehene was driven in a black Rolls-Royce into the great court of the British Museum, where

Nicholas Cullinan was waiting for him. He descended carefully in his flowing robes, amidst shouts of acclaim from courtiers, who lifted a huge umbrella over his head. Nicholas Cullinan guided the Asantehene up the museum steps and led him to the auditorium, already packed with the great and good of the museum world, the Ghanaian diaspora and many others. The Asantehene took the stage, flanked by his courtiers, and still protected by his umbrella. He talked through the twists and turns of Asante history, his every sentence punctuated by a shout of affirmation by the praise singer who stood by his side with a golden staff. He listed with gratitude pioneering British scholars – Robert Rattray, Ivor Wilks, Tom McCaskie – who had represented the Asante side of history. He spoke of a special debt to Malcolm McLeod, who together with Ivor Agyeman-Duah had worked successfully for the return of Asante heritage, 'the culmination of years of diplomacy ... a pathway through the logjam of cultural restitution' and had thereby helped his people to reunite with their ancestors and their souls. 'Respect for the past', he said, 'is the unbroken thread which keeps the Asante state together'.

The sting came at the end. We're proud of what we've achieved, the Asantehene said, 'but we do not pretend the agreement we reached is a solution to the issue of restitution ... All of us in this room are victims of a system in need of updating. We are either victims of a system which denies us justice or victims of a system which prevents us from administering justice and doing what we know to be the right thing.'[21] In other words, some of us were robbed, and others are held back by archaic laws which make it impossible to repair the damage (I asked Nicholas Cullinan later whether he saw himself as a 'victim' of current British legislation. He bridled at the suggestion and said 'the question is, how can you do something interesting within the set of circumstances that you have?').[22] Sometimes, in the midst of a turbulent period, it is hard to discern what has actually changed. But by any measure, an African king speaking as an honoured guest at the British Museum, celebrating the return of his treasure but also lambasting his hosts for not going further, was an extraordinary moment.

★★★

The British Museum has worked with the Manhyia Palace Museum for decades and hopes to carry on this partnership. The Fowler Museum in Los Angeles also wants to stay connected to Asante. 'This is just the beginning,' said Erica Jones. 'We don't just want to drop these [seven objects] off and fade away, we want to help the Palace Museum in any way they want,' whether through training or partnering on curatorial work.[23] Tristram Hunt says the V&A is also looking for more than 'a transactional exchange of objects, we're looking to help build technical skills, security, environmental skills.'[24] The Asantehene explained to me 'these major global institutions, there are many things we can learn from them ... we have learned to collaborate with people of like-minds.'[25]

The return of cultural objects raises lofty ambitions. Professor Kodzo Gavua in Accra told me he wanted 'them to foment healing, create new relationships and knowledge and fill the gap between the past and the present'. He leaned forwards and said, 'and all that is especially important here in the South because we think all good things come from the North, that's why our youth want to flee.'[26] No doubt my imagination is constrained by my own Western and secular outlook, but it feels like an enormous weight is being put on these objects, no matter how sacred, if we expect their return to somehow repair the profound rupture of colonialism.

The Manhyia Palace Museum. 'We want people to see what our civilisation was and how it can inspire the present,' says Ivor Agyeman-Duah.

Many in Kumasi do strive, valiantly, to fill that gap between past and present. Francis Kwarayire, a scholarly man employed by the Ghana Museum and Monuments Board, has the challenging task of conserving what little remains of the Asante traditional architecture which so impressed European visitors in the nineteenth century. Only a handful of buildings survive, 'the last material remains of the great Asante civilization' according to the United Nations cultural organisation UNESCO, which lists them as a World Heritage Site.[27] Tellingly, none are in Kumasi itself. That is partially the legacy of Garnet Wolseley, the man who ordered the city's 'total destruction', but also later wars and the galloping modernisation of recent decades. Instead, the listed buildings are scattered around surrounding towns and villages. They are made of earth and wood and would traditionally have had thatched roofs. All are fragile and require regular maintenance in the warm and humid climate.

Francis, with no car, and working out of a small, dilapidated office in the centre of Kumasi, does his best to keep across each site. He took me to Ejisu to see one of the most impressive buildings, the Besease shrine house, built in the mid-nineteenth century. The courtyard galleries, the ornate pillars decorated with bas-relief spiral and bird and animal patterns, the steeply pitched roof – all reminded me of what I had seen in the black-and-white photographs of nineteenth-century Asante. It was a refuge from the relentless ugliness of the concrete and breeze-block sprawl of today's Kumasi. Besease is still a functioning shrine; the elders come every Thursday to consult the *Tano Yaw* deity, to whom they sacrifice chickens and pour schnapps.

I admired Francis's determination to repair the buildings with indigenous materials and techniques, even though the surrounding forests and swamps, the historic source of timber and thatch, are disappearing. He was worried. 'The grants we get from UNESCO and the government are small, our expenses are high,' he told me. If only, he lamented, the Western museums who were returning regalia would help conserve the last Asante buildings.[28] He asked if tourists would come to see this building if they only knew about it. Undoubtedly. But Ghana, for all its cultural wealth and history, and strong diaspora networks, is not a major tourist destination. It would take a certain kind of visitor, engaged and curious, to come out to this small shrine house in Ejisu.

In Kumasi, in the Asafo neighbourhood, Francis took me to meet Frederick Ohene, a fourth-generation Asante goldsmith, who runs the 'King of Kings Jewellery' shop. Frederick is a powerfully built man in his forties, with a conspicuous gold tooth and another tooth decorated with a gold cross. 'Gold-working is my destiny, the family work, my grandfather and father showed me how to melt gold,' he said. He makes jewellery with an enormous blowtorch in a dark little workshop at the back of his shop, behind heavily barred windows, and hides his gold in a heavy duty safe. When he goes home, he checks his shop is secure via remote video. 'People will always want gold,' he says. 'When the economy goes down, the gold price goes up. My sons will take over from me.'[29]

In 2025 Ghana was Africa's leading gold producer, ahead of South Africa. 'There's gold everywhere in Ghana,' said President John Mahama.[30] But this is a mixed blessing. More than a third of Ghana's gold comes from the 'galamsey' – or 'gather them and go' – artisanal miners. They traditionally cleared land with picks and shovels but have graduated to mechanical excavators, high pressure hoses and mercury and are destroying forests and rivers at an alarming rate.[31] Frederick bought four acres of land outside Kumasi for 100,000 Ghanaian Cedis (about £5,000). He showed me a video of what happened next. The excavator smashed down the trees and dug up the soil, which his workers then hosed down with poisonous chemicals. Everything was trashed. After six months, Frederick would abandon this ruined plot, buy another one and repeat the process. 'In this work, you need a lot of money before you can get started. That's why the politicians are doing it,' said Frederick, matter-of-factly. I wondered if he had been interested in the return of the Asantehene's regalia, just up the road at the Manhyia Palace, and whether he might take inspiration from the objects which had come home. He laughed at me. 'I don't care,' he said. 'I heard about it on the radio but I won't go there to see it. It can't be mine, and I won't get anything from it. I'm not interested. Those who are in Ghana' – Frederick spoke of his country as an abstract concept which meant nothing to him – 'it belongs to them, I'm not part of them.' He laughed again.

★★★

At the end of 2024, I travelled back to Kumasi. It had been six months since the ceremony at the Manhyia Palace Museum and I was curious to see what people thought about the returned treasures. I spent much of that visit with Malcolm McLeod, who was advising the Asantehene on the museum's further progress. 'I'm happy here, I miss it dreadfully when I'm away,' Malcolm told me. The Asantehene had installed him in one of a matching pair of faux-stucco wedding cake mansions, which he keeps for favourite guests. Malcolm rattled around his mansion for several weeks, wondering what meal a reclusive cook might prepare for him and when the Asantehene's driver would turn up (the driver was also one of the Asantehene's umbrella bearers, so could only attend to Malcolm when not on court duty and yet Malcolm had been strictly barred, on royal honour, from taking his own taxis). Had he actually been paid, I asked, for all the work he had done? The thought had clearly not occurred to him. 'No,' he replied bemused, and explained that seeing the Asante regalia come back to Kumasi had been its own reward. In that case, I ventured, maybe his old employers the British Museum should have paid him, as a sort of diplomatic consultant. Malcolm laughed. 'No one has ever called me diplomatic before.'

On the edge of the Manhyia Palace grounds, I attended a durbar to mark the 100th anniversary of Prempeh's return from the Seychelles. 'From the Atlantic shores to the Indian Ocean shores, we are one,' said the guest of honour, the President of the Seychelles, Wavel Ramkalawan. 'It was an honour, though sad for us, to receive your great king.' Some of Prempeh's descendants who still live on the islands sat on the podium beside him. 'The British couldn't break the spirit of Asante!' shouted the master of ceremonies and people cheered. The Asantehene paraded past us on his palanquin, splendid once again in his finery and surrounded by legions of drummers, deafening horn-blowers – 'filling the air with their melodious horns,' said the MC generously – and gun bearers who fired haphazard and jolting blasts into the sky. Smoke filled the air and a group of men danced under a quivering lion skin.

Ivor Agyeman-Duah, meanwhile, was not resting on his laurels. A few days before the durbar, he had arrived in Kumasi with twenty-eight gold objects donated by the South African-based mining company AngloGold Ashanti. Their provenance was unclear – AngloGold had bought them from the Barbier-Mueller collection in Geneva some twenty years earlier – but they were believed to date from the nineteenth century and so they could have been taken by the British during the wars.[32] AngloGold Ashanti executives from Johannesburg, sweaty and incongruous in their tight suits amidst all the Asante robes of the durbar, made their way to the front and opened the boxes of gold for the Asantehene to inspect. 'We thank God they are all home,' intoned the MC, and the crowd cheered again.

Ivor was also in talks with the Wellcome Collection in the UK about returning a further fifty or sixty Asante objects: gold weights, necklaces, pipes and so on. 'They are very co-operative, very liberal and are saying we can take whatever we want,' he said.[33] In his practical and unideological way, he was ready to ride the wave of the global restitution movement as far as it would take him. 'We want to get back as many objects as is humanely possible,' he said. 'We are very interested in co-operating with whoever wants to work with us, whether it's loans or permanent returns. We just want people to see what our civilisation was, and how it can inspire the present.'[34] He told me the number of visitors to the Manhyia Palace Museum had doubled since the British Museum and V&A had returned their objects.[35]

The museum was building an extension to better display the new returns and host exhibitions and Ivor showed me round. Afterwards I made my way to the original building next door and climbed the stairs to the small upstairs rooms where the treasure from the British Museum, the V&A and the Fowler Museum was beautifully presented, on green cloth in glass display cases. The necklaces and rings, the *Mpomponsuo* sword and the *denkyemkye* helmet, the dagger, the elephant tail fly whisk. In London and Los Angeles – for all the unedifying story of how they got there – they had served as ambassadors for Asante culture. But what were they now? Mere museum artefacts or still possessed of their original sacred powers? When I asked the Asantehene this question, he was diplomatic. 'Both,' he said, 'before they left, they were sacred and since they returned, the custodians ensured that they are seen as that.'[36]

In the following days, as I spent many long hours in those upstairs rooms, I saw groups of school children in uniform file by, somewhat dutifully, more intrigued by the waxwork Asantehenes than by any gold regalia. I met people who'd come from all over Ghana, hoping to see the regalia with their own eyes, as well as other Ghanaians who had never heard the history of the Anglo-Asante Wars but were fascinated by what they'd learnt. I met a steady trickle of visitors from further afield: Seoul, Sydney, and Scarborough, which was where Dave came from, a retired journalist who had chosen Ghana for a holiday after googling 'safest country in Africa'. I asked a woman from Washington DC how she felt about the British decision to only loan the regalia. 'Offended', she said firmly. George Adu-Poku, an elderly clergyman born in Ghana but who now lives in London told me the treasures 'represent our history, our riches. I'm 100 per cent happy they've come back, it's a restoration of pride in the Asante kingdom. But it also represents reconciliation with the British.' His wife Eunice said, 'I'm getting upset, it's ours, they are thieves and they stole it, but don't worry, we won't give it back.' But she was laughing as she spoke.[37]

Outside, I sat on the museum's veranda overlooking the rubber trees. I imagine Prempeh would have sat here in his final years, listening to the peacocks and reflecting on his journeys across the oceans and how his kingdom had fallen and risen again. That was where I met Josephine Asuming, a young filmmaker of Ghanaian parents who lives in England. She had come all this way specifically to see the regalia. The British she said, 'were not fair, burning down the palace and then pretending it's yours. But we Ghanaians are quite civil people, we're chill, that's how we do it.' I thought of something Hew Locke had written at his exhibition in the British Museum. It was his final thought, the last caption on the wall before you reached the gift shop. 'Do objects belong here, or in their place of origin? What is their place of origin? I have my opinions.

Things change and shift and opinions differ. Everything is fluid.' At the Manhyia Palace Museum, I asked one of the guides, a young man called Sammy Amoah, about the significance of the treasures coming home. He paused and then said simply, 'It's important because it confirms history. That what we've been taught in books about our own past is true.'[38]

ACKNOWLEDGEMENTS

I am indebted to Ivor Agyeman-Duah for his advice, support and good company during my visits to Kumasi and for sharing so many insights on the history of Asante and its long and complex relationship with Britain. Malcolm McLeod has been unfailingly supportive and generous, opening doors to both the Asantehene's palace and obscure corners of the British Museum and its history.

In Kumasi, Peter King Appiah, Justice Brobbey, Gordon Frimpong, Francis Kwarayire, Peter Osei-Bonsu Safo Kantanka and Barima Owusu-Nyantekyi have been especially helpful. In Accra, I am grateful to Nii Kwate Owoo, still fired up after all these years, as well as Kodzo Gavua and Nana Oforiatta Ayim, for their stimulating thoughts on culture, colonialism and restitution. I was fortunate to work with some inspiring Ghanaian colleagues in the glory days of the BBC Africa Service. Ofeibea Quist-Arcton, Ama Annan and the late and sadly missed Kwabena Mensah; I learnt so much from you. A special thank you to my old boss from Bush House, Elizabeth Ohene, who sets an example through her integrity, but also her wit and sense of fun. It is always a pleasure to catch up with her and the erudite Professor George Ofosu-Amaah for food and conversation in Accra. Thank you also to former president John Kufuor.

At the British Museum I am extremely grateful to Julie Hudson. A big thank you also to Lloyd de Beer, as well as Nicholas Cullinan, Chris Gosden and Lizzie Loudon, and former curators Nigel Barley, Chris Spring and Neil Stratford. At the V&A, Sophie Brendel, Emefa Cole, Tristram Hunt, Angus Patterson and Jacques Schuhmacher were very supportive. So were Xavier Bray and Suzanne Higgott at the Wallace

Collection, Hannah Boulton and Sarah Davis at the Royal Collection and Terri Dendy at the National Army Museum.

I wrote this book at a time when the British Library was struggling to cope with the impact of a massive cyber-attack. Despite the prolonged frustrations and inconveniences, the librarians in the British Library reading rooms were as helpful and resourceful as ever. Humanities 1 and 2, and Asian and African Studies reading rooms, I leave you my blood, sweat and tears. I'm also grateful to the archivists at the National Archives in Kew and at the V&A's Art Library and V&A East.

Michael Graham-Stewart shared his knowledge, connections and extraordinary collection of historic photographs. Thank you also to Martin Bailey, Jarat Chopra, Lance Entwistle, Jean Fritts, Alex Herman, Christopher and Robert Hingley, Steven Hooper, Angela Palmer, Caroline Pheby, Justine Pick, Christine Pullen, Bell Ribeiro-Addy, John Ryle, Tim Teuten, Ken Timbers, Emily Upton, Hermione Waterfield, Patrick Watt and Sean Willcock. In the United States, Kwasi Ampene, Robin Cooper, Cory Gundlach, Erica Jones, Perrin Lathrop and Roslyn Walker went out of their way to assist me.

John Scanlon, CEO of the Elephant Protection Initiative, kindly gave me time away from the day job. My friend Simon Robinson and my father Adrian Phillips took time and trouble to read an early version of the manuscript, and both made many excellent suggestions which improved it. Adam Roberts accompanied me on a memorable excursion into the Kentish Weald in pursuit of an intriguing lead.

At Oneworld, Sam Carter has, once again, been a wonderful editor: perceptive in his criticism but also trusting and encouraging. His assistant, Hannah Haseloff has been resourceful and accommodating. Thank you also to Laura McFarlane, Paul Nash and Margot Weale. Olivia Ralphs was a most assiduous and patient copy-editor.

My greatest debt is to my family. To my daughters Emmeline and Mariella, who inspire me with their love of life and big hearts, but above all to my wife Nicole, without whom none of this would have been possible.

ILLUSTRATION LIST

1. Elmina Castle, Elmina, Ghana. Photograph by Peace Itemi, Unsplash.
2. Asante warrior, Kumasi 2024. Photograph by Barima Owusu-Nyantekyi.
3. Sir Garnet Wolseley, *c.* 1878. Photograph by John Thomson. University of St Andrews Libraries and Museums.
4. 'The Ashantee War – A Bush Fight', *The Graphic*, 3 January 1874.
5. 'The Fantee Women Carrying English Stores', *Comic Scenes in Ashantee*, (Manchester: J. Hargreaves, 1874). Courtesy of Michael Graham-Stewart.
6. 'The Ashantee War: The 42nd Highlanders in the Front – From a Sketch by our Special Artist', *The Illustrated London News*, 21 March 1874.
7. 'The Ashantee War: The Naval Brigade Clearing the Streets of Coomassie. From a Sketch by our Special Artist', *The Illustrated London News*, 21 March 1874.
8. 'The Sale of Loot – Sir Garnet Wolseley in the Auction Room', *The Graphic*, 18 April 1874.
9. 'London – King Coffee Calcalli's Umbrella at the South Kensington Museum', *The Graphic*, 25 July 1874.
10. Kumasi. Section-view of front of old houses. Walls with relief patterns and pillars. Gelatin silver print, *c.* 1888. © The Trustees of the British Museum.

11. 'Prince Henry in the Bush' from *The Downfall of Prempeh, A Diary Of Life with the Native Levy in Ashanti, 1895–96* by Robert Baden-Powell (London: Methuen, 1898).
12. 'Submission of King Prempeh, January 20th, 1896', from *The Downfall of Prempeh, A Diary of Life with the Native Levy in Ashanti, 1895–96* by Robert Baden-Powell (London: Methuen, 1898).
13. The Asante Ewer, originally made in England *c.* 1390–1399 and taken from Kumasi Palace in 1896 © The Trustees of the British Museum.
14. Asante Sword ornament, *c.* 1800–1895, taken from Kumasi Palace in 1896 © The Trustees of the British Museum.
15. 'Residency and Fort Kumassi in course of erection (view from back)', photograph courtesy of Malcolm McLeod.
16. Kumasi Fort today. Author's photograph.
17. 'Inmates of the Fort at Kumasi' from *The Ashanti Campaign of 1900* by Sir Cecil Hamilton Armitage and Arthur Forbes Montanaro (London: Sands & Co, 1901).
18. Yaa Asantewaa, 1901. Original photographer unknown. Author's photograph, taken at Prempeh II Jubilee Museum.
19. King Prempeh on board ship bound for exile, 1896. National Army Museum.
20. Princess Molly Prempeh, 2024. Author's photograph.
21. 'King Prempeh of Ashanti and followers (Political Prisoners) Mahé, Seychelles'. Photograph by S. Ohashi. Wikimedia Commons.
22. 'Ashanti chief at the procession at Kumasi Sports Ground in mourning for King George V'. Photograph by Mary S. R. Sinclair. Gelatin silver print, 2 March 1936. © The Trustees of the British Museum.
23. Opoku Ware. Photograph courtesy of Malcolm McLeod, 1981.
24. Asante *akrafokonmu*, private collection. Courtesy of Entwistle Archive.
25. Ceremonial hat and slippers put up for auction by Christie's in 2003. © Christie's Images / Bridgeman Images.

26. The Princeton Gold Head. Princeton University Art Museum, The John B. Elliott Class of 1951 Collection.
27. Diana Jackson's stool. Courtesy of Robert Hingley.
28. Lieutenant-General W. G. Knox KCB. Royal Artillery Museum.
29. Osei Tutu II. Courtesy of Manhyia Palace.
30. Asante Gold, disc pendant. © The Trustees of the British Museum.
31. Nigel Peverett as a young man. Courtesy of Nigel's family.
32. British Museum curator Julie Hudson shows Asantehene Osei Tutu II the returned treasures. Courtesy of Manhyia Palace.
33. Asantehene Osei Tutu II arrives at the British Museum for a lecture in July 2024. Author's photograph.
34. Manhyia Palace Museum, 2024. Author's photograph.

PLATE SECTION

1. Asantehene with the Golden Stool today. Photograph by Barima Owusu-Nyantekyi.
2. 'The First Day of the Custom' from *Mission from Cape Coast Castle to Ashantee* by Thomas Edward Bowdich (London: John Murray, 1819).
3. Golden ornament in shape of six-stringed harp, donated to British Museum by Bowdich. Lost-wax cast in gold, 1817. © The Trustees of the British Museum.
4. Golden *akrafokonmu*, donated to British Museum by Bowdich. Lost-wax cast in gold, 1817. © The Trustees of the British Museum.
5. 'The King of Ashantee's Palace at Coomassie Viewed from the East', *The Illustrated London News*, 25 April 1874.
6. 'Ashantee Golden Ornaments and Trophies', *The Illustrated London News*, 23 May 1874.
7. Asante trophy head in the Wallace Collection. © Wallace Collection, London, UK / Bridgeman Images.

8. The Golden Ram Head, in the Silver Room of the Royal Artillery Mess, Woolwich, photo given to author.
9. Golden *akrafokonmu*. Lost-wax cast in gold, c. 1800–1874. © The Trustees of the British Museum.
10. Golden *akrafokonmu* with spiral motifs. Lost-wax cast in gold, c. 1800–1874. © The Trustees of the British Museum.
11. Neck torc. Lost-wax cast in gold, c. 1800–1874. © The Trustees of the British Museum.
12. Golden crescent-shaped *akrafokonmu*. Lost-wax cast in gold, c. 1800–1874. © The Trustees of the British Museum.
13. Ceremonial sword or *Mpomponsuo* with leopard-skin sheaf and lost-wax cast hollow gold sword ornament, *abosodee*, in form of snake, c. 1700–1895. © The Trustees of the British Museum.
14. Ceremonial cap (*denkyemkye*) made from antelope hide with gold detailing, c. 1800–1895. © The Trustees of the British Museum.
15. Finger ring (*frumepu, frumoampun*). Lost-wax cast in gold, late nineteenth century. © The Trustees of the British Museum.
16. Gun bearer's cap (*krobonkye*) made from antelope hide with gold detailing, c. 1800–1874. © The Trustees of the British Museum.
17. *Awisiado* or *ewisiado* pendant (c. 1850–1873) set into R & S Garrard & Co dish (1874). © The Trustees of the British Museum.
18. Detail of R & S Garrard & Co mark on the dish. © The Trustees of the British Museum.
19. Detail of Asante pendant on dish. © The Trustees of the British Museum.
20. The Asante Ewer in situ at the Kumasi Palace, 1884. The National Archives.
21. Malcolm McLeod and Queen Yaa Asantewaa II, Kumasi, 2024. Author's photograph.
22. Ivor Agyeman-Duah at Homecoming. Author's photograph.

BIBLIOGRAPHY

INTERVIEWS, CORRESPONDENCE

Ghana
Ivor Agyeman-Duah, historian and museum director, Kumasi
Peter King Appiah, cultural centre administrator, Kumasi
Kodzo Gavua, professor of archaeology, Accra
John Kufuor, former president, Accra
Francis Kwarayire, civil servant, Kumasi
Nii Kwate Owoo, film maker, Accra
Nana Oforiatta Ayim, writer and art historian, Accra
Frederick Ohene, jeweller, Kumasi
Peter Osei-Bonsu Safo Kantanka, historian, Kumasi
Otumfuo Osei Tutu II, the Asantehene, Kumasi
Molly Prempeh, retired teacher, Kumasi

United Kingdom
Nigel Barley, British Museum
Lloyd de Beer, British Museum
Xavier Bray, Wallace Collection
Nicholas Cullinan, British Museum
Sarah Davis, Royal Collection
Mark Eddo, communications consultant
Lance Entwistle, art dealer
Chris Gosden, British Museum
Michael Graham-Stewart, art dealer
Anthony Guyan, antique dealer, TV production
Christopher Hingley, Christian pastor
Robert Hingley, corporate financier
Julie Hudson, British Museum
Tristram Hunt, V&A

Richard Luck, antique dealer
John Mack, British Museum
Malcolm McLeod, University of Glasgow, British Museum
Angela Palmer, artist
Angus Patterson, V&A
Meryl, Howard, Chloe and Ellie, relatives of Nigel Peverett
Christine Pullen, Royal Green Jackets Museum
Bell Ribeiro-Addy, MP
John Ryle, anthropologist
Tim Teuten, art dealer
Hermione Waterfield, Christie's
Chris Wingfield, Sainsbury Research Unit, University of East Anglia

United States
Kwasi Ampene, Tufts University
Erica Jones, Fowler Museum, Los Angeles
Cory Gundlach, Stanley Museum, Iowa
Rachel Kabukala, Nelson-Atkins Museum, Kansas City
Perrin Lathrop, Princeton University Art Museum
Roslyn Walker, Dallas Museum of Art

NEWSPAPERS AND MAGAZINES

African Times
Apollo Magazine
Army and Navy Gazette
Art Newspaper
Ashanti Pioneer
Belfast News Letter
Belfast Telegraph
Bury Free Press
Country Life
Daily Express
Daily Graphic
Evening Standard
Ghanaian Times
Globe
Guardian
Illustrated London News
Lloyd's Weekly Newspaper
London Daily Chronicle

London Gazette
London Review of Books
Los Angeles Times
Daily Mail
Daily Mirror
Morning Post
New Yorker
New York Times
Northampton Mercury
Nottinghamshire Guardian
NRK (Norway)
Observer
Palaver
Pall Mall Gazette
Princeton Alumni Weekly
Queen
Rifle Brigade Chronicle
Royal Gold Coast Gazette
Scotsman
Shipping and Mercantile Magazine
Southern Echo
Spectator
Stirling Observer
Surrey Mirror
Tatler
Daily Telegraph
The Times
Times Literary Supplement
West Africa Magazine
Wilts and Glos Standard

MISC

'International Exhibition of Navigation, Travelling, Commerce and Manufacturing', Liverpool Printing and Stationery Company, 1886

Locke, Hew, captions from exhibition 'What Have We Here?', British Museum 2024–2025

Asantehene Opoku Ware II, Address at Gold Jubilee Durbar, Kumasi, 16/11/85

Pigot's Directory

Prempeh letters displayed in the Manhyia Palace Museum

Vienna exhibition catalogue, Götter Geister Ahnen, Afrikanische Skulpturen in deutschen Privatsammlungen im Museum für Völkerkunde Wien, Neue Hofburg, 23 März bis 24 Juli, 1994

FILMS

'Whose Art Is It Anyway?' *Chronicle*, BBC 2, 27.5.81, Editor Andrew Pace, Producer Ben Shephard

The Return of a King to Seychelles, Ivor Agyeman-Duah, documentary on Osei Tutu II's visit to Seychelles, 2015

Researching and Curating African Collections at MAA, Devolving Restitution Series #4, 23/2/22, https://www.youtube.com/watch?v=wGPLPvWJAVI

WEBSITES

BBC News
Birmingham University, War Studies
British Museum Collections
Christie's
Dallas Art Museum
Dapper Foundation
Entwistle Gallery
Fathom Online
Fowler Museum
France 24
Hansard
Imperial War Museum
Ministry of Tourism, Culture and Creative Arts, Ghana
Mongabay
National Army Museum
National Museum of Scotland
Nelson-Atkins Museum
Noonans
Princeton University
Royal Collection
Royal Green Jackets Museum
Royal United Services Institute
Semafor Africa digital newsletter
SlaveVoyages

Sotheby's
UNESCO
V&A
Wallace Collection
https://aprivatefamily.org/edwin-arthur-cade/edwin-arthur-cade/
http://www.queenvictoriasjournals.org
https://victoriacrosstrust.org
All money conversions done through www.measuringworth.com

UNPUBLISHED SOURCES

Adu Boahen, Albert, *Prempeh in Exile*, paper read at National Cultural Centre, Kumasi, 1972.
Asantehene Opoku Ware II, letter to British High Commissioner.
British Museum, AOA Archive, Collection Files: Af 1874, Af 1891, Af 1896, Af 1900, Af 1901, Af 1902.
British Museum, Corporate Archive, Board of Trustees' Minutes, vol. 3 1971–74 (BM/1/1/G/2/4/1/3); vol. 4 1975–77, (BM/1/1/G/2/4/1/4); vol. 9 1991–94 (BM/1/1/G/2/4/1/9).
Ehrlich, Martha Judith, *A Catalogue of Ashanti Art taken from Kumasi in the Anglo-Ashanti War of 1874*, PhD Thesis, Indiana University, USA 1981.
Fowler Museum, '1874 Asante Objects_Fowler'.
Garrard's Gentlemen's Ledger, January 1869–January 1883, V&A Archives, AAD/1995/7/47.
Jackson, Diana, Journal of visit to Ghana, 1985.
Kumasi Traditional Council letter to Malcolm McLeod 16/5/75.
Kumasi Traditional Council Petition, 5/11/73.
Little, George, *Diary of the Ashantee War By An Eye Witness, from 1873–74*, V&A Art Library, OCLC Number 1344340049.
McLeod, Malcolm, letter to Asantehene, 8/11/76.
McLeod, Malcolm, RP Baffour Lecture, Kwame Nkrumah University of Science and Technology, Kumasi, November 2019.
McWhannell, Francis, *Smaller Pictures: Reconstructing the Lives and Communities of West African Professional Photographers of the Nineteenth Century*, MA Thesis, University of Auckland, 2020.
National Army Museum, 1976-07-37, Papers of Brig Gen Francis James Kempster (1855–1925).
Pope-Hennessy, John to Professor Laurence Gower, letter of 5/10/76.
Royal Artillery to Jarat Chopra, letter of 06/01/20.
Taylor, Ayowa Afrifa, *An Economic History of the Ashanti Goldfields Corporation, 1895–2004: Land, Labour, Capital and Enterprise*, PhD Thesis, LSE, 2006.
Wallace Collection Archives, Files on Asante objects.

NATIONAL ARCHIVES

CO 96/281
CO 879/6
CO 1069/31
DO 195/60
FCO 13/1189
FCO 65/1335
FCO 65/1503
FCO 65/1504
FCO 65/2555
FCO 65/3143
WO 32/7641
WO 32/7647
WO 33/26
WO 106/6390
WO 147/3

PUBLISHED SOURCES

Aboagye, Festus, *Indigenous African Warfare, Its Concept and Art in the Gold Coast, Asante and the Northern Territories up to the early 1900s*, Pretoria, Ulinzi African Publishing, 2010.

Adams, W., *The Modern Voyager and Traveller*, Volume 1, Africa, London, Fisher, 1834.

Adjaye, Joseph, *Diplomacy and Diplomats in 19th-Century Asante*, Asmara, Africa World Press, 1996.

Adu Boahen, Albert, *African Perspectives on Colonialism*, Baltimore, Johns Hopkins University Press, 1987.

Adu Boahen, Albert, 'A Nation in Exile: The Asante on the Seychelles Islands, 1900–24' in Enid Schildkrout, *The Golden Stool: Studies of the Asante Center and Periphery*, New York, American Museum of Natural History, 1987.

Adu Boahen, Albert, *Yaa Asantewaa and the Asante-British War of 1900–1901*, Accra, Sub-Saharan Publishers and James Currey, 2003.

Aidoo, Agnes Akosua, 'The Asante Succession Crisis 1883–1888', *Transactions of the Historical Society of Ghana*, vol. 13, no. 2, 1972.

Akyeampong, Emmanuel, 'Christianity, Modernity and the Weight of Tradition in the Life of 'Asantehene' Agyeman Prempeh I, c. 1888–1931', *Africa: Journal of the International African Institute*, 69, 1999.

Alexander, Henry, *African Tightrope, My Two Years as Nkrumah's Chief of Staff*, London, Pall Mall, 1965.

Ampene, Kwasi and Nyantakyi III, Nana Kwadwo, *Engaging Modernity: Asante in the Twenty-First Century*, Ann Arbor, University of Michigan Press, 2014.

Bibliography

Armitage, Cecil and Montanaro, Arthur, *The Ashanti Campaign of 1900*, London, Sands and Co, 1901.
Badawi, Zeinab, *An African History of Africa*, London, W. H. Allen, 2024.
Baden-Powell, Robert, *The Downfall of Prempeh, A Diary of Life with the Native Levy in Ashanti 1895–1896*, London, Methuen, 1896.
Beckett, Ian (ed.), *Wolseley and Ashanti, The Asante War Journal and Correspondence of Major General Sir Garnet Wolseley 1873–74*, Stroud, History Press for Army Records Society, 2009.
Beddoes, Henry, *Report on the Military Operations in Ashanti 1900*, London, Waterlow, 1901.
de Beer, Lloyd and Hudson, Julie, 'The British Museum and the Fourth Anglo-Asante War, 1895–1896' (forthcoming).
de Beer, Lloyd, Hudson, Julie and Agyeman-Duah, Ivor, *Object in Focus: The Asante Ewer*, London, British Museum Press, 2025.
Bernstein, Peter, *The Power of Gold, The History of An Obsession*, New Jersey, John Wiley & Sons Inc., 2012.
Biss, Harold, *The Relief of Kumasi*, London, Methuen, 1901.
Bowdich, Thomas Edward, *Mission from Cape Coast to Ashantee*, London, John Murray, 1819; London, Frank Cass, 1966.
Boyle, Frederick, *Through Fanteeland to Coomassie*, London, Chapman and Hall, 1874.
Brackenbury, Henry, *The Ashanti War of 1873–74*, Edinburgh, William Blackwood and Sons, 1874.
Bradley, Ian, *The Complete Annotated Gilbert & Sullivan*, Oxford, Oxford University Press, 1996.
Bradley, John, *The History of Seychelles*, Victoria, Clarion Press, 1940.
Burleigh, Bennet, *Two Campaigns, Madagascar and Ashantee*, London, Fisher Unwin, 1896.
Burne, Alfred, *The Royal Artillery Mess, Woolwich and Its Surroundings*, Portsmouth, WH Barrell, 1905.
Cambridge University Museum of Archaeology and of Ethnology, Thirty-Fourth Annual Report of the Antiquarian Committee to the Senate with List of Accessions for the years 1917 and 1918. Reprinted, with corrections, from the Cambridge University Reporter, 1919.
Camden, John Vincent (ed.), *A Selection from the Diaries of Edward Henry Stanley, 15th Earl of Derby, Between September 1869 and March 1878*, London, Royal Historical Society, 1994.
Carruthers, Jane, *Melton Prior, War Artist in Southern Africa, 1895–1900*, Johannesburg, Brenthurst Press, 1987.
Cherry, John and Stratford, Neil, *Westminster Kings and the Medieval Palace of Westminster*, British Museum Occasional Paper 115, British Museum, 1995.
Christie's catalogues, 1974, 1996, 2003, 2005.
Christie's, 'Catalogue of Old English Silver', London, 13/2/57.
Christie's, 'Tribal Art; Ashanti Gold and Goldweights', London, 18/3/80.
Claridge, William, *A History of the Gold Coast and Ashanti*, London, John Murray, 1915.
Clocte, Stuart, *The African Giant*, London, Collins, 1956.
Conway, Moncure, *Travels in South Kensington*, London, Trübner, 1882.

Daaku, Kwame Yeboa, *Trade and Politics on the Gold Coast 1600–1720*, Oxford, Clarendon Press, 1970.

Davidson, Basil, *The Black Man's Burden*, London, James Currey, 1992.

Davies, K. G., *The Royal African Company*, London, Longmans, Green and Co, 1957.

Dooner, William Toke, *Jottings En Route to Coomassie*, London, W. Mitchell, 1874.

Dupuis, Joseph, *Journal of A Residence in Ashantee*, London, Henry Colburn, 1824.

Edgerton, Robert, *The Fall of the Asante Empire, The Hundred-Year War for Africa's Gold Coast*, New York, The Free Press, 1995.

Ellis, Alfred Burdon, *A History of the Gold Coast of West Africa*, London, Chapman and Hall, 1893.

Fagg, William, 'A Golden Ram Head from Ashanti', *Man*, vol. 54, 1954.

Fagg, William, *The Epstein Collection of Primitive and Exotic Sculpture*, London, The Arts Council of Great Britain, 1960.

Fagg, William, 'Ashanti Gold', *The Connoisseur*, vol. 185, no. 743, 1974.

Fagg, William, and Plass, Margaret, *African Sculpture: An Anthology*, London, Studio Vista, 1964.

Figes, Orlando, *A People's Tragedy, The Russian Revolution 1891–1924*, London, Jonathan Cape, 1996.

Foster's, *A Catalogue of the Highly Important Collection of Benin Bronzes formed by the late G. W. Neville Esq*, 1 May 1930.

Freeman, Richard Austin, *Travels and Life in Ashanti and Jaman*, London, Archibald Constable, 1898.

Freeman, Richard Austin, *The Trail of Behemoth*, in *The Magic Casket*, London, Hodder & Stoughton, 1927.

Freeman, Thomas B., *Journal of Various Visits to the Kingdoms of Ashanti, Aku and Dahomi in Western Africa*, London, John Mason, 1844.

Fuller, Francis, *A Vanished Dynasty, Ashanti*, London, John Murray, 1921.

Gale, Thomas, 'The Struggle Against Disease in the Gold Coast: Early Attempts at Urban Sanitary Reform', *Transactions of the Historical Society of Ghana*, no. 1, vol. 16 (1995): 2.

Gere, Charlotte and Culme, John with William Summers, *Garrard the Crown Jewellers*, London, Quartet Books, 1993.

Gere, Charlotte and Rudoe, Judy, *Jewellery in the Age of Queen Victoria*, London, British Museum, 2010.

Glendining & Co, catalogues 1928, 1934.

Graham-Stewart, Michael and McWhannell, Francis, *Broad Sunlight, Early West African Photography*, London, Michael Graham-Stewart, 2020.

Green, Toby, *A Fistful of Shells*, London, Penguin, 2020.

Gros, Jules, *Voyages, aventures et captivité de J. Bonnat chez les Achantis*, Paris, Librairie Plon, 1884.

Hall, Wynyard Montagu, *Great Drama of Kumasi*, London, Putnam, 1939.

Heavens, Andrew, *The Prince and the Plunder*, Cheltenham, History Press, 2023.

Henty, George, *The March to Coomassie*, London, Tinsley Brothers, 1874.

Herodotus, *The Histories*, London, Everyman, 1997.

Higgott, Suzanne, *The Most Fortunate Man of His Day, Sir Richard Wallace, Connoisseur, Collector & Philanthropist*, London, The Wallace Collection, 2018.
Hodgson, Mary, *The Siege of Kumassi*, London, Arthur Pearson, 1901.
Hodgson, Pat, *The War Illustrators*, London, Osprey, 1977.
Hulme, Edward, *The Alphabet of Life*, London, Ex-Officers' Agencies & Supplies, 1949.
Huxley, Elspeth, *Four Guineas*, 1954 (The Reprint Society edition, London, 1955).
Jackson, P.R.S. *The Silver Room, The Royal Artillery Mess Woolwich*, Woolwich, 1976.
James, Jamie, *The Glamour of Strangeness*, New York, Farrar, Straus and Giroux, 2016.
Japin, Arthur, *The Two Hearts of Kwasi Boachi*, London, Vintage, 2001.
Joyce, Thomas Athol, *The British Museum Quarterly*, vol. 8, no. 1, 1933, The British Museum.
Kapuściński, Ryszard, *The Shadow of the Sun*, Allen Lane, 2001.
Killingray, David, 'The Mutiny of the West African Regiment in the Gold Coast 1901', *International Journal of African Historical Studies*, 16, 3, 1983.
Kirby, Brandon, 'A Journey into the Interior of Ashanti', *Proceedings of the Royal Geographical Society*, vol. 6, 1884.
Knox, William, *Personal Reminiscences of the Turco-Russian War 1877–8*, Lecture of 04/10/88, Aldershot Military Society, Aldershot, Gale & Polden, 1888.
Knox, William, *The Problem of Our Army Horse and his Rider and Driver*, Lecture of 23/02/09, Aldershot Military Society, London, Hugh Rees, 1909.
Kwadwo, Osei, *A Handbook on Asante Culture*, Kumasi, O. Kwadwo Enterprise, 2002.
Kwate Owoo, Nii, 'Hiding and Returning Asante Regalia' in *Fifteen Colonial Thefts*, Adjei, Sela and LeGall, Yann; London, Pluto Press, 2024.
Kyerematen, Alexander, *Guide to Ghana National Cultural Centre*, Kumasi, 1970.
Lehmann, Joseph, *All Sir Garnet: A Life of Field-Marshal Lord Wolseley*, London, Jonathan Cape, 1964.
Lloyd, Alan, *The Drums of Kumasi*, London, Panther, 1965.
Lovelace, Antonia, 'War Booty: Changing Contexts, Changing Displays: Asante "Relics" From Kumasi, Acquired by the Prince of Wales's Own Regiment of Yorkshire in 1896', *Journal of Museum Ethnography*, no. 12, 2000 (MEG Conference 1999: Glimpses of Africa Museums, Scholarship and Popular Culture, The Horniman Museum, London).
Manning, Stephen, *Britain at War with the Asante Nation*, Yorkshire, Pen and Sword Books, 2021.
Massie, Alastair, 'Community Consultation and the Shaping of the National Army Museum's Insight Gallery' in Henrietta Lidchi and Stuart Allen, *Dividing the Spoils, Perspectives on Military Collections and the British Empire*, Manchester, Manchester University Press, 2022.
Maurice, John Frederick, *The Ashantee War, A Popular Narrative*, London, Henry King, 1874.
McCaskie, Tom, 'Cultural Encounters: Britain and Africa in the Nineteenth Century' in Andrew Porter (ed.), *The Oxford History of the British Empire, Vol. III The Nineteenth Century*, Oxford, Oxford University Press, 1999.
McCaskie, Tom, 'The Life and Afterlife of Yaa Asantewaa', *Africa: Journal of the International African Institute*, vol. 7, no. 2, 2007.

McInnes, Ian and Fraser, Mark, *Ashanti 1895–96*, Chippenham, Picton, 1987.

McIntyre, W. D., 'The Ashanti Expedition of 1873–74', *The Historical Journal*, vol. 5, no. 1, 1962.

McLeod, Malcolm, 'T.E. Bowdich: An Early Collector in West Africa' in *Collectors and Collections*, British Museum Yearbook, London, British Museum Publications, 1977.

McLeod, Malcolm, 'A Note on an Asante Royal Chair of Iberian Origin' in Marion Johnson and Malcolm McLeod, *Akan-Asante Studies, Occasional Paper No. 3*, British Museum, 1979.

McLeod, Malcolm, *The Asante*, Museum of Mankind, British Museum, London, 1981.

McLeod, Malcolm, 'Richard II Part 3, at Kumase', in David Henige and Tom McCaskie, *Studies in Memory of Marion Johnson*, Madison, University of Wisconsin, 1990.

Meredith, Henry, *An Account of the Gold Coast of Africa: With A Brief History of the African Company*, London, Longman, Hurst, Rees, Orme and Brown, 1812.

Meriton-Jean, Sharon and Uranie, Sharon, 'Back to Her Roots', Seychelles News Agency, 17/2/2015.

Musgrave, George, *To Kumassi with Scott*, London, Wightman, 1896.

Myatt, Frederick, *The Golden Stool, An Account of the Ashanti War of 1900*, London, William Kimber, 1966.

Ojo, Olatunji, 'Ransoming White Captives: An Episode in Anglo-Asante Relations, 1869–1874', in *African Economic History*, vol. 42, 2014.

Phillips, Barnaby, *Loot, Britain and the Benin Bronzes*, London, Oneworld, 2021.

Pope-Hennessy, John, *Learning to Look*, London, Heinemann, 1991.

Prempeh I, Otumfuo, Nana Agyeman, *The History of Ashanti Kings and the Whole Country Itself and Other Writings*, Oxford, Oxford University Press, 2003.

Prempeh II, Otumfuo, Nana Osei Agyeman, *History of Ashanti* Ghana edition, Accra, Sub-Saharan Publishers, 2024.

Prior, Melton, *Campaigns of A War Correspondent*, London, Edward Arnold, 1912.

Ramseyer, Friedrich and Kühne, Johannes, *Four Years in Ashantee*, London, James Nisbet, 1875.

Rattray, Robert, *Ashanti*, Oxford, Clarendon Press, 1923.

Read, Charles, *Proceedings of the Society of Antiquaries*, Second Series, Vol. XVII, London, 1898.

Ricketts, Major H., *Narrative of the Ashantee War*, London, Simpkin and Marshall, T. Egerton and J. Ridgway, 1831.

Robbins, Warren and Ingram Nooter, Nancy, *African Art in American Collections*, Washington DC, Smithsonian, 1989.

Robinson, Ronald, Gallagher, John and Denny, Alice, *Africa and the Victorians*, London, Macmillan, 1965.

Russell, William Howard, *The Indian Mutiny, A Diary of the Sepoy Rebellion*, London, George Routledge, 1876.

Sarpong, Peter, *The Sacred Stools of the Akan*, Accra, Ghana Publishing Corporation, 1971.

Savoy, Bénédicte, *Africa's Struggle for Its Art*, Princeton, Princeton University Press, 2022.

Schaedler, Karl-Ferdinand, *Lexikon Afrikanische Kunst und Kultur*, Munich, Klinkhardt & Biermann, 1994.

Schaedler, Karl-Ferdinand, *Earth and Ore, 2,500 Years of African Art in Terra-Cotta and Metal*, Munich, Panterra Verlag, 1997.
Sinclair, Hugh, *Camp and Society*, London, Chapman and Hall, London, 1926.
Smith, Douglas, *Former People, The Last Days of the Russian Aristocracy*, London, Macmillan, 2012.
Soden Smith, Robert, 'Notes on Specimens of Wrought Gold, Forming A Portion of The Ashanti Indemnity', *Archaeological Journal*, vol. 31, 1874.
Sotheby's catalogues, 1999 and 2006.
Spiers, Edward, *The Victorian Soldier in Africa*, Manchester, Manchester University Press, 2004.
Spiers, Edward, 'Spoils of War: Custom and Practice', in Henrietta Lidchi and Stuart Allen, *Dividing the Spoils, Perspectives on Military Collections and the British Empire*, Manchester, Manchester University Press, 2022.
Spufford, Peter, *Money and Its Use in Medieval Europe*, Cambridge, Cambridge University Press, 1988.
Stanley, Henry M., *Coomassie and Magdala, The Story of Two British Campaigns in Africa*, London, Sampson Low, Marston, Low and Searle, 1874.
Stanley, Henry M., *Through the Dark Continent*, London, Sampson, Low, Marston, Searle & Rivington, 1890.
Stanley, Henry M., *Coomassie, The Story of the Campaign in Africa 1873–74*, London, Sampson Low, Marston and Company, 1896.
Stanley, Paul and Co, *Garrard's 1721–1911*, London, 1912.
Stone, I. R., 'The Education of Ashanti Children During the Exile in Seychelles', *Transactions of the Historical Society of Ghana*, vol. 14, no. 1, 1973.
Stopford, Albert, *The Russian Diary of An Englishman*, London, William Heinemann, 1919.
Thomas, Joseph Hammond, *A Full and Authentic Diary of the Ashanti Expedition*, William Emblow at the 'Pembrokeshire Advertiser', Pembroke, 1875.
Timbers, Ken, *The Royal Artillery Woolwich, A Celebration*, London, Third Millennium, 2008.
Tomlinson, Michael, *Regimental Heritage, A Pictorial Record of the Paintings and Silver of the Royal Regiment of Artillery*, London, Europa, 1984.
Toms, F. B. R., 'An Account of the Royal Artillery Regimental Plate in the R. A. Mess Woolwich', *Journal of the Royal Artillery*, vol. 32, 1905.
Tordoff, William, 'The Exile and Repatriation of Nana Prempeh of Ashanti (1896–1924)', *Transactions of the Historical Society of Ghana*, vol. 4, no. 2, 1960.
Tremearne, Arthur, *The Tailed Head-Hunters of Nigeria*, London, Seeley, Service and Co, 1912.
Vandervort, Bruce, *Wars of Imperial Conquest in Africa, 1830–1914*, London, UCL Press, 1998.
Vincent, William Thomas, *Warlike Woolwich*, Woolwich, A. W. and J. P. Jackson, 1875.
Walker, Roslyn (ed.), *The Power of Gold, Asante Royal Regalia from Ghana*, Dallas, Dallas Museum of Art, 2018.
War Office, *Manual of Military Law*, London, Her Majesty's Stationery Office, 1894.

Watt, Patrick, 'Ashantee Loot Is Unique: British Military Culture and the Taking of Objects in the Third Anglo-Asante War, 1873–1874', *British Journal for Military History*, vol. 9, no. 3, 2023.

Wilks, Ivor, *Asante in the Nineteenth Century*, Cambridge, Cambridge University Press, 1975.

Wilks, Ivor, *Forests of Gold, Essays on the Akan and the Kingdom of Asante*, Athens, Ohio University Press, 1993.

Willcocks, James, *From Kabul to Kumassi, Twenty-Four Years of Soldiering and Sport*, London, John Murray, 1904.

Williams, Susan, *White Malice*, London, Hurst, 2021.

Winwood Reade, William, *The Ashantee Campaign*, London, Smith, Elder & Co, 1874.

Wolseley, Garnet, *Narrative of the War with China in 1860*, London, Longman Green, 1862.

Wolseley, Garnet, *The Soldier's Pocket Book for Field Service*, London, Macmillan, 1874 and 1886.

Wolseley, Garnet, *The Story of A Soldier's Life*, Archibald Constable, London, 1903.

Wood, Diana 'Ryde Art Treasures Exhibition 1881–1882', Arcade no. 2 series, Historic Ryde Society, 2010.

Wood, Evelyn, *From Midshipman to Field Marshal*, Methuen, London, 1906.

Wood, Evelyn, *British Battles on Land and Sea*, London, Cassell, 1915.

Yarak, Larry, *Kwase Boakye and Kwame Poku: Dutch-Educated Asante "Princes"* in Enid Schildkrout, *The Golden Stool: Studies of the Asante Center and Periphery*, New York, American Museum of Natural History, 1987.

Yeebo, Yepoka, *Anansi's Gold, The Man Who Swindled the World*, London, Bloomsbury, 2023.

NOTES

Preface

1. These paragraphs are written based on information from several interviews with Ivor Agyeman-Duah and Julie Hudson in Kumasi and London and a phone conversation with John Kufuor, 06/05/2024. Kufuor was President of Ghana from 2001 to 2009.
2. Interview with Julie Hudson, British Museum, 03/07/2024.
3. Peter Bernstein, *The Power of Gold, The History of An Obsession*, John Wiley & Sons, 2000, p. 2.
4. Herodotus, *The Histories*, Everyman, 1997, pp. 381–2.
5. Presentation by Lloyd de Beer of the British Museum to University of East Anglia's Centre for African Art and Archaeology, 30/4/2025.
6. Kwame Yeboa Daaku, *Trade and Politics on the Gold Coast 1600–1720*, Clarendon Press, 1970, p. 8.
7. Thomas Edward Bowdich, *Mission from Cape Coast to Ashantee*, Frank Cass, 1966 (originally published by John Murray, 1819), p. 34.
8. Jules Gros, *Voyages, aventures et captivité de J. Bonnat chez les Achantis*. Librairie Plon, 1884, p. 246 (my translation of 'repoussant et de honteux').
9. National Archives, WO 106/6390, 'Précis of the Ashanti Expedition', Intelligence Department, War Office, 13/04/1874, p. 66.
10. Henry M. Stanley, *Coomassie and Magdala, The Story of Two British Campaigns in Africa*, Sampson Low, Marston, Low and Searle, 1874. Preface.
11. Major R. S. S. Baden-Powell, *The Downfall of Prempeh, A Diary of Life with the Native Levy in Ashanti 1895–1896*, Methuen, 1896, pp. 128–9.
12. Interview with Malcolm McLeod, London, 01/02/2024.
13. Interview with Nii Kwate Owoo, Kumasi, 02/05/2024.
14. Interview with Julie Hudson, British Museum, 03/07/2024. Julie puts the number of Asante gold pieces in the British Museum's collection as between 226 and 237 (there are doubts over the provenance and/or composition of eleven objects). She says the British Museum has 538 Asante objects that can definitely be linked to the wars (including all the gold pieces). Of these, 123 come from 1874, 280 come from 1896

and the remainder could come from either war. A search of the British Museum website in 2024 showed 2,899 Asante objects in total and that approximately half of these date from before 1900.
15 I met the Asantehene in Kumasi, 21/11/2024, and he subsequently provided written answers to my questions.
16 Phone conversation with John Kufuor, 06/05/2024.
17 Barnaby Phillips, *Loot, Britain and the Benin Bronzes*, Oneworld, 2021.

1. 'They Saw A Stool Descending from the Sky'

1 Peter Sarpong, *The Sacred Stools of the Akan*, Ghana Publishing Corporation, 1971, p. 30.
2 Zeinab Badawi, *An African History of Africa*, W. H. Allen, 2024. p. 288.
3 Otumfuo Nana Osei Agyeman Prempeh II, *History of Ashanti*, Sub-Saharan Publishers, 2024 (Ghanaian edition), p. 128.
4 Ibid., p. 133.
5 Otumfuo Nana Osei Agyeman Prempeh II, *History of Ashanti*, Sub-Saharan Publishers, 2024 (Ghanaian edition), p. 176.
6 Nana Agyeman Prempeh I, *The History of Ashanti Kings and the Whole Country Itself*. Oxford University Press, 2003, p. 109.
7 Osei Kwadwo, *A Handbook on Asante Culture*, O. Kwadwo Enterprise, 2002. p. iv.
8 Otumfuo Nana Osei Agyeman Prempeh II, *History of Ashanti*, Sub-Saharan Publishers, 2024 (Ghanaian edition), p. 188 (words underlined in green ink in original manuscript, 'clearly' by Prempeh II writes editor T. McCaskie).
9 Peter Sarpong, *The Sacred Stools of the Akan*, Ghana Publishing Corporation, 1971, pp. 8 and 26.
10 Robert Rattray, *Ashanti*, Oxford Clarendon Press, 1923, p. 289.
11 Told to author by Erica Jones, Senior Curator of African Arts, UCLA Fowler Museum, 25/06/2024.
12 Peter Bernstein, *The Power of Gold, The History of An Obsession*, John Wiley & Sons, p. 26.
13 Peter Spufford, *Money and Its Use in Medieval Europe*, Cambridge University Press, 1988, pp. 163 and 168.
14 Toby Green, *A Fistful of Shells*, Penguin, 2020, p. 115.
15 Ivor Wilks, *Forests of Gold, Essays on the Akan and the Kingdom of Asante*, Ohio University Press, 1993, p. 4 and Toby Green, *A Fistful of Shells*, p. 114.
16 Toby Green, *A Fistful of Shells*, p. 117.
17 Ivor Wilks, *Forests of Gold, Essays on the Akan and the Kingdom of Asante*, p. 5.
18 Introduction by Malcolm McLeod in Roslyn Walker (ed.), *The Power of Gold: Asante Royal Regalia*, Dallas Museum of Art, 2018.
19 Ivor Wilks, *Forests of Gold, Essays on the Akan and the Kingdom of Asante*, p. 77.
20 Introduction by Malcolm McLeod in Roslyn Walker (ed.), *The Power of Gold: Asante Royal Regalia*.

21 Captain Cecil Armitage and Lt Col Arthur Montanaro, *The Ashanti Campaign of 1900*, Sands and Co., 1901. Appendix V, p. 238.
22 Ivor Wilks, *Forests of Gold, Essays on the Akan and the Kingdom of Asante*, p. 77.
23 Malcolm McLeod, email to author, 19/5/2025.
24 Toby Green, *A Fistful of Shells*, p. 120.
25 Kwame Yeboa Daaku, *Trade and Politics on the Gold Coast 1600–1720*, Clarendon Press, 1970, p. 5.
26 Ivor Wilks, *Asante in the Nineteenth Century*, Cambridge University Press, 1975, p. 435.
27 Basil Davidson, *The Black Man's Burden*, James Currey, 1992, p. 58.
28 K. G. Davies, *The Royal African Company*, Longmans, Green and Co. 1957, p. 181.
29 Kwame Yeboa Daaku, *Trade and Politics on the Gold Coast 1600–1720*, p. 28.
30 Zeinab Badawi, *An African History of Africa*, W. H. Allen, 2024, p. 331.
31 Toby Green, *A Fistful of Shells*, p. 127.
32 Ibid., p. 177.
33 Tom McCaskie in Otumfuo Nana Osei Agyeman Prempeh II, *History of Ashanti*. Sub-Saharan Publishers, 2024 (Ghanaian edition), p. 120 (editor's introduction to chapter 3).
34 Otumfuo Nana Osei Agyeman Prempeh II, *History of Ashanti*, pp. 176–7.
35 Kwame Yeboa Daaku, *Trade and Politics on the Gold Coast 1600–1720*, p. 29.
36 Tom McCaskie in Otumfuo Nana Osei Agyeman Prempeh II, *History of Ashanti*, p. 209 (editor's introduction to chapter 4).
37 Osei Kwadwo, *A Handbook on Asante Culture*, O Kwadwo Enterprise, p. 103.
38 Tom McCaskie in Otumfuo Nana Osei Agyeman Prempeh II, *History of Ashanti*, p. 208 (editor's introduction to chapter 4).
39 Kwasi Ampene and Nana Kwadwo Nyantakyi III, *Engaging Modernity: Asante in the Twenty-First Century*, University of Michigan, 2014, p. 19.
40 Introduction by Malcolm McLeod in Roslyn Walker (ed.), *The Power of Gold: Asante Royal Regalia*, Dallas Museum of Art, 2018.
41 Warren Robbins and Nancy Ingram Nooter, *African Art in American Collections*, Smithsonian, 1989, pp. 197–200.
42 Toby Green, *A Fistful of Shells*, p. 111, citing the collector Tom Phillips.
43 Martha Judith Ehrlich, *A Catalogue of Ashanti Art taken from Kumasi in the Anglo-Ashanti War of 1874*, PhD Thesis, Indiana University, 1981, p. 16.
44 Introduction by Malcolm McLeod in Roslyn Walker (ed.), *The Power of Gold: Asante Royal Regalia*, Dallas Museum of Art, 2018.
45 Henry Meredith, *An Account of the Gold Coast of Africa: With A Brief History of The African Company*, Longman, Hurst, Rees, Orme and Brown, 1812, pp. 103–4.
46 Ivor Wilks, *Forests of Gold, Essays on the Akan and the Kingdom of Asante*, p. 95.

2. 'King of Kings'

1 Alan Lloyd, *The Drums of Kumasi*, Longman Green, 1964 (Panther edition, 1965), quoting Thomas Bowdich, p. 28.

2   Thomas Edward Bowdich, *Mission from Cape Coast to Ashantee*, Frank Cass, 1966 (originally published by John Murray, 1819), p. 6.
3   Otumfuo Nana Osei Agyeman Prempeh II, *History of Ashanti*, Sub-Saharan Publishers, 2024 (Ghanaian edition), p. 343.
4   Thomas Edward Bowdich, *Mission from Cape Coast to Ashantee*, p. 31.
5   Otumfuo Nana Osei Agyeman Prempeh II, *History of Ashanti*, p. 343 and Thomas Edward Bowdich, *Mission from Cape Coast to Ashantee*, p. 32.
6   Thomas Edward Bowdich, *Mission from Cape Coast to Ashantee*, pp. 34–8.
7   Ibid., p. 56.
8   Otumfuo Nana Osei Agyeman Prempeh II, *History of Ashanti*, p. 344.
9   Thomas Edward Bowdich, *Mission from Cape Coast to Ashantee*, p. 49.
10 Otumfuo Nana Osei Agyeman Prempeh II, *History of Ashanti*, pp. 326–7.
11 Alfred Burdon Ellis, *A History of the Gold Coast of West Africa*, Chapman and Hall, 1893, p. 115.
12 Otumfuo Nana Osei Agyeman Prempeh II, *History of Ashanti*, p. 328.
13 Ibid., p. 329.
14 Alfred Burdon Ellis, *A History of the Gold Coast of West Africa*, p. 119.
15 Ibid., pp. 117–18.
16 Figures taken from the SlaveVoyages.org website, hosted at Rice University. It estimates that more than 12.5 million Africans were taken in the Atlantic slave trade, of which 3.2 million were transported on British ships.
17 Tom McCaskie in Otumfuo Nana Osei Agyeman Prempeh II, *History of Ashanti*, p. 320 (editor's introduction to chapter 9).
18 Albert Adu Boahen, *African Perspectives on Colonialism*, Johns Hopkins University Press, 1987, p. 2.
19 Thomas Edward Bowdich, *Mission from Cape Coast to Ashantee*, p. 338.
20 Ibid., pp. 81 and 142.
21 Ibid., p. 149.
22 Ibid., p. 340.
23 Ibid., pp. 351–2.
24 https://www.encyclopedia.com/science/dictionaries-thesauruses-pictures-and-press-releases/lee-sarah-eglonton-wallis-bowdich, and Malcolm McLeod, 'T. E. Bowdich: An Early Collector in West Africa in Collectors and Collections', *British Museum Yearbook*, British Museum Publications, 1977.
25 Alan Lloyd, *The Drums of Kumasi*, p. 37.
26 Joseph Adjaye, *Diplomacy and Diplomats in 19th Century Asante*, University Press of America 1984 (Africa World Press edition, 1996) pp. 2–3.
27 Ivor Wilks, *Asante in the Nineteenth Century*, Cambridge University Press, 1975, p. 148.
28 Otumfuo Nana Osei Agyeman Prempeh II, *History of Ashanti*, p. 367.
29 Stephen Manning, *Britain at War with the Asante Nation*, Pen and Sword, 2021, p. 19.
30 Tom McCaskie in Otumfuo Nana Osei Agyeman Prempeh II, *History of Ashanti*, p. 322 (editor's introduction to chapter 9).
31 Joseph Dupuis, *Journal of A Residence in Ashantee*, Henry Colburn, 1824, Introduction.

32 Ivor Wilks, *Asante in the Nineteenth Century*, p. 168.
33 Joseph Dupuis, *Journal of A Residence in Ashantee*, p. 89.
34 Ibid., p. 162.
35 Ibid., p. 163.
36 Alfred Burdon Ellis, *A History of the Gold Coast of West Africa*, Chapman and Hall, 1893, p. 145.
37 Alan Lloyd, *The Drums of Kumasi*, p. 39.
38 Otumfuo Nana Osei Agyeman Prempeh II, *History of Ashanti*, p. 372.
39 Alfred Burdon Ellis, *A History of the Gold Coast of West Africa*, p. 145.
40 Otumfuo Nana Osei Agyeman Prempeh II, *History of Ashanti*, p. 372.
41 *Royal Gold Coast Gazette*, 07/05/1822 and 18/03/1823.
42 Major H. Ricketts, *Narrative of the Ashantee War*, Simpkin and Marshall, T. Egerton and J. Ridgway, 1831, pp. 55–8.
43 Ibid., p. 83.
44 *The Times*, 03/05/1824. A relic of the Battle of Nsamankow can be found in London's National Army Museum; an elephant tusk 'war trumpet' covered in fish hide and 'held in much veneration by the natives'. https://collection.nam.ac.uk/NAM.1963-10-187-1.
45 Otumfuo Nana Osei Agyeman Prempeh II, *History of Ashanti*, p. 375. In a footnote on this page, editor Tom McCaskie says it is more likely that Osei Bonsu died in October 1823 but that there is no conclusive evidence.
46 W. Adams, *The Modern Voyager and Traveller*, Volume 1, Africa, Fisher, Son and Co., 1834 edition. Preface.
47 *The Times*, 02/12/1826.
48 *The Times*, 02/12/1826 and Otumfuo Nana Osei Agyeman Prempeh II, *History of Ashanti*, p. 387 and Ivor Wilks, *Asante in the Nineteenth Century*, p. 439.
49 https://www.rct.uk/collection/search#/9/collection/69929/war-drum-of-the-king-of-ashanti.
50 *The Times*, 02/12/1826.
51 *The Times*, 02/12/1826.
52 Pigot's Directory, 1830 and https://escapetobritain.com/st-saviours-church-dartmouth/.
53 I am indebted to Patrick Watt of National Museums Scotland for thoughts and details on the MacCarthy skull. The missionaries are Chapman in 1843 and Friedrich Ramseyer in the 1860s.
54 Major H. Ricketts, *Narrative of the Ashantee War*, p. 176. A returned prisoner said the head belonged to 'Tooto Quamina, late king of Ashantee', aka Osei Bonsu.
55 W. Adams, *The Modern Voyager and Traveller*, Volume 1, p. 263.
56 W. Adams, *The Modern Voyager and Traveller*, Volume 1, Africa, pp. 260 and 263.
57 W. Adams, *The Modern Voyager and Traveller*, Volume 1, Africa, p. 261.
58 Ibid., p. 33.
59 Thomas Edward Bowdich, *Mission from Cape Coast to Ashantee*, pp. 274–84.
60 Ibid., architecture, p. 305; population estimate, p. 323; crafts, p. 311; female beauty, p. 318.

61 Ibid., pp. 114–15.
62 Ibid., p. 151.
63 Ibid., p. 147.
64 https://www.britishmuseum.org/collection and Kwasi Ampene and Nana Kwadwo Nyantakyi III, *Engaging Modernity: Asante in the Twenty-First Century*, University of Michigan, 2014, p. 118.
65 Thomas Edward Bowdich, *Mission from Cape Coast to Ashantee*, p. 311.
66 Joseph Dupuis, *Journal of A Residence in Ashantee*, p. 137.
67 Royal Gold Coast Gazette, 07/05/1822 and 21/05/1822.
68 Thomas B. Freeman, *Journal of Various Visits to the Kingdoms of Ashanti, Aku and Dahomi in Western Africa*, John Mason, London, 1844, pp. 141–2.
69 Ivor Wilks, *Asante in the Nineteenth Century*, Cambridge University Press, 1975, p. 200.

3. 'An End to All the Peace and Quiet'

1 Author's interview with Peter King Appiah, Kumasi, 29/04/2024.
2 Tom McCaskie in Otumfuo Nana Osei Agyeman Prempeh II, *History of Ashanti*, Sub-Saharan Publishers, 2024 (Ghanaian edition), fn p. 410 (editor's introduction to chapter 11).
3 Stephen Manning, *Britain at War with the Asante Nation*, Pen and Sword, 2021, p. 31.
4 Ian Beckett (ed.), *Wolseley and Ashanti, The Asante War Journal and Correspondence of Major General Sir Garnet Wolseley 1873–74*, History Press for Army Records Society, p. 5.
5 Stephen Manning, *Britain at War with the Asante Nation*, p. 33.
6 Henry Brackenbury, *The Ashanti War of 1873–74*, William Blackwood and Sons, 1874, pp. 21–22.
7 Ibid., p. 23.
8 Stephen Manning, *Britain at War with the Asante Nation*, p. 35.
9 Ivor Wilks, *Forests of Gold, Essays on the Akan and the Kingdom of Asante*, Ohio University Press, 1993, p. 169.
10 Otumfuo Nana Osei Agyeman Prempeh II, *History of Ashanti*, p. 433.
11 Tom McCaskie in Otumfuo Nana Osei Agyeman Prempeh II, *History of Ashanti*, fn p. 426 (editor's introduction to chapter 12).
12 Henry Brackenbury, *The Ashanti War of 1873–74*, William Blackwood and Sons, 1874, p. 30.
13 Joseph Adjaye, *Diplomacy and Diplomats in 19th Century Asante*, University Press of America, 1984 (Africa World Press 1996 edition), p. 200.
14 Festus Aboagye, *Indigenous African Warfare: Its Concept and Art in the Gold Coast, Asante, and the Northern Territories up to the Early 1900s*. Ulinzi African Publishing, 2010, p. 330.
15 Alan Lloyd, *The Drums of Kumasi*, Longman Green, 1964 (Panther edition, 1965), p. 63.
16 Otumfuo Nana Osei Agyeman Prempeh II, *History of Ashanti*, p. 442.
17 Olatunji Ojo, 'Ransoming White Captives: An Episode in Anglo-Asante Relations, 1869–1874', *African Economic History*, vol. 42, 2014, pp. 109–35.

18 *The Times*, 27/02/1883.
19 *The Times*, 27/02/1883.
20 Ian Beckett (ed.), *Wolseley and Ashanti, The Asante War Journal and Correspondence of Major General Sir Garnet Wolseley 1873–74*, pp. 10–11.
21 Stephen Manning, *Britain at War with the Asante Nation*, p. 37.
22 Ian Beckett (ed.), *Wolseley and Ashanti, The Asante War Journal and Correspondence of Major General Sir Garnet Wolseley 1873–74*, p. 12.
23 Stephen Manning, *Britain at War with the Asante Nation*, 2021, p. 46.
24 *The Times*, 10/07/1873.
25 *The Times*, 10/07/1873.
26 *The Times*, 10/07/1873.
27 Colonel Francis Festing's report in *The Times*, 16/07/1873.
28 *The Times*, 15/07/1873.
29 Stephen Manning, *Britain at War with the Asante Nation*, 2021, pp. 50–1.
30 *The Times*, 14/07/1873.
31 *The Times*, 16/07/1873.
32 W. D. McIntyre, 'The Ashanti Expedition of 1873–74', *The Historical Journal*, vol. 5, 1, 1962.
33 A. Adu Boahen, *African Perspectives on Colonialism*, Johns Hopkins University Press, 1987, p. 26.
34 Stephen Manning, *Britain at War with the Asante Nation*, pp. 8–9.
35 Captain Edmund Freemantle in *The Times*, 16/07/1873.
36 Stephen Manning, *Britain at War with the Asante Nation*, p. 58.
37 Otumfuo Nana Osei Agyeman Prempeh II, *History of Ashanti*, p. 443.
38 W. D. McIntyre, 'The Ashanti Expedition of 1873–74', *The Historical Journal*, vol. 5, 1, 1962.
39 Ian Beckett (ed.), *Wolseley and Ashanti, The Asante War Journal and Correspondence of Major General Sir Garnet Wolseley 1873–74*, p. 13.
40 Evelyn Wood, *From Midshipman to Field Marshal*, Methuen, 1906, vol. 1, pp. 254–5.
41 Field-Marshal Viscount Wolseley, *The Story of A Soldier's Life*, Archibald Constable, 1903, vol. 2, pp. 262–4.
42 Field-Marshal Viscount Wolseley, *The Story of A Soldier's Life*, Archibald Constable, 1903, vol. 2, p. 267.
43 Joseph Lehmann, *All Sir Garnet: A Life of Field-Marshal Lord Wolseley*, Jonathan Cape, 1964, p. 13.
44 William Winwood Reade, *The Ashantee Campaign*, Smith, Elder & Co., London, 1874, p. 146.
45 Ian Beckett (ed.), *Wolseley and Ashanti, The Asante War Journal and Correspondence of Major General Sir Garnet Wolseley 1873–74*, p. 16.
46 *The Times*, 16/09/1873 and 17/09/1873.
47 *The Times*, 16/09/1873.
48 Henry Brackenbury, *The Ashanti War of 1873–1874*, William Blackwood and Sons, 1874, vol. I, p. 145.
49 Alan Lloyd, *The Drums of Kumasi*, p. 81.

50 http://www.queenvictoriasjournals.org. Queen Victoria's journal, 30/03/1874.
51 National Archives, WO 147/3. Wolseley's journal, 12/9/1873.
52 *Spectator*, 20/09/1873.
53 *The Times*, 07/10/1873.
54 Ivor Wilks, *Forests of Gold, Essays on the Akan and the Kingdom of Asante*, p. 215.
55 Ivor Wilks, *Forests of Gold, Essays on the Akan and the Kingdom of Asante*, p. 222.
56 Joseph Adjaye, *Diplomacy and Diplomats in 19th Century Asante*, Africa World Press, 1996, p. 192.
57 Ivor Wilks, *Forests of Gold, Essays on the Akan and the Kingdom of Asante*, p. 221.
58 W. D. McIntyre, 'The Ashanti Expedition of 1873–74', *Historical Journal*, vol. 5, 1, 1962.
59 Alan Lloyd, *The Drums of Kumasi*, p. 108.

4. 'The White Men Have Guns Which Hit Five Ashantees At Once'

1 George Little, 'Diary of the Ashantee War by an Eye Witness, from 1873–74', V&A Art Library, OCLC Number 1344340049.
Number of soldiers onboard HMS *Himalaya* from National Archives, WO 106/6390.
'Précis of the Ashanti Expedition', Intelligence Dept, War Office, 13/04/1874.
2 Ibid.
3 *The Times*, 07/10/1873.
4 Ian Beckett (ed.), *Wolseley and Ashanti, The Asante War Journal and Correspondence of Major General Sir Garnet Wolseley 1873–74*, p. 15.
5 Stephen Manning, *Britain at War with the Asante Nation*, 2021, p. 61.
6 Ian Beckett (ed.), *Wolseley and Ashanti, The Asante War Journal and Correspondence of Major General Sir Garnet Wolseley 1873–74*, p. 100.
7 Field-Marshal Viscount Wolseley, *The Story of A Soldier's Life*, Archibald Constable, 1903, p. 279.
8 National Archives, WO 147/3 Wolseley's journal, 14–15 Oct.
9 W. D. McIntyre, 'The Ashanti Expedition of 1873–4', *Historical Journal*, vol. 1, 1962.
10 *The Times*, 1/12/1873.
11 National Archives, WO 147/3 Wolseley journal 03/11/73 and 04/11/73.
12 Wolseley to Colonel William Earle, 25/11/73, in Ian Beckett (ed.), *Wolseley and Ashanti, The Asante War Journal and Correspondence of Major General Sir Garnet Wolseley 1873–74*, pp. 230–1.
13 National Archives, WO 147/3 Wolseley journal, 27/09/73.
14 Field-Marshal Viscount Wolseley, *The Story of A Soldier's Life*, p. 257, vol. 2.
15 Field-Marshal Viscount Wolseley, *The Story of A Soldier's Life*, p. 135, vol. 2.
16 Joseph Lehmann, *All Sir Garnet, A Life of Field-Marshal Lord Wolseley*, Jonathan Cape, 1964, p. 123, quoting *Blackwood's Magazine* of January 1863.
17 Wolseley to Francis Wolseley, 23/09/73, in Ian Beckett (ed.), *Wolseley and Ashanti, The Asante War Journal and Correspondence of Major General Sir Garnet Wolseley 1873–74*, p. 84.

18 National Archives, WO 147/3 Wolseley's journal, 10/12/73.
19 Bruce Vandervort, *Wars of Imperial Conquest in Africa, 1830–1914*, UCL Press, 1998, p. 95, and Edward Spiers, *The Victorian Soldier in Africa*, Manchester University Press, 2004, p. 23.
20 Ian Beckett (ed.), *Wolseley and Ashanti, The Asante War Journal and Correspondence of Major General Sir Garnet Wolseley 1873–74*, pp. 104–5.
21 Stephen Manning, *Britain at War with the Asante Nation*, 2021, p. 57.
22 George Little, 'Diary of the Ashantee War by an Eye Witness, from 1873–74'. V&A Art Library, OCLC Number 1344340049, and uniform details from Ian Beckett (ed.), *Wolseley and Ashanti, The Asante War Journal and Correspondence of Major General Sir Garnet Wolseley 1873–74*, p. 37.
23 Henry Brackenbury, *The Ashanti War of 1873–74*, William Blackwood and Sons, 1874, vol. 1, p. 127.
24 Ian Beckett (ed.), *Wolseley and Ashanti, The Asante War Journal and Correspondence of Major General Sir Garnet Wolseley 1873–74*, p. 245.
25 Ian Beckett (ed.), *Wolseley and Ashanti, The Asante War Journal and Correspondence of Major General Sir Garnet Wolseley 1873–74*, p. 244, and Alan Lloyd, *The Drums of Kumasi*, p. 104.
26 Wolseley to Cambridge 21/11/73 in Ian Beckett (ed.), *Wolseley and Ashanti, The Asante War Journal and Correspondence of Major General Sir Garnet Wolseley 1873–74*, p. 220.
27 Joseph Lehmann, *All Sir Garnet, A Life of Field-Marshal Lord Wolseley*, Jonathan Cape 1964, p. 186.
28 Wolseley to Alison 06/1/74 in Ian Beckett (ed.), *Wolseley and Ashanti, The Asante War Journal and Correspondence of Major General Sir Garnet Wolseley 1873–74*, p. 328.
29 National Archives, WO 147/3 Wolseley's journal 16/1/74.
30 Joseph Hammond Thomas, A Full and Authentic Diary of the Ashanti Expedition, William Emblow at the 'Pembrokeshire Advertiser', Pembroke 1875, Diary entries 14–22 December 1873.
31 Joseph Hammond Thomas, A Full and Authentic Diary of the Ashanti Expedition, William Emblow at the 'Pembrokeshire Advertiser', Pembroke 1875, Diary entries 14–22 December 1873.
32 Joseph Hammond Thomas, A Full and Authentic Diary of the Ashanti Expedition, William Emblow at the 'Pembrokeshire Advertiser', Pembroke 1875, Diary entry 25 December 1873.
33 All other quotes in this paragraph are from George Little, 'Diary of the Ashantee War by an Eye Witness, from 1873–74', V&A Art Library, OCLC Number 1344340049.
34 Joseph Hammond Thomas, A Full and Authentic Diary of the Ashanti Expedition, William Emblow at the 'Pembrokeshire Advertiser', Pembroke 1875, Diary entry 1 January 1874.
35 Wolseley to Cardwell, 13/10/74, in Ian Beckett (ed.), *Wolseley and Ashanti, The Asante War Journal and Correspondence of Major General Sir Garnet Wolseley 1873–74*, p. 145.

36. Edward Spiers, *The Victorian Soldier in Africa*, p. 24, and George Little, 'Diary of the Ashantee War by an Eye Witness, from 1873–74', V&A Art Library, OCLC Number 1344340049.
37. Edward Spiers, *The Victorian Soldier in Africa*, 2013, p. 24.
38. Joseph Hammond Thomas, A Full and Authentic Diary of the Ashanti Expedition, William Emblow at the 'Pembrokeshire Advertiser', Pembroke 1875, Diary entry 18 January 1874.
39. Melton Prior, *Campaigns of A War Correspondent*, Edward Arnold, 1912, pp. 11 and 14.
40. Garnet Wolseley, *The Soldier's Pocket Book for Field Service*, Macmillan, 1874, pp. 93–7.
41. W. D. McIntyre, 'British Policy in West Africa: The Ashanti Expedition of 1873–4', *Historical Journal*, 5, 1, 1962, pp. 19–46.
42. Pat Hodgson, *The War Illustrators*, Osprey, 1977, p. 110.
43. Wolseley to Louisa Wolseley, 04/1/74 in Ian Beckett (ed.), *Wolseley and Ashanti, The Asante War Journal and Correspondence of Major General Sir Garnet Wolseley 1873–74*, p. 326 (with an explanation of Frances's editing in Beckett's Introduction, pp. 23–4).
44. National Archives, WO 147/3 Wolseley's journal, 18/09/73.
45. George Little, 'Diary of the Ashantee War by an Eye Witness, from 1873–74', V&A Art Library, OCLC Number 1344340049.
46. George Little, 'Diary of the Ashantee War by an Eye Witness, from 1873–74', V&A Art Library, OCLC Number 1344340049 and National Archives, WO 147/3 Wolseley's journal 19/1/74.
47. Friedrich Ramseyer and Johannes Kühne, *Four Years in Ashantee*, James Nisbet, 1875, p. 265.
48. Wolseley's journal, 13/1/74, in Ian Beckett (ed.), *Wolseley and Ashanti, The Asante War Journal and Correspondence of Major General Sir Garnet Wolseley 1873–74*, p. 334.
49. Wolseley's journal, 13/1/74, in Ian Beckett (ed.), *Wolseley and Ashanti, The Asante War Journal and Correspondence of Major General Sir Garnet Wolseley 1873–74*, p. 334 and Wolseley to King Kakari [sic], 02/1/74, in Ian Beckett (ed.), *Wolseley and Ashanti, The Asante War Journal and Correspondence of Major General Sir Garnet Wolseley 1873–74*, p. 317.
50. Wolseley to King Kofi Karikari, 13/1/74, National Archives, C/O 879/6.
51. Ian Beckett (ed.), *Wolseley and Ashanti, The Asante War Journal and Correspondence of Major General Sir Garnet Wolseley 1873–74*, pp. 302–3.
52. Wolseley to King Kakari, 13/10/73, in Ian Beckett (ed.), *Wolseley and Ashanti, The Asante War Journal and Correspondence of Major General Sir Garnet Wolseley 1873–74*, p. 137.
53. *The Times*, 6/2/1874, and National Archives, W/O 106/6390. I have used Measuringworth.com for currency conversion here and throughout this book.
54. Ayowa Afrifa Taylor, *An Economic History of the Ashanti Goldfields Corporation, 1895–2004: Land, Labour, Capital and Enterprise*, LSE Doctorate, 2006, p. 44.
55. Henry M. Stanley, *Coomassie and Magdala, The Story of Two British Campaigns in Africa*, Sampson Low, Marston, Low and Searle, 1874, p. 172 and Wolseley's journal, 24/1/74, in Ian Beckett (ed.), *Wolseley and Ashanti, The Asante War Journal and Correspondence of Major General Sir Garnet Wolseley 1873–74*, p. 348.

56 Otumfuo Nana Osei Agyeman Prempeh II, *History of Ashanti*, p. 436.
57 Friedrich Ramseyer and Johannes Kühne, *Four Years in Ashantee*, p. 237.
58 Ivor Wilks, *Asante in the Nineteenth Century*, p. 506.
59 Friedrich Ramseyer and Johannes Kühne, *Four Years in Ashantee*, p. 239.
60 Friedrich Ramseyer and Johannes Kühne, *Four Years in Ashantee*, p. 252.
61 Friedrich Ramseyer and Johannes Kühne, *Four Years in Ashantee*, p. 256, and Evelyn Wood, *British Battles on Land and Sea*, Cassell, 1915, vol. 2, p. 693.
62 Friedrich Ramseyer and Johannes Kühne, *Four Years in Ashantee*, James Nisbet, 1875, p. 267.

5. 'Every Doctor Looked Like A Butcher'

1 Joseph Hammond Thomas, A Full and Authentic Diary of the Ashanti Expedition, William Emblow at the 'Pembrokeshire Advertiser', Pembroke 1875, diary entry 18/1/74.
2 Joseph Hammond Thomas, A Full and Authentic Diary of the Ashanti Expedition, William Emblow at the 'Pembrokeshire Advertiser', Pembroke 1875, diary entry 23/1/74.
3 George Little, 'Diary of the Ashantee War by an Eye Witness, from 1873–74', V&A Art Library, OCLC Number 1344340049.
4 Henry Brackenbury, *Narrative of the Ashanti War*, William Blackwood and Sons, 1874, p. 82, vol. 2.
5 Wolseley to King Kakari, 24/1/74, in Ian Beckett (ed.), *Wolseley and Ashanti, The Asante War Journal and Correspondence of Major General Sir Garnet Wolseley 1873–74*, History Press for Army Records Society, p. 349.
6 Field-Marshal Viscount Wolseley, *The Story of A Soldier's Life*, Archibald Constable, 1903, p. 264.
7 Wolseley to Cambridge, 25/1/74, in Ian Beckett (ed.), *Wolseley and Ashanti, The Asante War Journal and Correspondence of Major General Sir Garnet Wolseley 1873–74*, p. 353.
8 Stephen Manning, *Britain at War with the Asante Nation*, 2021, p. 88.
9 Joseph Adjaye, *Diplomacy and Diplomats in 19th Century Asante*, Africa World Press, 1996, p.196.
10 Otumfuo Nana Osei Agyeman Prempeh II, *History of Ashanti*, Sub-Saharan Publishers, 2024 (Ghanaian edition), p. 444.
11 Friedrich Ramseyer and Johannes Kühne, *Four Years in Ashantee*, p. 267.
12 Ivor Wilks, *Asante in the Nineteenth Century*, Cambridge University Press, p. 506.
13 Festus Aboagye, *Indigenous African Warfare Its Concept and Art in the Gold Coast, Asante and the Northern Territories up to early 1900s*, Ulinzi African Publishing, 2010, p. 329.
14 Henry M. Stanley, *Coomassie and Magdala*, Sampson Low, Marston Low & Searle, 1874, pp. 166–7.
15 George Little, 'Diary of the Ashantee War by an Eye Witness, from 1873–74', V&A Art Library, OCLC Number 1344340049.

16 Joseph Hammond Thomas, A Full and Authentic Diary of the Ashanti Expedition, William Emblow at the 'Pembrokeshire Advertiser', Pembroke 1875, diary entry 21/1/74, and George Little, 'Diary of the Ashantee War by an Eye Witness, from 1873–74', V&A Art Library, OCLC Number 1344340049.
17 Edward Spiers, *The Victorian Soldier in Africa*, Manchester University Press, 2004, p. 26.
18 National Archives, WO 147/3 Wolseley's journal, 29/1/74.
19 Henry Brackenbury, *The Ashanti War of 1873–74*, William Blackwood and Sons, 1874, vol. 1, pp. 361–7.
20 George Little, 'Diary of the Ashantee War by an Eye Witness, from 1873–74', V&A Art Library, OCLC Number 1344340049.
21 National Archives, WO 147/3 Wolseley's journal, 30/1/74.
22 Edward Spiers, *The Victorian Soldier in Africa*, Manchester University Press, 2004, p. 28.
23 National Archives, WO 147/3 Wolseley's journal, 10/12/74, and Field-Marshal Viscount Wolseley, *The Story of A Soldier's Life*, p. 313.
24 Robert Ferguson, 'A Stirlingshire Soldier's Account of the War', in *Stirling Observer*, 04/04/74.
25 George Little, 'Diary of the Ashantee War by an Eye Witness, from 1873–74', V&A Art Library, OCLC Number 1344340049.
26 George Henty, *The March to Coomassie*, Tinsley Brothers, 1874, p. 385.
27 Sir Garnet Wolseley, *The Story of A Soldier's Life*, p. 342.
28 Melton Prior, *Campaigns of A War Correspondent*, Edward Arnold, 1912, p. 18.
29 Otumfuo Nana Osei Agyeman Prempeh II, *History of Ashanti*, p. 445.
30 Ian Beckett (ed.), *Wolseley and Ashanti, The Asante War Journal and Correspondence of Major General Sir Garnet Wolseley 1873–74*, p. 309.
31 Ian Beckett (ed.), *Wolseley and Ashanti, The Asante War Journal and Correspondence of Major General Sir Garnet Wolseley 1873–74*, p. 312.
32 Edward Spiers, *The Victorian Soldier in Africa*, 2004, p. 29.
33 George Little, 'Diary of the Ashantee War by an Eye Witness, from 1873–74', V&A Art Library, OCLC Number 1344340049.
34 Henry M. Stanley, *Coomassie and Magdala*, p. 197.
35 National Archives, WO 106/6390, 'Précis of the Ashanti Expedition', Intelligence Dept, War Office, 13/04/1874, pp. 53–4.
36 Joseph Hammond Thomas, A Full and Authentic Diary of the Ashanti Expedition, William Emblow at the 'Pembrokeshire Advertiser', Pembroke 1875, diary entry 9 February.
37 Ian Beckett (ed.), *Wolseley and Ashanti, The Asante War Journal and Correspondence of Major General Sir Garnet Wolseley 1873–74*, pp. 311–12.
38 Ibid.
39 National Archives, WO 147/3 Wolseley's journal, 31/1/74, and Wolseley to Louisa 1/02/74 in Ian Beckett (ed.), *Wolseley and Ashanti, The Asante War Journal and Correspondence of Major General Sir Garnet Wolseley 1873–74*, p. 383.
40 Field-Marshal Viscount Wolseley, *The Story of A Soldier's Life*, p. 343.

41 Ian Beckett (ed.), *Wolseley and Ashanti, The Asante War Journal and Correspondence of Major General Sir Garnet Wolseley 1873–74*, p. 310.
42 Edward Spiers, *The Victorian Soldier in Africa*, 2013, p. 29.
43 Otumfuo Nana Osei Agyeman Prempeh II, *History of Ashanti*, p. 446.
44 National Archives, WO 106/6390, 'Précis of the Ashanti Expedition', Intelligence Dept, War Office, 13/04/1874, pp 53–4.
45 George Little, 'Diary of the Ashantee War by an Eye Witness, from 1873–74', V&A Art Library, OCLC Number 1344340049.
46 George Little, 'Diary of the Ashantee War by an Eye Witness, from 1873–74', V&A Art Library, OCLC Number 1344340049.
47 George Little, 'Diary of the Ashantee War by an Eye Witness, from 1873–74', V&A Art Library, OCLC Number 1344340049.
48 Joseph Hammond Thomas, A Full and Authentic Diary of the Ashanti Expedition, William Emblow at the 'Pembrokshire Advertiser', Pembroke 1875, diary entry 03/02/74.
49 Wolseley to King Kakari 03/02/74 in Ian Beckett (ed.), *Wolseley and Ashanti, The Asante War Journal and Correspondence of Major General Sir Garnet Wolseley 1873–74*, p. 386.
50 Ian Beckett (ed.), *Wolseley and Ashanti, The Asante War Journal and Correspondence of Major General Sir Garnet Wolseley 1873–74*, p. 363.
51 George Little, 'Diary of the Ashantee War by an Eye Witness, from 1873–74', V&A Art Library, OCLC Number 1344340049.
52 National Archives, WO 147/3 Wolseley's journal, 04/04/74.
53 Joseph Lehmann, *All Sir Garnet, A Life of Field-Marshal Lord Wolseley*, Jonathan Cape 1964, p. 195.
54 Otumfuo Nana Osei Agyeman Prempeh II, *History of Ashanti*, p. 446.
55 Joseph Hammond Thomas, A Full and Authentic Diary of the Ashanti Expedition, William Emblow at the 'Pembrokshire Advertiser', Pembroke 1875, diary entry 04/02/74.
56 Edward Spiers, *The Victorian Soldier in Africa*, p. 30.
57 George Little, 'Diary of the Ashantee War by an Eye Witness, from 1873–74', V&A Art Library, OCLC Number 1344340049.

6. 'Blew Up the Palace and Left Coomassie in Flames'

1 *Observer*, 27/1/2024, https://www.theguardian.com/culture/2024/jan/27/vas-return-of-looted-ghana-gold-is-a-new-way-to-tackle-britains-painful-past.
2 Tristram Hunt in conversation with author, 27/02/24.
3 William Howard Russell, *The Indian Mutiny, A Diary of the Sepoy Rebellion*, George Routledge, 1876, p. 196.
4 Joseph Lehmann, *All Sir Garnet A Life of Field-Marshal Lord Wolseley*, Jonathan Cape, 1964, pp. 73–4.
5 Joseph Lehmann, *All Sir Garnet A Life of Field-Marshal Lord Wolseley*, Jonathan Cape, 1964, p. 106.

6   Sir Garnet Wolseley, *Narrative of the War with China in 1860*, Longman Green, 1862, p. 227.
7   Sir Garnet Wolseley, *The Story of A Soldier's Life*, p. 78.
8   Sir Garnet Wolseley, *Narrative of the War with China in 1860*, pp. 237–9.
9   Sir Garnet Wolseley, *The Soldier's Pocket-Book for Field Service*, pp. 165–6.
10 Sir Garnet Wolseley, *The Story of A Soldier's Life*, pp. 339–40.
11 Sir Garnet Wolseley, *Narrative of the War with China in 1860*, pp. 224–5.
12 Ian Beckett (ed.), *Wolseley and Ashanti, The Asante War Journal and Correspondence of Major General Sir Garnet Wolseley 1873–74*, p. 365, and National Archives, WO 147/3 Wolseley's journal, 04/02/74.
13 Edward Spiers, *The Victorian Soldier in Africa*, p. 31.
14 George Little, 'Diary of the Ashantee War by an Eye Witness, from 1873–74', V&A Art Library, OCLC Number 1344340049.
15 George Little, 'Diary of the Ashantee War by an Eye Witness, from 1873–74', V&A Art Library, OCLC Number 1344340049.
16 George Little, 'Diary of the Ashantee War by an Eye Witness, from 1873–74', V&A Art Library, OCLC Number 1344340049.
17 Henry Brackenbury, *The Ashanti War of 1873–74*, William Blackwood and Sons, 1874, Vol. 2, p. 230.
18 Wolseley to Secretary of State for Colonies, 07/02/74, reproduced in Henry M. Stanley, *Coomassie and Magdala, The Story of Two British Campaigns in Africa*, Sampson Low, Marston, Low and Searle, 1874, pp. 235–7.
19 Otumfuo Nana Osei Agyeman Prempeh II, *History of Ashanti*, Sub-Saharan Publishers, 2024 (Ghanaian edition), p. 446.
20 Wolseley to King Kakari 04/02/74 in Ian Beckett (ed.), *Wolseley and Ashanti, The Asante War Journal and Correspondence of Major General Sir Garnet Wolseley 1873–74*, p. 388.
21 Robert Ferguson, 'A Stirlingshire Soldier's Account of the War', in *Stirling Observer* 04/04/1874.
22 George Little, 'Diary of the Ashantee War by an Eye Witness, from 1873–74', V&A Art Library, OCLC Number 1344340049.
23 George Little, 'Diary of the Ashantee War by an Eye Witness, from 1873–74', V&A Art Library, OCLC Number 1344340049.
24 Henry Brackenbury, *The Ashanti War of 1873–74*, p. 247.
25 National Archives, WO 147/3 Wolseley's journal, 05/02/74.
26 National Archives, WO 147/3 Wolseley's journal, 05/02/74.
27 Sir Garnet Wolseley, *The Story of A Soldier's Life*, p. 314
28 Wolseley to Louisa Wolseley 30/1/74 in Ian Beckett (ed.), *Wolseley and Ashanti, The Asante War Journal and Correspondence of Major General Sir Garnet Wolseley 1873–74*, p. 383.
29 Wolseley to Secretary of State for Colonies 07/02/74 reproduced in Henry M. Stanley, *Coomassie and Magdala, The Story of Two British Campaigns in Africa*, pp. 235–7.
30 Ian Beckett (ed.), *Wolseley and Ashanti, The Asante War Journal and Correspondence of Major General Sir Garnet Wolseley 1873–74*, p. 366.

31 Ian Beckett (ed.), *Wolseley and Ashanti, The Asante War Journal and Correspondence of Major General Sir Garnet Wolseley 1873–74*, p. 364.
32 National Archives, WO 147/3 Wolseley's journal, 05/02/74.
33 Wolseley to Secretary of State for Colonies 07/02/74 reproduced in Henry M. Stanley, *Coomassie and Magdala, The Story of Two British Campaigns in Africa*, pp. 235–7.
34 Henry Brackenbury, *The Ashanti War of 1873–74*, William Blackwood and Sons, p. 237.
35 Henry M. Stanley, *Coomassie and Magdala*, Sampson Low, Marston Low & Searle, 1874, pp. 236–7.
36 Henry M. Stanley, *Coomassie and Magdala*, p. 237.
37 Henry M. Stanley, *Coomassie and Magdala*, p. 237.
38 William Winwood Reade, *The Ashantee Campaign*, Smith, Elder & Co, London, 1874, p. 391.
39 William Winwood Reade, *The Ashantee Campaign*, p. 294.
40 Henry M. Stanley, *Coomassie and Magdala, The Story of Two British Campaigns in Africa*, p. 230.
41 William Toke Dooner, *Jottings En Route to Coomassie*, W. Mitchell, 1874, p. 60.
42 Henry M. Stanley, *Coomassie and Magdala, The Story of Two British Campaigns in Africa*, p. 231.
43 George Henty, *The March to Coomassie*, Tinsley Brothers, 1874, p. 409.
44 Frederick Boyle, *Through Fanteeland to Coomassie*, London, Chapman and Hall, 1874, pp. 342–3.
45 Henry M. Stanley, *Coomassie and Magdala, The Story of Two British Campaigns in Africa*, pp. 233–4.
46 William Winwood Reade, *The Ashantee Campaign*, p. 314.
47 Melton Prior, *Campaigns of A War Correspondent*, Edward Arnold, 1912, p. 25.
48 Patrick Watt, 'Ashantee Loot is Unique: British Military Culture and the Taking of Objects in the Third Anglo-Asante War, 1873–1874', *British Journal for Military History*, vol. 9, no. 3, 2023.
49 John Frederick Maurice, *The Ashantee War, A Popular Narrative*, Henry King, 1874, p. 302.
50 Jules Gros, *Voyages, aventures et captivité de J. Bonnat chez les Achantis*. Paris, Librairie Plon, 1884, pp. 241–2. My translation: Bonnat, 'Les bontés du roi pour moi et mes compagnons pendant notre captivité avaient éteint dans mon coeur toute rancune.'
51 Henry Brackenbury, *The Ashanti War of 1873–74*, William Blackwood and Sons, 1874, Vol. 2, pp. 240–3.
52 Otumfuo Nana Osei Agyeman Prempeh II, *History of Ashanti*. Sub-Saharan Publishers, 2024 (Ghanaian edition), p.446
53 Jules Gros, *Voyages, aventures et captivité de J. Bonnat chez les Achantis*. Paris, Librairie Plon, 1884, pp. 245–6. My translation. Bonnat, 'Pendant ce pillage organisé, rien ne m'aurait été plus facile que de remplir mes poches d'or et de riches curiosites d'art dont j'aurais pu disposer avantageusement plus tard ... Je ne voulus rien prendre et sortis les main vides. Ce pillage nocturne avait à mes yeux quelque chose de repoussant et de honteux; je ne voulus pas en être complice.'
54 Sir Garnet Wolseley, *The Story of A Soldier's Life*, p. 360.

55 Sir Garnet Wolseley, *The Story of A Soldier's Life*, p. 282.
56 National Archives, WO 33/26, 'Journal of the Engineer Operations on the Gold Coast during the recent Expedition'.
57 https://victoriacrosstrust.org/grave/mark-sever-bell/.
58 Frederick Boyle, *Through Fanteeland to Coomassie*, Chapman and Hall, 1874, p. 359.
59 National Archives, WO 33/26, 'Journal of the Engineer Operations on the Gold Coast during the recent Expedition'.
60 George Henty, *The March to Coomassie*, 1874, p. 413.
61 Wolseley to Secretary of State for Colonies 07/02/74 reproduced in Henry M. Stanley, *Coomassie and Magdala, The Story of Two British Campaigns in Africa*, pp. 235–7.
62 Wolseley to Louisa Wolseley 07/02/74 in Ian Beckett (ed.), *Wolseley and Ashanti, The Asante War Journal and Correspondence of Major General Sir Garnet Wolseley 1873–74*, p. 391.
63 Sir Garnet Wolseley, *The Story of A Soldier's Life*, p. 359.
64 George Little, 'Diary of the Ashantee War by an Eye Witness, from 1873–74', V&A Art Library, OCLC Number 1344340049.

7. 'Gold Is Always Pretty'

1   National Archives, WO 147/3 Wolseley's journal 06/02/74.
2   George Little, 'Diary of the Ashantee War by an Eye Witness, from 1873–74', V&A Art Library, OCLC Number 1344340049.
3   Stephen Manning, *Britain at War with the Asante Nation*, Pen and Sword, 2021, p. 104.
4   Alfred Burdon Ellis, *A History of the Gold Coast of West Africa*, Chapman and Hall, 1893, p. 349.
5   Joseph Hammond Thomas, *A Full and Authentic Diary of the Ashanti Expedition*, William Emblow at the 'Pembrokshire Advertiser', Pembroke 1875, diary entry 08/02/74.
6   George Little, 'Diary of the Ashantee War by an Eye Witness, from 1873–74', V&A Art Library, OCLC Number 1344340049.
7   Otumfuo Nana Osei Agyeman Prempeh II, *History of Ashanti*, Sub-Saharan Publishers, 2024 (Ghanaian edition), p. 447.
8   Ian Beckett (ed.), *Wolseley and Ashanti, The Asante War Journal and Correspondence of Major General Sir Garnet Wolseley 1873–74*, History Press for Army Records Society, pp. 370–371.
9   Ian Beckett (ed.), *Wolseley and Ashanti, The Asante War Journal and Correspondence of Major General Sir Garnet Wolseley 1873–74*, pp. 301–2.
10 Ian Beckett (ed.), *Wolseley and Ashanti, The Asante War Journal and Correspondence of Major General Sir Garnet Wolseley 1873–74*, pp. 369–70.
11 National Archives, WO 147/3 Wolseley's journal 09/02/74.
12 John Frederick Maurice, *The Ashantee War, A Popular Narrative*, Henry King, 1874, pp. 370–3.

13 Jules Gros, *Voyages, aventures et captivité de J. Bonnat chez les Achantis*. Paris, Librairie Plon, 1884, p. 247. Author's translation. 'lui serra le coeur'.
14 William Claridge, *A History of the Gold Coast and Ashanti*, John Murray, 1915, p. 152.
15 Otumfuo Nana Osei Agyeman Prempeh II, *History of Ashanti*, p. 447.
16 National Archives, WO 147/3 Wolseley's journal, 12/02/74 and 13/02/74.
17 Otumfuo Nana Osei Agyeman Prempeh II, *History of Ashanti*, p. 447.
18 'Treaty of Fommanah' in Ian Beckett (ed.), *Wolseley and Ashanti, The Asante War Journal and Correspondence of Major General Sir Garnet Wolseley 1873–74*, pp. 399–401.
19 Wolseley to Cambridge in Ian Beckett (ed.), *Wolseley and Ashanti, The Asante War Journal and Correspondence of Major General Sir Garnet Wolseley 1873–74*, p. 398, and National Archives, WO 32/7641, Camp Frommanah, Wolseley to Secretary of State for War, 13/02/74.
20 *The Times*, 05/02/1874.
21 John Vincent Camden (ed.), *A Selection from the Diaries of Edward Henry Stanley, 15th Earl of Derby, Between September 1869 and March 1878*, 5th Series, vol. 4, Royal Historical Society, London, 1994.
22 National Archives, WO 33/26.
23 George Little, 'Diary of the Ashantee War by an Eye Witness, from 1873–74', V&A Art Library, OCLC Number 1344340049, and National Archives, WO 33/26, Lieutenant Jekyll 29/06/74, and Ian Beckett (ed.), *Wolseley and Ashanti, The Asante War Journal and Correspondence of Major General Sir Garnet Wolseley 1873–74*, pp. 38–9.
24 *Illustrated London News*, 07/03/1874.
25 *Illustrated London News*, 14/03/1874.
26 National Archives, WO 106/6390. 'Précis of the Ashanti Expedition', Intelligence Dept, War Office, 13/04/1874.
27 Melton Prior, *Campaigns of A War Correspondent*, 1912, Edward Arnold, pp. 28–9.
28 Joseph Hammond Thomas, *A Full and Authentic Diary of the Ashanti Expedition*, William Emblow at the 'Pembrokshire Advertiser', Pembroke 1875, diary entries for Feb 9th and Feb 7th.
29 National Archives, WO 147/3 Wolseley's journal, 19/02/74.
30 George Little, 'Diary of the Ashantee War by an Eye Witness, from 1873–74', V&A Art Library, OCLC Number 1344340049.
Joseph Hammond Thomas, *A Full and Authentic Diary of the Ashanti Expedition*, William Emblow at the 'Pembrokshire Advertiser', Pembroke 1875, diary entries 21/02/74 and 23/02/74.
31 Alan Lloyd, *The Drums of Kumasi*, p. 182, and National Archives, WO 147/3 Wolseley's journal, 19/02/74.
32 Wolseley to Cambridge, 22/02/74, in Ian Beckett (ed.), *Wolseley and Ashanti, The Asante War Journal and Correspondence of Major General Sir Garnet Wolseley 1873–74*, p. 404.
33 National Archives, WO 147/3 Wolseley's journal, 22/02/74. Frederick Boyle, *Through Fanteeland to Coomassie*, Chapman and Hall, 1874, p. 379.
34 Frederick Boyle, *Through Fanteeland to Coomassie*, pp. 379–80.
35 John Frederick Maurice, *The Ashantee War, A Popular Narrative*, Henry King, 1874, p. 376.

36 Frederick Boyle, *Through Fanteeland to Coomassie*, Chapman and Hall, 1874, p. 379.
37 Other notable sales at the Cape Coast auction include the 'King's state dagger', more than 30 cm long and with a golden sheaf, also £114, and a blue velvet cap ornamented with golden figures of armed men and gold beads around a border of green silk, £26. Frederick Boyle, *Through Fanteeland to Coomassie*, p. 380, and *The Graphic*, 11/04/1874. Clutterbuck named in Patrick Watt, '"Ashantee Loot is Unique": British Military Culture and the Taking of Objects in the Third Anglo-Asante War, 1873–74', *British Journal for Military History*, vol. 9, no. 3, 2023.
38 Frederick Boyle, *Through Fanteeland to Coomassie*, p. 383.
39 *Daily Graphic*, 18/04/1874.
40 National Archives, WO 147/3 Wolseley's journal, 23/02/74 and 24/02/74.
41 Frederick Boyle, *Through Fanteeland to Coomassie*, p. 390.
42 Wolseley to Louisa Wolseley in Ian Beckett (ed.), *Wolseley and Ashanti, The Asante War Journal and Correspondence of Major General Sir Garnet Wolseley 1873–74*, p. 406.
43 National Army Museum warehouse, Stevenage, visited by author, 16/1/2025.
44 Wolseley to Louisa Wolseley in Ian Beckett (ed.), *Wolseley and Ashanti, The Asante War Journal and Correspondence of Major General Sir Garnet Wolseley 1873–74*, p. 406.
45 John Frederick Maurice, *The Ashantee War, A Popular Narrative*, p. 377.
46 Frederick Boyle, *Through Fanteeland to Coomassie*, p. 386.
47 Wolseley to Louisa Wolseley in Ian Beckett (ed.), *Wolseley and Ashanti, The Asante War Journal and Correspondence of Major General Sir Garnet Wolseley 1873–74*, p. 406.
48 John Frederick Maurice, *The Ashantee War, A Popular Narrative*, p. 378.
49 National Archives, WO 147/3 Wolseley's journal, 16/02/74.
50 Frederick Boyle, *Through Fanteeland to Coomassie*, p. 383.
51 National Archives, WO 147/3 Wolseley's journal, 25/02/74.
52 Orlando Figes, *A People's Tragedy, The Russian Revolution 1891–1924*, Jonathan Cape, 1996, pp. 462–3. Douglas Smith, *Former People, The Last Days of the Russian Aristocracy*, Macmillan, 2012, pp. 105–7. Albert Stopford, *The Russian Diary of an Englishman*, William Heinemann, 1919, pp. 207–8.

8. 'Worthy to Find A Resting Place in the British and South Kensington Museums'

1 http://www.queenvictoriasjournals.org/, 10/03/1874.
2 *Daily Telegraph*, 09/03/1874, and Patrick Watt, '"Ashantee Loot is Unique": British Military Culture and the Taking of Objects in the Third Anglo-Asante War, 1873–74', *British Journal for Military History*, vol. 9, no. 3, 2023.
3 *Illustrated London News*, 21/03/1874.
4 *Daily Telegraph*, 09/03/1874.
5 National Archives, WO 33/26, 11 March, Secretary of State for War to Wolseley.
6 National Archives, C/O 879/6 13/3/1874, Maxwell to Kimberley.
7 *Daily Telegraph*, 23/03/1874.
8 National Archives, WO 147/3 Wolseley's journal 04/03/74.
9 http://www.queenvictoriasjournals.org/, 22/03/1874.

10 *The Graphic*, 02/05/1874.
11 *The Graphic*, 02/05/1874, and Charlotte Gere and Judy Rudoe, *Jewellery in the Age of Queen Victoria*, British Museum, 2010, p. 191.
12 Ian Beckett (ed.), *Wolseley and Ashanti, The Asante War Journal and Correspondence of Major General Sir Garnet Wolseley 1873–74*, History Press for Army Records Society, pp. 375–6.
13 https://collection.nam.ac.uk/_1974-10-100-1.
14 Field-Marshal Viscount Wolseley, *The Story of A Soldier's Life*, Archibald Constable, 1903, p. 370.
15 Ian Bradley, *The Complete Annotated Gilbert & Sullivan*, Oxford University Press, 1996, p. 220.
16 National Archives, WO 106/6390. 'Précis of the Ashanti Expedition', Intelligence Dept, War Office, 13/04/1874.
17 Edward Spiers, Talk at National Army Museum, 27/04/2018, and Stephen Manning, *Britain at War with the Asante Nation*, Pen and Sword, 2021, p. 106.
18 George Little, 'Diary of the Ashantee War by an Eye Witness, from 1873–74', V&A Art Library, OCLC Number 1344340049, and Joseph Hammond Thomas, *A Full and Authentic Diary of the Ashanti Expedition*, William Emblow at the 'Pembrokshire Advertiser', Pembroke 1875, diary entries 17 March–2 April 1874.
19 Joseph Lehmann, *All Sir Garnet, A Life of Field-Marshal Lord Wolseley*, Jonathan Cape, 1964, p. 204.
20 *Daily Telegraph*, 23/04/1874, and *Lloyd's Weekly*, 12/04/1874.
21 *The Graphic*, 28/02/1874.
22 William Winwood Reade, *The Ashantee Campaign*, Smith, Elder & Co, 1874, p. 402.
23 'Death of Winwood Reade', *Daily Telegraph*, 27/04/1875.
24 Henry M. Stanley, *Through the Dark Continent*, Sampson, Low, Marston, Searle & Rivington, 1890, p. 1, and *Illustrated London News*, 25/04/1874.
25 For more on the Maqdala campaign, see Andrew Heavens, *The Prince and the Plunder*, History Press, 2023.
26 For examples of officers who served in both campaigns, see *The Times*, obituaries of Major General Sir Edward Woodgate, 26/03/1900, and Colonel Walter Wynter, 29/08/1924.
27 Henry M. Stanley, *Coomassie, The Story of the Campaign in Africa 1873–74*, 1896. Preface.
28 Henry M. Stanley, *Through the Dark Continent*, pp. 1–2.
29 Melton Prior, *Campaigns of A War Correspondent*, 1912, Edward Arnold, p. 286.
30 Jane Carruthers, *Melton Prior, War Artist in Southern Africa, 1895–1900*, Brenthurst Press, 1987, p. 28.
31 *Illustrated London News*, 5/11/1910, quoted in Jane Carruthers, *Melton Prior, War Artist in Southern Africa, 1895–1900*, Brenthurst Press, 1987, p. 39.
32 https://www.iwm.org.uk/memorials/item/memorial/11771.
33 *Illustrated London News*, archive in V&A Art Library.
34 *Illustrated London News*, 28/03/1874.
35 *Illustrated London News*, 23/05/1874.
36 *Garrard's 1721–1911*, Stanley Paul and Co., 1912, p. 117.

37. Ibid., p. 98.
38. Ibid., p. 104.
39. Ibid., p. 110.
40. Ibid., p. 118.
41. *The Times*, 18/04/1874.
42. John Vincent Camden (ed.), *A Selection from the Diaries of Edward Henry Stanley, 15th Earl of Derby, Between September 1869 and March 1878*. 5th Series, Vol. 4, Royal Historical Society London, 1994, p. 172.
43. https://www.rct.uk/collection/search#/6/collection/62823/state-sword-afena.
44. http://www.queenvictoriasjournals.org/, 02/04/1874.
45. Charlotte Gere and John Culme with William Summers, *Garrard the Crown Jewellers*, Quartet Books, 1993, pp. 36–7. On the trophy head, https://www.rct.uk/collection/ RCIN 62901, and *The Globe*, 30/04/1874.
46. *Northampton Mercury*, 02/05/1874. Also mentioned, without details, in *Morning Post*, 29/04/74.
47. Charlotte Gere and John Culme with William Summers, *Garrard the Crown Jewellers*, Quartet Books, 1993, pp. 36–7.
48. British Museum archive, AF 1874, 5–18. 1–14. Garrard and Co.
49. *Daily Telegraph*, 10/03/1874.
50. The *akrafokonmu* were also worn by royal servants, officials and negotiators (Malcolm McLeod, email to author, 19/5/25).
51. *The Times*, 18/04/1874.
52. *The Globe*, 30/04/1874.
53. Charlotte Gere and Judy Rudoe, *Jewellery in the Age of Queen Victoria*, British Museum, 2010, p. 512, fn 10.
54. *Nottinghamshire Guardian*, 24/04/1874.
55. *Northampton Mercury*, 02/05/1874.
56. https://www.britishmuseum.org/collection/object/E_Af1973-07-1-2. The second dish is referred to in *Catalogue of Old English Silver*, Christie Manson and Woods, 13 February 1957, Lot 128, Property of Mrs J. Dix, 'The back engraved with the Cecil Crest and monogram of Francis Horace Pierrepont Cecil, 2nd son of the 3rd Marquess of Exeter, died 1889' (see chapter 17).
57. Hew Locke, 'What Have We Here?', British Museum, 2024–2025.
58. https://www.britishmuseum.org/collection/object/E_Af1973-07-1-2.
59. *The Times*, 18/04/1874.
60. *Northampton Mercury*, 02/05/1874.
61. The V&A would subsequently acquire four more pieces of loot taken by Wolseley's expedition; a piece of sheet-gold ornament bought from a Lt Col John Vesey for £20 in December 1874, another badge bought for £10 in 1883 with no record of the seller, a gold ring donated by the artist Victor Ames in 1921 and a gold eagle donated by a Mr W. C. Smith in 1936. (V&A press release 25/1/2024 and further details on prices, Vesey, Ames, Smith at https://collections.vam.ac.uk/ and from captions in Manhyia Palace Museum, Kumasi.)
62. https://www.britishmuseum.org/collection/object/E_Af1951-35-1-a-b.

63 *The Times*, 23/06/1890 and https://collections.vam.ac.uk/item/O72980/robert-henry-soden-smith-ma-medallion-hope-pinker-henry/.
64 Robert Soden Smith, 'Notes on specimens of wrought gold, forming a portion of the Ashanti indemnity', V&A Art Library 913329592.
65 Robert Soden Smith, V&A Art Library 913329592.
66 Marjorie Caygill, 'Creating a Great Museum: Early Collectors and the British Museum' on Columbia University's Fathom Online learning site, https://web.archive.org/web/20110608160247/http://www.fathom.com/course/21701728/session3.html, and https://www.britishmuseum.org/collection.
67 British Museum AOA Archive, Collection File: Af 1874, 5-18. 1-14. Garrard and Co.
68 British Museum AOA Archive, Collection File: Af 1874, 5-18. 1-14. Garrard and Co. British Museum AOA Archive, Collection File: Af 1874, 5-18. 1-10. Garrard and Co.
69 British Museum AOA Archive, Collection File: Af 1874.0528.1-2 Pask, and https://www.britishmuseum.org/collection.
70 British Museum AOA Archive, Collection File: Af, Ash.1-89. Crown Agents for the Colonies.
71 National Museum of Scotland Accession Register, 1875-16.1-19.
72 Interview with author, 03/10/2024.
73 https://www.wallacecollection.org/. Wallace Collection, W112 and W113.
74 https://www.wallacecollection.org/. Wallace Collection, S50.
75 Suzanne Higgott, email to author, 08/02/2024.
76 This total calculated from a list Garrard sent to the Wallace Collection on 24/05/35, in Wallace files for Asante objects. Suzanne Higgott calculates that Wallace spent at least £1,341 on the Asante artefacts.
77 Suzanne Higgott, email to author, 08/02/2024.
78 Suzanne Higgott, email to author, 08/02/2024.
79 https://www.wallacecollection.org/. Wallace Collection, OA 1683, and William Fagg, 'Ashanti Gold', *The Connoisseur*, Jan 1974, Vol. 185, Number 743.
80 *The Times*, 18/04/1874.
81 *Illustrated London News*, 23/05/1874.
82 *The Globe*, 30/04/1874.
83 Robert Soden Smith, 'Notes on specimens of wrought gold, forming a portion of the Ashanti indemnity', V&A Art Library 913329592.
84 William Fagg, 'Ashanti Gold', *The Connoisseur*, Jan 1974, Vol. 185, Number 743.
85 William Fagg to Wallace, 27/03/63, in Wallace files on Asante objects.
86 Malcolm McLeod, conversation with author, 24/11/2022, and https://www.wallacecollection.org/. Wallace Collection, OA 1683.
87 Martha Ehrlich, *A Catalogue of Ashanti Art taken from Kumasi in the Anglo-Ashanti War of 1874*, 1981, PhD Thesis, Indiana University.
88 William Fagg, 'Ashanti Gold', *The Connoisseur*.
89 Suzanne Higgott, *The Most Fortunate Man of His Day, Sir Richard Wallace, Connoisseur, Collector & Philanthropist*, The Wallace Collection, 2018, p. 292.
90 *Daily Telegraph*, 23/03/1874.

91 The *Graphic*, 25/07/1874.
92 Moncure Conway, *Travels in South Kensington*, Trübner, 1882. p. 70.
93 Ibid., p. 71.
94 https://hansard.parliament.uk/Commons, 04/05/1874.
95 *The Times*, 23/12/1881; Suzanne Higgott, *The Most Fortunate Man of His Day, Sir Richard Wallace, Connoisseur, Collector & Philanthropist*, The Wallace Collection, 2018, 292; 'Ryde Art Treasures Exhibition 1881–1882', Arcade no. 2 series, Historic Ryde Society, Diana Wood, 2010.

9. 'Kumasi Was Falling Into A Ruinous State'

1 https://digital.nmla.metoffice.gov.uk/.
2 *Bury Free Press*, 02/07/1881; *Nottinghamshire Guardian*, 1/07/1881.
3 *The Times*, 27/06/1881.
4 Ivor Wilks, *Forests of Gold, Essays on the Akan and the Kingdom of Asante*, Ohio University Press, 1993, p. 194.
5 http://www.queenvictoriasjournals.org/, 30 June 1881. On Barrow being a large man, see photograph of him in Roslyn Walker, 'A Cast Gold Spider, Brandon Kirby, and Kwaku Dua II: A History', in Roslyn Walker (ed.), *The Power of Gold, Asante Royal Regalia from Ghana*, Dallas Museum of Art, 2018, p. 53.
6 *The Times*, 11/02/1881.
7 *The Times*, 08/02/1881.
8 *The Times*, 13/05/1881.
9 William Claridge, *A History of the Gold Coast and Ashanti*, John Murray, 1915, vol. 2. pp. 241–2.
10 *Bury Free Press*, 02/07/1881, *The Times*, 27/06/1881 and 28/06/1881. *The Times* says Barrow brought the entire 2,000 ounces of gold with him, but Hansard, 07/07/1881, says that he brought 1,200. Other newspapers (e.g. *Bury Free Press*) report, with more details, that he brought 1,400.
11 *The Times*, 27/06/1881.
12 William Claridge, *A History of the Gold Coast and Ashanti*, p. 225.
13 William Claridge, *A History of the Gold Coast and Ashanti*, p. 243.
14 *The African Times*, 1/02/1882 and 1/10/1885.
15 *The Times*, 23/12/1881 and http://www.queenvictoriasjournals.org/ 30/06/1881.
16 Otumfuo Nana Osei Agyeman Prempeh II, *History of Ashanti*, Sub-Saharan Publishers, 2024 (Ghanaian edition), p. 456.
17 Otumfuo Nana Osei Agyeman Prempeh II, *History of Ashanti*, p. 471.
18 Tom McCaskie in Otumfuo Nana Osei Agyeman Prempeh II, *History of Ashanti*. Introduction to chapter 13 pp. 451–2.
19 Ronald Robinson, John Gallagher with Alice Denny, *Africa and the Victorians*, Macmillan, 1965, p. 385.
20 Wolseley to Secretary of State for Colonies, 07/02/74, reproduced in Henry M. Stanley, *Coomassie and Magdala, The Story of Two British Campaigns in Africa*, Sampson Low, Marston, Low and Searle, 1874, pp. 235–7.

21 Stephen Manning, *Britain at War with the Asante Nation*, Pen and Sword, 2021, p. 107.
22 Otumfuo Nana Osei Agyeman Prempeh II, *History of Ashanti*, p. 450.
23 W. D. McIntyre, 'British Policy in West Africa: The Ashanti Expedition of 1873–4', *Historical Journal*, 5, 1 (1962), 19–46.
24 W. D. McIntyre, 'British Policy in West Africa: The Ashanti Expedition of 1873–4'.
25 Thomas Gale, 'The Struggle Against Disease in The Gold Coast: Early Attempts at Urban Sanitary Reform', *Transactions of the Historical Society of Ghana*, vol. 16, no. 2, 1995.
26 Otumfuo Nana Osei Agyeman Prempeh II, *History of Ashanti*, p. 453.
27 Emmanuel Akyeampong, Introduction to Albert Adu Boahen, *Yaa Asantewaa and the Asante-British War of 1900–1901*, Sub-Saharan Publishers and James Currey, 2003, p. 11.
28 Captain Brandon Kirby, 'A Journey into the Interior of Ashanti', *Proceedings of the Royal Geographical Society*, 1884, vol. 6, pp. 447–50, and Roslyn Walker, 'A Cast Gold Spider, Brandon Kirby, and Kwaku Dua II: A History' in Roslyn Walker (ed.), *The Power of Gold, Asante Royal Regalia from Ghana*, Dallas Museum of Art, 2018.
29 Quoted in Ivor Wilks, *Forests of Gold, Essays on the Akan and the Kingdom of Asante*, Ohio University Press, 1993, p. 130.
30 'Native of Accra' from Ghana National Archives, kindly shared with me by Lloyd de Beer.
31 These photos can be seen at National Archives CO 1069/31.
32 Michael Graham-Stewart and Francis McWhannell, *Broad Sunlight, Early West African Photography*, Michael Graham-Stewart, 2020, p. 76, and Christraud Geary, 'African Photographer Frederick Grant and Registering Copyright in 1884' in Roslyn Walker (ed.), *The Power of Gold, Asante Royal Regalia from Ghana*, Dallas Museum of Art, 2018. More on Frederick Grant, including the possibility he was not African, is in Francis McWhannell, 'Smaller Pictures: Reconstructing the Lives and Communities of West African Professional Photographers of the Nineteenth Century', MA Thesis, University of Auckland, 2020.
33 Biographical details on Brandon Kirby kindly supplied by Roslyn Walker, 29/09/2024, by email.
34 Roslyn Walker, 'A Cast Gold Spider, Brandon Kirby, and Kwaku Dua II: A History' in Roslyn Walker (ed.), *The Power of Gold, Asante Royal Regalia from Ghana*, Dallas Museum of Art, 2018. Spider and pendant in Dallas Art Museum. https://dma.org/art/collection/object/5339962; https://dma.org/art/collection/object/5339963; for Brandon Kirby 1898 Cape Town marriage https://www.1820settlers.com/genealogy/settlerbrowsemarrs.
35 Captain Brandon Kirby, 'A Journey into the Interior of Ashanti', *Proceedings of the Royal Geographical Society*, 1884, vol. 6, pp. 447–50.
36 Tom McCaskie in Otumfuo Nana Osei Agyeman Prempeh II, *History of Ashanti*. Introduction to chapter 14, p. 481, and Otumfuo Nana Osei Agyeman Prempeh II, *History of Ashanti*, p. 486, and Tom McCaskie in Nana Agyeman Prempeh I, *The History of Ashanti Kings and the Whole Country Itself*, Oxford University Press, 2003, p. 11.

37 Otumfuo Nana Osei Agyeman Prempeh II, *History of Ashanti*, p. 487.
38 *The Times*, 11/05/1886.
39 Programme quoted in Malcolm McLeod's RP Baffour Lecture at Kumasi's Kwame Nkrumah University of Science and Technology, November 2019, and Official Catalogue International Exhibition of Navigation, Travelling, Commerce and Manufacturing, Liverpool Printing and Stationery Company, 1886, pp. 123–4.
40 *The Times*, 17/07/1886. Five million people from: https://www5.open.ac.uk/research-projects/making-britain/content/colonial-and-indian-exhibition-1886.
41 Ronald Robinson, John Gallagher with Alice Denny, *Africa and the Victorians*, p. 2.
42 *The Times*, 17/07/1886.
43 Tom McCaskie in Nana Agyeman Prempeh I, *The History of Ashanti Kings and the Whole Country Itself*, p. 11.
44 Otumfuo Nana Osei Agyeman Prempeh II, *History of Ashanti*, p. 502.
45 Agnes Akosua Aidoo, 'The Asante Succession Crisis 1883–1888', *Transactions of the Historical Society of Ghana*, vol. 13, no. 2, 1972, pp. 163–80, and Richard Austin Freeman, *Travels and Life in Ashanti and Jaman*, Archibald Constable, 1898, p. 129.
46 Richard Austin Freeman, *Travels and Life in Ashanti and Jaman*, pp. 101–2.
47 Richard Austin Freeman, *Travels and Life in Ashanti and Jaman*, pp. 109–11.
48 'The Trail of Behemoth' in Richard Austin Freeman, *The Magic Casket*, Hodder & Stoughton, 1927.
49 Quoted by Emmanuel Akyeampong, Introduction to Albert Adu Boahen, *Yaa Asantewaa and the Asante-British War of 1900–1901*, p. 12.
50 Albert Adu Boahen, *African Perspectives on Colonialism*, Johns Hopkins University Press, 1989, p. 24.
51 Albert Adu Boahen, *African Perspectives on Colonialism*, p. 24.

10. 'Prepared to Sacrifice Myself to Save the Lives of My People'

1 Tom McCaskie in Otumfuo Nana Osei Agyeman Prempeh II, *History of Ashanti*, Sub-Saharan Publishers, 2024 (Ghanaian edition), pp. 697–8.
2 Tom McCaskie in Otumfuo Nana Osei Agyeman Prempeh II, *History of Ashanti*, Introduction to chapter 15, p. 497.
3 Jamie James, *The Glamour of Strangeness*, Farrar, Straus and Giroux, 2016, p. 71.
4 Larry Yarak, 'Kwase Boakye and Kwame Poku: Dutch-Educated Asante "Princes"', in Enid Schildkrout (ed.), *The Golden Stool: Studies of the Asante Center and Periphery*, American Museum of Natural History, 1987, and see Arthur Japin's 1997 novel, *The Two Hearts of Kwasi Boachi*, Vintage, 2001.
5 Ian Beckett (ed.), *Wolseley and Ashanti, The Asante War Journal and Correspondence of Major General Sir Garnet Wolseley 1873–74*, History Press for Army Records Society, p. 506.
6 Tom McCaskie in Otumfuo Nana Osei Agyeman Prempeh II, *History of Ashanti*. Introduction to chapter 15, p. 496.

7   Richard Austin Freeman, *Travels and Life in Ashanti and Jaman*, Archibald Constable, 1898, p. 369.
8   Government statement of 14/02/95 to the House of Commons, reported in *The Times*, 22/04/95, and https://hansard.parliament.uk/commons/1895-02-14/debates/.
9   *The Times*, 18/04/1895.
10 *The Times*, 21/11/1895.
11 Jonathan Harris, Solicitor to the Ashanti Embassy, letter in *The Times*, 03/10/1895.
12 *The Times*, 18/10/1895.
13 Ivor Wilks, *Forests of Gold, Essays on the Akan and the Kingdom of Asante*, Ohio University Press, 1993, p. 225.
14 Ronald Robinson, John Gallagher with Alice Denny, *Africa and the Victorians*, Macmillan, 1965, pp. 395 and 399.
15 Otumfuo Nana Osei Agyeman Prempeh II, *History of Ashanti*, p. 522.
16 Albert Adu Boahen, *African Perspectives on Colonialism*, Johns Hopkins University Press, 1987, p. 53, and Ivor Wilks, *Asante in the Nineteenth Century*, Cambridge University Press, 1975, pp. 301–5.
17 Otumfuo Nana Osei Agyeman Prempeh II, *History of Ashanti*, pp. 524–6.
18 Stephen Manning, *Britain at War with the Asante Nation*, Pen and Sword, 2021, p. 117.
19 *The Times*, 30/06/1902, Sir Francis Scott obituary, and Alan Lloyd, *The Drums of Kumasi*, Longman Green, 1964, p. 203.
20 *The Times*, 14/10/1895.
21 Lansdowne to Scott, 22/11/95, in NAM 1976-07-37, papers of Brigadier General Francis Kempster.
22 Otumfuo Nana Osei Agyeman Prempeh II, *History of Ashanti*, p. 523 (McCaskie fn citing N/A CO 96/262).
23 Colonel Hugh Sinclair, *Camp and Society*, Chapman and Hall, 1926, p. 203.
24 *The Times*, 18/11/1895 and 21/11/1895.
25 *The Times*, 13/11/1895.
26 Otumfuo Nana Osei Agyeman Prempeh II, *History of Ashanti*, p. 526.
27 Albert Adu Boahen 'Prempeh I in Exile', Paper read at National Cultural Centre, Kumasi, 1972.
28 Otumfuo Nana Osei Agyeman Prempeh II, *History of Ashanti*, p. 528.
29 Tom McCaskie in Nana Agyeman Prempeh I, *The History of Ashanti Kings and the Whole Country Itself*, Oxford University Press, 2003, p. 19.
30 Joseph Adjaye, *Diplomacy and Diplomats in 19th Century Asante*, Africa World Press, 1996 (originally University Press of America, 1884), p. 199.
31 *The Times*, 09/12/1895.
32 'Confidential Mobilization Committee' 9/11/95, and hand-written note to Colonel Francis Kempster, also 9/11/95, which says 'Viscount Wolseley has selected you' to be second-in-command of Asante expedition. Both documents in National Army Museum 1976-07-37, Papers of Brig Gen Francis Kempster.
33 *The Times*, 09/12/1895, and Stephen Manning, *Britain at War with the Asante Nation*, Pen and Sword, 2021, p. 120.

34 http://www.queenvictoriasjournals.org/ 17/11/95.
35 Alan Lloyd, *The Drums of Kumasi*, pp. 195–6.
36 Robert Baden-Powell, *The Downfall of Prempeh, A Diary of Life with the Native Levy in Ashanti, 1895–1896*, Methuen, 1898. Naval and Military Press Reprint, 2016, pp. 36–7.
37 Robert Edgerton, *The Fall of the Asante Empire, The Hundred-Year War for Africa's Gold Coast*, The Free Press, 1995, p. 177.
38 Stephen Manning, *Britain at War with the Asante Nation*, p. 118; Robert Edgerton, *The Fall of the Asante Empire, The Hundred-Year War for Africa's Gold Coast*, p. 177. Antonia Lovelace, 'War Booty: Changing Contexts, Changing Displays: Asante "Relics" From Kumasi, Acquired by the Prince Of Wales's Own Regiment of Yorkshire in 1896', *Journal of Museum Ethnography*, no. 12, (MEG Conference, 1999: Glimpses of Africa Museums, Scholarship and Popular Culture, The Horniman Museum, London (May 2000)), pp. 147–60.
39 Colonel Hugh Sinclair, *Camp and Society*, p. 209.
40 *The Times*, 02/1/1896, and Alan Lloyd, *The Drums of Kumasi*, p. 197, and Ian McInnes and Mark Fraser, *Ashanti 1895–96*, Picton, 1987, p. 56 and p. 95.
41 Robert Baden-Powell, *The Downfall of Prempeh, A Diary of Life with the Native Levy in Ashanti, 1895–1896*, p. 57.
42 Robert Baden-Powell, *The Downfall of Prempeh, A Diary of Life with the Native Levy in Ashanti, 1895–1896*, p. 58.
43 *The Times*, 08/1/1896.
44 Robert Baden-Powell, *The Downfall of Prempeh, A Diary of Life with the Native Levy in Ashanti, 1895–1896*, p. 67.
45 Diary of Lt Hood in Ian McInnes and Mark Fraser, *Ashanti 1895–96*, Picton, 1987, p. 58.
46 Alan Lloyd, *The Drums of Kumasi*, p. 199.
47 Robert Baden-Powell, *The Downfall of Prempeh, A Diary of Life with the Native Levy in Ashanti, 1895–1896*, p. 107.
48 Robert Baden-Powell, *The Downfall of Prempeh, A Diary of Life with the Native Levy in Ashanti, 1895–1896*, p. 110.
49 Robert Baden-Powell, *The Downfall of Prempeh, A Diary of Life with the Native Levy in Ashanti, 1895–1896*, p. 114
50 http://www.telegraph.co.uk/history/10132546/Bennet-Burleigh-the-wild-man-of-the-Victorian-press.html. *Daily Telegraph*, obituary, 18/06/1914 and *The Times*, obituary 18/06/1914.
51 Bennet Burleigh, *Two Campaigns, Madagascar and Ashantee*, Fisher Unwin, 1896, p. 502.
52 Bennet Burleigh, *Two Campaigns, Madagascar and Ashantee*, p. 506.
53 Bennet Burleigh, *Two Campaigns, Madagascar and Ashantee*, pp. 502–3.
54 Robert Baden-Powell, *The Downfall of Prempeh, A Diary of Life with the Native Levy in Ashanti, 1895–1896*, p. 115.
55 Lt Hood in Ian McInnes and Mark Fraser, *Ashanti 1895–96*, p. 51.
56 Otumfuo Nana Osei Agyeman Prempeh II, *History of Ashanti*, p. 529.

57 Robert Baden-Powell, *The Downfall of Prempeh, A Diary of Life with the Native Levy in Ashanti, 1895–1896*, p. 117.
58 National Archives, WO 32/7647, 'Report of Interview between Colonel Sir F C Scott and King Prempeh at Kumassi on 17th January'.
59 Robert Baden-Powell, *The Downfall of Prempeh, A Diary of Life with the Native Levy in Ashanti, 1895–1896*, p. 118.
60 NCO diary, West Yorkshire Regiment in Ian McInnes and Mark Fraser, *Ashanti 1895–96*, Picton, 1987, p. 93.

11. 'I Beg the Governor Not to Take My People and Myself Away'

1 Bennet Burleigh, *Two Campaigns, Madagascar and Ashantee*, Fisher Unwin, 1896, pp. 513–16. Robert Baden-Powell, *The Downfall of Prempeh, A Diary of Life with the Native Levy in Ashanti, 1895–1896*, Methuen, 1898, Naval and Military Press Reprint, 2016, pp. 123–5. Otumfuo Nana Osei Agyeman Prempeh II, *History of Ashanti*, Sub-Saharan Publishers, 2024 (Ghanaian edition), p. 531.
2 NCO Diary, West Yorkshire Regiment in Ian McInnes and Mark Fraser, *Ashanti 1895–96*, Picton, 1987, pp. 94–5.
3 National Archives, WO 32/7647, 'Report of Interview between Governor of Cape Coast Colony and King Prempeh at Kumassi on January 20th, 1896'. 'Slowly and painfully' from Otumfuo Nana Osei Agyeman Prempeh II, *History of Ashanti*, p. 533. Robert Baden-Powell, *The Downfall of Prempeh, A Diary of Life with the Native Levy in Ashanti, 1895–1896*, p. 125.
4 Otumfuo Nana Osei Agyeman Prempeh II, *History of Ashanti*, pp. 530–1.
5 George Musgrave, *To Kumassi with Scott*, Wightman, 1896, p. 178.
6 Tom McCaskie in Otumfuo Nana Osei Agyeman Prempeh II, *History of Ashanti*, p. 687.
7 Colonel Hugh Sinclair, *Camp and Society*, Chapman and Hall, 1926, p. 216.
8 Unattributed newspaper clipping in NAM 1976-07-37. Papers of Brigadier General Francis Kempster.
9 Robert Baden-Powell, *The Downfall of Prempeh, A Diary of Life with the Native Levy in Ashanti, 1895–1896*, p. 130.
10 William Claridge, *A History of the Gold Coast and Ashanti*, John Murray, 1915, vol. 2, p. 415.
11 Robert Baden-Powell, *The Downfall of Prempeh, A Diary of Life with the Native Levy in Ashanti, 1895–1896*, pp. 128–9.
12 Nana Agyeman Prempeh I, *The History of Ashanti Kings and the Whole Country Itself*, Oxford University Press, 2003, p. 158.
13 Bennet Burleigh, *Two Campaigns, Madagascar and Ashantee*, Fisher Unwin, 1896, p. 524.
14 George Musgrave, *To Kumassi with Scott*, pp. 182–3.
15 Colonel Hugh Sinclair, *Camp and Society*, Chapman and Hall, 1926, p. 217.
16 Otumfuo Nana Osei Agyeman Prempeh II, *History of Ashanti*, p. 534.
17 Lt Hood in Ian McInnes and Mark Fraser, *Ashanti 1895–96*, p. 52.
18 Captain Raymond Reade in Ian McInnes and Mark Fraser, *Ashanti 1895–96*, p. 14.

19 Robert Baden-Powell, *The Downfall of Prempeh, A Diary of Life with the Native Levy in Ashanti, 1895–1896*, p. 131.
20 Lieutenant Hood Diary in Ian McInnes and Mark Fraser, *Ashanti 1895–96*, p. 60.
21 Antonia Lovelace, 'War Booty: Changing Contexts, Changing Displays: Asante "Relics" From Kumasi, Acquired by the Prince Of Wales's Own Regiment of Yorkshire in 1896', *Journal of Museum Ethnography*, no. 12, (MEG Conference, 1999: Glimpses of Africa Museums, Scholarship and Popular Culture, The Horniman Museum, London (May 2000)), pp. 147–60.
22 N/A WO 32/7647 General Orders Ashanti Expeditionary Force, Kumassi 20 January 1896, and William Claridge, *A History of the Gold Coast and Ashanti*, p. 573.
23 N/A WO 32/7647 General Orders Ashanti Expeditionary Force, Kumassi 21 January 1896.
24 N/A WO 32/7647 'Inventory of Specie. Gold dust, ornaments etc taken from Palace of King Prempeh of Kumassi'.
25 N/A WO 32/7647 'Proceedings of a Board Assembled in the Headquarters Mess, Kumassi'.
26 Photograph from York Army Museum archives, kindly shared by Lloyd de Beer.
27 Antonia Lovelace, 'War Booty: Changing Contexts, Changing Displays: Asante "Relics" From Kumasi, Acquired by the Prince Of Wales's Own Regiment of Yorkshire in 1896', pp. 147–60.
28 Bennet Burleigh, *Two Campaigns, Madagascar and Ashantee*, p. 533.
29 N/A WO 32/7647 Governor's Orders, and *The Times*, 17/03/1896.
30 Bennet Burleigh, *Two Campaigns, Madagascar and Ashantee*, pp. 524 and 527.
31 Bennet Burleigh, *Two Campaigns, Madagascar and Ashantee*, p. 528.
32 Otumfuo Nana Osei Agyeman Prempeh II, *History of Ashanti*, p. 534.
33 Bennet Burleigh, *Two Campaigns, Madagascar and Ashantee*, p. 528 and N/A WO 32/7647 Governor's Orders.
34 Antonia Lovelace, 'War Booty: Changing Contexts, Changing Displays: Asante "Relics" From Kumasi, Acquired by the Prince Of Wales's Own Regiment of Yorkshire in 1896', pp. 147–60, and album of photos taken by Captain Phillips, shown to author, in private collection.
35 Captain Raymond Reade in Ian McInnes and Mark Fraser, *Ashanti 1895–96*, p. 15.
36 Ian McInnes and Mark Fraser, *Ashanti 1895–96*, p. 121.
37 Robert Baden-Powell, *The Downfall of Prempeh, A Diary of Life with the Native Levy in Ashanti, 1895–1896*, p. 138.
38 Bennet Burleigh, *Two Campaigns, Madagascar and Ashantee*, pp. 530–1.
39 http://www.queenvictoriasjournals.org/ 22/1/1896.
40 *Southern Echo*, 05/02/1896.
41 *The Times*, 27/1/1896 and William Tordoff, 'The Exile and Repatriation of Nana Prempeh I of Ashanti (1896–1924)', *Transactions of the Historical Society of Ghana*, vol. 4, no. 2, 1960, and Alan Lloyd, *The Drums of Kumasi*, 1965, p. 207.
42 William Tordoff, 'The Exile and Repatriation of Nana Prempeh I of Ashanti (1896–1924)', *Transactions of the Historical Society of Ghana*, vol. 4, no. 2, 1960, and George Musgrave, *To Kumassi with Scott*, p. 213.

43 George Musgrave, *To Kumassi with Scott*, p. 213.
44 *The Times*, 05/02/1896.
45 Robert Baden-Powell, *The Downfall of Prempeh, A Diary of Life with the Native Levy in Ashanti, 1895–1896*, 2016, p. 149.

12. 'Simply A Policy of Robbery'

1 Interview with author 04/10/2024.
2 https://www.britishmuseum.org/collection/object/H_1896-0727-1. The story of the Asante Ewer or Jug is well described by Martin Bailey in *Apollo Magazine*, December 1993, 'Two Kings, Their Armies and Some Jugs: The Ashanti Ewer' and in *The Art Newspaper*, November 2023, 'The Long and Curious Journey of the British Museum's Asante Ewer', and John Cherry and Neil Stratford, British Museum Occasional Paper 115, 'Westminster Kings and the Medieval Palace of Westminster', The British Museum, 1995.
3 Lloyd de Beer, Julie Hudson and Ivor Agyeman-Duah, *Object in Focus: The Asante Ewer*, British Museum Press, 2025 (page reference not available at time of publication).
4 *The Times*, 19/03/1929 for Read's wealth (£61, 459) left to widow, and for more on Read see Barnaby Phillips, *Loot, Britain and the Benin Bronzes*, Oneworld, 2021, p. 124.
5 British Museum AOA Archive, Collection File: Af1896, 0727.1.Barter.
6 Charles Read, *Proceedings of the Society of Antiquaries*, Second Series, Vol. XVII, 1898, pp. 82–7.
7 Antonia Lovelace, 'War Booty: Changing Contexts, Changing Displays: Asante "Relics" From Kumasi, Acquired by the Prince Of Wales's Own Regiment of Yorkshire in 1896', pp. 147–60. Note that the date on the plaque is slightly wrong, for Governor Maxwell only arrived in Kumasi on 18 January and handed out various objects on the 20th, after Prempeh's arrest.
8 National Archives, CO 1069/31.
9 Presentation by Lloyd de Beer of the British Museum to University of East Anglia's Centre for African Art and Archaeology, 30/4/2025, citing British Museum, AOA Archive, 'Collection of Capt. C.H. Armitage'. This document says the jug had been 'carried in the van of [the] Ashanti army when it attacked the fort on 28 April 1900 to ensure victory' only for it be 'captured by loyal Ashanti levies and presented to Capt. Armitage' (see events of Chapter 13).
10 https://www.britishmuseum.org/collection/object/E_Af1933-2, and John Cherry and Neil Stratford, British Museum Occasional Paper 115, 'Westminster Kings and the Medieval Palace of Westminster', The British Museum, 1995.
11 Malcolm McLeod, 'Richard II Part 3, At Kumase', in *Studies in Memory of Marion Johnson*, (eds.), David Henige and Tom McCaskie, University of Wisconsin, 1990.
12 Thomas Athol Joyce, *The British Museum Quarterly*, vol. 8, no. 1, 1933, p. 52.
13 Malcolm McLeod, 'A Note on an Asante Royal Chair of Iberian Origin' in Marion Johnson and Malcolm McLeod, *Akan-Asante Studies*, Occasional Paper No. 3, British Museum, 1979.

14. Diary of Thomas H. Berney, York Army Museum Archive, PD 00085, pp. 78–85, quoted by Lloyd de Beer, Julie Hudson and Ivor Agyeman-Duah in *Object in Focus: The Asante Ewer*, British Museum Press, 2025 (page reference not available at time of publication).
15. Diary of Captain Thomas H. Berney, York Army Museum Archive, PD 00085, pp. 71–2, quoted by Lloyd de Beer, Julie Hudson, Ivor Agyeman-Duah in *Object in Focus: The Asante Ewer*, British Museum Press, 2025 (page reference not available at time of publication).
16. https://www.bbc.co.uk/ahistoryoftheworld/objects/Q6VjNPE3Q-W4c-F752ZyJg.
17. See Chapter 7 and https://collection.nam.ac.uk/, 1963-10-300.
18. Ian McInnes and Mark Fraser, *Ashanti 1895–96*, Picton, 1987, p. 5.
19. *The Times*, 24/03/1931 Charles Barter obituary
20. *The Times*, 24/03/1931 Charles Barter obituary, and https://www.birmingham.ac.uk/research/centres-institutes/war-studies/lions-led-by-donkeys.
21. *Daily Telegraph*, 05/03/1896.
22. *The Times*, 05/03/1896.
23. Antonia Lovelace, 'War Booty: Changing Contexts, Changing Displays: Asante "Relics" From Kumasi, Acquired by the Prince Of Wales's Own Regiment of Yorkshire in 1896', pp. 147–60, and phone conversation with Caroline Pheby, York Army Museum, 07/10/2024.
24. Emmanuel Akyeampong, 'Christianity, Modernity and the Weight of Tradition in the Life of Asantehene Agyeman Prempeh I, c. 1888–1931', *Africa: Journal of the International African Institute*, 69, 1999, pp. 279–311, and Nana Agyeman Prempeh I, *The History of Ashanti Kings and the Whole Country Itself*, Oxford University Press, 2003, pp. 185–91.
25. Author's conversation with Lloyd de Beer, London 29/1/2025, and with Julie Hudson 16/6/2025. Julie says the lions and knobs on the rim of the bowl are of European origin and that the metal for the bowl was also probably imported from Europe.
26. Thomas Edward Bowdich, *Mission from Cape Coast Castle to Ashantee*, John Murray 1819, p. 279.
27. Robert Baden-Powell, *The Downfall of Prempeh, A Diary of Life with the Native Levy in Ashanti, 1895–1896*. Methuen, 1898. Naval and Military Press Reprint, 2016, p. 24.
28. *The Times*, 1/1/1914 and 04/12/1919.
29. Alastair Massie, 'Community Consultation and the shaping of the National Army Museum's Insight Gallery' in Henrietta Lidchi and Stuart Allen, *Dividing the Spoils, Perspectives on Military Collections and the British Empire*, Manchester University Press, 2022, pp. 246–7, fn 26, and https://collections.rusi.org/category/museum. In the National Army Museum, the brass bowl is NAM. 1963-10-182-1.
30. https://hansard.parliament.uk/Commons 12/03/96.
31. https://hansard.parliament.uk/Commons 12/03/96.
32. Photograph of the 1896 RUSI display kindly shared with the author by Lloyd de Beer; *London Evening Standard*, 02/04/1896.
33. Lloyd de Beer and Julie Hudson, 'The British Museum and the Fourth Anglo-Asante War, 1895–6' (forthcoming).

34 https://hansard.parliament.uk/Commons, 20/04/96.
35 https://hansard.parliament.uk/Commons, 28/1/97.
36 https://hansard.parliament.uk/Commons, 24/02/98, in which Davitt is quoting the *Lagos Weekly Record*.
37 War Office, *Manual of Military Law*, Her Majesty's Stationary Office, 1894, pp. 312–13.
38 Alexander Herman Art Newspaper, 'Law, Restitution and the Benin Bronzes', *The Art Newspaper*, 21/12/18, and Barnaby Phillips, *Loot, Britain and the Benin Bronzes*, Oneworld, 2021 pp. 102–4.
39 Kitchener cited by Edward Spiers, 'Spoils of War: Custom and Practice', in Henrietta Lidchi and Stuart Allen, *Dividing the Spoils, Perspectives on Military Collections and the British Empire*, Manchester University Press, 2022, p. 35.
40 https://hansard.parliament.uk/Commons, 28/1/97.
41 National Archives, CO 96/281 Gold Coast No. 21913. I'm indebted to Lloyd de Beer for kindly sharing this information with me.
42 I'm grateful to Justine Pick of Birmingham University for insights on Mary Endicott Chamberlain.
43 Charles Read, *Proceedings of the Society of Antiquaries*, Second Series, Vol XVII, 1898, pp. 82–7.
44 British Museum, AOA Archive, Collection File: Af1900, 0427.1–63 Gold Coast Government.
45 *Illustrated London News*, 14/03/1896 and https://www.britishmuseum.org/collection/object/E_Af1900-0427-7-a-b.
46 National Archives, CO 96/285, Gold Coast No.7309, p. 90, quoted by Lloyd de Beer and Julie Hudson in 'The British Museum and the Fourth Anglo-Asante War, 1895–96' (forthcoming).
47 https://www.britishmuseum.org/collection/object/E_Af1900-0427-1.
48 British Museum, AOA Archive, Collection File: Af1900, 0427.1-63 Gold Coast Government.
49 Lloyd de Beer and Julie Hudson in 'The British Museum and the Fourth Anglo-Asante War, 1895–96' (forthcoming).
50 British Museum, AOA Archive, Collection File: Af1901,01–17.1 Gold Coast Government, and https://www.britishmuseum.org/collection/object/E_Af1901-0117-1.
51 British Museum, AOA Archive, Collection File: Af1902, 11-15.1. Crown Agents for the Colonies. This gold vessel was also loaned back to the Manhyia Palace Museum in Kumasi in 2024.
52 William Fagg and Margaret Plass, *African Sculpture: An Anthology*, Studio Vista, 1964, p. 115.
53 https://www.britishmuseum.org/collection/object/E_Af1900-0427-44.
54 *The Queen*, 04/07/1896.
55 *Illustrated London News*, 14/03/1896.
56 Malcolm McLeod, 'A Note on an Asante Royal Chair of Iberian Origin' in Marion Johnson and Malcolm McLeod, *Akan-Asante Studies*, Occasional Paper No. 3, British Museum, 1979.

57 Emmanuel Akyeampong, 'Christianity, Modernity and the Weight of Tradition in the Life of Asantehene Agyeman Prempeh I, c. 1888–1931', *Africa: Journal of the International African Institute*, 69, 1999, pp. 279–311.

13. 'Why Am I Not Sitting on The Golden Stool?'

1 Major Frederick Myatt, *The Golden Stool, An Account of the Ashanti War of 1900*, William Kimber, 1966, p. 186.
2 Stephen Manning, *Britain At War with the Asante Nation*, Pen and Sword, 2021, p. 125.
3 Captain Cecil Armitage and Lt Col Arthur Montanaro, *The Ashanti Campaign of 1900*, Sands and Co., 1901. Appendix 2, p. 217.
4 Otumfuo Nana Osei Agyeman Prempeh II, *History of Ashanti*, Sub-Saharan Publishers, 2024 (Ghanaian edition), p. 535.
5 Adu Boahen, *Yaa Asantewaa and the Asante-British War of 1900–01*, Sub-Saharan Publishers and James Currey, 2003, pp. 31–3.
6 Otumfuo Nana Osei Agyeman Prempeh II, *History of Ashanti*, p. 536.
7 Henry M. Stanley, *Coomassie and Magdala*, Sampson Low, Marston Low & Searle, 1874, p. 18.
8 Henry Brackenbury, *Narrative of the Ashanti War*, William Blackwood and Sons, 1874, vol. 2, p. 351.
9 Wynyard Montagu Hall, *Great Drama of Kumasi*, Putnam, 1939, p. 3.
10 I am indebted to Ayowa Afrifa Taylor for her compelling 'An Economic History of the Ashanti Goldfields Corporation 1895–2004: Land, Labour, Capital and Enterprise', LSE Doctorate, 2006. This information is taken from p. 42. Physical description of Cade, p. 66.
11 Captain Cecil Armitage and Lt Col Arthur Montanaro, *The Ashanti Campaign of 1900*, Sands and Co., 1901, p. 239.
12 Ayowa Afrifa Taylor, 'An Economic History of the Ashanti Goldfields Corporation 1895–2004: Land, Labour, Capital and Enterprise', p. 68 on Asante mining skill and 1895 purchase.
13 Ayowa Afrifa Taylor, 'An Economic History of the Ashanti Goldfields Corporation 1895–2004: Land, Labour, Capital and Enterprise'; early growth of Ashanti Goldfields Corporation, pp. 72–6.
14 Wynyard Montagu Hall, *Great Drama of Kumasi*, p. 3.
15 Ayowa Afrifa Taylor, 'An Economic History of the Ashanti Goldfields Corporation 1895–2004: Land, Labour, Capital and Enterprise', p. 54.
16 Edwin Arthur Cade's letters are on this remarkable website: https://aprivatefamily.org/edwin-arthur-cade/edwin-arthur-cade/.
17 Ayowa Afrifa Taylor, 'An Economic History of the Ashanti Goldfields Corporation 1895–2004: Land, Labour, Capital and Enterprise', p. 79, https://aprivatefamily.org/edwin-arthur-cade/edwin-arthur-cade/ says he died of dengue fever.
18 Adu Boahen, *Yaa Asantewaa and the Asante-British War of 1900–01*, p. 33.
19 William Tordoff, 'The Exile and Repatriation of Nana Prempeh of Ashanti (1896–1924)', *Transactions of the Historical Society of Ghana*, vol. 4, no. 2 (1960).

20 William Tordoff, 'The Exile and Repatriation of Nana Prempeh of Ashanti (1896–1924)'.
21 Alan Lloyd, *The Drums of Kumasi*, Longmans, 1964, p. 14.
22 Alan Lloyd, *The Drums of Kumasi*, pp. 13–14.
23 Frederic Hodgson obituary, 07/08/1925, *The Times*.
24 Alan Lloyd, *The Drums of Kumasi*, p. 14.
25 Otumfuo Nana Osei Agyeman Prempeh II, *History of Ashanti*, p. 537.
26 Lady Hodgson, *The Siege of Kumassi*, Arthur Pearson, 1901, pp. 52–5.
27 Otumfuo Nana Osei Agyeman Prempeh II, *History of Ashanti*, pp. 537–8; Alan Lloyd, *The Drums of Kumasi*, p. 214.
28 Otumfuo Nana Osei Agyeman Prempeh II, *History of Ashanti*, p. 538.
29 Adu Boahen, *Yaa Asantewaa and the Asante-British War of 1900–01*, p. 35.
30 Henry R. Beddoes, *Report on the Military Operations in Ashanti 1900*, Waterlow, 1901, Hodgson to Chamberlain, 7/4/00 pp. 88–9.
31 Lady Hodgson, *The Siege of Kumassi*, p. 80.
32 Lady Hodgson, *The Siege of Kumassi*, p. 80.
33 https://hansard.parliament.uk/Commons, 17/05/00.
34 Adu Boahen, *Yaa Asantewaa and the Asante-British War of 1900–01*, p. 78.
35 Adu Boahen, *Yaa Asantewaa and the Asante-British War of 1900–01*, p. 39.
36 Adu Boahen, *Yaa Asantewaa and the Asante-British War of 1900–01*, p. 118.
37 Tom McCaskie, 'The Life and Afterlife of Yaa Asantewaa', *Africa: Journal of the International African Institute*, vol. 7, no. 2, 2007, pp. 151–79.
38 Tom McCaskie, 'The Life and Afterlife of Yaa Asantewaa', 151–79.
39 Captain Cecil Armitage and Lt Col Arthur Montanaro, *The Ashanti Campaign of 1900*, Sands and Co., 1901, pp. 7–9.
40 Otumfuo Nana Osei Agyeman Prempeh II, *History of Ashanti*, p. 539.
41 *The Times*, 05/04/1900.
42 Otumfuo Nana Osei Agyeman Prempeh II, *History of Ashanti*, p. 540.
43 Lady Hodgson, *The Siege of Kumassi*, p. 114.
44 Otumfuo Nana Osei Agyeman Prempeh II, *History of Ashanti*, p. 541.
45 Captain Cecil Armitage and Lt Col Arthur Montanaro, *The Ashanti Campaign of 1900*, Sands and Co., 1901, pp. 84–5.
46 Major Frederick Myatt, *The Golden Stool, An Account of the Ashanti War of 1900*, William Kimber, 1966, p. 79.
47 For more details of the three-month siege, read Lady Hodgson, *The Siege of Kumassi*, pp. 114–87, and Alan Lloyd, *The Drums of Kumasi*, pp. 224–5.
48 Lady Hodgson, *The Siege of Kumassi*, Arthur Pearson, 1901, p. 187
49 Captain Cecil Armitage and Lt Col Arthur Montanaro, *The Ashanti Campaign of 1900*, p. 114.
50 This extraordinary photograph is printed in: Captain Cecil Armitage and Lt Col Arthur Montanaro, *The Ashanti Campaign of 1900*, p. 133 as well as Paul Steiner, *Dark and Stormy Days at Kumassi 1900*, Partridge, 1901, p. 149 (with date of photo) and is also displayed in the Kumasi Fort museum.
51 Lady Hodgson, *The Siege of Kumassi*, p. 187.

14. 'Gold Was A Perfect Curse'

1. Lady Hodgson, *The Siege of Kumassi*, Arthur Pearson, 1901, p. 201.
2. Lady Hodgson, *The Siege of Kumassi*, p. 224.
3. Otumfuo Nana Osei Agyeman Prempeh II, *History of Ashanti*, Sub-Saharan Publishers, 2024 (Ghanaian edition), p. 542.
4. Major Frederick Myatt, *The Golden Stool, An Account of the Ashanti War of 1900*, William Kimber, 1966, p. 104.
5. Alan Lloyd, *The Drums of Kumasi*, Longmans, 1964, p. 234.
6. Robert Edgerton, *The Fall of the Asante Empire*, The Free Press, 1995, p. 204.
7. *The Times*, 24/07/1900.
8. Alan Lloyd, *The Drums of Kumasi*, p. 238.
9. Author's visits to Kumasi Fort, 20/11/2024 and 23/11/2024.
10. Lady Hodgson, *The Siege of Kumassi*, p. 195.
11. *The Times*, 24/07/1900.
12. Adu Boahen, *Yaa Asantewaa and the Asante-British War of 1900–01*, Sub-Saharan Publishers and James Currey, 2003, p. 96, quoting Willcocks to Chamberlain GNA Adm, 11/1/728.
13. Brigadier-General James Willcocks, *From Kabul to Kumassi, Twenty-Four Years of Soldiering and Sport*, John Murray, 1904, pp. 371–3.
14. Tom McCaskie in introduction to chapter 15 in Otumfuo Nana Osei Agyeman Prempeh II, *History of Ashanti*, p. 499.
15. Henry R. Beddoes, *Report on the Military Operations in Ashanti 1900*, Waterlow, 1901, p. 14.
16. Captain Cecil Armitage and Lt Col Arthur Montanaro, *The Ashanti Campaign of 1900*, Sands and Co., 1901, p. 182.
17. Henry R. Beddoes, *Report on the Military Operations in Ashanti 1900*, Willcocks to Chamberlain, p. 84.
18. Henry R. Beddoes, *Report on the Military Operations in Ashanti 1900*, Waterlow, 1901, Willcocks to Chamberlain, p. 85.
19. Asante recollections of Kwabena Kyere in Otumfuo Nana Osei Agyeman Prempeh II, *History of Ashanti*, Appendix, pp. 567–8.
20. Major Frederick Myatt, *The Golden Stool, An Account of the Ashanti War of 1900*, p. 171.
21. Harold J. C. Biss, *The Relief of Kumasi*, Methuen, 1901, pp. 310–11.
22. Asante recollections of Kwabena Kyere in Otumfuo Nana Osei Agyeman Prempeh II, *History of Ashanti*, Appendix, p. 569.
23. Samuel Hingley's letter to *The Times*, 16/02/1935.
24. Samuel Hingley's BBC radio talk of 02/11/1937 is quoted in the preface of Wynyard Montagu Hall, *Great Drama of Kumasi*, Putnam, 1939.
25. Brigadier-General James Willcocks, *From Kabul to Kumassi, Twenty-Four Years of Soldiering and Sport*, p. 425, and Wynyard Montagu Hall, *Great Drama of Kumasi*, Putnam, 1939, p. 350.

26 *The Times*, 16/03/1901, and Wynyard Montagu Hall, *Great Drama of Kumasi*, p. 350.
27 Wynyard Montagu Hall, *Great Drama of Kumasi*, p. 350.
28 https://hansard.parliament.uk/Commons/, 03/08/00 and 13/12/00.
29 https://hansard.parliament.uk/Commons/, 19/03/01.
30 *The Times*, 08/02/1901.
31 Brigadier-General James Willcocks, *From Kabul to Kumassi, Twenty-Four Years of Soldiering and Sport*, p. 425.
32 Henry R. Beddoes, *Report on the Military Operations in Ashanti 1900*, p. 33, p. 45, pp. 47–9.
33 James Willcocks, *The London Gazette*, 4 December 1900; Major Frederick Myatt, *The Golden Stool, An Account of the Ashanti War of 1900*, p. 99; David Killingray, 'The Mutiny of the West African Regiment in The Gold Coast 1901', *International Journal of African Historical Studies*, 16, 3, 1983.
34 Wynyard Montagu Hall, *Great Drama of Kumasi*, p. 349.
35 Arthur Tremearne, *The Tailed Head-Hunters of Nigeria*, Seeley, Service and Co., 1912, p. 218.
36 Wynyard Montagu Hall, *Great Drama of Kumasi*, p. 349.
37 *The Times*, 21/04/1901.
38 Many details of the mutiny taken from David Killingray, 'The Mutiny of the West African Regiment in The Gold Coast 1901'.
39 *Army and Navy Gazette*, 14/7/1906.
40 *The Times*, 14/05/1901.

15. 'Consider How Wretched I Am'

1 Author's interview with Molly Prempeh, 04/05/24, Kumasi, and Sharon Meriton-Jean and Sharon Uranie, Seychelles News Agency, 'Back To Her Roots', 17/02/2015.
2 Prempeh's ignorance of war from Nana Agyeman Prempeh I, *The History of Ashanti Kings and the Whole Country Itself*, Oxford University Press, 2003, p. 165.
3 William Tordoff, 'The Exile and Repatriation of Nana Prempeh of Ashanti (1896–1924)', *Transactions of the Historical Society of Ghana*, vol. 4, no. 2, 1960.
4 Albert Adu Boahen, 'Prempeh in Exile', Kumasi National Festival of Arts 1972.
5 Albert Adu Boahen, 'A Nation in Exile: The Asante on the Seychelles Islands, 1900–24' in Enid Schildkrout assisted by Carol Gelber, *The Golden Stool: Studies of the Asante Center and Periphery*, American Museum of Natural History, 1987.
6 John Bradley, *The History of Seychelles*, Clarion Press, 1940, p. 305.
7 William Tordoff, 'The Exile and Repatriation of Nana Prempeh of Ashanti (1896–1924)'.
8 William Tordoff, 'The Exile and Repatriation of Nana Prempeh of Ashanti (1896–1924)'.
9 John Bradley, *The History of Seychelles*, p. 305.
10 William Tordoff, 'The Exile and Repatriation of Nana Prempeh of Ashanti (1896–1924)'.

11. Albert Adu Boahen, 'A Nation in Exile: The Asante on the Seychelles Islands, 1900–24'.
12. *The Times*, 3/4/1923 & 11/5/1923.
13. Albert Adu Boahen in Nana Agyeman Prempeh I, *The History of Ashanti Kings and the Whole Country Itself*, Oxford University Press, 2003, p. 28.
14. Albert Adu Boahen, 'A Nation in Exile: The Asante on the Seychelles Islands, 1900–24'.
15. I. R. Stone, 'The Education of Ashanti Children During the Exile in Seychelles', *Transactions of the Historical Society of Ghana*, vol. 14, no. 1, 1973.
16. There is an excellent analysis of Prempeh's motivations in Emmanuel Akyeampong, 'Christianity, Modernity and the Weight of Tradition in the Life of "Asantehene" Agyeman Prempeh I, c. 1888–1931', *Africa: Journal of the International African Institute*, vol. 69, no. 2, 1999, pp. 279–311.
17. Nana Agyeman Prempeh I, *The History of Ashanti Kings and the Whole Country Itself*.
18. Ivor Wilks in Nana Agyeman Prempeh I, *The History of Ashanti Kings and the Whole Country Itself*, pp. 57–83, on the history of the text itself.
19. Albert Adu Boahen, 'A Nation in Exile: The Asante on the Seychelles Islands, 1900–24'.
20. Emmanuel Akyeampong, 'Christianity, Modernity and the Weight of Tradition in the Life of "Asantehene" Agyeman Prempeh I, c. 1888–1931'.
21. Albert Adu Boahen, 'Prempeh in Exile', Kumasi National Festival of Arts, 1972.
22. William Tordoff, 'The Exile and Repatriation of Nana Prempeh of Ashanti (1896–1924)'.
23. William Tordoff, 'The Exile and Repatriation of Nana Prempeh of Ashanti (1896–1924)'.
24. Nana Agyeman Prempeh I, *The History of Ashanti Kings and the Whole Country Itself*, pp. 148–50.
25. Sir Francis Fuller, *A Vanished Dynasty, Ashanti*, John Murray, 1921, p. 214.
26. Wynyard Montagu Hall, *Great Drama of Kumasi*, Putnam, 1939, p. 350.
27. Sir Francis Fuller, *A Vanished Dynasty, Ashanti*, p. 225 and p. 227.
28. Tom McCaskie, 'Cultural Encounters: Britain and Africa' in Andrew Porter (ed.), *The Oxford History of the British Empire, Vol. III The Nineteenth Century*, Oxford University Press, 1999, p. 680.
29. Sir Francis Fuller, *A Vanished Dynasty, Ashanti*, dedication at start of book, v.
30. Sir Francis Fuller, *A Vanished Dynasty, Ashanti*, p. 219.
31. Otumfuo Nana Osei Agyeman Prempeh II, *History of Ashanti*, Sub-Saharan Publishers, 2024 (Ghanaian edition), p. 549.
32. Sir Francis Fuller, *A Vanished Dynasty, Ashanti*, p. 229.
33. William Tordoff, 'The Exile and Repatriation of Nana Prempeh of Ashanti (1896–1924)'.
34. Nana Agyeman Prempeh I, *The History of Ashanti Kings and the Whole Country Itself*, p. 24.
35. Emmanuel Akyeampong, 'Christianity, Modernity and the Weight of Tradition in the Life of "Asantehene" Agyeman Prempeh I, c. 1888–1931'.
36. Emmanuel Akyeampong, 'Christianity, Modernity and the Weight of Tradition in the Life of "Asantehene" Agyeman Prempeh I, c. 1888–1931', and Tom McCaskie in Nana Agyeman Prempeh I, *The History of Ashanti Kings and the Whole Country Itself*, p. 8 and p. 14 on the importance of Prempeh's mother.

37 Otumfuo Nana Osei Agyeman Prempeh II, *History of Ashanti*, p. 552.
38 Letter printed Manhyia Palace Museum, Albert Adu Boahen, 1972.
39 Otumfuo Nana Osei Agyeman Prempeh II, *History of Ashanti*, p. 554.
40 Otumfuo Nana Osei Agyeman Prempeh II, *History of Ashanti*, p. 555.
41 William Tordoff, 'The Exile and Repatriation of Nana Prempeh of Ashanti (1896–1924)'.
42 Wynyard Montagu Hall, *Great Drama of Kumasi*, p. 361.
43 Hansard, 14/02/24.
44 Ivor Agyeman-Duah, *The Return of a King To Seychelles*, documentary film on Osei Tutu II's visit to Seychelles, 2015, and John Bradley, *The History of Seychelles*, pp. 300–18, for a useful summary of political prisoners on the Seychelles.
45 William Tordoff, 'The Exile and Repatriation of Nana Prempeh of Ashanti (1896–1924)'.
46 *The Times*, 14/04/1924.
47 Malcolm McLeod's RP Baffour Lecture at Kumasi's Kwame Nkrumah University of Science and Technology, November 2019.
48 *London Daily Chronicle*, 29/5/1924.
49 Emmanuel Akyeampong, 'Christianity, Modernity and the Weight of Tradition in the Life of "Asantehene" Agyeman Prempeh I, c. 1888–1931'.
50 William Tordoff, 'The Exile and Repatriation of Nana Prempeh of Ashanti (1896–1924)'.
51 Emmanuel Akyeampong, 'Christianity, Modernity and the Weight of Tradition in the Life of "Asantehene" Agyeman Prempeh I, c. 1888–1931'.
52 Elspeth Huxley, *Four Guineas*, 1954, p. 141.
53 Tom McCaskie, 'The Life and Afterlife of Yaa Asantewaa', *Africa: Journal of the International African Institute*, vol. 7, no. 2, 2007, pp. 151–79, and Otumfuo Nana Osei Agyeman Prempeh II, *History of Ashanti*, p. 560 (McCaskie says two boxes of bones, while Prempeh II says four).
54 Wynyard Montagu Hall, *Great Drama of Kumasi*, pp. 361–2.
55 Emmanuel Akyeampong, 'Christianity, Modernity and the Weight of Tradition in the Life of "Asantehene" Agyeman Prempeh I, c. 1888–1931', and Emmanuel Akyeampong in Nana Agyeman Prempeh I, *The History of Ashanti Kings and the Whole Country Itself*, p. 55.
56 *The Times*, 23/02/1935.

16. 'Return All Stolen Property to the People of Ashanti!'

1 British Museum, Corporate Archive, Board of Trustees' Minutes, vol. 3, 1971–74, pp. 1634–5 (BM/1/1/G/2/4/1/3), 06/04/74.
2 *The Times*, obituary 16/07/1895
3 *The Times*, obituary 30/07/1925; First Peer to Die in An Automobile Accident from: https://americanaristocracy.com/people/herbert-francis-eaton.
4 Author's conversation with Christie's source, 11/1/2023.
5 https://www.britishmuseum.org/collection/object/E_Af1973-07-1-2. Mrs J.

Coram-Wright described here as Lord Cheylesmore's step-daughter, but in BM Trustees Minutes of 16/09/72, she is referred to as his step-granddaughter, which seems more realistic.

6. British Museum, Corporate Archive, Board of Trustees' Minutes, vol. 3, 1971–74, p. 1391 (BM/1/1/G/2/4/1/3), 24/02/73.
7. National Archives, FCO 65/1335 FCO to BHC, Accra, 08/02/73.
8. National Archives, FCO 65/1335, FCO to British Museum, 09/02/73.
9. Asantehene Opoku Ware II to BHC, 02/1/74, and Kumasi Traditional Council Petition of 05/11/73, documents shared with author.
10. *Palaver*, 7–13/11/1973.
11. National Archives, FCO, 65/1504 9/9/74 BHC Accra to FCO and FCO 13/1189 briefing on Opoku Ware biography.
12. National Archives, FCO, 65/1335, BHC to FCO, 07/11/73 and FCO 65/1503 BHC to FCO 26/1/74.
13. Major-General H. T. Alexander, *African Tightrope*, Pall Mall, 1965, pp. 94 and 149.
14. *The Times*, 18/4/2000.
15. Susan Williams, *White Malice*, Hurst, 2021, p. 443.
16. *Daily Graphic*, 20/11/1961.
17. *Daily Graphic*, 14/11/1961.
18. *Ashanti Pioneer*, 15/11/1961.
19. *Daily Telegraph*, 15/11/1961.
20. *The Times*, 15/11/1961.
21. Royal Collection, https://www.rct.uk/collection/92604/stool.
22. *Ashanti Pioneer*, 22/11/1961 and *Daily Telegraph*, 14/11/1961.
23. National Archives, DO 195/60.
24. Author's email correspondence with Sarah Davis of the Royal Collection, 03/12/2024, 06/12/2024 and 22/1/2025.
25. Author's email correspondence with Sarah Davis of the Royal Collection, 03/12/2024, 06/12/2024 and 22/01/2025.
26. A.A.Y Kyerematen, guide to Ghana National Cultural Centre, Kumasi 1970, and *The Times*, 20/11/1961 and *Daily Express*, 21/11/1961.
27. Photo shared with the author by Sarah Davis, 16/12/2024, and listed in Royal Collection as Walery: 164 Regent St, London. Saloon, Marlborough House. [Marlborough House, c.1890s. Volume A], 1890 to 1899.
28. National Archives, FCO 65/1503 FCO to BHC, Accra 03/04/74.
29. National Archives, FCO 65/1503, FCO to BHC, Accra, 03/04/74.
30. National Archives, FCO 65/1504, FCO to BHC, Accra, 03/05/74.
31. National Archives, FCO 65/1503, BHC Accra to FCO 07/02/74.
32. National Archives, FCO 65/1503, Asantehene's address of 04/02/74.
33. National Archives, FCO 65/1503, BHC Accra to FCO 08/02/74.
34. National Archives, FCO 65/1503, BHC Accra to FCO 03/05/74.
35. National Archives, FCO 65/1503, Internal comms 13/05/74.
36. National Archives, FCO 65/1504, BHC Accra to FCO 29/05/74.
37. National Archives, FCO 65/1504, BHC Accra to FCO 23/08/74.

38   https://hansard.parliament.uk/Lords, 10 December 1974.
39   John Pope-Hennessy, *Learning to Look*, Heinemann, 1991, p. 202.
40   Basil Davidson, 'Hidden Treasure', *West Africa Magazine*, 02/02/63.
41   John Pope-Hennessy, *Learning to Look*, p. 217.
42   British Museum, Corporate Archive, Board of Trustees' Minutes, Vol. 3, 1971–1974, p. 1443, no. 21 (BM/1/1/G/2/4/1/3). (12/05/73) on the need for Fagg to retire.
43   John Pope-Hennessy, *Learning to Look*, p. 217.
44   Author's interview, near Jedburgh, 24/11/2022.
45   Stephen Manning, *Britain at War with the Asante Nation, 1823–1900*, Pen and Sword, 2021, pp. 44–6.
46   Author's interview, near Jedburgh, 24/11/2022.
47   Bénédicte Savoy, *Africa's Struggle for Its Art*, Princeton University Press, 2022, p. 3.
48   Bénédicte Savoy, *Africa's Struggle for Its Art*, p. 139.
49   Bénédicte Savoy, *Africa's Struggle for Its Art*, p. 140.
50   British Museum, Corporate Archive, Board of Trustees' Minutes, vol. 3, 1971–74, no. 28, pp. 1, 692–3 (BM/1/1/G/2/4/1/3), 20/07/74.
51   British Museum, Corporate Archive, Board of Trustees' Minutes, vol. 3, 1971–74, pp. 1708–9 (BM/1/1/g/2/4/1/3), 14/09/74.
52   National Archives, FCO 65/1503, 'Centenary of the Sagrenti War – The Call for the Return of the Asante Regalia', University Press, Kumasi.
53   National Archives, FCO 65/1504 FCO to BHC Accra, 14/10/74, and British Museum, Corporate Archive, Board of Trustees' Minutes, vol. 3, 1971–74, no. 2, pp. 1, 714–5 (BM/1/1/G/2/4/1/3), 26/10/74.
54   British Museum, Corporate Archive, Board of Trustees' Minutes, vol. 3, 1971–74, pp. 1708–9 (BM/1/1/G/2/4/1/3), 14/09/74.
55   Basil Davidson, 'Hidden Treasure' in *West Africa Magazine*, 02/02/63.
56   Letters from John Russell of the *Sunday Times* to Wallace 8/1/1957, and John Ingamells to Winfried Lierenfield, 28/12/1979, refer to the objects not being on display. Both in Wallace files on Asante objects; Martha Ehrlich, *A Catalogue of Ashanti Art taken from Kumasi in the Anglo-Ashanti War of 1874*, 1981, PhD Thesis, Indiana University.
57   Wallace curator to British Museum, email, in Wallace files on Asante objects.
58   Email from Alexander Collins at the Wallace, 15/04/2024.
59   Author's interview, near Jedburgh, 24/11/2022.
60   British Museum, Corporate Archive, Board of Trustees' Minutes, vol. 3, 1971–74, pp. 1708–9 (BM/1/1/G/2/4/1/3), 14/09/74.
61   British Museum, Corporate Archive, Board of Trustees' Minutes, vol. 3, 1971–74, no. 28, pp. 1, 692–3 (BM/1/1/G/2/4/1/3), 20/07/74.
62   Letter to McLeod from Manhyia Kumasi Traditional Council, 16/05/75, and British Museum, Corporate Archive, Board of Trustees' Minutes, vol. 4, 1976–77, no. 23, pp. 2, 150–1 (BM/1/1/G/2/4/1/4), 24/07/76.
63   British Museum, Corporate Archive, Board of Trustees' Minutes, vol. 4, 1976–77, no. 24, pp. 2, 168–9 (BM/1/1/G/2/4/1/4), 25/09/76.
64   British Museum, Corporate Archive, Board of Trustees' Minutes, vol. 4, 1976–77, no. 24, pp. 2, 168–9 (BM/1/1/G/2/4/1/4, 25/09/76.

65 JPH to Professor Laurence Gower, 05/10/1976.
66 British Museum, Corporate Archive, Board of Trustees' Minutes, vol. 4, 1976–77, no. 24, pp. 2, 168–9 (BM/1/1/G/2/4/1/4), 25/09/76.
67 British Museum, Corporate Archive, Board of Trustees' Minutes, vol. 4, 1976–77, no. 27, pp. 2, 197–8 (BM/1/1/G/2/4/1/4), 30/10/76, and McLeod to Asantehene, 08/11/1976.
68 British Museum, Corporate Archive, Board of Trustees' Minutes, vol. 4, 1976–77, no. 27, pp. 2, 197–8 (BM/1/1/G/2/4/1/4), 30/10/76.
69 Author's interview, British Museum, 03/07/2024.
70 Malcolm McLeod, email to author, 10/06/2024.
71 National Archives, FCO 13/1189.
72 'Whose Art Is It Anyway?' *Chronicle*, BBC 2, 27.5.81, Editor, Andrew Pace, Producer, Ben Shephard.
73 National Archives, FCO 13/1189 and *The Times*, 16/03/1981.
74 'Whose Art Is It Anyway?' *Chronicle*, BBC 2, 27.5.81, Editor, Andrew Pace, Producer, Ben Shephard.
75 National Archives, FCO 65/2555, Paul Channon, Minister for Arts to Asantehene, 07/09/81.
76 Author's interview, London, 1/02/2024.
77 *New York Times*, 15/10/1984.
78 *New York Times*, 15/10/1984.
79 Author's interview, London, 1/02/2024.

17. 'The Most Marvellous Experience of Our Lives'

1 Martha Judith Ehrlich, *A Catalogue of Ashanti Art taken from Kumasi in the Anglo-Ashanti War of 1874*, PhD Thesis, Indiana University, 1981, p. vii.
2 Martha Judith Ehrlich, *A Catalogue of Ashanti Art taken from Kumasi in the Anglo-Ashanti War of 1874*.
3 V&A archives, Garrard's Gentlemen's Ledger, AAD/1995/7/47, January 1869–January 1883.
4 *The Times*, 30/04/1946.
5 Martha Judith Ehrlich, *A Catalogue of Ashanti Art taken from Kumasi in the Anglo-Ashanti War of 1874*, Appendix II, p. 463.
6 Martha Judith Ehrlich, *A Catalogue of Ashanti Art taken from Kumasi in the Anglo-Ashanti War of 1874*, Appendix I, p. 447.
7 Christie, Manson and Woods, Catalogue of Old English Silver, 13/02/57, Lot 128. For more on Ernest Ohly, and his father William, see Barnaby Phillips, *Loot, Britain and the Benin Bronzes*, Oneworld, 2021, chapter 13.
8 Christie, Manson and Woods, Catalogue of Old English Silver, 13/02/57, Lot 129, 'a circular silver-gilt sideboard-dish, made for the above gold badge ... 24in. diam'.
9 It was owned by John J. Klejman, Jay C. Leff and Alan Brandt, who sold it to Lance Entwistle.

10   Author's conversation with Lance Entwistle, 09/04/2024.
11   https://dapper.fr/.
12   Author's conversation with Lance Entwistle, 09/04/2024.
13   *The Times*, 07/11/1961, and *Country Life*, 18/01/1962, and *Ashanti Pioneer*, 'Ashanti and Benin Arts Auctioned', 22/11/1961, and Lady Coryndon obituary, *The Times*, 22/03/1961.
14   *The Times*, 20/10/1965.
15   *The Times*, 07/11/1967.
16   The sales catalogue is still online at https://www.christies.com/en/auction/art-africain-oceanien-et-precolombien-18652/, and the Asante objects are Lot 271.
17   *The Globe*, 30/04/1874.
18   *Illustrated London News*, 23/5/1874.
19   They are given a higher estimated value in the paper catalogue than the online catalogue, which values them at 30–40,000 euros. Perhaps the online catalogue was amended after subsequent events, to minimise the embarrassment. Christie's had sold this same hat and slippers in 1980, 'Tribal Art, Ashanti Gold and Goldweights', 18/3/80, in London, when it advertised them as 'The Property of a Gentleman', and they were bought by a Belgian collector, Nellie Van Den Abbeele, for £12,000. In 2003, Van Den Abbeele's collection was being sold off, and so Christie's had a second chance to auction them.
20   Author's conversation with informed source, 11/01/2023. Christie's was not entirely successful at suppressing the news; *Le Parisien*, 10/12/2003, published a brief report, saying that Christie's had reported the theft of rare gold and leopard-skin objects of 'an indigenous people of Ghana', worth 50,000 euros.
21   Author's conversation with former Christie's employee, 22/02/2023.
22   Email from French police, 23/09/2024.
23   Email from Lydia Poitevin, Communications Director, Christie's Paris, 31/01/2025.
24   https://www.christies.com/en/calendarParis, 6 December 2005, lots 155–157, and *The Times*, 07/02/1950.
25   https://www.sothebys.com/en/auctions/ecatalogue/2006/african-oceanic-and-pre-columbian-art-n08246/lot.274.html, and William Fagg, *The Epstein Collection of Primitive and Exotic Sculpture*, The Arts Council of Great Britain, 1960.
26   Personal correspondence with Christie's contact, 17/10/2024.
27   British Museum, AOA Archive, Collection File: Af1891, 11-14, 1-2. Phillips Brothers, and https://www.britishmuseum.org/collection/object/, Af1891-0114-1.
28   University of Cambridge, Museum of Archaeology and of Ethnology Thirty-Fourth Annual Report of the Antiquarian Committee to the Senate with List of Accessions for the years 1917 and 1918. Reprinted, with corrections, from the *Cambridge University Reporter*, 1919. https://collections.maa.cam.ac.uk/objects/. Accession 1918.83 at MAA, and for the explanation of 1874, 'Researching and Curating African Collections at MAA, Devolving Restitution #4', https://www.youtube.com/watch?v=wGPLPvWJAVI, Dr Mary-Ann Middlekoop at 31 minutes.
29   Wallace Collection, Correspondence file on Asante Objects.

30 Author's phone conversation, 12/04/2024.
31 Wallace Collection, Correspondence file on Asante Objects.
32 Author's Zoom call, 10/04/2024.
33 https://paw.princeton.edu/memorial/john-brailsford-elliott-51.
34 *Princeton Alumni Weekly*, 02/03/1971.
35 https://rgjmuseum.co.uk/object-archive-item/ashanti-king/, and email correspondence with Christine Pullen, curator, 31/01/2024.
36 Colonel R. F. Meysey-Thompson, obituary, *Rifle Brigade Chronicle*, 1926.
37 The Royal Signals Museum cannot say how it acquired its chair. Captain Reginald Curtis of the Telegraph Battalion of the Royal Engineers received an Asante chair in Kumasi in 1896, according to Ian McInnes and Mark Fraser, *Ashanti 1895–6*, Picton, 1987, pp. 36–7. The Royal Collection says that one of the two chairs Queen Elizabeth II returned to Ghana in 1961 had belonged to Captain Curtis (email from Sarah Davis of Royal Collection to author, 29/11/2024).
38 Author's interview, 14/08/2024.
39 Neil Ascherson, 'How It Felt To Be There', *London Review of Books*, vol. 34, no. 15, 02/08/2012.
40 https://www.gracesguide.co.uk/Walter_Claude_Johnson.
41 John Ryle, 'Africa: The Art of a Continent', at the Royal Academy of Arts, *Times Literary Supplement*, 20/10/1995.
42 Author's visit to John Ryle, 13/06/2024.
43 Stuart Cloete, *The African Giant*, Collins, 1956, p. 233.
44 Email from Malcolm McLeod, 05/11/2024.
45 Christie's Catalogue, Antiquities and Primitive Art 11/12/74, Lot 47A. Christie's sold the elephant tail flywhisk again, in November 1996, for $2,300 see https://www.christies.com/en/lot/lot-1104103.
46 British Museum, Corporate Archive, Board of Trustees' Minutes, vol. 3, 1971–74, no. 2, pp. 1714–5 (BM/1/1/G/2/4/1/3), 26/10/74, and National Archives, FCO 65/1504, BM to FCO 14/10/74.
47 *The Times*, 03/12/1974.
48 Author's interview with Hermione Waterfield, 11/01/2023.
49 Email from Malcolm McLeod, 05/11/2024.
50 Edward Hulme, *The Alphabet of Life*, Ex-Officers' Agencies, 1949, pp. 44–54.
51 *Daily Mirror*, 05/06/1950, and *Surrey Mirror*, 01/07/1966.
52 https://www.noonans.co.uk/auctions/calendar/670/catalogue/449013/.
53 Author's email correspondence with Angela Palmer, 29/10/2024 and 15/11/2024.
54 I visited Ejisu with Malcolm McLeod and Gordon Frimpong on 20/11/2024.
55 Samuel Hingley, letter to *The Times*, 16/03/1935.
56 Hingley obituary, 'Death of Lt Col S H Hingley, Distinguished Military Career, Veteran of Spanish-American War' in National Archives, FCO 65/3143.
57 Author's phone conversation with Christopher Hingley in Bulawayo, 27/03/2024, and interview in London with Robert Hingley, 24/04/2024.
58 Diana Jackson's journal, 1985 Journey to Ghana, p. 11.
59 Diana Jackson's journal, 1985 Journey to Ghana, p. 12.

60 National Archives, FCO 65/3143, British High Commission to Mrs Jackson, 25/01/85 and 26/03/85.
61 National Archives, FCO 65/3143 FCO 22/07/85.
62 Robert Hingley, interview in London, 24/04/2024.
63 Diana Jackson's journal, 1985 Journey to Ghana, p. 15.
64 *Wilts and Glos Standard*, undated, 'Cirencester widow entertained by Ashanti King', in Mrs Jackson's papers.
65 Diana Jackson's journal, 1985 Journey to Ghana, p. 16.
66 Diana Jackson's journal, 1985 Journey to Ghana, p. 26.
67 Diana Jackson's journal, 1985 Journey to Ghana, p. 54.
68 Address by Otumfuo, Opoku Ware II, Golden Jubilee Durbar, Kumasi, 16/11/1985.
69 Diana Jackson's journal, 1985 Journey to Ghana, p. 60.
70 Author's phone call with Christopher Hingley, 27/03/2024.
71 *Wilts and Glos Standard*, undated, 'Cirencester widow entertained by Ashanti King', in Mrs Jackson's papers.

18. 'You Express The Views of A Civilian'

1 William Fagg, 'Ashanti Gold', *The Connoisseur*, January 1974, vol. 185, no. 743, and William Fagg, 'A Golden Ram Head from Ashanti', *Man*, vol. 54, February 1954.
2 Width and weight from the *Daily Telegraph* and *The Times*, both 14/04/1874.
3 William Fagg, 'Ashanti Gold'.
4 Lt Col F. B. R. Toms, 'An Account of the Royal Artillery Regimental Plate in the R.A Mess Woolwich', *Journal of the Royal Artillery*, vol. 32, 1905.
5 Lt Col F. B. R. Toms, 'An Account of the Royal Artillery Regimental Plate in the R.A Mess Woolwich'.
6 *Shipping and Mercantile Gazette*, 21/03/1874 and *Daily Telegraph*, 14/04/1874.
7 *The Times*, 14/04/1874.
8 William Thomas Vincent, *Warlike Woolwich*, A. W. and J. P. Jackson, 1875, p. 53.
9 *The Times*, 21/05/1874. James Smyth was the celebrated Royal Artillery bandmaster 1854–81.
10 Lt Col Alfred Burne, *The Royal Artillery Mess, Woolwich and its Surroundings*, WH Barrell Portsmouth, 1905, p. 195.
11 Lt Col P. R. S. Jackson, *The Silver Room, The Royal Artillery Mess Woolwich*, 1976, p. 72.
12 https://www.rct.uk/collection/70496.
13 Lt Col P. R. S. Jackson, *The Silver Room, The Royal Artillery Mess Woolwich*, p. 31, and Lt Col F B R Toms, 'An Account of the Royal Artillery Regimental Plate in the R.A Mess Woolwich'.
14 Lt Col Alfred Burne, *The Royal Artillery Mess, Woolwich and its Surroundings*, WH Barrell Portsmouth, 1905, p. 195.
15 *The Queen*, 07/06/1890.

16 Lt Col F. B. R. Toms, 'An Account of the Royal Artillery Regimental Plate in the R.A Mess Woolwich'.
17 Michael Tomlinson, *Regimental Heritage, A Pictorial Record of the Paintings and Silver of the Royal Regiment of Artillery,* Europa, 1984, p. 80, and confusion on Haile Selassie date from Lt Col P. R. S. Jackson, *The Silver Room, The Royal Artillery Mess Woolwich*, p. 31.
18 William Knox, obituary, *Daily Telegraph*, 18/12/1916.
19 Major William Knox, 'Personal Reminiscences of the Turco-Russian War 1877–8', Lecture 04/10/88, *Aldershot Military Society*.
20 Major-General William Knox, The Problem of Our Army Horse and his Rider and Driver', 23/02/09, *Aldershot Military Society*, Hugh Rees, Pall Mall, London.
21 Funeral of Lord Wolseley, *The Times*, 01/04/1913.
22 *Pall Mall Gazette*, 22/12/1915 and 29/12/1915 as examples. Knox was posthumously revealed as author of 'Letters from Mars' in *Pall Mall Gazette*, 16/12/1916.
23 *The Times*, 29/05/1916.
24 *Daily Telegraph*, 19/12/16 and *The Times*, 19/12/1916.
25 *Tatler*, 22/04/1936.
26 Description of mess dinners from conversation with Royal Artillery officer. Edward VII visited the RA Mess 1904, George V in 1913 and 1928 (the ram's head was displayed on both occasions), George VI dined there in 1950, Elizabeth II visited in 1958, 1969 and 1993 and dined there in 1976 and 2000.
27 Rawlings died in 2020. I regret I was therefore unable to ask him his thoughts on the ram's head while researching this book.
28 Brigadier Ken Timbers, *The Royal Artillery Woolwich, A Celebration*, Third Millennium 2008.
29 General Sir Thomas Morony, Introduction in Michael Tomlinson, *Regimental Heritage, A Pictorial Record of the Paintings and Silver of the Royal Regiment of Artillery*.
30 Author's interview with retired Royal Artillery officer, London 25/10/2023.
31 Letter from Asst Regimental Secretary, Royal Artillery to Jarat Chopra 06/01/2020.
32 Author's conversation with museum director, 21/02/2024.

19. 'The Past Should Not Dictate The Present'

1 Author's interview with Malcolm McLeod, London, 01/02/2024.
2 Author's interview with Malcolm McLeod, London, 01/02/2024 and 16/05/2025.
3 The trustees agreed to the loan on 18/01/2024.
4 I met the Asantehene in Kumasi, 21/11/24, and he subsequently provided written answers to my questions.
5 Author's interview with Malcolm McLeod, London, 01/02/2024.
6 Author's interview with Ivor Agyeman-Duah, Kumasi, 02/05/2024.
7 'Notes of An Interview Held at Cape Coast Castle', 17 December 1895, in NAM

1976-07-37, Papers of Brig Gen Francis Kempster.
8 William Tordoff, 'The Exile and Repatriation of Nana Prempeh I of Ashanti', *Transactions of the Historical Society of Ghana*, vol. 4, no. 2, 1960.
9 Emmanuel Akyeampong, 'Christianity, Modernity and the Weight of Tradition in the Life of 'Asantehene' Agyeman Prempeh I, c. 1888–1931', *Africa: Journal of the International African Institute*, vol. 69, no. 2, 1999.
10 Author's interview with Ivor Agyeman-Duah, Kumasi, 02/05/2024.
11 Author's interview with Ivor Agyeman-Duah, Kumasi, 22/11/2024.
12 https://x.com/Asante_nation/status/1750470628551856233.
13 Author's interview with Ivor Agyeman-Duah, Kumasi, 02/05/2024.
14 Professor Kodzo Gavua's lecture to 'Museum Lab' students, attended by author, University of Ghana, Legon, 19/11/2024.
15 Author's Zoom conversation with Professor Kwasi Ampene, 24/03/2024.
16 I visited the National Army Museum storage on 16/01/2025.
17 According to the 1934 RUSI catalogue, Edward VII transferred the umbrella to RUSI from Windsor Castle in 1903. The National Army Museum received most of its Asante objects from RUSI in 1963, including the umbrella and Wolseley's collection. https://collections.rusi.org/official-catalogue-of-the-royal-united-service-museum-whitehall-london-s-w-1934/.
18 Otumfuo, Nana Agyeman Prempeh I, *The History of Ashanti Kings and the Whole Country Itself*, Oxford University Press, 2003, pp. 189–90.
19 Author's interview with Ivor Agyeman-Duah, Kumasi, 02/05/2024.
20 Author's interview with Ivor Agyeman-Duah, Kumasi, 02/05/2024.
21 Thomas Edward Bowdich, *Mission from Cape Coast to Ashantee*, Frank Cass, 1966 (originally published by John Murray, 1819), p. 279.
22 Martha Judith Ehrlich, 'A Catalogue of Ashanti Art taken from Kumasi in the Anglo-Ashanti War of 1874', PhD Thesis, Indiana University, 1981, p. 126.
23 Author's interview with Ivor Agyeman-Duah, Kumasi, 02/05/2024.
24 Kwasi Ampene and Nana Kwadwo Nyantakyi III, *Engaging Modernity: Asante in the Twenty-First Century*, University of Michigan, University Lithoprinters, 2014, p. 18.
25 Author's Zoom conversation with Professor Kwasi Ampene, 24/03/2024.
26 See Barnaby Phillips, *Loot, Britain and the Benin Bronzes*, Oneworld, 2021, chapter 15.
27 Author's Zoom conversation with Professor Kwasi Ampene, 24/03/2024.
28 https://www.theartnewspaper.com/2022/11/08/british-museum-chair-george-osborne-defies-restitution-movement-in-speech.
29 Off the record interview with British Museum curator, 05/07/2024.
30 https://www.bbc.co.uk/news/entertainment-arts-66543589. For detailed coverage of these thefts, listen to the BBC podcast 'Thief at The British Museum' and read Rebecca Mead, 'Stones of Contention', *New Yorker*, 13/05/2024.
31 Off the record interview with British Museum curator, 01/09/2023.
32 https://www.bbc.co.uk/news/entertainment-arts-66543589.
33 British Museum, Corporate Archive, Board of Trustees' Minutes, vol. 9, 1991–4, p. 5, 212, no. 12 (BM/1/1/G/2/4/1/9), 05/10/91.

34 https://www.britishmuseum.org/collection/object/E_Af1925-1024-1, and *The Times*, 12/10/1925.
35 Author's email correspondence with Malcolm McLeod, 19/5/2025.
36 Author's email correspondence with John Mack, 01/12/2024.
37 British Museum, Corporate Archive, Board of Trustees' Minutes, vol. 9, 1991–4, pp. 5, 273–4. no. 9 (BM/1/1/G/2/4/1/9), 25/01/92.
38 Karl-Ferdinand Schaedler, *Lexikon Afrikanische Kunst und Kultur*, Klinkhardt and Biermann, 1994, p. 31, and *Götter Geister Ahnen, Afrikanische Skulpturen in deutschen Privatsammlungen Im Museum für Völkerkunde Wien*, Neue Hof burg, 23 März bis 24 Juli, 1994, Villa Stuck, 1994, number 240, and Karl-Ferdinand Schaedler, *Earth and Ore, 2,500 Years of African Art in Terra-Cotta and Metal*, Panterra Verlag, 1997, p. 185.
39 Important African and Oceanic Art, including the Collection of Dr Karl-Ferdinand Schädler, Sotheby's New York, Tuesday May 25, 1999, Lot 29 (p. 24 of catalogue).
40 Author's phone call with Nigel Barley, 05/11/2024.
41 Author's phone call with Hermione Waterfield, 7/8/2025.
42 Further details of this story have been confirmed to me by two people in Britain, and the Indianapolis Museum of Art. Doran Ross died in 2020. The Indianapolis Museum of Art's curator who was in charge of African collections in 1999, Ted Celenko, has also died.
43 *The Times*, 24/07/1993 and 28/07/1993.
44 British Museum, Corporate Archive, Board of Trustees' Minutes, vol. 9, 1991–1994, p. 5, 328, no. 3b (BM/1/1/G/2/4/1/9), 16/05/92.
45 British Museum, Corporate Archive, Board of Trustees' Minutes, vol. 9, 1991–1994, p. 5, 352, no. 13 (BM/1/1/G/2/4/1/9), 20/06/92.
46 I'm grateful to the Peverett family for some of this information.
47 British Museum, Corporate Archive, Board of Trustees' Minutes, vol. 9, 1991–1994, p. 5, 328, no. 3b (BM/1/1/G/2/4/1/9), 16/05/92.
48 British Museum, Corporate Archive, Board of Trustees' Minutes, vol. 9, 1991–1994, p. 5, 352, no. 13 (BM/1/1/G/2/4/1/9), 20/06/92, and British Museum, Corporate Archive, Board of Trustees' Minutes, vol. 9, 1991–1994, p. 5, 419, no. 10 (BM/1/1/G/2/4/1/9), 07/11/92.
49 Author's phone call with Anthony Guyan, 30/01/2025.
50 Author's phone call with Richard Luck, Hastings antique dealer, 07/07/2025.
51 Author's interview with Nigel's ex-wife Meryl and three children, Howard, Chloe and Ellie, 12/06/2025.
52 Author's phone call with Mark Eddo, 05/06/2024.
53 https://www.nrk.no/stor-oslo/to-menn-domt-for-kronjuvel-tyveri-1.10972497, and https://www.bbc.co.uk/news/world-europe-19919062.
54 British Museum, Corporate Archive, Board of Trustees' Minutes, vol. 9, 1991–1994, p. 5212, no. 12 (BM/1/1/G/2/4/1/9), 05/10/91.
55 British Museum, Corporate Archive, Board of Trustees' Minutes, vol. 9, 1991–1994, p. 5328, no. 3b (BM/1/1/G/2/4/1/9), 16/05/92.
56 British Museum, Corporate Archive, Board of Trustees' Minutes, vol. 9, 1991–1994, p. 5419, no. 10 (BM/1/1/G/2/4/1/9), 07/11/92.

57 British Museum, Corporate Archive, Board of Trustees' Minutes, vol. 9, 1991–1994, pp. 5, 588–9, no. 15 (BM/1/1/G/2/4/1/9), 02/10/93.
58 'Whose Art Is It Anyway?' *Chronicle*, BBC 2, 27.5.81, Editor, Andrew Pace, Producer, Ben Shephard.

20. 'A Happy Day for Asante, for the Black African Continent'

1 Peacocks given to Opoku Ware II on a visit to Persia, according to Yao Andoh. Author's email from Malcolm McLeod, 15/6/2024.
2 Ryszard Kapuściński, *The Shadow of the Sun*, Allen Lane, 2001 p. 24.
3 Elspeth Huxley, *Four Guineas*, 1954, p. 135.
4 Speeches made on 01/05/2024 in Kumasi.
5 https://www.dailymail.co.uk/news/article-13423083/museums-treasures-preserved-centuries-Elgin-Marbles.html.
6 Interview with Julie Hudson, British Museum, 03/04/2024.
7 Angus Patterson, LinkedIn post, May 2024.
8 Author's interview with Peter King Appiah, Kumasi, 29/04/2024.
9 Nii Kwate Owoo, 'Hiding and Returning Asante Regalia' in *Fifteen Colonial Thefts*, Sela Adjei and Yann LeGall, Pluto Press, 2024, p. 91.
10 Author's interview with Nii Kwate Owoo, Kumasi 02/05/2024.
11 Author's interview with Nii Kwate Owoo, Kumasi 02/05/2024.
12 Author's interview with Nii Kwate Owoo, Kumasi 02/05/2024.
13 Author's interview with Nii Kwate Owoo, Kumasi 02/05/2024.
14 https://www.motac.gov.gh/return-stolen-cultural-artefacts/, and https://ghanaiantimes.com.gh/president-reaffirms-support-for-restitution-reparation/.
15 Author's WhatsApp chat with Nii Kwate Owoo, 05/12/2024.
16 *The Times*, 18/4/2000.
17 Author's interview with Tristram Hunt, V&A, 04/11/2024.
18 Author's interview with Nana Oforiatta Ayim, Accra, 25/11/2024.
19 Author's interviews with Ivor Agyeman-Duah, Kumasi, 02/05/2024.
20 Author's interview with Peter King Appiah, Kumasi, 29/04/2024.
21 Author's interview with Professor Kodzo Gavua, University of Ghana, Legon, on 19/11/2024.
22 Author's interview with Professor Kodzo Gavua, University of Ghana, Legon, on 19/11/2024.
23 Author's Zoom call with Professor Kodzo Gavua, Accra, 24/05/2024.
24 Author's Zoom call with Professor Kodzo Gavua, Accra, 24/05/2024.
25 https://fowler.ucla.edu/wp-content/uploads/2022/03/FowlerMuseumRelease_Permanent-Return-of-Asante-Objects-to-Ghana.pdf.
26 Author's Zoom call with Erica Jones, 18/01/2024.
27 Glendining & Co., 'Valuable Coins, Commemorative Medals and Gold Ethnographical Ornaments', 30/11/28.

28 I visited Rousdon House in April 2024, which is now divided up into private apartments. A photograph of the museum was kindly shared with the author by Tim Teuten.
29 For more on the Peek family of Rousdon: https://www.lymeregis-hotel.com/wp-content/uploads/2019/01/Peek-room-description.pdf.
30 The Fowler Museum kindly shared with me their own document on the history of the seven objects – '1874 Asante Objects_Fowler' and many details are taken from there. Also see *The Times*, 03/12/28 on the sale.
31 Ibid.
32 Glendining's catalogue, 17/12/1934, Lots 136–41; https://art.nelson-atkins.org/objects/26090/royal-stool. Rachel Kabukala, the museum's Africa curator, says it has identified the stool 'as a priority' for provenance research (email to author, 14/08/2024).
33 Author's Zoom call with Erica Jones, 18/01/2024.
34 Author's Zoom call with Professor Kwasi Ampene, 24/03/2024.
35 Author's Zoom call with Erica Jones, 26/02/2024.
36 Author's Zoom call with Erica Jones, 18/01/2024.
37 https://www.latimes.com/entertainment-arts/story/2024-02-05/ucla-fowler-museum-looted-african-art-asante-king.
38 Author's Zoom calls with Erica Jones, 18/01/2024 and 26/02/2024.
39 Author's Zoom call with Professor Kwasi Ampene, 24/03/2024.
40 Author's Zoom calls with Erica Jones, 18/01/24 and 26/02/2024.
41 Author's Zoom call with Cory Gundlach, 18/10/2024.
42 Author's Zoom call with Professor Kwasi Ampene, 24/03/2024.
43 Author's interview with Peter Osei-Bonsu Safo Kantanka, Kumasi, 30/04/2024.

21. 'Which History We Remember'

1 Author's interview with Nicholas Cullinan, British Museum, 07/02/2025.
2 An account of the dinner given to the author, 19/07/2024.
3 Author's interview with Tristram Hunt, V&A, 04/11/2024.
4 Author's phone call with Chris Gosden, 06/12/2024.
5 Author's interview with Tristram Hunt, V&A, 04/11/2024.
6 Author's interview with Nicholas Cullinan, British Museum, 07/02/2025.
7 Michael Mosbacher, 'Our Museums Are Now at Risk of Being Looted', *Daily Telegraph*, 28/01/2024.
8 Author's phone call with Chris Wingfield, 3/6/2025.
9 Conversations with British Museum curator May 2024, and trustee December, 2024.
10 Hew Locke, 'What Have We Here?', Exhibition at the British Museum, 2024–2025.
11 I saw the portrait of Yaa Asantewaa in September 2024. It was still there at the end of 2025.
12 Author's interview with Nicholas Cullinan, British Museum, 07/02/2025.

13 The 1992 Act says 'The Wallace Collection Board shall neither add any object to their collection nor dispose of any object the property in which is vested in them and which is comprised in their collection'.
14 The Oriental Armoury, the Wallace Collection, 13/01/2023.
15 Author's interview with Dr Xavier Bray, 03/10/2024.
16 *Daily Express* and *Belfast News* Letter, 08/02/1965.
17 *The Times* and *The Scotsman*, 08/02/1965.
18 *Belfast Telegraph*, 30/03/1966. The flag had been held in the Imperial War Museum in London but belonged to the Royal Collection. Email from Sarah Davis of Royal Collection 29/11/24 that this was the last object de-accessioned.
19 Author's interview with Bell Ribeiro-Addy, Houses of Parliament, 07/10/2024.
20 Author's interview with Tristram Hunt, London, 04/11/2024.
21 The Asantehene's address at the British Museum, quotes from author's notes, 19/07/2024.
22 Author's interview with Nicholas Cullinan, British Museum, 07/02/2025.
23 Author's Zoom call with Erica Jones, 26/02/2024.
24 Author's interview with Tristram Hunt, London, 04/11/2024.
25 I met the Asantehene in Kumasi, 21/11/2024, and he subsequently provided written answers to my questions.
26 Author's interview with Kodzo Gavua, Accra, 19/11/2024.
27 https://whc.unesco.org/en/list/35/.
28 I visited Ejisu with Francis, 02/05/2024.
29 Author's interview with Frederick Ohene, 30/04/2024.
30 Semafor Africa Newsletter, 14/5/2025 and 26/5/2025.
31 For the devastation wrought by gold mining in Ghana today, see e.g., https://news.mongabay.com/2023/02/mechanization-of-illegal-gold-mining-threatens-ghanas-forests/; https://www.theguardian.com/world/2024/nov/25/polluted-rivers-taxes-ghana-illegal-gold-mining-boom; https://www.bbc.co.uk/news/articles/cn9dn8xq92jo.
32 https://www.france24.com/en/live-news/20241121-historic-gold-regalia-returned-to-ghana-s-king.
33 Author's interview with Ivor Agyeman-Duah, London, 24/05/2024.
34 Author's interview with Ivor Agyeman-Duah, London, 24/05/2024.
35 The Manhyia Palace Museum says it attracted 87,000 visitors (of which 77,700 were Ghanaian) from January to October 2024, compared to 46,000 in the same period of the previous year. The museum was closed throughout April 2024.
36 I met the Asantehene in Kumasi 21/11/2024 and he subsequently provided written answers to my questions.
37 Author's interviews at the Manhyia Palace Museum, 20/11/2024 and 21/11/2024.
38 Author's interviews at Manhyia Palace Museum, 20/11/2024 and 21/11/2024.

INDEX

Note: The following abbreviations are used. f = photographs; n = endnotes.

Aban (Palace of Culture) 26–7
Aberdare, Lord 125
Abinsi (Royal Mail steamer) 203
abolitionists (enslavement) 16–17, 18, 19
abua (pipe) 108
Abyssinia expedition (1868) 101, 102–3, 247–8
Accra (Ghana) *xxxi, xxxii–xxxiii, xxxvii*, 122–3, 124, 125, 132, 194, 199, 276
Act for the Abolition of the Slave Trade (1807) (British) 16–17, 18, 19, 53
Adanse Hills 61–3, 139
Adanse people 86, 135, 140
Adjaye, Joseph (historian) 18, 32, 41, 62, 136
Adu Boahen, Albert *xii*, 35–6
Adu 'Bofuo' Bobi (Asanti general) *xii*, 33
Adu-Poku, George and Eunice, 297
Adu Yaw (Asante envoy) 88
'Africa Fest' 265, 266
African Company of Merchants 16, 17, 18, 19
African Times 122
Africa's Struggle For Its Art (Savoy) 218–19
Africa and the Victorians (Robinson, Gallagher and Denny) 122, 133
Afua Kobiri, Queen Mother 121
agriculture 5, 9, 129, 186, 189, 198
Agyeman Badu (brother of Prempeh I) 200
Agyeman-Duah Ivor (Ghanaian scholar, great-grandson of Kwame Boatin) *xiii, xvii, xxxi, xxxii* n.1, *xxxv, xxxvi*
    campaign for return of regalia 256–7, 258–9, 260, 261, 262
    return of regalia from British Museum (2024) 272, 276, 291, 292, 296
Akan ethnic group 2–3, 4–5, 9, 10, 94, 262, 281
Akkere, Native Officer 185
akrafokonmu ('soul washer badges') *xxxii*, 111, 120, 209–10, 221, 287
    sales of 106, 107–8, 228–9, 231
    thefts of 264*f*, 265
Akua'ba (carved female figures) 9
Akwaboa (village) 74
Akwamu people *xxii*, 22, 275

Akwidaa (village) 110
akyeame (spokesmen) 9
Akyeampong, Emmanuel (historian) 123, 166, 205
Akyem people *xxii*, 22, 33, 86
Albert Edward, Prince of Wales (son of Queen Victoria, later Edward VII) 99, 101, 112, 188, 214, 247
Alexander, Major-General Henry 212
Alexander II, Czar of Russia 247
Alfred, Prince, Duke of Saxe-Coburg and Gotha (son of Queen Victoria) 101–2, 105–6
Ali, Muhammad (boxer) 2
Alison, Brigadier-General Sir Archibald (Wolseley's deputy) *xiii*, 51, 65, 67
'All Sir Garnet' (phrase) 100
alluvial gold 5, 6
Amankwa Tia (Asante general) *xiii*, 35, 36–7, 47, 58, 59, 66
American Museum of Natural History (New York) 224
Americas, The 8, 9
ammunition 7, 32, 47, 136
Amoafo, Battle of (1874) *xvi, xiii, xx, xxiii*, 64–7, 76, 79, 80, 91, 246
Amoah, Sammy (guide) 298
Ampene, Professor Kwasi 259, 261–2, 280, 281, 282
ancestors and ancestral world 41
Anderson Robert (former director, British Museum) 269
Andooa (King of Elmina) 80
Anglican Church of St Paul's (Seychelles) 196
Anglo-Asante Wars (1824–1900) *xvi, xxii, xxiv, xxxii, xxxvi* n.14, 22, 29, 212, 280, 289, 297
Anglo-Burmese War, Second (1852–1853) 49
AngloGold Ashanti 296
Annowo ('Palaver Hall/Ground') (Cape Coast Castle) 92, 141
Anomabu Fort (battle) (1806) 15, 16
Ansa, John Owusu *xiii*
antelope-skin helmet (*denkyemkye*) *xxxii*
'Anthropological Department in Ashanti' 201
Appiah, Peter King (Head of Research, Centre for National Culture) 29, 42, 273, 277
Arab traders *xxxiii*, 4
Archaeological Journal 109
architecture (Asante traditional) 293–4

Index

Armitage, Sir Cecil (British soldier/colonial official) *xiii*, 156, 157, 174, 177, 178, 179
'Armitage Jug' 156 n.9, 157, 158
Army and Navy Gazette 191
art and artworks 9–10
Arthur, Prince (third son of Queen Victoria) 247
artillery guns 5, 35, 66–7, 185
Asafo Agyei (King of Dwaben) 86
Asaman (land of the ancestors) 41
Asamoa Nkwanta (General, Skrafokra ('soldier's guardian spirit')) *xiii*, 63
Asante in the 19th Century (Wilks) *xix*
Asante Army *xi*, 7, 13, 20–1, 33–4, 104
    Battle of Amoafo (1874) 64–5, 66
    Battle of Odaso (1874) 67–9
    invasion of Asante (British) (1873–1874) 47, 50, 56, 58, 62, 73, 76–7
    invasion of the Gold Coast (1873) 33–5, 36, 38–9
    siege of Kumasi Fort (1900) 183, 184, 185, 186–7
Asante-Dutch treaty (1837) 132
'Asante Ewer' *xiii*, 153–4, 156, 158, 213
Asantehene (Kings of Asante) *xi–xii*, 3–4, 10, 106, 119, 157, 205, 275, 277, 297
    see also under individuals
Asantehene's Palace (Kumasi) *xvi*, *xxiii*, *xxxiv*, 15, 27, 106, 145–6, 170
    destruction of (1874) 75–9, 81–2, 92, 121–2, 126, 153, 156–7, 159
Asantehewaa (Queen Mother) 8, 62, 74, 121, 127
    humiliation of Yaa Akyia 141, 142*f*, 144, 150
    exile of Yaa Akyia 195, 196, 200, 204
'Asante Kingdom of Gold' (exhibition) (British Museum/American Museum of Natural History) *xxvi*, 223, 224
Asante, People and Kingdom of *xii*, *xx*, *xxi*, *xxii*, *xxxii*, *xxxiii*, *xxxiv*, 74, 102, 122–3, 125–6, 139
    adaption to modern world 165–6, 198–9, 201, 202, 276
    annexation 198–9, 241–2
    dispersal of cultural wealth 261–2, 276, 277–8, 281, 282, 287, 293–4
    historical background 2, 7, 8–10, 12*f*, 16–24, 29, 30–31
    proposal to become British Protectorate 128–9
Asare, Rev. N.V. 121
Asen People 15, 30, 33
'Ashantee Band' 53
'Ashantee earring' 100
'Ashantee March' (piano music) (Pridham) 100
'Ashanti Camp School' 197
Ashanti Field Force (Kumasi) 187, 188
Ashanti Goldfields Corporation *xiv*, 172, 188, 198
Ashanti Pioneer 212, 229
Asiedu, Oheneba 225
asipim chairs (oak/mahogany) 157–8, 159, 279
Assyrians, The 109
Asuming, Josephine (filmmaker) 297
Athenaeum Club (London) 285, 290
Atta Kwami (painter) 255
Atuarbo 190
auctions (looted/plundered goods) *xiv*, *xix*, *xxiii*
    Cape Coast Castle (1874) 84*f*, 92, 93 n.37, 94–6, 246, 259

Christie's (Paris) 229, 230*f*, 231
Sotheby's (New York) 265, 266
Wolseley in Peking (1860) 72, 73
Aya Kese (ornamental brass bowl) 160, 259–60

Baden-Powell, Lady Olave (wife of Robert Baden-Powell) 237
Baden-Powell, Major Robert *xiii*, *xxxiv*, 160, 164, 237, 249, 259–60, 279
    Invasion of Asante (British) (1895–1896) 137, 139, 140, 141, 144, 145, 146–7, 149, 150
Baerbock, Annalena *xxvii*
Banda people 113
Banqueting House (London) 162
Bantama (royal mausoleum, 'Fetish Temple') 23, 77, 122, 146–7, 160, 204, 260
Barbier-Mueller collection (Geneva) 296
Barbot, Jean 10
Bare (village) 177
Barima Agyeman Badu (son of Prempeh and heir apparent) 144
Barley, Nigel (curator) 265
Barnett, Captain E.A. 127
Barracouta, HMS 35
Barrow, Captain Knapp 119, 120 n.10, 121, 123
Barter, Major Charles (British soldier) *xiii*, 147–8, 154–5, 156, 158
Bathurst, Earl (Secretary of State for War and the Colonies) 23
Beatrice, Princess (youngest daughter of Queen Victoria) 115, 136, 149
Bekwai 10, 140, 171, 186
Bell, Lieutenant Mark Sever 82
Benin Bronzes *xviii*, 94, 113–14, 153, 162, 184, 259, 261–2, 287–8
    auction of 164, 229
    return of *xxvii*, *xxxvi*, 219, 268, 277, 281–2
Berlin Conference (1884–1885) 126
Berlin (meeting) (1884–1885) *xxiv*
Berney, Captain Thomas 147, 158
Besease shrine house (Ejisu) 293, 294
Biemso (Obassa) 186
Birimian rocks 171
Bishop, Captain Frederick 184–5
Black Lives Matter *xxvi*, 259
Black Unity and Freedom Party 275
Black Watch *see* Royal Highland Regiment
Blonde, HMS 149
Boahen, Albert Adu (historian) 16–17, 170, 175, 176, 196
Boakye Tenten (husband of Afua Kobiri) 121
Boatin, Paul (grandfather of Ivor Agyeman-Duah) 258
Boatin, Thomas (son of Kwame Boatin) 257–8
Bokhara (mail ship) 136
Bonnat, Marie-Joseph (French trader) *xiii*, 57–8, 61, 80, 81, 87
Bonny (steamship) 33
bosumuru boaman ('greatest of the State Umbrellas') 221
Bowdich, Sarah (wife of Thomas, zoologist/author) 18
Bowdich, Thomas (British official, nephew of Governor John Hope Smith) *xi*, *xiii–xiv*, *xxi–xxii*, *xxxiii–xxxiv*, 40, 128, 160, 206, 261

expedition (1817) 13, 14, 15, 17–18, 19, 20, 24–5, 27
Boyle, Frederick (correspondent) xiv, 78, 82, 92, 93, 94–5, 102
Brackenbury, Henry (Wolseley's military secretary) xiv, 39, 51, 74, 75, 91–2, 171, 246
  capture of Kumasi 74, 75, 76–7, 80–1
Brake, Colonel Herbert 190–1
Brandford Griffith, Governor William xxiv, 120, 127, 128, 132
brass and bronzework 94–5
Bray, Dr Xavier xiv, 289
bridges 50, 76, 85
Bristol Courier, The 79
British Army xiv, xv, xxxiv, 101, 105, 178, 188, 249
  battles with Asante Army, 63, 65, 66, 67, 68
  capture of Kumasi 72, 73, 74, 75, 77, 82, 85–6, 90–1, 95
  Invasion of Asante (British) (1873–1874) 31, 38, 42, 51, 53, 56, 58, 59
  Invasion of Asante (British) (1895–1896) 135, 136, 137, 145–7, 148, 150
British Empire *see* colonialism; imperialism
British Empire Exhibition (1924) xxv, 202–3
British High Commission (Accra) 210, 211
British and Medieval Antiquities and Ethnography (British Museum) 110
British Museum Act (1963) 219, 220, 221, 286, 291
British Museum (London) xii–xv, xvii–xviii, xxii, xxv–xxvii, xxxi–xxxii, xxxv–xxxvi n.14, 22, 25, 27, 286, 290
  acquisition of Asante regalia 108 n.61, 109–11, 113, 228, 231, 237–8, 239, 242
  campaign for return of Asante regalia (1974) 209–10, 214, 215, 216–17, 218, 219, 220, 221–4
  campaign for return/loan of Asante regalia (2023–2024) 255–9, 260, 262–3, 272, 274–6, 278–9
  looting and plundering (colonial), 153–5, 156, 157, 158, 160, 163–5
  return of regalia 284f, 285–6, 287–9, 291–2, 297
  thefts from 263, 264f, 265–6, 267f, 268, 269
British, The xii–xv, xviii, xxi–xxii, xxvii, 6, 7, 8, 10, 109, 122–3, 188
  enslavement 16–17
  exploitation of gold trade, 171–3
  relations with Asanti 13–14, 15, 18–20, 22, 29–36, 41, 89, 194, 258
Brodrick, William ((Under) Secretary of State for War) 148, 191
Buckle, Mr 21
Buller, Captain Redvers (intelligence officer) 80, 92, 150
burials and graves 185, 204
Burleigh, Bennet (correspondent) xiv, 139, 140, 148, 149
Burnett, Andrew 256
'Burning of Coomassie, The' (picture) (Prior) 90
Burroughs, Colonel Charles 190, 191
Busby, Margaret (Ghanaian-born publisher) 177
Buswell, Archdeacon Henry 196
Butler, Captain William 86
Buxton, Sidney (Under Secretary of State for the Colonies) 132

Cade, Edwin Arthur (gold miner) xiv, 171–2, 188
Calabar (mailboat) 35

Cambridge, Duke of (Commander-in-Chief of British Army) 51, 62, 88–9, 92, 95
Cambridge Museum of Archaeology and Anthropology *see* Museum of Archaeology and Anthropology (Cambridge)
camps (military) 50
candlesticks (silver) 115
cannons 7–8
Canton 115
Cape Coast and Cape Coast Castle xiv, xxi, xxii, xxiii, 7, 22, 26, 132, 138, 149, 190
  Anglo-Asante Wars 32, 33, 35, 46, 53, 100
  auction (23 February 1874) 84f, 85, 91, 92–6, 158, 246, 259
  Bowdich expedition to Kumasi 13, 17, 18
  Invasion of 1881 120, 121, 122
Cape Coast Castle peace treaty (1831) xxii, 22, 23
Cape of Good Hope 38
capital punishment 40–1
Cardwell, Lord Edward (politician) xiv, 34, 37, 46, 88, 101
Carnarvon, Lord 122
Carter, Colonel Charles 184
Carthaginians xxxiii
Casely Hayford, Joseph 202
cash crops 128, 198
casket (silver) 126
cassava 9
'Catalogue of Ashanti Art taken from Kumasi in the Anglo-Ashanti War of 1874, A' (Ehrlich) 227–8
Caygill, Marjorie 109–10
Cayley, Captain Walter 148
Cecil, Francis Horace Pierrepont (son of William) 107
Cecil, William, Marquess of Exeter 107–8, 209, 228–9
'Centenary of the Sagrenti War - The Call for the Return of the Asante Regalia' (Otumfuo Opoku Ware II) 219
Central Africa 189
Central African Rifles 190–1
Centre for National Culture (Kumasi) 29, 42, 273, 277
ceremonial sword (*Mpomponsuo*) xxxii, 15
chair (Asante) 235
chair (Asantehene's) 112
chair ('King's State Seat') 279
Chamahs people (Shama) 39
Chamberlain, Joseph (politician) xiv, xxiv–xxv, 133–4, 195, 198
  acquisition of Asante regalia 159, 160, 161, 162, 163, 164
  siege of Fort Kumasi (1900) 172, 175, 176, 178, 186, 188
Chamberlain, Mrs Mary Endicott (3rd wife of Joseph) 163
Chapple, Dr William (MP) 202
Charles II of England xxxiii
Charles III, King 255, 256, 289, 290
Cheylesmore, Major-General Lord 210
China 263
Chinery, Mrs D. 116
'cholera belt' 50
Chopra, Jarat (lawyer) 251
Chopra of Multan, Diwan Mulraj (Sikh governor of Punjab) 251
Christianity 5, 196, 197, 199, 205, 258
Christian Victor of Schleswig-Holstein, Prince 136, 150

Christie's London/Paris (auction house) 210, 228, 229, 230, 231, 233, 237
Christy Fund 111
Church, Corporal 85–6
Church of England 196
Churchill, Winston 189
Church Mission Society 196
Civil War (Ashanti) (1884–1888)
Claridge, William (historian) 120–1
Cloete, Stuart (novelist) 237
Clutterbuck, Dr James (surgeon-major) 93
cocoa trade 172, 198
cocoyam 9
coffee pot (silver) 158
coiled gold disc (Captain F Bishop) 184–5
coins (Roman) 266
Coldstream Guards 137
'Collection of Gold and Other Objects from Ashanti, A' (exhibition) (1874) *xxiii*, 114–15
Collet, Sir Mark Wilks 231
Colley, Colonel George 52–3, 68
'Colonial and Indian Exhibition' (London) 126, 127
colonialism *xxvi, xxxv, xxxvi*, 133, 170–1, 198, 211, 217, 259
   acquisition of Asante regalia 71, 114–15, 122–3, 126–7, 128–9, 141, 145
   decolonialisation 212, 275, 281–2, 285–6, 290, 292
   restitution 262–3, 277–8
   return of regalia 218, 236, 272
Colonial Office (British) *xxiv–xxv*, 35, 93, 119, 132, 133, 194
   acquisition of Asante regalia 159, 161, 163, 164, 165
Columbia 287
Commerell, Commodore John 38–39, 40
Confederates (United States) 48–9, 139
'Confidential Mobilization Committee' 136
Congreve rockets 22
Connoisseur, The (art magazine) 236
Conrad, Joseph 71
Constantinople 4
Convention People's Party 274
Conway, Moncure (American abolitionist) 114
Coomassie (Ghana) *see* Kumasi
Coomassie and Magdala (Stanley) 102–3
Coram Wright, Mrs J. (step-daughter of Lord Cheylesmore) 210
Coromandel (troopship) 136
coronation ceremonies *xxiv*, 127, 129
Coryndon, Lady Phyllis 229
Côte d'Ivoire *xxxi*, 2, 233
Country Life 229
Cowan, Lieutenant F. 237
craftsmanship (Asante) 9–10, 94–5, 106–110, 113, 128, 165, 166f, 175
Cree, James 125
crops 9
Crown Agents for the Colonies 111, 147, 159, 163, 164, 165
'Cruising And Christmas Day' (25th December) 53
crypt (St Paul's Cathedral) 104
Cullinan Diamond 105
Cullinan, Nicholas (Director of British Museum) *xiv*, 285, 286, 287, 291
Curragh Incident (1914) 280

Daaku, Kwame Yeboa (historian) 6, 8
Dadease people 135
dagger (gold sheath/hilt/ornaments) 221, 296
dagger (*sikay*) *xxxii*
Daily Express 213
Daily Graphic 93, 212
Daily Mail 273
Daily Mirror 238
Daily Telegraph xiv, 78, 92, 99, 106, 139, 159, 212, 286–7
Dallas Museum of Art 125
Dalrymple, Captain William 86
Dapper Foundation 229
Davidson, Basil (historian) 6, 216–17, 220
Davis, Alexandra (student) 225
Davitt, Michael (MP) 162, 163
Dawson, Joseph (Fante interpreter) *xiv*, 57, 62, 75
deaccessioning 219, 286, 290
dealers 263
deaths (Asante) 36, 58, 66–7, 69, 185, 186, 189–90
deaths (British) 36, 47, 56, 76, 85, 149, 185
De Beer, Lloyd (curator) 153–4, 159, 160
Deletaille, M Emile (art dealer) 264
Dendy, Terri (curator) 259
denkyemkye (horned cap) ('King Prempeh's Crown') 163, 164, 296
Denkyira kingdom *xi, xvii, xxi, xxii*, 2–3, 7, 8, 22, 30, 33, 160
Denmark *xxii*, 7, 8, 26, 30
Denny, Alice 122, 133
Derby, Earl of 105
'derived rococo' sword vessel 165, 166f
Desanges, Louis (artist) 104
deserters 54
'Diary of the Ashantee War by an Eye Witness' (Little) *xvii*, 45–6, 49, 51, 53, 54, 56, 101
   battles with Asante Army, 61, 63, 64, 65, 66, 68, 69
   capture of Kumasi, 74, 75, 78, 82, 85–6, 90, 91
Dillon, John (MP) 161
diplomacy *xvii*, 62–3, 74, 290, 291, 295, 297
'Disaster on the River Prah' 39–40, 110–11
Disraeli, Benjamin *xiv, xxiii*, 38, 89, 100
Dix, Mrs J. 228, 229
Dompoase 184
donkeys 51
Donkor, Kimathi (artist) 288
Driberg, Tom (MP) 213
Druid, HMS 110
drum (Asante) 154
drum (with skull) 148, 281
Dugdale, Captain Henry (Rifle Brigade) 80
Duncan, John (soldier) 23
Dunkwa 34
Dupuis, Joseph (British envoy) *xiv, xxii*, 18–19, 20, 26, 40
Dwaben kingdom 10, 86
Dwarka (transport ship) 195
dysentery 7, 10, 31, 36, 50, 59, 63, 85, 125, 189

Eardley-Wilmot, Lieutenant Frederick 47
earrings (Greek) 266
Easter Uprising (Dublin) (1916) 290
Eddo, Mark 269

Edo people *see* Benin Bronzes
education (Western) 196–7, 199
Ehrlich, Martha (scholar of Asante regalia) 113, 220, 227–8, 261
Ejisu (town) 176–7, 204, 293
elephants 51
elephant tail flywhisk 237, 281, 296
elephant tusk (with skull attached) 281
Elgin Marbles 262, 268, 290
Elizabeth II, Queen *xxvi*, 212–14, 237, 251, 256, 260, 289–90
Elliott, Sir Bignell 264
Elliott, John (collector) 234
Elmina and Elmina Castle (São Jorge da Mina) *xii, xvii, xx, xxii, xxiv–xxv, xxxviiif*, 5, 6, 7, 8, 21, 26, 40, 46, 50, 59, 66, 88
  British acquisition of 32, 33, 35–7
  exile of Prempah I and family, 148, 150–1, 161, 199
Elmina, King of 34
Enchantress (paddle-wheel steamer) 90
enslavement *xxi*, 124, 133, 157, 160, 170, 189, 199, 287, 290
  abolition of 16–17, 18, 19, 24, 30, 31, 33, 47–8, 53, 114
  establishment of C17th trade 6, 7, 8, 10
Entwistle, Lance (dealer) 229
envoys (Asante) *xxiii, xxiv*, 76, 87, 88, 120, 125, 131–4, 136, 145
envoys (British) *xiv, xxii*, 18–19, 127
Epstein, Sir Jacob (sculptor) 231
Esen Kwaku (Asante envoy) 88
Ethiopia 248, 252, 268, 289–90
ethnographic collections (museums) *xiv, xvii*, 113, 154–5, 209, 216, 217, 279
Europe and Europeans 35–6, 42
Ewe people 33, 37, 277
exhibitions *xii*, 126–7

Fagg, William (ethnographic curator) *xiv*, 113, 165, 210, 217, 218, 228, 231, 238, 245
Fante people *xi, xxi, xxii*, 140, 150, 170, 171–2, 178
  British and 32, 33, 34, 35, 37, 39
  capture of Kumasi 74, 75, 80, 82
  Invasion of Asante (British) (1873–1874) 46, 47, 52*f*, 53–4, 62, 63, 67–8, 87, 92, 93
  relations with Asante people 10, 13, 15–16, 17, 18, 19, 20, 22
Farah, Nuruddin (novelist) 235–6
Fegan, Dr Henry 92
Ferguson, Robert (private) 65, 75
Festing, Lieutenant Colonel Francis 35, 36
'Fetish Pond' 69
Feyiase, Battle of (1701) *xi, xxi*, 2–3
Fifth Anglo-Asante War ('Yaa Asantewaa War') (1900–1901) *xvi, xix, xxv, xxxii*, 176–8
Fighting in the Ashantee Forest (painting) (Desanges) 104
First Anglo-Asante War (1824–1831) *xxii*, 22, 131
First World War (1914–1918) 199, 249
Fischer, Dr Hartwig (art historian) *xiv–xv, xxvii*, 255, 256, 262, 263, 269
Fisher, Son & Co (publisher) 22
flag (Irish republican) 290
Floyd, George *xxvi*

Focal Team on Reparation and Restitution (Ghana) 275, 277, 278
folklore (Asanti) 30, 32
Fomena, Battle of *xxiii*, 63–4, 77, 86–7, 105, 110, 111
'Fommanah, Treaty of (Fomena)' (1874) 88–9, 92–3, 100, 115, 121, 132, 143, 144, 173, 227
Foreign Office (United Kingdom) 210, 211, 213, 214, 215, 222, 223
Forte, HMS 190, 191
forts and castles 7, 10, 16, 19
Fourth Anglo-Asante War (1896) *xxiv*
Fowler Museum (Los Angeles) *xxvii*, 265, 278–9, 280–1, 292, 296
France *xviii, xxvi*, 7, 33, 72, 80, 128–9, 133, 134, 145,
  stolen regalia 229, 230*f*, 231
Franks, Augustus Wollaston (Keeper (curator)) *xv, xviii*, 110–11, 155, 231
Freedom of the City of London 189
Freeman, Richard Austin (writer) *xv*, 127, 128, 132
Freeman, Thomas Birch (Methodist minister) *xv*, 26, 27
Freemasons Lodge (Mauritius) 238
Freetown (Sierra Leone) 173, 190, 191
Frimpong, Gordon 239
'From Cape Coast to Coomassie, An Illustrated Narrative of the Ashantee' (*Illustrated London News*) 104
Full and Authentic Diary of the Ashanti Expedition, A (Thomas) *xix*
Fuller, Sir Francis (Chief Commissioner of Asante) 198–9, 200
funerals (Asanti) 24, 204–5
funerals (at sea) 101
furniture (Asanti) 213

'galamsey' ('gather them and go' artisanal miners) 294
Gallagher, John 122, 133
Ga people *xxii*, 22, 275
Garden City, The *see* Kumasi (Coomassie) (Asante capital)
Garrard's (Crown jewellers) *xxiii*, 104–7, 108, 110, 111, 112, 113, 209, 228–9, 232, 279
Gathorne-Hardy Gathorne, 1st Earl of Cranbrook 89
Gatling machine guns 40, 137
'Gentleman's Ledger' (Garrard) 228
geologists 171
George IV, King 22
George V, King 200, 202, 203
Germany *xxvii*, 7, 33, 128–9
Ghana Armed Services 212
Ghana Military Museum 168*f*
Ghana Museum and Monuments Board 293
Ghana, Republic of *xxi, xxvi, xxxi*, 10, 29, 211, 222, 237, 258
  government position on return to regalia 274, 275–6, 277, 278, 281
  stolen regalia 262, 263
  traditional architecture 293–5
Gibraltar 101
Gifford, Lieutenant Lord Edric 230
Gilbert and Sullivan (operas) 101
gilt-silver dishes (Cecil family) 107–8
Gisborough, Baron 216
Gladstone, William (politician) *xv*, 34, 41, 46, 89, 119

Glendining & Co (auction house) 279, 280
Globe, The 106–7, 113
Glover, John (naval officer/colonial official) *xv*, 37, 86
God's axes (*Nyame Akuma*) 6
Gold Coast Colony *xxv*, 31, 128, 129, 131, 133, 134, 135, 198
Gold Coast Constabulary 123
Gold Coast Leader 204
Gold Coast Protectorate 62, 63, 87, 114, 120–1, 122, 128, 197, 203, 211
Gold Coast Regiment 170, 199
Gold Coast Supreme Court (Accra) 133
Gold Coast, The ('Costa da Mina') *xv*, *xvii*, *xix*, *xxxiii*, 7, 8, 10, 16, 50
 Asante invasion of (1873) *xi*, *xiii*,
 British presence on *xxii–xxiii*, *xxiii–xiv*, *xxv*, 30, 32, 33, 37
 independence of *xxvi*
Gold Coast Times, The 124
Golden Axe (Asante sacred object) 119–21, 125
Golden Jubilee Durbar (November 1985) 241
'Golden Spoil from Ashantee' (*The Times*) 105
Golden Stool of Ashanti, The (*Sika Dwa*) *xii*, *xvi*, *xvii*, *xxi*, *xxiv*, *xxv*, 14, 22, 146, 212
 reverence and desecration of 3–4, 119, 200–1
 Kirby's visit to Asante 122, 123, 125
 return of Prempeh 204, 205, 241
 siege of Fort Kumasi (1900), 170, 174, 175–6, 177, 178, 188
gold and gold trade *xi*, *xiii*, *xxi*, *xxxiii*, *xxxiv*, 76, 87, 294
 Asanti power and 8–9, 14, 24, 25, 26, 121, 144
 Britain and 171–4, 188
 establishment and growth of 3, 4–5, 6–7, 30, 57–8, 124, 132, 157
gold heads (fakes) 233
gold leaf (found by Captain Graves) 232
gold-ring (in form of frog) 229
goldsmiths 9, 24, 25
'gold weights' (*mbrammoo*) 9
'Good Shepherd, The' (crystal statuette) 112
Goronwy-Roberts, Baron (Foreign Office minister) 216
Grant, Frederick ('Native of Accra', photographer) *xv*, 124, 125, 156
Grant, General Sir James Hope 72
Graphic, The 102, 114, 212
Graves, Captain 232
Greece 262, 263, 266
Grenadier Guards 137, 139
Griffiths, Antony (keeper) 267, 269
Griffiths, James (Colonial Secretary) 238
Grossmith, George 101
Grosvenor, Captain 92
groundnuts 9
Guggisberg, Governor Sir Gordon 201–2
'guinea' (coin) *xxxiii*, 7
gun bearer's cap (*krobonkye*) 231
Gundlach, Cory (curator) 282
Guyan, Anthony (antique dealer) 266, 267

Hague Convention (1899) *xxv*, 162–3
Hall, Wynyard 171, 172

'Hamadikky, King' (King of Dixcove) 110
Hamilton, Bruce Meade 184, 249
'Happy Ashantee' (comic sketch) 102
Hare, Lieutenant 82
Harper, Charles (Chief Commissioner for Asante) 201
Harvey, Captain John Audley 279
hat (Asante green leather with crocodiles) 237–8
hat (cap of leather) 280
hat (leopard-skin) 229, 230*f*, 230 n.19, 231
Hausas (Houssas) (Muslim soldiers) 34, 46, 47, 86, 137, 139, 170, 177–8, 187, 246
Havelock-Allan, Sir Henry 161
head (gold-cast) (Wallace Collection) 113–14, 220
'Head of a King...' (Princeton Head) 233, 234*f*, 235
Heart of Darkness (Conrad) 71
heat apoplexy 138, 149
Heilbuth, Ferdinand (artist) 112
'Hell Prison Cell' (Kumasi Fort) 169–70
Henry III of England *xxxiii*
Henry the Navigator (Portuguese prince) 155–6
Henry, Prince of Battenberg ('Liko', son-in-law of Queen Victoria) *xv*, 130*f*, 136, 138, 149
Henty, George (novelist/war correspondent) *xv*, 56, 65, 78, 82, 102, 103
Herodotus *xxxiii*
Hertford, 4th Marquess of 111, 112
Higgott, Suzanne 112, 114
Higgs, Dr Peter (curator) 263
High Commission, British (Accra) 211, 214, 215, 241
High Court (Kumasi) 185
Himalaya, HMS (troop ship) 45, 49, 53, 91, 101
Hingley, Anthony (son of Samuel) 240
Hingley, Christopher (nephew of Diana Jackson) 242
Hingley, Lieutenant-Colonel Samuel (British officer) *xv*, 187, 240*f*, 241
History of Ashanti (Agyeman Prempeh II) *xii*, *xvii*, 3, 7, 15, 20, 21, 58, 74, 125
 Asanti people and war 31–2, 33, 37
 British-Asanti battles 66, 67, 68–9
 British-Asanti relations 197, 199, 200, 201
 Invasion of Asante (British) (1873–1874) 121, 122
 Invasion of Asante (British) (1895–1896) 133–4, 135, 140, 146
 regalia 80–1, 88
 siege of Fort Kumasi (1900) 170–1, 174, 175, 177, 178
History of Ashanti Kings and the Whole Country Itself, The (Agyeman Prempeh I) 197
History of the Gold Coast (Claridge) 120–1
Hodgson, Sir Frederick (colonial official) *xvi*, *xxv*, 173–7, 178, 180, 188, 189, 191, 194
Hodgson, Lady Mary (wife of Frederick) *xvi*, 173–4, 175–6, 178, 179, 183, 185
Hodson, Governor Sir Arnold 205
'Homecoming; Adversity and Commemoration' ceremony (Kumasi, 1 May 2024) *xxvii*, 271–3, 282, 286
Home, Captain Robert (Officer, Royal Engineers) *xvi*, 81
Hood, Lieutenant Arthur 139, 140, 146, 147
Hope Smith, Governor John (uncle of Thomas Bowdich) 13, 17, 18, 19, 20
hostages 33, 61, 62, 80
How I Found Livingstone (Stanley) 103

Hudson, Julie (curator) xvi, xxxi, xxxii n.1, xxxiii n.2, xxxv, xxxvi n.14, xxxvii, 27, 160
   return of regalia 222–3, 257, 270f, 272, 273
Hugette (mother of Princess Molly Prempeh) 194
Hulme, Edward 238
human sacrifice 24, 59, 74, 78, 88, 113, 123
   British attitudes towards 40–2, 132, 133, 134, 146–7, 174, 189
Hunt, Tristram (historian and director of V&A) xvi, 71, 272, 276, 285, 286, 290, 292
Huppenbauer, David (missionary) 124
Huxley, Elspeth 204
Huyshe, Captain George 56

Illustrated London News xviii, 55, 66, 70f, 90, 99, 103–4, 113, 165, 230
imperialism xiv, xv, xxiv, 48, 103, 128–9, 198
   exhibitions of looted regalia 126–7, 202–3
   European 133
   Invasion of Asante (British) (1873–1874) 114–15, 122–3
   Invasion of Asante (British) (1895–1896) 141, 145, 161, 162, 166, 236
   return of regalia 236, 272, 287–8, 288–9
indemnity (Asante) 216, 227–8, 279
   Invasion of Asante (British) (1873–1874) xxiii, 57, 62, 87–8, 92–3
   failure of Asante to pay 134, 144, 145, 170, 173, 175, 178
   sale of regalia 101, 105, 107, 110, 111
Independence of Ghana (1957) xii, xvii, xxvi, 2, 211, 274, 276, 281
Indianapolis Museum of Art 265, 266
infectious diseases *see* dysentery; malaria; smallpox; yellow fever
'Inmates of the Fort of Kumasi' (photograph) 179, 180f
intelligence reports 67, 68
'International Exhibition of Navigation, Commerce and Industry' (Liverpool) 126
'Interpreters Stool' (Stool of N'cheti) 240f, 241–2
Invasion of Asante (British) (1873–1874) xvii, xix, xx, xxiv, xxvi, xxvii, 42, 122, 134, 214
   Adanse Hills camp and Wolseley's demands 61–3
   attacks by Asante army 33–6
   British-Asante battles 63–9, 76
   capture and fall of Kumasi 70f, 71–82, 99, 102–3, 127–8
   need for native carriers 51, 52f, 52–3, 54, 55, 67–8, 80
   reaction of Asante 56–9
   return of looted regalia 256, 261–2, 278, 279, 280
   use of journalists 55–6
   voyage and arrival of HMS *Himalaya* 45–6, 49–51, 53
   Wolseley's Asante journal 46–8, 50, 52, 64, 65, 67, 75, 76, 87–8, 94, 100
Invasion of Asante (British) (1895–1896) xiii, xiv, 56–9, 158, 160–1, 175, 184
   arrival of troops 138–9
   Asante envoys visit London, 131–4, 136
   ceremony of submission and humiliation 143–5
   meeting with Asante at Kumasi 139–41
   preparation for a new expedition 134–5, 136–8
   removal of Asantehene and family to Elmina 144, 148–9, 150–1
   removal of regalia from Palace and Bantama 145–8
   invasion of the Gold Coast (Asanti) (1873) 33–6
'Inventory of Specie. Gold Dust, ornaments etc from Palace of King Prempeh' (Ordnance Store Department) 147
Irish Nationalist Party 161, 162
Isle of Wight 115, 116, 149
ivory 7, 24, 113–14

Jackson, Deirdre (daughter of Diana) 241
Jackson, Diana (daughter of Samuel Hingley) 240f, 241–2
Jackson, Dorothy (daughter of Samuel Hingley) xv
jawbones (human) 23
Jeweller and Metalworker 107
jewellery (Roman) 266, 269
Johnson, Walter Claude (engineer) 236
Jones, Erica (curator) 279, 280, 281, 292
Joseph, B.H. and Co (jewellers) 100
journalists and correspondents xv, xix, xx, xxxiv, 38, 102–3, 133, 149, 150
   Invasion of Asante (British) (1873–1874) 55–6, 65–6, 77–8, 79–80, 88, 90, 145
Juabin people 135
jungle fighting 60f

Kabalega of Bunyoro, King 196
Kagoshima (Japan) 115
Katamanso (Dodowa), Battle of (1826) xi, xxii, 22, 23, 30, 57
Kempster, Colonel Francis 143
kente cloth 9–10
Kenyon, Dame Kathleen 218–19
Kimberley Earl *see* John Wodehouse
'King of Kings Jewellery' (shop in Kumasi) 294
'King Koffees Coffee-pot' 94
'King Prempeh, the Queen Mother & War Chiefs quitting Kumasi at dawn' (photograph) 149
'King Prempe's Mine' (Ekwanta) 171
King's Own Yorkshire Light Infantry 148
Kintampo 124
Kirby, Brandon (colonial adventurer) xvi, 123–5, 127, 156
Kitchener, Lord 163
knife (Asante) 115
knife (handle overlaid with gold) 280
knife (iron with wood handle) 247
Knox, General Sir William George (British soldier) xvi, 244f, 245–6, 247–8, 248–50
Koch, Ed (Mayor of New York) 224
Kodzo Gavua (Associate Professor of Archaeology) xv, 259, 277–8, 292
Kofi Afrane (King of Ejisu) 176
Kofi Karikari (10th Asantehene (1867–1874, older brother of Mensa Bonsu, 'King Coffee') xi, xiii, xiv, xxii, xxiii, xxxiv, 42, 48, 56, 119, 132, 170
   abdication and death of 122, 125
   capture and fall of Kumasi 75–6, 80, 81, 86–7, 88, 94, 100, 108
   indemnity payment 57–9, 107, 110, 126, 171
   prophecy of war 32, 33, 37, 56
   stolen regalia of 229, 230f, 231, 232, 237, 246, 247, 280

responses to Wolseley's demands 61–3, 64, 67, 68, 69, 74–5, 76–7
Kofi Nti (son of Kofi Karikari) *xvi*, 132, 173
Koh-i-Noor diamond 104–5
Kokofu people 10, 135
kola nuts 30, 140, 198
Korsah, Timothy (Fante interpreter) 196
kuduo (brass vessels) 95
Kufuor, John (President of Ghana 2001–2009, 'Gentle Giant') *xvi, xxxi–xxxii, xxxv, xxxvi*, 239, 280, 285
Kühne, Johannes 56–7
Kumasi (Coomassie) (Asante capital) *xi–xiv, xvii–xix, xxii, xxv, xxxv*, 113, 190, 193, 199, 204
   Asanti relations with The British *xxi, xxxiii*, 13–14, 16, 17, 21, 24–5, 32, 33, 37, 40–1, 56
   British attack (1873–1874) *xv, xxiii, xxxiv*, 42, 47, 59, 61–2, 67, 68, 69, 85, 86, 256
   capture and fall of 70*f*, 71–82, 90, 91, 99, 102–3, 110, 115
   decolonialisation 212, 214–15
   Invasion of Asante (British) (1895–1896) *xiii, xxiv*, 134, 138–41, 146, 147
   origins of 3, 9, 10
   restoration of 121, 123, 124, 127–8
   return of regalia (2023–2024) *xxxii, xxxvii*, 108, 229, 230*f*, 231, 271, 276, 280
Kumasi Fort, Siege of (1900) *xvi, xiii, xviii, xxv*, 168*f*, 169–70, 173–9, 180*f*, 183–5, 194
Kumasihene (King of Kumasi) *xii, xxvi*, 3, 204
Kumasi Railway 198
Kumasi Traditional Council 210, 211
Kwabena Baako (sword bearer and war captain) 176
Kwabena Dwumo (King of Mampong (Mamponhene)) (commander of Asante army) *xvi*, 63, 66
Kwabena Kyere (Ashanti chief) *xvi, xxv*, 186–7
Kwabena Nkwantabisa (Adansehene) 197
Kwabena Oben (King of Adanse) 86
Kwadwo Appia (Offinsohene) 197
Kwadwo Otibu (Asen chief) 16
Kwaku Dua I (9th Asantehene (1834–1867)) *xi, xxii*, 30, 31–2, 40–1, 64, 78, 94, 131–2
Kwaku Dua II (12th Asantehene (1884)) *xii, xxiv*, 123, 124–5
Kwaku Essien (prince of Bekwai, fictional character) 128
Kwaku Suo (Asante envoy) 88
Kwame Boatin (Kyidomhene, later Henry Boatin) (Asante aristocrat, great-grandfather of Ivor Agyeman-Duah) *xvii, xiii*, 257, 258, 272–3
Kwame Gyansah (Asante chief) 203–4
Kwamena Elsa (Akan king) 5
Kwame Poku (nephew of Kwaku Dua I) 132
Kwarayire, Francis (conservator) 293
Kwasi Boakye (son of Kwaku Dua I) 132
Kwasi Gyambibi (father of Agyeman Prempeh I) *xvii*, 144, 200
Kyerematen, Alexander (historian) 213, 245

Lake, Edward (assistant to Winwood Reade) 79
Lambert, Messrs. (display company) 247
Landseer, Sir Edwin (artist) 112
Lansdowne, Marquess of (Secretary of State for War) 134

Lathrop, Perrin (curator) 234–5
'Laughing N*****, The' (song) 102
Lee, Baroness Jennie 216
Leeds City Museum 159
Lee, Robert E. 48–9
Le Rocher (Seychelles) 195
Lethbridge, Inspector H.B., 127
'Letters from Mars' (Knox) 249–50
Lincoln, Abraham 49
lions (golden) 229
Little, George (British soldier) *xvii*, 45–6, 49, 51, 53, 54, 56, 101
   battles with Asante Army 61, 63, 64, 65, 66, 68, 69
   capture of Kumasi 74, 75, 78, 82, 85–6, 90, 91
Livingstone, David 103
Lloyd, Alan (historian) 41–2, 136–7, 139, 173
Lloyd George, David (MP) 188–9
Locke, Hew (artist) 107–8, 287–8, 297
logistics officers 50–1
London Review of Books, The 235
looting and plundering (African) 34, 35, 183, 185–6, 190
looting and plundering (colonial) *xii, xiii, xvi, xviii, xxiii –xxvii, xxxii, xxxiv* n.8, *xxxv–xxxvi*, 7, 15, 27, 71
   attitudes to 141, 145–6, 148, 211, 213, 216, 219
   auction (23 February 1874) 87*f*, 92, 93 n.37, 94–6
   British Museum and 153–5, 156, 157, 158, 160, 163–5
   Kumasi 75, 77, 78–81, 90–2, 93 n.37, 94–6, 99, 104–7, 114, 162–3
   Parliament debate on 159–63
   Qaisarbagh Palace (Lucknow) 71–2, 73
   return of regalia 256, 261–2, 275, 277, 279, 280, 281–2, 289–90, 291
   Summer Palace (Peking) 72–73
   treasures brought back from expeditions 153–8, 228, 229, 231, 239
Los Angeles Times 281
lost wax (*cire perdue*) method 9, 113, 124, 157
Lough, Thomas (MP) 191
Louise, Princess, Duchess of Argyll (daughter of Queen Victoria) 105
Luard, Mr G.M.C. 232
Luce, Richard (Foreign Office minister) 223
Luck, Richard (antique dealer) 268
lute-harp (*sika sankuo*) 27

MacAleese, Daniel (MP) 162
MacCarthy, Sir Charles (soldier/colonial official, 'Mankata') *xvii, xxii*, 19–20, 22, 23, 93, 238, 240, 246
McCaskie, Tom (British historian) *xvii*, 8, 16, 22 n.45, 123, 135–6, 176, 186, 198, 212, 276, 291
Mack, John (Keeper of Ethnography, British Museum) 264, 265
Maclean, Lieutenant (Naval Brigade) 80
McLeod, Professor Malcolm (British anthropologist) *xxxv, xxxvii*, 10, 157, 165, 203, 264, 272, 276, 285
   adviser to the Asantehene 255, 256, 295
   appointment of 217–18, 219, 220, 221, 222, 223, 224–5
   return of regalia 237, 239, 291
McNeill, Colonel John 46
Macron, Emmanuel *xxvi*

Madam Victoria (wife of Otumfuo Opoku Ware II) 211, 224
Madeira 39, 49, 90
magistrate's court (Kumasi) 170
Mahama, John (President of Ghana (2012–2017; 2025–) xvii, 294
mail ships 35, 40
maize 9
malaria 7, 10, 18, 31, 36, 50, 150, 170, 172
Mampong 10
Manchester Guardian 188
Mandingo, Private Morlai (Sierra Leonean leader) 190
Mandinka people 126
Manhyia Palace and Museum (Kumasi) xiii, xxvi, 4, 27, 86, 204, 211, 238, 239, 255, 257, 262
    return of regalia xxvii, xxxvii, 270f, 275, 282, 292, 295, 296, 298
manillas (brass bracelets) 5
Manso-Nkwanta people 135
Manual of Military Law (War Office) 162
Maqdala cross (regalia) 248, 252, 268
Maqdala xvi, 114, 115, 287, 289
Marlborough House (London) 214
Martini-Henry (breech-loading single-shot rifle) 137
Martyrdom of Man, The (Winwood Reade) xx
mask (gold) 229
mask (gold, fake) 233
matrilineal system of inheritance 8
Maurice, Lieutenant Frederick (Wolseley's private secretary) xvii, 80, 87, 92, 94–5, 108, 246
Maxim (recoil-operated machine gun) 137, 179, 191
Maxwell, Governor William Maxwell xvii, xxiv, xxxiv, 161, 164, 170, 257
    auction of regalia (1874) 147, 148, 154, 158
    takes over as Governor of Gold Coast 134–5, 141, 143–4, 145
medics 50–1
Medieval Europe Gallery (British Museum) 153
Mensa Bonsu (11th Asantehene (1874–1883), younger brother of Kofi Karikari) xii, xxiv, 62, 68, 119–20, 121, 123
Mexico 109
Meysey-Thompson, Lieutenant Richard Frederick 235
military adventurism 30, 31–2
Military Museum (Kumasi) 169
mining pits ("gold holes") 5–6
'mischief Pickles' (Fante boy) 63
missionaries 33, 41, 58, 124, 131, 170, 174, 178, 183
Mission from Cape Coast Castle to Ashantee (Bowdich) xiv, 18
Mitchell, Mrs E. (Treasury Solicitor) 221
'Modern Voyager and Traveller, The' (Fisher Son & Co.) 22, 23–4
Montagu of Beaulieu, Lord (Conservative peer) 216
Mont Fleuri cemetery (Seychelles) 194
Moore and Burgess (blackface minstrels) 102
Mpomponsuo sword 163–4, 221, 222, 261, 296
Mulraj's sword (regalia) 251, 252
Museum of Archaeology and Anthropology (Cambridge) 217, 231–2
Museum für Völkerkunde (Berlin) 164
Museum für Völkerkunde (Vienna) 265

Museum of Mankind (London) 209, 210, 217, 223, 263–4
Museums and Galleries (1992) (United Kingdom) 288
museums xxvi–xxvii, 281
    thefts from 263, 264f, 265–6, 267f, 268
'museum for the world' 288, 289
Musgrave, George (journalist) 145, 150
music (Asanti) 25
musket guns ('Long Danes') 6, 7–8, 9, 14, 20–1, 32, 36, 39, 65, 67, 69
Mwanga of Buganda, King 196

Nana Afua Kobiri (Asantehemaa) xiii, 58, 62, 68, 74
Nana Akufo-Addo (President of Ghana (2017–2025) xiii, 4, 275
Nana Oforiatta Ayim (writer and art historian) 276
Nana Ofori Atta, King of Akyem Abuakwa 202
Nana Osei Bonsu ('whale') (7th Asantehene (1804–1824, formerly Osei Tutu Kwame) xi, xix, xxi, xxii, 221
    British-Asante relations 13, 14, 15–16, 17–20, 21 n.44, 22 n.45, 23, 25–6, 27
Nathan, Governor Matthew 191
National Archives (United Kingdom) 143
National Army Museum (United Kingdom) 94, 158, 160, 260
National Heritage Act (1983) (United Kingdom) 286
nationalism 222
National Museum (Accra) 213, 276
National Museum of Scotland 111
Native Committee of Chiefs 170–1
Native Houssa Artillery 246
'native levies' 47
Native Levy 38, 137, 138–9
necklace (circular pendant in form of crab/golden) 229
necklace (gold with earrings) 232
necklace (royal golden) 279
necklace (shell pendants) 231–2
neck torc (golden) 221
Nelson-Atkins Museum (Kansas City) 280
Netherlands, The xxi, xxii, xxvii, 6, 7–8, 26, 32, 37, 132
Neville, George William (banker) 164
New World see Americas, The
New York Herald xxxiv, 102
Nigeria xxvii, 86, 184, 185–6, 219, 262, 268, 277
Nightingale, Florence 105
Nkrumah, Kwame (first president of Ghana) xvii, xxvi, 211–12, 213, 274
Norman, Lady (wife of Baron Montagu Norman) 231
Norman, Baron Montagu (grandson of Sir Mark Wilks Collet) 231
Northampton Mercury 107, 108
'Notes on specimens of wrought gold, forming a portion of the Ashanti indemnity' (Smith) 109
Nottinghamshire Guardian 107
Nsamankow, Battle of (1824) xvii, xxii, 20 n.44, 21
Nsuta 10
Ntim Gyakari (Denkyira king) 2–3
Nyan Kumasi Assin (camp) 54

Oba of Benin 277, 282
Obuasi (mines) 171–3
Odaso, Battle of xxiii, 67–9, 73, 76, 82, 94, 139

Index 375

Ohene, Frederick (Asante goldsmith) 294
Ohly, Ernest (ethnographic art dealer) 228
Okomfo Anokye (priest/adviser) ('Cardinal Wolsey of Ashanti') xi, xvii, 1–4, 160, 221
'Okomfo Anokye Sword Site' (Kumasi) 1
Old Creole (language) xviii, 193, 194, 197, 257
Ommanney, Sir Montagu (Senior Crown Agent for the Colonies) 159
Opanin Kwabena Boadu (elder) 176
Opoku Ware (2nd Asantehene, Di Sika great-nephew of Osei Tutu) ('the one who ate gold'/Katakyie ('the Impregnable Warrior')) (c. 1720–1750) xi, xxi, 8–9, 221
Opoku Ware II (15th Asantehene (1970–1999)) xii, xxvi, 214, 237, 241, 242, 256, 260, 262, 269, 272
Ordah river 85
Ordnance Store Department 147
Osborne, George 262
Osei-Bonsu Safo Kantanka, Peter (historian) 282
Osei Kwadwo (Asantehene) 237
Osei Tutu (1st Asantehene) (c. 1700–1717) xi, xvii, xxi, 2–3, 7, 8, 25, 279
Osei Yaw Akoto (8th Asantehene (1824–1834)) xi, 22, 23
Otumfuo Opoku Ware II (Asantehene, nephew of Prempeh II) 210, 211, 215, 216, 219–20, 220–1, 223–5
Otumfuo Osei Tutu II (16th and current Asantehene (1999–)) xii, xvii, xxvii, xxxv, xxxvi, xxxvii, 4, 222, 252, 254f
   return of regalia 270f, 272, 273, 275, 277–8, 280, 281, 284f, 285, 290–1, 292, 295
   negotiations for loan/return of regalia, 255–9, 260–1, 262–3, 268–9
Owoo, Nii Kwate (filmmaker) xviii, xxxv–xxxvi, 274–5, 277
Owuso Koko Kuma (Asante negotiator) 56–7
Owusu Ansa, Albert (brother of John envoy) 131, 143, 145, 257
Owusu Ansa, John (envoy) 131, 132, 145, 257
Owusu Ansa (son of Osei Bonsu and father of John and Albert) 131

paddle-wheel steamers 90
Paget, General Sir Arthur (British soldier) xviii, 279–80
Pakistan xxxi
Palaver, The 211
Pall Mall Gazette 249
Palmer, Angela (artist) 239
palm oil 30, 128
Pan-Africanism xvii
pardons 52
parliamentary committees (1865) 34
Parthenon Marbles *see* Elgin Marbles
Pask, James Morton (sailor) 110–11
Patterson, Angus (curator) 273
peace pipe (*abua*) xxxii
peace treaties xxii, 22, 23, 57, 62
Peacey, Miss L. 232
Pearce, David 158
Pearce, Captain Francis 158
Peduase Lodge (presidential guesthouse) (Ghana) xxxi, xxxii
Peek, Cuthbert (son of Sir Henry) 279
Peek, Sir Henry (MP) 279

Peek, Wilfred (grandson of Sir Henry) 279
pendant (t-shaped gold casting) 124–5
Penwell, Charles (soldier) 85–6
'Petit Coffee' (possibly Kofi, son of Boakye Atonsa (Akomforehene)) 198
Petitot, Jean (enamel painter) 72
Peverett, Nigel (antique dealer) 266, 267f, 268
Philippa of Lancaster (daughter of John of Gaunt) 155
Phillips Brothers (jewellers) 231
photography and photographers 124, 125, 156
Pindar (Greek poet) xxxiii
pineapples 9
Pine, Grovenor Richard 30–1
Pirates of Penzance, The (Gilbert and Sullivan) 101
plate (silver) 158
Ponsonby, General Sir Henry 105
Pope-Hennessy, John (British art historian) xviii, 216, 217, 218, 219, 220–1
Pope Hennessy, Governor John (grandfather of John Pope-Hennessy) 218
porters 51, 52f, 52–3, 54, 55, 189
Portsmouth (England) 101
Portugal xxi, 4–5, 6, 7, 90, 155–6, 157, 158
potters and pottery 24
Prahsu 50, 51, 56
Prempeh, Agyeman (13th Asantehene (1888–1931) 'Mr Edward Prempeh') xvii, xviii, xix, xxiv, xxv, xxvi, xxvii, xxxiv, 164, 165–6, 171, 260
   ceremony of submission and humiliation 143–5
   conversion to Christianity 196, 197, 199
   enstoolment of 127, 128, 129
   exile of Asantehene and family to Elmina 148–9, 150–1, 159, 160, 161, 257
   exile to Freetown, Sierra Leone 173, 175, 176, 178, 192f, 257
   exile to The Seychelles 193, 194f, 195f, 196–8, 199–200, 202, 257, 273
   Invasion of Asante (British) (1895–1896) 131, 132, 133–4, 135–6, 139, 140, 141, 142f
   return to Asante homeland 198, 200, 202, 203–4, 205f, 206, 256, 271, 295, 297
Prempeh II, Agyeman (Nana Osei Tutu, 14th Asantehene (1931–1970)) xii, xxvi, 3, 7, 15, 20, 21, 42, 58, 74, 113
   Asanti people and war 31–2, 33, 37, 121, 122, 125
   British-Asante battles 66, 67, 68–9
   British-Asante relations 197, 199, 200, 201
   Invasion of Asante (British) (1873–1874) 121, 122
   Invasion of Asante (British) (1895–1896) 133–4, 135, 140, 146
   regalia 80–1, 88, 231–2
   restoration of monarchy 205f, 212, 213, 241
   siege of Fort Kumasi (1900) 170–1, 172, 174, 175, 177, 178, 183
Prempeh II Jubilee Museum (Kumasi) 42, 211, 213–14, 260
Prempeh, Princess Molly (great-granddaughter of Agyeman Prempeh I) xviii, 193–4
Pridham, John (composer) 100
Princeton University Art Museum 233, 234f
prints (antique) 266, 267f, 268
Prior, Melton (war correspondent/artist) xviii, 55, 66, 79, 90–1, 99, 103–4

prize agents 72, 76, 79–80, 81, 88, 92, 93, 105
'prize money' *see* looting and plundering (colonial)
protectorates (British) *xxiv*, 30, 31, 34, 40, 46, 62, 87, 131, 134, 184
proverbs (Asante) 9
punch bowl (silver) 157
'purchase' system (abolition) (1871) 38

Qaisarbagh Palace (Lucknow) 71–2
Quainoo, Emmanuel (curator) 185
Queen Idia ivory masks (kingdom of Benin) 113–14, 219
Queen, The (magazine) 165
quinine 50, 90

Racoon, HMS 150, 151
Ramkalawan, Wavel (President of the Seychelles) 295
Ramseyer, Friedrich (Swiss missionary) *xviii*, 33, 58–9, 63, 174, 178, 183
Ramseyer, Rosa (wife of Friedrich, Swiss missionary) *xviii*, 61, 174, 178, 183
ram's head (golden) 245–6, 247, 248, 252
Rattlesnake, HMS 38, 39
Ratton, Charles (dealer) 233, 238
Rattray, Robert (British colonial official/anthropologist) *xviii*, 201, 203, 291
Rawlings, Flight Lieutenant Jerry (President of Ghana 1979; 1981–2000) 241, 250
Read, Sir Charles Hercules (Keeper) *xviii*, 154–5, 156, 163–5
Red Crescent Society 248
Redmond, William (MP) 161, 188
regalia (Asante) *xvii–xix*, *xxii*, *xxvi–xxvii*, 8, 15, 22, 25, 27, 57, 164, 175, 231
  auction at Cape Coast Castle (23 February 1874) 84f, 87, 88, 92–6
  auctions of Asante objects 229, 230f, 231
  campaign for return of (1974) 209, 210–11, 213–16, 218–25, 260
  campaign for return/loan of Asante regalia (2023–2024) 255–7, 258–3, 268–9, 270f, 279, 285, 286–7, 290–2, 294, 295–7
  deception and fraud 233, 234f, 235
  exhibitions of looted regalia 121, 122, 124–5, 126, 127, 128
  identifying/cataloguing Asante objects in museums/collections 231–3, 234f
  individuals returning Asante objects 237–9, 240f, 241–2
  items returned on loan (2024) 231, 273–4
  looting and plundering (colonial) 78–9, 80–1, 104–7, 108 n.61, 112–13, 140, 145–8, 149, 159, 163
  negotiations for loan/return of 255–9
  private owners and collections of 227, 236–7
  regeneration of 260–1
  regimental military museums and 235
  tracking lost objects 227–9
regimental military museums 235
'Report of Interview between Governor of Cape Coast Colony and King Prempeh at Kumassi, January 20th 1896' 143
repoussé (decorative gold) 279
restitution *xxxv*, *xxxvi*, 218, 256, 260, 262, 263, 268, 274, 277–8

decolonialisation 286, 290, 291, 296
Reuters (news agency) 120, 134, 145, 177, 189
Ribeiro-Addy, Bell (MP) 290
Richard, Henry (politician, 'Apostle of Peace') *xviii*, 114–15
Ricketts, Governor Major Henry John 20–1
Rifle Brigade (2nd Battalion) *xix*, 81, 91, 101, 235, 246
  Invasion of Asante (1874–1875) 45, 46, 49, 53, 63, 64, 65, 67
ritual killing ground ('Great Golgotha', Kumasi) 77–8
Robinson, Ronald 122, 133
rockets (weaponry) 22, 35, 65, 66
Romer, Emick (Norwegian silversmith) 158
Rosebery, Lord 132
Ross, Doran (scholar of Ghanian art) 265
Rothschild, Cécile de 233
Roupell, Captain Ernest 184
Rowe, Governor Sir Samuel 120, 123, 125
Roxo, Joao Rodrigues 6
Royal African Company (British) 6–7
Royal African Corps (army) 20, 21
Royal Artillery Institution 251
Royal Artillery (Larkhill) *xvi*, 47, 245–52
Royal Artillery Mess (Woolwich) 246–7, 250
Royal Collection (Windsor) 22, 213–14, 247, 289–90
Royal Engineers (British) *xvi*, *xxxiv*, 50–1, 67–8, 81–2, 85, 89, 135, 138, 147, 235
Royal Family (Asante) 8, 74
Royal Geographical Society 123, 124, 125
Royal Gold Coast Gazette 20, 26
Royal Green Jackets Museum 235
royal harem 204
Royal Highland Regiment (42nd, Black Watch) 46, 49, 54, 64, 65, 67, 69, 73–5, 93, 134, 279
Royal Hussars 99
Royal Marines, British 34, 35, 46, 50, 55
royal mausoleum *see* Bantama (royal mausoleum)
Royal Military Exhibition (1890) (Chelsea) 248
Royal Mint (England) *xxxiii*
Royal Navy 37, 39, 49, 50, 64, 67, 86, 90, 92, 93
Royal Order of Ashantee (gold ornament) 120
Royal Scottish Museum *see* National Museum of Scotland
Royal Signals Museum 235 n.37
Royal State robe (King of Ashantee) 116
Royal United Services Institution *xxv*, 94, 160, 161–2
Royal Welch Fusiliers 46, 49, 54, 232, 237
rubber trade 198
Russell, Henry (trader/Private Secretary) 239
Russell, William Howard 71
Russo-Turkish War (1877) 248
'Ryde Art Treasures Exhibition' (Ryde Town Hall, Isle of Wight) 115, 116
Ryle, John (anthropologist/writer) 235–6

Sagrenti War *see* Invasion of Asante (British) (1873–1874)
Sainsbury Gallery (British Museum) 153
St Saviour's Church (Dartmouth) 23
Samori Toure (African Mandinka king) *xviii*, 133–4, 164
Sarmatian, HMS (troopship) 49
Sarr-Savoy Report (2018) (France) *xxvi*
Savoy, Bénédicte (academic) 218–19
Schaedler, Karl-Ferdinand (private collector) 265

Scott, C.P. (critic) 188
Scott, Colonel Sir Francis (British soldier) xviii, xxiv–xxv, 134, 136, 137–8, 139, 140–1, 143, 147, 184
'Scramble for Africa' 36
sculpture (King of Ashantee) 94, 95, 96
Second Anglo-Afghan War (1878–1880) 101
Second Anglo-Asante War (1863) xxii
Selassie, Emperor Haile 248, 289–90
Seychelles islands xii, xiii, xvii, xviii, xx, xxv, xxvii, xxxiv
  exile of Prempeh (13th Asantehene) 193, 194f, 196–8, 199–200, 202, 256, 257, 296
Shama 38–9, 40, 46
Sherwood, Captain Oliver 147
ship's bell 158
Sierra Leone xii–xiii, xvi–xvii, xx, xxv, 19, 20, 30, 47–8, 120, 126, 173, 190–1
  exile of Prempeh (13th Asantehene) 173, 175, 176, 178, 192f, 194, 257
Sika Akuma *see* Golden Axe
Sika Dwa *see* Golden Stool of Ashanti, The
sika mena (elephant's tail whisk) 279
Sinclair, Major Hugh 135, 138, 145, 146, 157–8, 160
skulls (Akwidaa) 110–11
skull (Sir Charles MacCarthy's) 23, 239, 246
slippers (gold) 229, 230f, 230 n.19, 231
slippers (State Sandals mounted in gold and silver) 280
smallpox 36, 59, 125, 189
Smith, Robert Soden xix, 108–9, 113
Smithsonian museums (United States) xxvii
Sniders (breech-loading rifles) 36, 37, 51, 59, 66, 67, 69, 137
Society of Antiquaries 155
Soldier's Pocket-Book for Field Service, The (Wolseley) 38, 73
Sotherby's (auction house) 228, 229, 265, 266
South Kensington Museum *see* Victoria and Albert Museum (V&A) (London)
sovereignty 32, 119–20, 129, 133, 212, 277–8
Spain 158
Special Service Corps 137, 138, 148, 154
Spectator, The 40
Speedway Travel (Kumasi) 224
spider (gold casting) 124–5
Spufford, Peter 4
stamps (colonial era) 213
standards (Asante military) 100
Standard, The (newspaper) xv, 56, 65, 78, 82, 102
Stanley, Harry (High Commissioner, Accra) 215–16
Stanley, Henry Morton (explorer/journalist) xix, xxxiv, 55, 63, 65–6, 66–7, 77, 78, 102–3, 171
Stanley Museum of Art (University of Iowa) 281–2
Starmer, Keir 290
Stationers' Company 124
Stewart, Captain Donald (Resident Commissioner, Kumasi) 169, 170
stools (Royal/wooden) 9–10, 76, 78–9, 99, 126, 155, 213
  return of 236–7, 238–9, 240f, 241–2, 260, 280
Story of A Soldier's Life, The (Wolseley) 48, 62, 67 n.40, 76
sugar 6
Summer Palace (Peking) 72, 112, 115
'Surf Boats' 53
Sweden 7
Switzerland 33, 58
swords (ceremonial) 78, 80, 94–6, 114–16, 215, 221, 222

'talking drum' (*atumpan*) 235
Tamar, HMS (troopship) 49
Tano Yaw (deity) 293
Tatler (magazine) 250
Taylor, Mrs Helen 232
Taylor, Mabel 232
telegraph lines 89–90, 139, 147, 235, 236
Telegraph, The 82, 102
Tewodros, Emperor of Ethiopia 102–3, 248, 289–90
Third Anglo-Asante War ('Sagrenti War') (1873) xxii, xxvi, xxvii
Thomas, James Henry (Colonial Secretary) 202, 203
Thomas, John (father of Joseph) xix
Thomas, Lieutenant Joseph (British soldier) xix, 61, 67, 69, 85, 91, 101
Thompson, Sir Richard (British Museum trustee) 223
Thorne, Captain H.A. 235
three elephants ring 165
tian tsui ('dotting with kingfishers') 112
Tibet 163
Timbers, Brigadier Ken 250
Timbuktu 124, 155
timeline xxi–xxvii
Times, The xx, 213, 223, 238, 250, 264
  Battle of Katamanso (1826) 23
  Battle of Nsamankow (1824) 20–1
  exile of Prempeh 203, 205, 206
  looted regalia 121, 126, 127, 133, 135
  capture and fall of Kumasi 71, 77, 78, 89
  Invasion of Asante (1874–1875) 35, 38, 39, 40, 46, 47, 55, 65
  return of regalia to London 102, 105, 106, 107, 108, 113, 116, 160
  siege of Fort Kumasi (1900) 187, 191
Tipu Sultan ('Tiger of Mysore') 115, 116
tobacco 9
Torrane, Governor Colonel George xix, 16, 24
'Trail of Behemoth, The' (Freeman) 128
trans-Saharan trade 4
Treasury, HM 111
Treaty of Trade and Friendship (1817) xxi–xxii, 17, 18–19, 25
Trinidad xvi
troopships 45, 49
tropical helmets 49, 69
Trump, Donald xxvii
tuberculosis (phthisis) 189
Tufts University (Massachusetts) 259, 261–2, 280, 282
Turner, Willy (British diplomat) 214, 215
Twi (Akan language) 2, 3, 194, 275

Uganda 196, 202
umbrella (Royal State, 'King Koffee') 98f, 99, 100, 114, 115, 126, 259
UNESCO 293
United States xxvi, xxvii, xxxvii, 48, 139, 229
'universal museum' 288, 289
University of Ghana (Accra) xv, 218
University of Iowa 281–2
Ussher, Herbert Taylor (administrator) 32

vase (Japanese) 266
vases (pre-Colombian) 264, 265, 269

Victoria and Albert Museum (V&A) (London) *xii*, *xvii*, *xviii*, *xix*, *xxvii*, *xxxii*, *xxxv–xxxvi*, 268
    purchases and exhibitions of regalia 98*f*, 108 n.61, 109, 111, 114–15, 228, 247
    return of regalia 239, 260, 272, 276, 278–9, 285, 286, 288, 289, 290, 292, 296
Victoria, Princess of Wales 126
Victoria, Queen (1819–1901) *xix*, *xxiv*, 40–1, 80, 104, 123, 129, 141, 147, 176, 188
    exhibitions of regalia 115, 126
    Invasion of Asante (British) (1873–1874) *xxiii*, 89, 100, 101, 259
    purchase of regalia 105–6, 113, 114
    regalia as gifts 78, 94, 99, 119–120, 121, 179, 246
    son-in-law visits Kumasi 130*f*, 132, 136–7, 149, 150
Vigilant (paddle-wheel steamer) 90
Vincent, William Thomas (historian) 247
Volta River 33
Volta (Royal Mail steamer) 119
Von Luschan, Felix 164
Vyazemsky, Boris (elder son of Leonid) 95–6
Vyazemsky, Dmitry (younger son of Leonid) 95
Vyazemsky, Leonid (Russian aristocrat) *xix*, 95, 102
Vyazemsky, Maria (wife and widow of Leonid) 96

Wallace, Amélie (wife of Richard) 112
Wallace Collection *xiv*, *xix*, 111–116, 216, 219, 220, 232, 233, 237, 288–9
Wallace, Richard (British aristocrat) *xix*, 111–14, 115–16, 228, 232
Wantage, Lord 228
war cry (Asanti) 29
'Wardour Street' list (random objects) 157
war drum and sticks (Asante) 78, 160
'War of the Golden Stool' *see* 'Yaa Asantewaa War'
War Office (British) 37–8, 46, 57, 89, 101, 135, 137–8, 143, 160, 162
Wassa kingdom 86
Waterfield, Hermione 210, 233, 238, 265
Watherston & Son of Pall Mall (jewellers) 164
Watson, Sir Francis (curator) 233
'wear cloth' (Asante) 257
Wellcome, Sir Henry 279–80
Wellcome Trust 279, 281, 296
Wellington, Duke of 104
West Africa Magazine 216–17
West African Frontier Force 184, 186
West Africa Regiment 190–1
West Africa *xxxiii*, *xxxvi*, 31, 36, 46, 48, 262
West Indian people 34, 46, 47, 79, 87, 137, 241
'West Yorkshire Jug' 154–5, 156 n.7, 157, 158
West Yorkshire Regiment (2nd Battalion) 137–8, 145–6, 147, 148, 150, 159–60, 171
Wetherall, Ensign 21
whipping posts 55
Wilks, Ivor (British historian) *xix*, 5–6, 26–7, 31, 40, 41, 133, 210, 291
Willcocks, Colonel James (British soldier) *xx*, 184, 185, 186, 188, 189, 190, 239
Williams, Jonathan (deputy of Hartwig Fischer) 263
Williams, Mr J. T. (Colonial Secretary) 21

Willis Rooms (St James's) 104
Wilson, David (former director, British Museum) 269
Windsor Castle 121
wine cups (Chinese) 112
Wingfield, Chris (curator/academic) 287
Winniett, Governor William 40–1
Winwood Reade, William (British writer/correspondent) *xx*, 38, 55–6, 65, 77, 78, 79, 102
Wodehouse, John, Earl of Kimberley (politician) *xvi*, 34, 35, 37, 41, 46, 77, 119, 122
Wolseley, Frances (daughter of Sir Garnet) 55, 94
Wolseley, Sir Garnet (Administrator and Commander-in-Chief of the Gold Coast) *xii–xx*, *xxii–xxiii*, *xxxiv*, 149, 215, 227, 246, 279
    Adanse Hills camp and Wolseley's demands 61–3, 139
    Asante journal 46–8, 50, 52, 64, 65, 67, 75, 76, 87–8, 94
    attitude towards Black people *xi*, 47–8, 62, 64, 103
    auction at Cape Coast Castle (23 February 1874) 84*f*, 87, 92, 93 n.37, 94–6, 259
    autobiography 48, 62, 67 n.40, 76
    capture and fall of Kumasi 71, 73, 74–7, 85, 86, 88–90, 91–2, 110, 127, 160, 293
    character 28*f*, 37–8, 39, 40, 42
    complicated relationship with journalists 55–6, 65–6
    funeral of 249
    Invasion of Asante (British) (1873–1874) 44*f*, 46–8, 50, 52, 54–7, 67–9, 120, 122, 125, 137, 256, 279–80
    looting and plundering (colonial) 71–3, 75–6, 79–82, 84*f*, 90–1, 107, 110–11, 158–9, 162–3, 211, 230
    promotion/honours on return to England 100–1, 126, 136
Wolseley, Louisa (wife of Sir Garnet) 67, 72, 76, 82, 94
'Wolseley Ring' 39, 91–2
woman's breast (gold) 246
Wood, Major-General Sir David 246
wooden drum (Asanti) 22
Wood, Sir Evelyn (British army officer) *xx*, 37, 104, 149–50, 249
Wood, Lieutenant Henry (Wolseley's aide-de-camp) 99, 114, 214, 259
World Heritage Sites (Kumasi) 293
Worosa (King of Banda) 113, 237
wristlets (gold) 221

Yaa Akyia (mother of Agyeman Prempeh I/wife of Kwasi Gyambibi, 'Elizabeth') *xx*, 127, 141, 142*f*, 144, 150, 196, 200
Yaa Asantewaa II (current Queen Mother) 239
Yaa Asantewaa (Queen Mother of Ejisu) *xv*, *xvi*, *xx*, *xxv*, 186–7, 195, 197–9, 204, 238–9, 240*f*, 241–2, 260, 288
'Yaa Asantewaa War' (5th and final Anglo-Asante War (1900–1901) *xvi*, *xix*, *xxv*, *xxxii*, 183–7
Yam Custom 261
Yam Festival (Asanti) 24
Yao Andoh (private secretary) 221, 222, 225
yellow fever 7, 10, 50, 101
Yoruba people 86, 184
You Hide Me (documentary film) (Owoo) *xviii*, 274, 275

Zanzibar 103
Zimbabwe *xxxi*